Romans

Romans

FRANK J. MATERA

Baker Academic
a division of Baker Publishing Group
Grand Rapids, Michigan

Published by Baker Academic
a division of Baker Publishing Group
PO Box 6287, Grand Rapids, MI 49516-6287
www.bakeracademic.com

Printed in the United States of America

Library of Congress Cataloging-in-Publication Data

Matera, Frank J.
    Romans / Frank J. Matera.
       p.   cm. — (Paideia: commentaries on the New Testament)
    Includes bibliographical references and index.
    ISBN 978-0-8010-3189-2 (pbk.)
    1. Bible. N.T. Romans—Commentaries. I. Title.
  BS2665.53.M38 2010
  227'.107—dc22
                                              2010021385

Baker Publishing Group publications use paper produced from sustainable forestry practices and post-consumer waste whenever possible.

This work is dedicated to Joseph A. Fitzmyer, SJ,
on the occasion of his ninetieth birthday
and to my colleagues in
The School of Theology and Religious Studies at
The Catholic University of America, Washington, DC

Contents

◩

Contents

Figures

日

Foreword

Paideia: Commentaries on the New Testament is a series that sets out to comment on the final form of the New Testament text in a way that pays due attention both to the cultural, literary, and theological settings in which the text took form and to the interests of the contemporary readers to whom the commentaries are addressed. This series is aimed squarely at students—including MA students in religious and theological studies programs, seminarians, and upper-divisional undergraduates—who have theological interests in the biblical text. Thus, the didactic aim of the series is to enable students to understand each book of the New Testament as a literary whole rooted in a particular ancient setting and related to its context within the New Testament.

The name "Paideia" reflects (1) the instructional aim of the series—giving contemporary students a basic grounding in academic New Testament studies by guiding their engagement with New Testament texts; (2) the fact that the New Testament texts as literary unities are shaped by the educational categories and ideas (rhetorical, narratological, etc.) of their ancient writers and readers; and (3) the pedagogical aims of the texts themselves—their central aim being not simply to impart information but to form the theological convictions and moral habits of their readers.

Each commentary deals with the text in terms of larger rhetorical units; these are not verse-by-verse commentaries. This series thus stands within the stream of recent commentaries that attend to the final form of the text. Such reader-centered literary approaches are inherently more accessible to liberal arts students without extensive linguistic and historical-critical preparation than older exegetical approaches, but within the reader-centered world the sanest practitioners have paid careful attention to the extratext of the original readers, including not only these readers' knowledge of the geography, history, and other context elements reflected in the text but also their ability to respond correctly to the literary and rhetorical conventions used in the text. Paideia commentaries pay deliberate attention to this extratextual repertoire in order to highlight the ways in which the text is designed to persuade and move its readers. Each rhetorical unit is explored from three angles: (1) introductory matters; (2) tracing the train of thought or narrative or rhetorical flow of the argument; and (3) theological issues raised by the text that are of interest to the contemporary Christian. Thus, the primary focus remains on the text and not its historical context or its interpretation in the secondary literature.

Our authors represent a variety of confessional points of view: Protestant, Roman Catholic, and Greek Orthodox. What they share, beyond being New Testament scholars of national and international repute, is a commitment to reading the biblical text as theological documents within their ancient contexts. Working within the broad parameters described here, each author brings his or her own considerable exegetical talents and deep theological commitments to the task of laying bare the interpretation of Scripture for the faith and practice of God's people everywhere.

Mikeal C. Parsons
Charles H. Talbert

Preface

It was professor Jean Giblet of the University of Louvain (Belgium) who first introduced me to the study of Romans during the 1967–68 academic year. Although I did not comprehend all that he was saying then, I am forever grateful for the gift of his careful scholarship and engaging pedagogy that inspired my own love for God's word. About the same time, I read Karl Barth's great commentary on Romans. Reading that commentary—to which I have returned at different points in my life—was like listening to a sermon delivered from a lofty mountain. It confronted me with the utter transcendence of God's word. In writing this commentary, I have tried to communicate something of the power and passion of this letter that I experienced in the lecture halls of Louvain and from reading Barth's Romans commentary.

Writing a commentary on Romans is a humbling and never-ending task, even when one has completed the commentary! It is a humbling task because one eventually realizes that there is no way to completely master or exhaust this remarkable text. It is a never-ending task because even after the commentary is finished, the interpreter of Romans is deeply aware of the ongoing challenges and possibilities of this letter that still need to be addressed. This, at least, has been my experience. But there is a moment when every commentator must bring the work to completion, trusting in what has been done and looking forward to exploring this letter in other ways.

At the completion of my own work I express my gratitude to my research assistant, Mr. Paul Jeon, who has carefully read this manuscript several times and contributed to it in numerous ways over the past two years. I also extend my gratitude to my friend and colleague Professor Christopher Begg, who has generously read portions of this commentary in manuscript form and made valuable suggestions for improving it, even when he had more important things to do. Finally, I am grateful to my students at the Catholic University of America, and to all those who have patiently listened to my lectures on Paul and Romans, thereby enabling me to grow in my own understanding of Paul and this great letter.

I express my appreciation to the Catholic University of America Press for permission to quote from Origen, *Commentary on the Epistle to the Romans*, vols. 102–3 of the Fathers of the Church series.

Frank J. Matera
June 29, 2009
The Solemnity of the Apostles Peter and Paul

Abbreviations

General

def.	definition	OT	Old Testament
Eng.	English	s.v.	*sub verbo*, under the word
lit.	literally	trans.	translated by
NT	New Testament		

Bible Texts and Versions

LXX	Septuagint	NJPS	*Tanakh: The Holy Scriptures; The New JPS Translation according to the Traditional Hebrew Text*
NAB	New American Bible		
NET	New English Translation		
NETS	New English Translation of the Septuagint	NRSV	New Revised Standard Version
		RSV	Revised Standard Version

Ancient Corpora

OLD TESTAMENT

Gen.	Genesis	Judg.	Judges
Exod.	Exodus	Ruth	Ruth
Lev.	Leviticus	1–2 Sam.	1–2 Samuel
Num.	Numbers	1–2 Kings	1–2 Kings
Deut.	Deuteronomy	1–2 Chron.	1–2 Chronicles
Josh.	Joshua	Ezra	Ezra

Neh.	Nehemiah	1–2 Cor.	1–2 Corinthians
Esth.	Esther	Gal.	Galatians
Job	Job	Eph.	Ephesians
Ps./Pss.	Psalm/Psalms	Phil.	Philippians
Prov.	Proverbs	Col.	Colossians
Eccles.	Ecclesiastes	1–2 Thess.	1–2 Thessalonians
Song	Song of Songs	1–2 Tim.	1–2 Timothy
Isa.	Isaiah	Titus	Titus
Jer.	Jeremiah	Philem.	Philemon
Lam.	Lamentations	Heb.	Hebrews
Ezek.	Ezekiel	James	James
Dan.	Daniel	1–2 Pet.	1–2 Peter
Hos.	Hosea	1–3 John	1–3 John
Joel	Joel	Jude	Jude
Amos	Amos	Rev.	Revelation
Obad.	Obadiah		

OLD TESTAMENT PSEUDEPIGRAPHA

Jon.	Jonah	2 Bar.	*2 Baruch (Syriac Apocalypse)*
Mic.	Micah		
Nah.	Nahum	1 En.	*1 Enoch (Ethiopic Apocalypse)*
Hab.	Habakkuk		
Zeph.	Zephaniah	2 En.	*2 Enoch (Slavonic Apocalypse)*
Hag.	Haggai		
Zech.	Zechariah	*Jub.*	*Jubilees*
Mal.	Malachi	L.A.E.	*Life of Adam and Eve*

APOCRYPHAL/DEUTEROCANONICAL BOOKS

		Pss. Sol.	*Psalms of Solomon*
2 Esd.	2 Esdras	*Sib. Or.*	*Sibylline Oracles*
1–2 Macc.	1–2 Maccabees		
Sir.	Sirach/Ecclesiasticus		

DEAD SEA SCROLLS

Wis.	Wisdom of Solomon	CD	*Damascus Document*
		1QH	*Hodayot* (Thanksgiving Psalms)

NEW TESTAMENT

Matt.	Matthew	1QS	*Rule of the Community/ Manual of Discipline*
Mark	Mark		
Luke	Luke	4QMMT	*Some Observances of the Law*
John	John		
Acts	Acts		

APOSTOLIC FATHERS

Rom.	Romans	1 Clem.	*1 Clement*

Ancient Authors

AUGUSTINE

Conf.   *Confessions*

C. Jul.   *Contra Julianum*

CICERO

Rab. Perd.   *Pro Rabirio Perduellionis Reo*

JOHN CHRYSOSTOM

Hom. Rom.   *Homiliae in epistulam ad Romanos*

JOSEPHUS

Ag. Ap.   *Against Apion*

J.W.   *Jewish War*

JUSTIN

1 Apol.   *First Apology*

ORIGEN

Comm. Rom.   *Commentarii in Romanos*

SUETONIUS

Claud.   *Divus Claudius*

Series, Collections, and Reference Works

ANF   *The Ante-Nicene Fathers.* Edited by Alexander Roberts and James Donaldson. 10 vols. New York: Christian Literature Co., 1885–96. Repr., Grand Rapids: Eerdmans, 1957.

BDAG   *A Greek-English Lexicon of the New Testament and Other Early Christian Literature.* Edited by F. W. Danker. 3rd ed. Chicago: University of Chicago Press, 2000.

DBI   *Dictionary of Biblical Interpretation.* Edited by John H. Hayes. 2 vols. Nashville: Abingdon, 1999.

EDNT   *Exegetical Dictionary of the New Testament.* Edited by H. Balz and G. Schneider. 3 vols. Grand Rapids: Eerdmans, 1990–93.

FC   Fathers of the Church

IDB   *Interpreter's Dictionary of the Bible.* Edited by G. A. Buttrick. 4 vols. Nashville: Abingdon, 1962.

NPNF[2]   *Nicene and Post-Nicene Fathers.* 2nd series. Edited by P. Schaff and H. Wace. 14 vols. Repr., Peabody, MA: Hendrickson, 1994.

OCD   *Oxford Classical Dictionary.* Edited by S. Hornblower and A. Spawforth. 3rd ed. Oxford: Oxford University Press, 1996.

OTP   *Old Testament Pseudepigrapha.* Edited by James H. Charlesworth. 2 vols. Garden City, NY: Doubleday, 1983–85.

Romans

Introduction

Romans is the first of the Pauline Letters in the NT. Although it enjoys this pride of place because it is the longest of the letters, its placement is well deserved since it is the most detailed presentation of Paul's gospel, and since it has influenced the course of Christian theology more than any other writing of the NT. For example, in the patristic era Augustine drew upon this letter to develop his theology of grace. Martin Luther's reading of Romans eventually led to the Reformation. And, at the beginning of the twentieth century, Karl Barth's commentary on Romans exploded on the theological scene and sounded the death knell of nineteenth-century German liberal theology.

Romans has played a crucial role in theology. Romans 1:18–3:20 and Rom. 7 have become foundational for Christian anthropology because of their descriptions of the human condition under the power of sin. Romans 3:21–5:11 is indispensable for the Christian understanding of Christ's redemptive death and the doctrine of justification by faith. Paul's Adam-Christ comparison in Rom. 5:12–21 is the starting point for the church's doctrine of original sin. Romans 6 has played a central role in Christianity's understanding of ethics and the sacramental life. Romans 8 is a key text for pneumatology and eschatology. Romans 9–11 has been a locus classicus for the Augustinian and Calvinist teaching on predestination. And more recently, this text has challenged Christians to rethink their understanding of the relationship between Israel and the church. Finally, Rom. 12:1–15:13 is central to how believers understand the relationship between justification by faith and the morally good life that expresses itself through love. In a word, there is hardly a chapter of Romans that has not played a vital role in the development of Christian doctrine.

Because Romans has exercised such an important role in Christian theology, those who study it inevitably find themselves to be partners in a conversation that has been in progress for nearly two millennia. Origen, Augustine,

Chrysostom, Aquinas, Luther, Calvin, and Barth, to mention only a few, have been major participants in this conversation. Given the stature of these and other great commentators, it is important to approach Romans with a sense of humility. That such great minds have wrestled with this letter should make all commentators aware that they are heirs to a rich exegetical tradition. To paraphrase Matthew's Gospel, every commentator of Romans "is like the master of a household who brings out of his treasure what is new and what is old" (Matt. 13:52). With one eye on the past and the other on the present, then, commentators must learn what has been said as well as what is being said.

My own commentary is modest in scope and theological in orientation. Its purpose is to provide students at the master's level with an initial reading of this great letter that will enable them to progress to more learned commentaries. Each section of this commentary begins with a discussion of introductory matters of which readers need to be aware. Next, I seek to explain the train of thought in each unit. Finally, I conclude each section with a discussion of the theological issues that the text raises. This is the kind of commentary, then, that should enable readers to appreciate the overall message and argument of Romans.

Introductory Matters

There is little or no question about the authorship and literary integrity of Romans. Apart from the voices of a few exegetes such as Walter Schmithals (1975), there is little discussion about its literary integrity. Accordingly, although some have questioned if chapter 16 belongs to the original letter, there is no support for viewing Romans as a composite letter composed of earlier letters or fragments of letters. Rather, the most critical introductory issues surrounding Romans concern its occasion and purpose. Was there a specific occasion or reason why Paul wrote this letter to a community he did not establish and had not visited? Closely related to this question is another that can be posed in two ways. If there was a specific occasion, what was Paul's reason for writing to the Romans? If there was none, why did he write? In this section, I consider these and other introductory issues. In the first section, I summarize what we can know about Paul's circumstances when he wrote this letter. In the second, I summarize what we know about the circumstances of the Romans when they received this letter. In the third, I will consider why Paul wrote Romans. Finally, I conclude with a few observations about the manuscript tradition of Romans.

Paul's Circumstances

Romans provides us with important information about Paul's circumstances at the time that he was writing this letter. According to Rom. 16:23, Paul was staying at the house of Gaius. Since Paul mentions Gaius and Crispus as two of the people whom he baptized when he was at Corinth (1 Cor. 1:14), we can assume that Paul wrote Romans from Corinth, unless the Gaius mentioned here is a different person. Moreover, since Paul tells the Romans that Macedonia and Achaia (the northern and southern Roman provinces of Greece) have decided to contribute to the collection that he is about to bring to Jerusalem (Rom. 15:26), this indicates that Paul's conflict with the Corinthian community (which was the occasion for Paul to write 2 Corinthians) had been resolved in his favor. If we date this conflict to the mid-fifties, as most commentators do, Paul is writing after the Corinthian crisis, about AD 56. We find some corroborating evidence for this in Acts 20:1–6, which relates that Paul stayed in Greece (Achaia, where Corinth is located) for three months (20:3) before sailing for Syria from Philippi, after the Feast of Unleavened Bread (20:6), which occurs in the spring. If the information of Acts is correct, Paul spent three months in Corinth, during which time he wrote Romans in the late winter and early spring of AD 56.

Paul informs the Romans that he has often tried to visit them (1:13) but has been prevented from doing so because of the demands of his missionary work in the eastern basin of the Mediterranean world, that is, modern-day Greece and Turkey (15:17–19, 22). But now that he has completed his missionary work in the East, he hopes to open a new mission in the West, in Spain. Consequently, his plan is to visit Rome and then go to Spain (15:24). But before Paul can come to Rome, he has an important ministry to complete. Having taken up a collection among his Gentile churches for many years, he must bring that collection to Jerusalem (15:25–29). The pillar apostles (James, Cephas/Peter, John) requested this collection at the time of the Jerusalem conference (Gal. 2:9–10), and Paul readily agreed to their wishes since he viewed the collection as a visible sign of unity between his Gentile congregations and the Jewish-Christian congregation at Jerusalem (Rom. 15:27; 2 Cor. 9:11–15). As he writes Romans, however, Paul is apprehensive about the kind of reception he will receive at Jerusalem, and so he asks the Romans to join him in prayer for the success of his ministry to Jerusalem (15:30–33).

The Acts of the Apostles corroborates some of these events inasmuch as it tells us of Paul's intention to go to Jerusalem and then visit Rome (19:21). Acts, however, says nothing about Paul's intention to go to Spain, and it is strangely silent about the collection for Jerusalem, unless 24:17 is a reference to the collection. What Acts does tell us, however, is that Paul was not able to complete his plans in the way that he outlined them in Romans. For in addition to corroborating Paul's decision to go to Jerusalem and then to Rome, Acts narrates what had not yet happened at the time that Paul wrote Romans: his extended imprisonment in Jerusalem and Caesarea (Acts 22–26) before being transferred as a prisoner to Rome (Acts 27–28), where he remained under house arrest for two years (28:30–31). Although the writings of the NT say nothing further about Paul's journey to Spain, the first letter of Clement does: "After he had been seven times in chains, had been driven into exile, had been stoned, and had preached in the east and in the west, he won the genuine glory for his faith, having taught righteousness to the whole world and having reached the farthest limits of the west" (*1 Clem.* 5.6–7, trans. Holmes 2007).

Paul's circumstances at the time of writing Romans can be summarized in this way. He writes from Corinth, from the home of Gaius, during the winter and spring of AD 56. He has completed his work in the East, and he intends to open a mission in Spain. On his journey to Spain, he will visit the Christ-believers at Rome. But before visiting them, he must bring the collection that he has been taking up among his Gentile congregations to the poor among the Christ-believers of Jerusalem. But what were the circumstances of the Roman Christians? Why was Paul writing to a community that he did not establish and had never visited?

The Circumstances of the Romans

It is more difficult to determine the circumstances of the Romans than it is to describe Paul's circumstances. The reason for this is that Paul is not writing to describe the circumstances of the Romans so much as he is responding to their circumstances. Thus, although we can deduce Paul's circumstances from what he writes about himself, we must infer the circumstances of the Romans from what Paul writes to them. Because of the need to infer what is happening, scholars have described the circumstances of the Romans in different ways.

The different ways in which scholars have constructed the situation of the Romans is part of "the Romans Debate" that Karl P. Donfried (1991) has chronicled in a series of collected essays and that James C. Miller (2001) and A. Andrew Das (2007) have updated. This modern debate, which shows no sign of abating, attempts to understand the circumstances that occasioned Paul's Letter to the Romans. The presupposition of the debate is that since Romans is a real letter, our understanding of it is dependent upon grasping the circumstances of those to whom it was written. A. J. M. Wedderburn (1991a, 5) writes: "If this knowledge is in the case of Romans either not accessible or is at least disputed, then our understanding of what Paul is saying in Romans is of necessity flawed, uncertain and provisional."

Before trying to summarize the main contours of this debate, it will be helpful to make two points. First, Christianity appears to have come to Rome soon after the death and resurrection of Christ. Although the writings of the NT give no indication how this happened, it is likely that this new faith was brought to Rome by believers who went there for a variety of reasons, business as well as missionary. Inasmuch as the synagogue provided a ready-made audience for this faith that proclaimed Jesus as the Messiah, some of the earliest Christians at Rome probably came from the Jewish synagogues. Second, although the superscription of this letter, "To the Romans," can give the impression that Paul was writing to a single community, it is evident from his greetings in Rom. 16 that the Roman Christians belonged to different house churches. This may be the reason why Paul does not greet "the church at Rome" but writes "to those in Rome, God's beloved" (1:7). But who were these believers to whom Paul was writing? Were they Jewish Christians who continued to practice the Mosaic law, or Gentile Christians who had been proselytes and still practiced the law, or Gentile believers who never practiced the law, or some mixture of the above? Were there divisions among the Roman Christians whom Paul was addressing? If so, were they between or within the Roman house churches? Finally, what was the attitude of the Roman Christians toward Paul?

The ethnic makeup of the Romans. The ethnic makeup of the Roman Christians has been a point of contention among commentators. While the traditional approach views the Roman Christians as a mixed group composed of Gentile and Jewish believers, recent studies have focused on its Gentile component. Wedderburn (1991a, 50–54), for example, says that it is unwise to make a sharp distinction between Gentile and Jewish believers since some of the Gentiles may have been law-observant. Das (2007) goes further, vigorously arguing that Paul was writing exclusively to Gentiles. Although this debate may appear to be merely academic, it has an important bearing on the interpretation of the letter and the attitude of Christians toward Jews. For whereas older commentators often maintained that Paul was arguing against Jewish arrogance, some recent commentators see Paul as railing against Gentile arrogance.

The resolution of this question is difficult since it is possible to find evidence for both positions. For example, in the opening and closing of the letter it appears that Paul is and has been addressing a Gentile audience (1:6; 15:15–16). Moreover, in 11:13 Paul explicitly speaks to Gentiles. But in the body of the letter Paul addresses Jewish concerns that deal with Israel and its law. In 2:17 he engages an imaginary Jewish interlocutor, and in 7:1 he writes that he is speaking to those who know the law. Furthermore, although the majority of those whom he greets in Rom. 16 are Gentiles, some are Jewish (Prisca and Aquila, Andronicus and Junia, and Herodion). In my view, then, although Das has made the strongest case to date for a purely Gentile audience, Paul's appeal to his audience to welcome one another as Christ has welcomed them (15:7), which precedes his description of Christ as a minister to Jews and Gentiles (15:8–9), suggests that even if Paul's audience was composed predominantly of Gentile believers, it included some Jewish Christ-believers as well.

Divisions among the Romans. Related to the issue of the ethnic makeup of the Roman Christians is the question of whether there were divisions among the Roman believers. This topic arises because of Paul's discussion of the "weak" and the "strong" in 14:1–15:13, which has often been interpreted as a division between Jewish believers (the weak) who continue to observe dietary and calendar prescriptions of the law and Gentile believers (the strong) who do not. But the evidence is not as clear as it may appear at first since it is possible that there were also Gentile proselytes who continued to observe the law. In my own view, the weak probably included Jewish and Gentile Christ-believers who continued to observe certain cultic aspects of the law.

How the Romans perceived Paul. How the Romans perceived Paul is another aspect of the question that deals with the circumstances of the Romans. It is evident from the long list of greetings in chapter 16 that Paul knew many of the people in the house churches at Rome, and that some of them were his friends and associates (Prisca and Aquila, Epaenetus, Andronicus and Junia, Ampliatus, Urbanus, Stachys, Persis, Rufus and his mother). We can assume that these people held a favorable opinion of Paul. Likewise, inasmuch as Paul identifies himself as one of the strong (15:1), we can assume that most of the strong at Rome would have agreed with the gospel that he preached. The weak, however, probably mistrusted Paul's gospel because it encouraged the strong to act in a way that offended their convictions about food and certain days. Moreover, it is apparent from 3:8, and from the rhetorical objections that Paul lodges against his own gospel (6:1, 15; 7:7, 13), that there were misgivings about his gospel of justification on the basis of faith apart from doing the works of the law. On balance, then, it would seem that although there was goodwill toward Paul on the part of some of the Roman believers, there were others who had heard reports about the apostle that led them to mistrust his law-free gospel.

The situation of the Romans can be summarized in this way. Christianity had come to Rome long before Paul wrote to the Romans. While the original believers may have been converts from Judaism, there was a large Gentile contingent in Rome at the time Paul wrote. These Roman Christians belonged to different household churches, in which there may have been tensions between Jewish Christians and law-observant Gentile Christians, on the one hand, and Gentile believers who did not observe the law, on the other. While the latter group was probably sympathetic to Paul's gospel, the former was probably wary of the apostle's teaching.

The Purpose and Function of Romans

Given this description of the circumstances of Paul and the Romans, what can we say about the purpose and function of Romans? As with the other questions I have addressed, this one receives a variety of answers that are summarized in the works of Donfried, Wedderburn, Das, and Miller. In what follows, I focus on four proposals. The first three deal with Paul's circumstances, whereas the fourth concerns itself with the circumstances of the Romans: (1) Paul writes to summarize his gospel; (2) Paul writes to prepare his defense at Jerusalem; (3) Paul writes to enlist the support of the Romans for his mission to Spain; (4) Paul writes to resolve the problem of the weak and the strong.

A summary of Paul's gospel. Prior to Ferdinand Christian Baur's 1836 essay, which deals with the purpose and occasion of Romans, most commentators viewed Romans as something akin to a compendium of the apostle's theology, especially his teaching on justification by faith (R. Morgan, *DBI* 2:416). There was good reason for this. In this letter, more than any other, Paul presents his gospel in an orderly fashion by focusing on humanity's need for redemption and God's response to this need. This is why, even after Baur's essay, many scholars continued to argue that Paul used the occasion of this letter to summarize the essential points of his gospel. The classic essays of T. W. Manson (1991) and Günther Bornkamm (1991) provide two examples of this approach. In recent years, however, as scholars have studied the "frame" of Romans (the letter opening and the letter closing) and Paul's discussion of the weak and the strong (14:1–15:13), this position has fallen from favor (Miller 2000; Toney 2008).

A defense speech with Jerusalem in view. A few scholars have argued that Paul's immediate purpose was to enlist the support of the Romans for his upcoming visit to Jerusalem and to rehearse the kind of speech he would give in defense of his gospel before a hostile Jewish-Christian audience in that city (Jervell 1991). While this is an intriguing position, it has never been able to explain why Paul wrote this letter-speech to the Romans.

A letter of introduction in view of Paul's mission to Spain. Others have seen Paul's upcoming mission to Spain as the key to interpreting Romans (Jewett 2007, 87–91). In their view, Paul is traveling to Rome to enlist the help of the Romans for his mission to Spain. However, since the majority of the Roman Christ-believers do not know him, and since there are rumors circulating about him, Paul must present his gospel to them in order to gain their goodwill. Accordingly, he introduces himself to the Romans by explaining the gospel he preaches among the Gentiles. Romans, then, is a kind of ambassadorial letter in which Paul presents his apostolic credentials to the Romans. But if this is the case, it is strange that he waits until the very end of the letter to reveal his plans to go to Spain.

The weak and the strong. Unlike the first three proposals, which deal with Paul's circumstances (his desire to summarize his gospel, his defense at Jerusalem, his Spanish mission), this proposal interprets Romans in terms of the circumstances of the Roman Christians. In light of Paul's discussion of the weak and the strong (14:1–15:13), scholars have constructed a number of scenarios to explain what was happening at Rome, the most popular being "the Claudius Hypothesis" (Marxsen 1968, 95–104). According to this scenario, when the Jewish Christians returned to Rome after the Roman emperor Claudius had expelled the Jews from Rome in AD 49 because of disputes over a certain "Chrestus," they encountered a new situation. The Gentile Christians who had not been expelled from Rome were in the ascendancy, and they were now lording their position over the returning Jewish Christians who continued to practice the Mosaic law. Aware of this problem, Paul tries to relieve the tension between these two groups since it endangers his gospel, which seeks to unite Gentile and Jew in Christ. While stimulating, this proposal labors under the burden of explaining why Paul wrote the first eleven chapters of Romans.

Given the inability of any one proposal to explain "the purpose" for Romans, Wedderburn (1991a, 140–42) is probably correct when he argues that it is better to talk about the "reasons" for Romans rather than "the reason" for Romans. Paul undoubtedly had multiple reasons for writing Romans: his upcoming visit to Jerusalem, his mission to Spain, the tensions within the Roman community, the rumors and slanders about his gospel, and his desire to preach his gospel to the Romans. Accordingly, since his missionary work in the East was done, he writes this extended letter, which approaches the form of a letter-essay (Stirewalt 1991), to present himself to the Romans for some or all of the reasons listed above.

This said, it seems to me that although we cannot know with complete assurance Paul's inner purpose(s) for writing this letter, we can know what L. Ann Jervis (1991, 34) calls the "communicative function" of Romans, by which she means "the overriding intention of the communication without suggesting that one is peeking into Paul's mind." In this respect, Jervis is correct when she writes: "The function of Romans is to preach the gospel by letter to the Christian converts at Rome" (164). This is why Paul says that he is eager to preach the gospel to those at Rome (1:15), and why he reminds the Romans of the grace of apostleship that has been given to him to preach to the Gentiles, among whom are the Romans (1:6; 15:15–21). Consequently, although Paul hopes to preach the gospel when he comes to Rome, he is *already* preaching to the Romans through this letter, which will be read in their assemblies before his arrival. Romans continues to function in this way today whenever it is read in the liturgical assembly. For when it hears Romans proclaimed, the assembly hears the gospel of Paul.

> ### The Expulsion of the Jews from Rome
>
> "Since the Jews constantly made disturbances at the instigation of Chrestus, he [the Roman Emperor Claudius] expelled them from Rome." (Suetonius, *Claud.* 25, trans. Graves 1979)
>
> "There [at Corinth] he found a Jew named Aquila, a native of Pontus, who had recently come from Italy with his wife Priscilla, because Claudius had ordered all the Jews to leave Rome." (Acts 18:2)

The Text of Romans

While a few papyri dating from as early as the second and third centuries contain portions of Romans, the full text is found only in parchment manuscripts,

Figure 1. MS 0220 (Rom. 4:23–5:3; 5:8–13), Egypt, third century AD. This fragment of a vellum (sheepskin) manuscript shows wording from Rom. 4:23–5:3 written in an uncial script (i.e., all capital letters). In manuscripts of this period, there was no punctuation and no spacing between words.

the most important of which are uncials (manuscripts written in capital letters), although there are two important minuscules (manuscripts written in small and usually cursive letters), 33 and 1739, that are of high quality.

The following summary of papyri and parchment manuscripts is drawn from Kurt and Barbara Aland (1989), and from Bruce M. Metzger and Bart D. Ehrman (2005). In discussing the comparative value of the papyri and parchment manuscripts, I have employed the Alands' (335–36) five categories: (I) "Manuscripts of a very special quality." These are "manuscripts with a very high proportion of the early text." Papyri and manuscripts of the Alexandrian text type belong to this category. (II) "Manuscripts of a special quality." These contain "a considerable portion of the early text" but manifest "alien influences," especially from the Byzantine tradition. (III) "Manuscripts with a small but not a negligible proportion of early readings, with a considerable encroachment of polished readings." (IV) "Manuscripts of the Western text, or the D text." This text tends to be more expansive. (V) "Manuscripts with a purely or predominantly Byzantine text." Although this text offers a more polished reading, it is usually viewed as the least reliable for establishing the earliest text.

Among the papyri ($\mathfrak{P}^{10, 26, 27, 31, 40, 46, 61, 94, 113}$), four date from the third century ($\mathfrak{P}^{27, 40, 46, 113}$), one from the fourth ($\mathfrak{P}^{10}$), and the others ($\mathfrak{P}^{26, 31, 61, 94}$) ranging from the fifth to the seventh centuries. The most complete and important of these papyri is the Chester Beatty Papyrus $\mathfrak{P}^{46}$, which contains Rom. 5:17–6:14; 8:15–15:9; 15:11–16:27 and dates from about AD 200. The Alands identify it as a "free text" of category 1. $\mathfrak{P}^{46}$ is important for the textual history of Romans because it places the doxology, which is usually found at the end of Romans (16:25–27), after chapter 15.

Among the uncials that contain the full, or nearly the full, text of Romans, I highlight nine:

Manuscript number	Latin name	Traditional letter designation	Date	Category
01	Sinaiticus	ℵ	4th century	category I
02	Alexandrinus	A	5th century	category I (in Paul)
03	Vaticanus	B	4th century	category I
04	Ephraemi Syri Rescriptus	C	5th century	category II
010	Augiensis	Fᵖ	9th century	category II
012	Boernerianus	Gᵖ	9th century	category III
020	Angelicus	Lᵃᵖ	9th century	category V
044	Athous Lavrensis	Ψ	8th/9th century	category III

The following papyri and manuscripts belong to category I, making them especially important for establishing the earliest text of Romans: all of the papyri except 𝔓⁶¹ (category II) and 𝔓⁹⁴ (not categorized because it is too brief), the uncials 01, 02, 03, and the minuscules 33 and 1739. The most important textual problem in Romans concerns the doxology (16:25–27), which occurs in different places in the manuscript tradition, thereby raising the question of the letter's original form. I will discuss this problem in the introductory matters that pertain to the letter closing (15:14–16:27).

Tracing the Train of Thought

One of the distinguishing characteristic of this commentary series is its focus on the author's train of thought. Accordingly, rather than provide readers with a detailed exegetical analysis of individual words and verses, I seek to clarify Paul's overall argument, unit by unit. But Paul's thought is complex, and even when one understands his train of thought in a particular unit, it is necessary to see how the many literary units that constitute Romans are related to one another in the service of Paul's overall argument. While I have tried to review his overall argument throughout this commentary, especially when embarking on new sections of the letter, it will be helpful to summarize the overall movement of Romans before attending to a closer reading of the letter's individual units. In this way, those who read all or part of this commentary will have an understanding of the letter's argument. Below is the outline that guides my reading of the text.

The Letter Opening (1:1–17)

Romans begins with a letter opening in which Paul introduces himself, summarizes the gospel he preaches, announces his desire to visit the Romans, and explains why he is not ashamed of the gospel. In explaining why he is not ashamed of the gospel, Paul announces the theme that underlies his gospel: the righteousness of God, by which he means God's saving justice as revealed in Christ for the salvation of all, Gentile as well as Jew. This carefully constructed letter opening is longer than any other Pauline greeting because Paul is introducing himself to a community he did not establish and most of whose members have never seen or heard him, although some have heard rumors and scandalous remarks about his law-free gospel. In the letter closing, Paul will return to several of the themes he announces in the letter opening, especially his apostolic commission and plans to visit Rome, thereby enclosing the body of the letter in a frame that consists of an opening and closing that interpret each other as well as the entire letter.

Gentiles and Jews in the Light of God's Wrath (1:18–3:20)

Having announced that he is not ashamed of the gospel because it reveals God's righteousness, Paul proclaims that the wrath of God is presently being revealed against the impiety and unrighteousness of those who are suppressing the truth of God. The righteousness and the wrath of God can be compared to two sides of a coin. "The wrath of God is to unbelief the discovery of His righteousness, for God is not mocked. The wrath of God is the righteousness of God—apart from and without Christ" (Barth 1933, 43).

Paul's purpose in this part of Romans is to show that all, without exception, Jew as well as Gentile, are in need of the saving righteousness that God has manifested in Christ because all, Jew as well as Gentile, are under the domination of a cosmic power that Paul identifies as "sin." Although Paul will not explain how "sin" has attained this status until chapter 5, this part of Romans seeks to persuade Paul's audience of the sinful plight in which humanity finds itself and so its need for the saving righteousness that God reveals in Christ.

Three Text Types

The *Alexandrian text* is considered to be the earliest and most reliable text type. Among its chief witnesses are the Bodmer papyri, especially $\mathfrak{P}^{66}$ and $\mathfrak{P}^{75}$ (which contain early fragments of Luke and John), Codex Sinaiticus (ℵ), and Codex Vaticanus (B).

The *Western text*, which often manifests distinctive and expansive readings, appears to have been used in Italy, Gaul, and North Africa. Its chief witness is the text of D, comprising Codex 05 (Bezae Cantabrigiensis) for the Gospels and Codex 06 (Claromontanus) for the Epistles.

The *Byzantine text* (variously referred to as the Syrian text, the Koine text, the Ecclesiastical text, the Antiochian text, the Majority text) is witnessed to by the majority of NT manuscripts. It was the imperial text of Constantinople and was used throughout the Byzantine Empire. Since it tends to introduce stylistic improvements, it is less reliable for establishing the earliest text.

An Outline of Romans

The letter opening (1:1–17)

  Formal greeting and introduction (1:1–7)

  Thanksgiving and travel plans (1:8–17)

Gentiles and Jews in the light of God's wrath (1:18–3:20)

  Gentile failure to acknowledge God (1:18–32)

  The revelation of God's wrath (1:18)

  Why God's wrath is being revealed (1:19–23)

  How God's wrath is being revealed (1:24–31)

  Final condemnation (1:32)

  God's impartial judgment of Gentiles and Jews (2:1–16)

  God's just and impartial judgment (2:1–11)

  An example of God's impartiality (2:12–16)

  Jewish failure to observe the law (2:17–29)

  Reliance on the law is insufficient (2:17–24)

  Reliance on circumcision is insufficient (2:25–29)

  Gentiles and Jews under the power of sin (3:1–20)

  Questions and responses (3:1–8)

  All under the power of sin (3:9–20)

Gentiles and Jews in the light of God's righteousness (3:21–4:25)

  A righteousness accessible to all through faith (3:21–31)

  Abraham, the father of all who believe (4:1–25)

  "It was credited to him as righteousness" (4:1–12)

  "Abraham believed" (4:13–22)

  Conclusion (4:23–25)

The experience of salvation in the light of God's righteousness (5:1–8:39)

  Transferred from the realm of sin to the realm of grace (5:1–21)

  Humanity's new relationship to God as its ground for hope (5:1–11)

  The reason for this new relationship and hope (5:12–21)

  No longer slaves of sin and death (6:1–23)

  Why believers should not remain in sin (6:1–14)

  A change of allegiance from sin to righteousness (6:15–23)

  Released from a law frustrated by sin (7:1–25)

  An example from the law (7:1–6)

  The law is not sinful (7:7–12)

  The law did not bring death (7:13–23)

  Conclusion (7:24–25)

Paul develops his argument in four movements. First, he points to the failure of the Gentile world to acknowledge the truth and glory of God, even though it knew something of God from the created world (1:18–32). Consequently, God is presently manifesting his wrath against the sinful Gentile world by handing the Gentiles over to their own sinfulness so that the punishment of sin is to live in one's sin. Second, before turning to the situation of the Jewish world, Paul points to the impartiality of God (2:1–16). God does not judge

Life and hope in the realm of the Spirit (8:1–39)

The Spirit as the source of life (8:1–17)

The Spirit as the source of hope (8:18–30)

The irrevocable character of God's love (8:31–39)

God's righteousness and the destiny of Israel (9:1–11:36)

The mystery of divine election (9:1–29)

Paul's concern for Israel (9:1–5)

The principle of election (9:6–13)

A first objection and Paul's response (9:14–18)

A second objection and Paul's response (9:19–29)

The reason for Israel's failure (9:30–10:21)

Israel's failure to attain righteousness (9:30–10:4)

The righteousness that comes from faith (10:5–13)

Israel's disobedience (10:14–21)

God's irrevocable call (11:1–36)

A remnant remains (11:1–6)

The hardening of "the rest" of Israel (11:7–10)

The purpose of Israel's misstep (11:11–12)

A warning to Gentile believers (11:13–24)

The revelation of the mystery of Israel (11:25–32)

God's inscrutable wisdom (11:33–36)

God's righteousness and the moral life of the justified (12:1–15:13)

Love and obedience in the new age (12:1–13:14)

Paul's fundamental moral exhortation (12:1–2)

Living as one body in Christ (12:3–8)

Genuine love (12:9–21)

Subordination to those in authority (13:1–7)

Love as the fulfillment of the law (13:8–10)

The moral life in light of the end (13:11–14)

Welcoming one another according to the example of Christ (14:1–15:13)

An exhortation not to judge one another (14:1–12)

An exhortation not to scandalize one another (14:13–23)

An exhortation to support the weak (15:1–6)

An exhortation to receive one another (15:7–13)

The letter closing (15:14–16:27)

Paul's travel plans (15:14–33)

Commendation of Phoebe and greetings to those in Rome (16:1–16)

A warning (16:17–20)

Greetings from those with Paul (16:21–23)

[Grace (16:24)]

Doxology (16:25–27)

people on the basis of who they are but on the basis of what they do or fail to do. Having reminded his audience of God's impartiality, Paul in the third movement indicts the Jewish world for its failure to do the law in which it rightly boasts, for reliance on the law and circumcision are insufficient if one does not do the law (2:17–29). Paul begins the fourth movement by asking, if this is the situation in which the Jewish world finds itself, then what advantage is there in being a Jew (3:1–20)? After assuring his audience that there are many advantages, he comes to the climax of his argument. Although the Jewish world enjoys the advantage of the law and circumcision, it is no better off, because all are under the power of "sin" (3:9). Consequently no one will be justified before God by doing the works of the law (3:20) because all are under the power of "sin."

Although this description of the human plight may seem excessive, Paul is *not* giving a sociological analysis of the human condition. Standing on a higher mountain, he is *revealing* the situation of humanity apart from Christ when the human situation is analyzed in light of the saving righteousness that the gospel proclaims.

Gentiles and Jews in the Light of God's Righteousness (3:21–4:25)

Having argued that all, Jews as well as Gentiles, find themselves in a predicament from which they cannot free themselves because they are under the power of "sin," Paul returns to the theme of God's saving righteousness, which he introduced in 1:17. In one of the most important passages of Romans, he declares that God has manifested his saving righteousness in Christ's death on the cross. This death has resulted in redemption, justification, atonement, and the forgiveness of sins (3:21–26). Consequently, there is no room for boasting before God, because all, Jew as well as Gentile, are justified on the basis of faith apart from doing the works of the Mosaic law (3:27–31). To show that his gospel confirms the law rather than nullifies it, in chapter 4 Paul recounts the story of Abraham. In light of the gospel he exegetes the text: "Abraham believed God, and it was credited to him as righteousness" (Gen. 15:6). Noting that God acquitted Abraham on the basis of Abraham's trusting faith in God's promises before Abraham was circumcised, Paul presents Abraham as a model for Gentiles as well as Jews who walk in the way of faith that Abraham exhibited when he was still uncircumcised. Paul concludes this chapter with a description of Abraham's faith that was a type of resurrection faith inasmuch as Abraham believed God's promise even when his body and the womb of his wife Sarah were, for all practical purposes, dead. Such faith shows that Abraham was already believing in the God and Father of Jesus Christ, who raises the dead.

The Experience of Salvation in the Light of God's Righteousness (5:1–8:39)

After establishing the universal need for salvation and showing that God has responded to this need by manifesting his saving righteousness in Jesus Christ, Paul provides his audience with an extended discussion of the meaning and implication of God's righteousness for the Christian life. Paul develops this part of Romans in four movements. In the first, he describes how the justified have been transferred from the realm of "sin" to the realm of God's "grace"

(5:1–21). This movement begins with a description of the new situation in which believers find themselves (5:1–11): they are at peace with God because they have been justified and reconciled to God. Having been justified and reconciled to God, they can be all the more confident that they will be saved. Accordingly, believers live in hope of final salvation, a theme to which Paul will return at the end of chapter 8. To explain how this situation came about and how sin entered the world, Paul draws a comparison between Adam's act of disobedience that brought "sin" and "death" into the world, and Christ's singular act of obedience that brought "grace" and "life" into the world.

The second movement of Paul's discussion deals with the problem of sin in the Christian life (6:1–23). Since Paul's gospel proclaims that when sin increased, God's grace increased all the more (5:20), doesn't this imply that there is no need to stop sinning? Paul responds to this objection in two ways. First, he argues that believers died to sin when they participated in Christ's death through their baptism. Consequently, they have died to the power of sin over their lives (6:1–14). Second, he reminds them that they are no longer slaves of "sin," which pays a wage of "death," but slaves of righteousness, which gives them the gift of eternal life (6:15–23). Consequently, although it is possible for the justified to sin, continuing to sin is incongruous with the gospel that Paul preaches.

In the third movement of this part of the letter, Paul takes up the question of the Mosaic law (7:1–25). Does Paul's gospel imply that there is something sinful about the law (7:7)? Did the law bring people to death (7:13)? Paul emphatically denies these charges against his gospel by affirming that the law is holy (7:12) and spiritual (7:14). The culprit is not the law but the power of indwelling sin that frustrates the human person's desire to do what is good. In one of the most important and disputed passages of Romans, Paul describes the plight of the conflicted self that knows God's will but cannot do it because of the power of indwelling sin (7:13–23). The chapter comes to its climax with a cry of desperation: "Miserable one that I am, who will rescue me from this body doomed to death?" (7:24).

In chapter 8, the fourth movement of Paul's argument, the apostle answers this cry. What the law could not do, God has done by sending his own Son into the realm of the flesh to combat sin in its own realm. After explaining how God has dealt with sin by sending his own Son (8:1–4), Paul describes the new life of those who are in the realm of God's Spirit rather than in the realm of the flesh (8:5–17). Empowered by the Spirit, they can now live in a way that is pleasing to God. In the second half of chapter 8 (8:18–30), Paul returns to the theme of eschatological hope that he introduced in 5:1–11. Because the justified have received the gift of God's Spirit, they can be confident that God, who raised Jesus from the dead, will raise them as well. In addition to this, Paul affirms that the whole of creation is waiting for the revelation of God's children (which will occur at the general resurrection of the dead) so that creation itself can be set free from its bondage to futility. The chapter ends with a dramatic statement of God's irrevocable love for the justified, which assures them that nothing can separate them from God's love for them (8:31–39).

God's Righteousness and the Destiny of Israel (9:1–11:36)

After the ecstatic statement of confidence that concludes chapter 8, it might appear that Paul has said all that needs to be said about the righteousness of God. But this is not the case. Before he can complete his proclamation of God's saving righteousness, Paul must deal with two issues: (1) the failure of Israel to believe in the saving righteousness that God has revealed in Christ, and (2) the moral life of the justified. Paul deals with the first of these issues in Rom. 9–11, and with the second in 12:1–15:13.

As nearly all contemporary commentators insist, Rom. 9–11 is an integral part of Paul's exposition of the gospel since the fundamental question that drives the discussion is the faithfulness and integrity of God: Has God been faithful to Israel? Given the content of Paul's gospel, which proclaims justification on the basis of faith rather than on the basis of doing the works of the Mosaic law, it might appear (1) that God's ways have changed, (2) that God has not been faithful to the covenant promises made to Israel, and (3) that God has rejected his people. If this is the case, God is no longer reliable; God can no longer be trusted; God is not righteous. Accordingly, Rom. 9–11 is Paul's most profound discussion about God.

Paul develops this part of Romans in three movements. In the first, he considers the mystery of divine election by which God created Israel and continues to work on Israel's behalf (9:1–29). After expressing his deep concern for his people, Paul reviews the history of Israel to show how God created and has sustained Israel on the basis of divine election (9:6–13). He then confronts two objections to the principle of election: first, election implies injustice on God's part (9:14–18); second, God should not find fault, because no one can oppose God's will (9:19–29). In response to the first objection, he recalls the account of the hardening of Pharaoh to show that everything depends on God's mercy. In response to the second, he argues that it is not the place of the creature to question the Creator. He then explains that just as God created Israel on the basis of election, so God is presently creating a people from the Gentiles as well as the Jews. The word of God has not failed (9:6); for God is acting as God has always acted, on the basis of election and mercy.

In the second movement of his argument, Paul contends that the problem is not with God but with Israel's refusal to recognize God's saving righteousness revealed in Christ (9:30–10:21). The movement begins by highlighting the paradox that the Gentiles, who did not pursue righteousness, have attained it; yet Israel, which zealously pursued righteousness on the basis of the law, has failed to attain that righteousness (9:30–33). Paul's response is that Israel's zeal for the law was misguided because it did not recognize that Christ was the goal and terminus of the law. Consequently, Israel found itself pursuing its own righteousness rather than the righteousness God revealed in Christ (10:1–4). Paul concludes this movement by describing what he means by the righteousness that comes from faith (10:5–13) and by affirming that Israel has indeed heard the gospel (10:14–21). As Isaiah prophesied long ago, Israel has been, and remains, disobedient. The problem, then, is not the unfaithfulness of God but the disobedience of Israel.

In the third movement, Paul affirms God's irrevocable call of Israel (11:1–36). God has not rejected Israel, for although Israel has been disobedient, a faithful remnant remains, but a hardening has come upon the rest of Israel (11:1–10). However, this hardening is part of the divine plan. By it salvation has come to the Gentiles in order to make disobedient Israel jealous so that it will embrace the righteousness revealed in Jesus Christ (11:11–12). Consequently, Paul warns his Gentile readers who have been grafted into the olive tree, which is Israel, not to boast against unbelieving Israel because God is able to graft those who have not believed into the tree from which they were cut off (11:13–24). After this warning, Paul reveals a mystery: all Israel will be saved (11:25–32). Filled with awe as he contemplates the divine plan that will bring Jew and Gentile to salvation, Paul concludes this part of his letter with a hymn-like passage that celebrates God's inscrutable wisdom (11:33–36).

God's Righteousness and the Moral Life of the Justified (12:1–15:13)

Although Paul has completed what is sometimes called the "doctrinal" portion of his letter, he has not finished his exposition of the gospel. For in the final part of Romans he must draw out the implications of his gospel for everyday life. Paul develops this part in two movements. First, he presents the Romans with a general moral exhortation (12:1–13:14) before addressing a concrete issue pertinent to the Roman house congregations (14:1–15:13).

Paul sounds the leitmotif for his moral exhortation in 12:1–2 when he presents the moral life as an act of worship. The moral life that Paul envisions is integrally connected to the gospel he preaches inasmuch as it is a grateful response to what God has done in Christ. Consequently, living a morally good life becomes a way in which the justified offer themselves as living sacrifices to God. Following this initial exhortation, Paul embarks upon the first part of his paraenesis (12:3–13:14). Here he encourages the Romans to work for the good of one another by exercising the gifts that have been entrusted to them for their mutual benefit. He then provides the Romans with a description of genuine love, exhorting them not to avenge themselves but to leave retribution to God. Next, Paul exhorts the Romans to be subject to those in authority and pay taxes to those to whom they are due. He concludes this section by reminding his audience that all of the commandments find their fulfillment in the commandment to love one's neighbor, and he encourages them to prepare themselves for the struggle that the moral life entails since the day of their salvation is at hand.

In the second section of his paraenesis, Paul addresses the problem of the "weak" and the "strong" (14:1–15:13). Although commentators differ in the way they interpret the historical situation behind this section, the general thrust of Paul's argument suggests that he is addressing opposing factions among the Roman Christians, some of whom continue to practice certain dietary and calendar prescriptions of the law, and others who do not. Although Paul identifies himself as belonging to the strong, he exhorts the strong not to scandalize the weak and, if necessary, to curb their freedom in these matters. The entire section comes to a climax when Paul calls upon the weak and the strong to welcome each other as Christ has welcomed them (15:7–13).

The Letter Closing (15:14–16:27)

The letter closing returns to several of the themes that Paul introduced in the letter opening, thereby forming a frame around the body of the letter. It begins with Paul repeating his plans to visit Rome, which he announced in the letter opening (15:14–33). But this time he reveals that his visit is only one stage of a greater journey that will bring him to Spain, where he will open a new mission. Before he comes to Rome and goes to Spain, however, he must travel to Jerusalem to deliver the collection he has been taking up among his Gentile congregations for the poor among the Jewish believers in Jerusalem. After announcing his travel plans, Paul commends Phoebe (who may be the bearer of the letter) to the Romans before greeting several of the Roman Christians (16:1–16). The letter concludes with a warning about those who would cause divisions (16:17–20), greetings from those who are with Paul at Corinth (16:21–23), a grace wish that is not present in all manuscripts (16:24), and a benediction (16:25–27), which is found in different places in the manuscript tradition.

Theological Issues

Although Romans is an "occasional letter," inasmuch it was occasioned by the circumstances of Paul and the Romans, it remains a profoundly theological document that deals with issues central to humanity's relationship with God. This is not to say that Romans is a theological essay or a systematic compendium of Paul's theology. But it is a religious document composed by a man who has reflected deeply on the significance of the saving justice that God manifested in Christ. In doing so, Paul presents us with a series of insights that are foundational for the Christian understanding of the human person (anthropology), God's redemptive work in Christ (Christology and soteriology), the new community of believers whom God has called and sanctified in Jesus Christ (ecclesiology), the new life that believers live in and through the power of God's Spirit (ethics), and the hope of this sanctified community (eschatology). In effect, Romans provides us with the outline of a redemptive story that encompasses humanity's predicament prior to Christ, its redemption in Christ, and its hope for the final salvation and glorification it will enjoy when it participates in the glory that the risen Christ already enjoys.

God Who Is Righteous

From start to finish, Romans is about God. The gospel that Paul proclaims is God's own good news, God's gospel (1:1). The content of this gospel is God's Son; it is a gospel about Christ (1:4). This gospel is the power of God that brings people to salvation (1:16), for in the proclamation of the gospel, God's own righteousness (that is, God's saving justice, God's way of righting wrong, God's faithfulness and integrity) is revealed (1:17). In the face of sin, this righteousness is manifested as wrath, which results in condemnation for those who willfully refuse to acknowledge the truth and glory of God (1:18; 2:5). But God's judgments are always just because God is an impartial judge (2:11).

To deal with sin, God manifests his saving righteousness in the death of his Son on the cross (3:21–26). In doing so, God proves his love for sinners (5:8) by justifying the ungodly (5:6). Consequently, although God rightly manifests wrath in the face of sin, this wrath is the prelude to, and the manifestation of, God's saving righteousness in Christ. For where sin increased, God's grace abounded all the more (5:20). Because of the saving righteousness that God has manifested in Christ, there is nothing that can separate the justified from the love that God has for them (8:31–39).

Paul's most profound discussion about God occurs in Rom. 9–11, where he vigorously argues for the faithfulness and integrity of God. For if God's word has failed, and if God has rejected his people, then the God and Father of Jesus Christ is no longer the God of Abraham, Isaac, and Jacob. This is why Paul is firmly convinced that Israel's blindness is only temporary and is presently serving a greater purpose. For in God's own way and in God's own time, Israel will be saved. There is a depth to the wealth of God's wisdom and knowledge, then, that humans can never plumb, making God's decrees unfathomable and God's ways inscrutable (11:33). God is ultimately the source of hope—the God of hope (15:13)—because only God can give life to the dead and call into being what does not exist (4:17). In justifying the ungodly and raising the dead, God exhibits his love and creative power in a new and powerful way.

Christ the Eschatological Adam

In speaking of Christ, Paul talks about God as well; for it is in Christ that God reveals his saving righteousness. At the outset of this letter, Paul affirms Christ's Davidic lineage and so his messianic pedigree (1:3). Although Paul uses *Christos* as though it were a proper name, he is aware of its messianic significance, and in at least one instance he employs the term in its titular sense (9:5). Consequently, its messianic meaning remains close at hand. Christ is the agent of God's redemptive work, the anointed one for whom Israel hoped. But in the light of Christ's resurrection, Paul is keenly aware that Jesus is defined by what God has done in his Anointed more than by traditional messianic expectations. In light of the resurrection, Paul views Christ as the Son/Son of God (1:4, 9; 5:10; 8:3, 29, 32), the Lord (1:7; 4:24; 5:1; 10:9), the Lord of the dead as well as of the living (14:9).

Paul's understanding of Jesus, however, should not be limited to the titles he applies to him, since Romans focuses on what God has done in Christ (soteriology) more than on who Christ is (Christology). In addition to identifying Jesus as Christ, Son, and Lord, then, we can rightly call him the Justifier, the Redeemer, the Reconciler, and the Savior since he is the one in whom God justifies, redeems, reconciles, and saves humanity (3:24; 5:9–10). God, then, is revealed in Christ, and Christ is identified through God's saving work.

Paul presents Jesus as the eschatological Adam, the new human being who obediently does God's will. Although this Adam Christology occurs most explicitly in 5:12–21, it is a subtext that runs throughout this letter. For inasmuch as humanity has fallen short of God's glory because it has refused to acknowledge God, it found itself in the sphere of sin and death, the sphere of the old Adam, a realm in which it is impossible to please God. Consequently, it became necessary for God to send his own Son to do what the law, frustrated by sin, could not do, in order to transfer humanity to the realm of the eschatological Adam, who was perfectly obedient to God. The destiny of this new human being is the destiny of all who live in him. For just as God raised Christ from the dead and made him the eschatological Adam, so God will raise those who live in the sphere of the new human being. The justified, then, are coheirs with Christ and will be glorified with him, provided they suffer with him (8:16–17).

The Spirit of God and Christ

If God is the primary actor in the drama of salvation that Paul presents in Romans, and if Christ is the agent by whom God accomplishes this drama, then it is the Spirit of God and the risen Christ that enable the justified to live the new life that God makes possible in Christ. At the outset of Romans, Paul affirms that Jesus was appointed as Son of God in power by God's Spirit at the resurrection from the dead (1:4). Accordingly, even though Paul affirms the preexistence of Christ (Phil. 2:6), he understands that the resurrection was the moment of Christ's enthronement as Son of God in power by God's Spirit. Because the risen Lord was endowed with this Spirit in a powerful way at his resurrection from the dead, Paul can speak of the Spirit as the Spirit of Christ as well as the Spirit of God (Rom. 8:9). In writing this, Paul is not implying that there are two Spirits. Rather, he is suggesting that since the risen Lord enjoys the fullness of God's Spirit, this Spirit can be called the Spirit of Christ as well as the Spirit of God.

Thanks to God's redemptive work in Christ, believers enjoy this gift of the Spirit, and this assures them that just as God raised Jesus from the dead, so God will raise them from the dead as well (8:11). The Spirit, then, is the foretaste as well as the assurance of resurrection life. To be in the Spirit is to be in the realm of the eschatological Adam. Those who live in the realm of the Spirit are no longer determined by the powers of sin and death; they no longer need to live according to the flesh, which represents all that is mortal and destined to die.

Humanity Justified and Reconciled to God

Our discussion of the Spirit has brought us to our final topic: God's redemptive work in Christ on behalf of humanity. Apart from Christ, humanity was in a sinful predicament from which it could not extricate itself. This predicament came about because the creature rebelled against the Creator. This rebellion, in turn, introduced the power of sin into the world, which brought another cosmic power, the power of death (5:12). Accordingly, Adamic humanity found itself under the domination of a cosmic power called "sin" (3:9), which frustrated its desire to do God's will as expressed in the law (7:13). The end result, according to Paul's analysis of the human condition, is that Adamic humanity was in a predicament from which it could not free itself. For even though the law was holy and good (7:12), it could not bring humanity to righteousness so long as those who tried to observe the law were under the power of sin.

The purpose of God's work in Christ, then, was to do what humanity could not do for itself: to justify and reconcile it to God. This is why Paul's teaching on justification has been and remains central to Romans. By manifesting his saving justice in Christ's death and resurrection, God has justified humanity, thereby declaring it innocent. In doing this, God reconciled humanity and established it in a new covenant relationship with himself. Consequently, the justified and reconciled can be confident of their final salvation at the general resurrection of the dead. Already justified and reconciled, then, believers live in hope that they will be saved (8:24). In the meantime, they have already been transformed and sanctified by the gift of the Spirit that has been bestowed upon them. Inasmuch as they live in the realm of the Spirit, they are already part of a new creation that will be fully revealed at the resurrection of the dead. The essential response of the justified, then, is the obedience of faith (1:5). The justified must entrust themselves to what God has done in Christ and live accordingly. For even though they have been justified by God's grace, they must stand before the judgment seat of God (14:10).

Romans 1:1–17

The Letter Opening

⊡

Introductory Matters

Before embarking upon our reading of Rom. 1:1–17, it will be helpful to consider three introductory matters: (1) the relationship between the frame and the body of the letter, (2) the distinctive nature of the introductory material in Romans, and (3) the limits and structure of the letter opening.

The Relationship between the Frame and the Body of the Letter

The opening and concluding verses of Romans (1:1–17; 15:14–16:27) form a frame that encloses the body of the letter (1:18–15:13), in which Paul proclaims his gospel of God's righteousness. Although readers are rightly interested in the body of the letter because of its teaching on justification by faith, in recent years the frame of the letter has taken on a more significant role in the discussion of Romans (Miller 2000). For while the body of the letter contains the gospel that Paul proclaims, it is in the frame of the letter that the apostle makes his most explicit comments about his personal circumstances and reasons for writing to the Christ-believers at Rome. For example, in the letter opening Paul reveals that although he has been prevented from doing so in the past, he has often desired to visit the Christians at Rome (1:9–15). Then in the letter conclusion, after having presented his audience with an exposition of the gospel he preaches, he returns to the theme of this visit. This time, however, he explains (1) why he has been prevented from visiting Rome in the past;

(2) he reveals that after visiting Rome he will inaugurate a mission to Spain; and (3) he discloses that he is about to visit Jerusalem, where he will deliver the gracious gift that his Gentile congregations have designated for the poor among the holy ones in Jerusalem (15:14–33). Moreover, his extensive list of greetings in chapter 16 indicates that he is acquainted with several members of the various house churches at Rome.

According to A. J. M. Wedderburn (1991a, 5), an adequate explanation of Romans must explain the relationship between Paul's circumstances as related in the frame of the letter (his impending visits to Jerusalem, Rome, and Spain) and the gospel of God's righteousness that Paul expounds in the body of the letter. In other words, why does Paul provide his audience with such a detailed exposition of his gospel? Is there some relationship between the gospel he proclaims in the letter body and his circumstances and those of the Romans as disclosed in the frame of the letter?

Most contemporary scholars insist that the body of the letter should be read in light of the circumstances of Paul and the Romans as related in the letter frame. The letter frame, then, is not merely an appendage to Romans; it is intimately related to the body of the letter. Paul writes at a time when his missionary activity in the East has ended, and he is about to embark upon a new mission in the West. But if his mission to Spain is to succeed, he will need the assistance of the Romans, who must be persuaded of the gospel he presents in this letter. Consequently, there is an intimate relationship between the letter frame and the letter body inasmuch as the body of the letter proclaims the Pauline gospel of God's righteousness with a view to Paul's impending visits to Jerusalem and Rome, and his mission to Spain.

The Distinctive Nature of the Introductory Material

The letter opening of Romans has many distinctive features. First, it presents its audience with the most elaborate greeting of any Pauline letter. Second, it contains an extended section that deals with Paul's proposed visit to Rome. Third, it concludes with a concise and powerful summary of the gospel that Paul will develop in the body of the letter.

To appreciate the significance of the elaborate letter greeting in Romans, it is helpful to know that the greetings of the non-disputed Pauline Letters follow a standard form: sender to receiver, grace and peace. In most instances, this greeting consists of one or two verses. For example, in 1 Thess. 1:1 Paul associates himself with two cosenders: "Paul, Silvanus, and Timothy, to the church of the Thessalonians in God the Father and the Lord Jesus Christ. Grace to you and peace." But in Romans he begins with a careful description of his credentials as a slave and apostle of Christ Jesus without mentioning any cosenders (1:1). Next he summarizes the gospel he preaches (1:2–4) and highlights the apostleship he has received (1:5–6). Finally, he extends the traditional greeting of grace and peace to those at Rome (1:7), but without any reference to the church at Rome. The essential elements of the letter greeting (sender, receiver, grace and peace wish) occur in 1:1 and 1:7, and it would have been sufficient for Paul to limit the greeting to these verses. But since he has never visited Rome, and since the Romans have probably heard conflicting and damaging reports about the gospel he preaches, Paul carefully introduces himself in a formal way, as if he were an ambassador presenting his diplomatic credentials. The only other letter greeting comparable to Romans is Gal. 1:1–5, in which Paul insists upon his apostolic credentials and summarizes the truth of the gospel he preaches because some have challenged his gospel and apostolic credentials. Although Romans is not a polemical letter, Paul finds himself in an analogous situation inasmuch as some at Rome are suspicious of the gospel he preaches.

Like the letter greeting, the thanksgiving of this letter differs from the form of other Pauline thanksgivings, although it should be noted that the form of Paul's thanksgivings tends to be more flexible than the form of his letter greetings. The purpose of the Pauline thanksgiving is to establish a relationship between Paul and the recipients of the letter and to signal some of the themes he will develop in the rest of the letter. For example, in 1 Cor. 1:3–9 Paul thanks God for the many gifts of speech and knowledge that God has bestowed upon that church, and he prays that God will strengthen its members so that they may be blameless on the day of the Lord. By this thanksgiving Paul establishes an initial relationship with the community and highlights some of the issues he will discuss in the letter: the nature of knowledge, the gifts of the Spirit, and the eschatological dimension of the Christian life. In Romans the thanksgiving proper is found in 1:8, but it includes an initial presentation of Paul's travel plans (1:9–15) and a thematic statement of the gospel he will develop in the body of the letter (1:16–17). Although Paul normally narrates his travel plans at the end of his letters, there is an intimate relationship between his impending visit to Rome and the message he preaches that leads him to announce his travel plans at the beginning of this letter. This is a further indication of the relationship between the letter frame and the body of the letter. Because Paul presents his gospel in light of his coming visits to Jerusalem and Rome, he signals his intention to come to Rome in the opening of the letter, reserving the announcement of his plans to visit Spain until the end of the letter.

Finally, just as the letter greeting and thanksgiving of Romans are distinctive, so is Paul's summary of the gospel in 1:16–17. No other letter begins with such a powerful statement of the gospel. Nor is any thematic statement so consistently developed throughout the rest of the letter as is this statement. At the outset of this letter, Paul signals that he is writing about the power of the gospel in which God's saving righteousness is revealed. This break in form is not without purpose. Since the Romans have never seen or heard Paul, he knows that if they are to receive him in the way he hopes they will, he must provide them with a convincing exposition of the gospel he preaches. Consequently, he focuses their attention on the central theme that he will develop in the rest of the letter: God's saving righteousness. This theme has profound consequences for Paul's understanding of what it means to be in a right relationship with God, how God has dealt with Israel, how Gentile and Jewish believers ought to interact with each other, and how Christ-believers should relate to one another and conduct themselves in the world. The righteousness of God summarizes the central content of the teaching that Paul presents to the Romans.

The Limits and Structure of the Letter Opening

In addition to the issues raised above, we must consider two issues surrounding the limits and structure of the letter opening. How far does the introduction extend? How is it structured?

Although there is general agreement that the greeting of the letter consists of 1:1–7, there is less agreement about the limits and nature of the material that follows. For example, does the introduction include the thematic statement about the righteousness of God (1:16–17), or is it limited to 1:1–15? While most commentators (Byrne, Dunn, Stuhlmacher) include the thematic statement within the introductory material, Joseph Fitzmyer (1993, 253) does not. Even more disputed is how the material in 1:8–17 should be identified. Brendan Byrne (1996) labels it "Thanksgiving and Theme." James Dunn (1988) titles it "Personal Explanations and Summary Statement of the Letter's Theme," and Peter Stuhlmacher (1994) calls it "The Letter's Introduction and Announcement of Its Theme." Still others employ the categories of ancient rhetoric to identify the material. Thus Robert Jewett (2007) identifies 1:1–12 as the *Exordium*, which he subdivides into two pericopes, "The Inauguration of

---

Romans 1:1–17 in the Rhetorical Flow

▶ **The letter opening (1:1–17)**

Formal greeting and introduction (1:1–7)

Paul's self-identification (1:1)

A slave of Christ Jesus (1:1a)

A called apostle set apart for the gospel of God (1:1b)

The gospel Paul preaches (1:2–4)

Promised through the prophets in the Scriptures (1:2)

About God's Son (1:3–4)

Paul's apostleship (1:5–6)

The source of Paul's apostleship (1:5a)

The purpose of Paul's apostleship (1:5b)

The audience of Paul's apostleship (1:6)

Grace and peace wish (1:7)

Thanksgiving and travel plans (1:8–17)

Paul's prayer of thanksgiving (1:8)

Paul's intention to visit Rome (1:9–15)

His long-standing desire to visit Rome (1:9–10)

Why Paul wants to visit them (1:11–15)

Paul's confidence in the gospel (1:16–17)

The power of God (1:16a)

Salvation for all (1:16b)

The Jews first, then the Gentiles (1:16c)

Supporting reasons (1:17)

Paul's Communication with Believers in Rome" (1:1–7), and "Thanksgiving and *Causa*" (1:8–12), followed by *Narratio* (1:13–15) and *Propositio* (1:16–17). While these rhetorical categories are helpful, my structure employs the more traditional categories proper to letter writing. Moreover, I have chosen to include 1:16–17 with the introductory material since these verses are so intimately related to what precedes. In 1:15 Paul announces his eagerness to preach the gospel to those in Rome *because* he is not ashamed of the gospel, which is the power of God that reveals the righteousness of God (1:16–17).

Tracing the Train of Thought

The letter opening of Romans consists of two units: a greeting (1:1–7) followed by a thanksgiving in which Paul assures the recipients of his long-standing desire to visit and preach the gospel to them (1:8–17). The first unit consists of four subunits: Paul's self-identification (1:1), a summary of the gospel he preaches

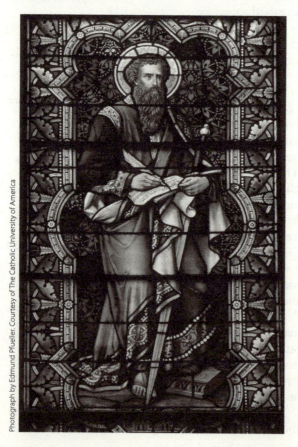

Photograph by Edmund Pfueller, Courtesy of The Catholic University of America

Figure 2. St. Paul the apostle, Caldwell Chapel, The Catholic University of America, Washington, DC. The sword, which appears in most artistic representations of St. Paul from around the fourteenth century, is usually taken to symbolize his martyrdom.

(1:2–4), a statement about his apostleship (1:5–6), and a greeting of grace and peace (1:7). The second unit consists of three subunits. In the first, Paul offers a prayer of thanksgiving (1:8). In the second, he explains his long-standing desire to visit the recipients of the letter in order to preach the gospel to them (1:9–15). In the third, which is grammatically joined to the second, he explains why he is not ashamed to preach the gospel to them (1:16–17). In the letter opening, then, Paul summarizes the gospel he preaches and announces his intention to visit Rome to preach the gospel of God's righteousness to them.

1:1–7. There is an intimate relationship between Paul's understanding of himself and the gospel he preaches. He proclaims the gospel because he is an apostle of Christ Jesus. Consequently, in the opening verse Paul presents himself in two ways. First, he is **a slave of Christ Jesus** (1:1a). Second, he is **an apostle called and set apart for God's own gospel** (1:1b).

By calling himself a slave of Christ Jesus, Paul affirms that his allegiance belongs to the one whose followers he formally persecuted. Although slaves constituted the lowest class of ancient society, Paul is not ashamed to be called Christ's slave because, as he will explain in chapter 6, those who have been freed from sin are free to be slaves to righteousness, which leads to life. This is why Paul makes use of this off-putting metaphor to describe his relationship to Christ.

Paul is Christ's slave because he has been called to be an apostle and set apart for "God's own gospel" (*euangelion theou*, which I construe as a subjective genitive). While Luke narrates Paul's call three times (Acts 9, 22, 26), Paul's own account is sparse in detail (Gal. 1:15–17). His call, however, is central to his understanding of his apostolic identity. While Paul was still in his mother's womb, God designated him to be an apostle to the Gentiles. Paul knows that he has been "set apart" (*aphōrismenos*; see Gal. 1:15, where he employs the same word) for God's own gospel. Just as Israel and the prophets had been set apart for service to the all-holy God of Israel, so Paul has been set apart for God's gospel: God's own good news about what God has accomplished in the saving death and resurrection of his Son.

Having identified himself as set apart for God's gospel, Paul describes the gospel in two ways. First, God **previously promised** this gospel **through his prophets in the holy Scriptures** (1:2a). Second, the subject of this gospel is **Jesus Christ our Lord** (1:4b). The continuity between the prophetic promises and the gospel about Jesus Christ is an essential aspect of this letter. Paul will argue that this gospel confirms rather than nullifies the law (3:31), and despite Israel's disobedience, God has not repudiated his people (11:1). Although the gospel is new and effects a new creation (2 Cor. 5:17), it was promised in Israel's prophetic scriptures. According to Gal. 3:8, God announced the gospel to Abraham.

Making use of what may have been a creedal formula familiar to the Roman Christians (Jewett 2007, 103–8), Paul summarizes the gospel he preaches in two phrases. The gospel is about God's Son, who was **born of David's seed, according to the flesh** (1:3), but then **appointed Son of God in power by the Spirit of holiness at the resurrection of the dead** (1:4a). In terms of his earthly descent, Jesus was the Davidic Messiah (2 Tim. 2:8). Therefore, although Paul does not develop the theme of Jesus's messiahship elsewhere, he is aware of it and of Israel's messianic hopes (Rom. 9:5). The inverted name, "Christ Jesus," then, can be understood as "Messiah Jesus"—Paul's way of highlighting Jesus's messiahship. The second, more developed phrase, speaks of Jesus's being appointed Son of God in or with power by the Spirit of holiness (i.e., the Holy Spirit) at the resurrection of the dead. Paul is not saying that Jesus became the Son of God at his resurrection but that God appointed or enthroned Jesus as Son of God *with full power* at his resurrection. For, although Christ preexisted with God, he entered into the realm of the flesh, where humanity did not recognize him because he did not insist on his godly status (Phil. 2:6–11). It was only at the resurrection, by the power of God's Spirit, that Jesus was enthroned with the full power that rightly belongs to him as God's Son. The expression "a Spirit of holiness" does not occur elsewhere in Paul's writings, an indication that this text may have come from an earlier creedal formula. It is attested in Isa. 63:10–11, however, and Fitzmyer (1993, 236) points to parallels in the Qumran literature (1QS 4.21; 8.16; 9.3; CD 2.12; 1QH 7.6–7; 9.32). The expression "at the resurrection" (lit., "from the resurrection of the dead") has the general resurrection of the dead in view and is consonant with Paul's theology, which understands Christ's resurrection as the firstfruits of the general resurrection of the dead (1 Cor. 15:20).

The manner in which Paul concludes this summary of his gospel ("Jesus Christ our Lord") leads to a discussion of his apostleship. It is through Jesus Christ our Lord that **we have received the favor of apostleship to bring about the obedience that consists in faith among all the Gentiles on behalf of his name** (1:5). Paul's apostleship, then, has its origins in the risen Lord, the Son of God, whom Paul proclaims in his gospel. Although he uses the word "apostleship" (*apostolēn*) only two other times (1 Cor. 9:2; Gal. 2:8), Paul's apostleship plays a central role in his thought, and he found it necessary to insist upon his apostolic status more than once (1 Cor. 9:1; Gal. 1:1). This apostleship, however, is not his own choice but a matter of God's "grace" or "favor" (*charis*) inasmuch as God has graciously called Paul in Christ. The purpose of Paul's apostleship is to bring about the *hypakoēn pisteōs* among all the Gentiles. This expression can be understood in several ways (Cranfield 1975, 66): as an objective genitive ("obedience to faith"), as a subjective genitive ("the obedience that faith works"), or as a genitive of apposition ("the obedience that consists in faith"). Given the close relationship that Paul establishes between faith and obedience in this letter, the genitive of apposition ("the obedience that consists in faith") is preferable. More than an intellectual consent to the truth, faith is a total entrusting of oneself to God that results in complete obedience to God. The recipients of Paul's preaching are the Gentiles, a point he will repeat in 1:14–15 and in 1:15–16.

Paul identifies the Romans as being among the Gentiles whom he is trying to bring to the obedience of faith: **Among them are you, who have been called by Jesus Christ** (1:6). The precise meaning of this phrase, however, is disputed. Does it suggest that Paul's audience is exclusively Gentile (Das 2007, 54–64)? Or does it mean that the Roman congregations, composed of both Gentile and Jewish believers, live among the Gentiles (Esler 2003, 111–15)? Whatever the answer, Paul identifies his recipients as "called by Jesus Christ," just as he was called to be an apostle.

Having identified himself, summarized his gospel, and explained the purpose of his apostleship, Paul finally extends his traditional greeting: **To all those in Rome, God's beloved, called and consecrated, grace and peace be to you from God our Father and Jesus Christ our Lord** (1:7). Somewhat surprisingly, there is no mention of the church at Rome, although Paul will extend greetings to the church in the house of Prisca and Aquila (16:3–4). This omission may reflect the composition of the Christian community at Rome, which appears to have been made up of a number of house churches. Paul, however, does identify the recipients of the letter in several other ways. They are "beloved of God" (*agapētois theou*), "called" (*klētois*), and "consecrated" (*hagiois*). Just as God set Paul apart for the gospel, so God called and consecrated them for service because they are God's beloved. It is fitting, then, that Paul extends to them the two blessings that summarize the gift of their new life: *charis*, the divine favor that God bestows on them; *eirēnē*, the peace and reconciliation they now enjoy with God because of Christ's saving death and resurrection.

1:8–17. Having greeted and introduced himself to the Romans in a formal manner since most of them have not seen or heard him, Paul undertakes the rhetorical task of establishing an initial bond between himself and his recipients in order to secure their trust and goodwill. He begins with a thanksgiving prayer in 1:8 that quickly takes up the topic of his planned visit to Rome. But rather than immediately announcing that he is coming to Rome, Paul carefully, almost apologetically, explains his long-standing desire to visit them. He will not disclose the full purpose of his visit, however, until chapter 15, after they have heard, through this letter, the gospel he preaches.

The thanksgiving functions like a *captatio benevolentiae* that enables Paul to gain the goodwill of his audience: **First, I thank my God, through Jesus Christ, for all of you, because your faith is proclaimed throughout the world** (1:8). To say that their faith is proclaimed throughout the world is not flattery. Just as the Romans have heard about Paul, so Paul has heard of them, as the list of greetings in chapter 16 reveals. Paul makes a similar statement about the faith of the Thessalonians (1 Thess. 1:8). But whereas he was the founding father of the Thessalonian community, he can make no such claim about the congregations of Christ-believers at Rome. Others have already proclaimed the gospel there, and their work has borne fruit. Paul is not coming "to plant" the gospel or to reprimand the Romans, although he will offer them his advice regarding a delicate situation (14:1–15:13). Their faith is strong, as his statement of confidence in the letter closing affirms (15:14).

Paul assures his audience that, although he has never seen them, he constantly remembers them and prays that he may succeed in visiting them. To reinforce this statement, he calls upon God as his witness (as he does in 2 Cor. 1:23; 11:31; Gal. 1:20; Phil. 1:8) and situates what he says in the wider context of his apostolic ministry: **The God whom I worship spiritually by proclaiming the gospel about his Son is my witness how I constantly remember you, always petitioning in my prayers if at last somehow I might, by God's will, succeed in coming to you** (1:9–10). Here Paul uses the kind of cultic language that he will employ in 15:16, where he speaks of serving the gospel in a priestly capacity so that he can present his Gentile converts as a pleasing sacrificial offering to God. Paul's ministry is a spiritual and priestly task, and he views his proclamation of the gospel as an act of worship, just as he views the moral life of the redeemed as an act of worship (12:1). However, whereas earlier Paul spoke of "God's own gospel" (a subjective genitive), here he speaks of "the gospel about his Son" (an objective genitive). The Son of God is the content of the gospel of God that Paul preaches. Paul's continual prayer that he may finally succeed in visiting the Romans indicates that this is a long-standing desire on his part. But to this point, God has not yet allowed this visit.

In 1:11–15 Paul provides the Romans with several reasons why he wants to visit them. This section falls into three parts: why Paul longs to see them (1:11–12); a disclosure of his past attempts to visit them (1:13); and why he is eager to preach the gospel to them (1:14–15).

Paul begins with a clause (a *gar* explanatory clause) that explains why he constantly prays that he might be able to visit the Romans: **For I long to see you that I might impart to you some spiritual gift in order to strengthen you** (1:11). But lest they perceive his intended visit as one-sided or heavy-handed, Paul clarifies what he means: **that is, to be encouraged by you through our mutual faith, yours and mine** (1:12). Although the precise meaning of the "spiritual favor" (*charisma pneumatikon*) Paul hopes to impart is not clear, his statement about his eagerness to preach the gospel at Rome (1:15) suggests that his proclamation of the gospel will be his spiritual gift to them. The doxology of 16:25–27, which has a complicated textual history, appears to confirm this interpretation: "To the one who is able to strengthen you in accordance with my gospel and the proclamation of Jesus Christ" (16:25). It is by his proclamation of the gospel, then, that Paul will strengthen the Romans. But lest they misunderstand his intentions, he explains what he means: his faith will encourage their faith, and their faith will encourage his faith. Paul makes a similar point in 15:24, where he expresses his hope that he will be able to enjoy their company before being sent forth by them to Spain. Consequently, in addition to strengthening them by the gospel he preaches, Paul hopes to be encouraged by their faith, which has been proclaimed throughout the world.

Next, Paul employs a disclosure formula and explains that he has often attempted to visit the Romans but has been prevented from doing so: **I do not want you to be unaware, brothers and sisters, that I have often proposed to come to you so that I might have some fruit even from you as from the rest of the Gentiles, but until now I have been prevented from doing so** (1:13). Paul will not reveal until 15:18–24 why he has been prevented from visiting them. Then he will explain that he has been detained because of his missionary work in the East. Paul's purpose, then, is to strengthen and be encouraged by the community and to reap some "fruit" (*karpon*) at Rome as well. The metaphor of "fruit" suggests that Paul hopes to gain some converts from among those at Rome who do not yet believe. In 16:5 he employs the related metaphor of the "firstfruit" (*aparchē*) to speak of Epaenetus as his first convert in Asia.

The mention of the Gentiles in 1:13 leads to Paul's climatic statement in which he explains why he is coming to Rome: **For I am obligated to Greeks and barbarians, to those who are wise and to those who are foolish. This explains my eagerness to preach the gospel even to you who are in Rome** (1:14–15). Paul's desire to visit Rome is rooted in the obligation he has to all the Gentiles, inasmuch as he is the apostle to the Gentiles, a point he will make again in 15:15–16. These neatly balanced verses can be displayed in this way:

to Greeks	and	to barbarians
to those who are wise	and	to those who are foolish

In this couplet, Paul is speaking of the Gentile world, which he views from two perspectives. On the one hand, some are "Greeks" in the sense that they have been hellenized and so are the beneficiaries of Greek culture. Such people view themselves as wise. On the other hand, some are "barbarians" in the sense that they do not participate in this culture. From the perspective of those who are hellenized, such people are without wisdom; they are foolish. From Paul's perspective, both groups belong to "the nations," and so they are part of his missionary field. Inasmuch as he is the apostle to the Gentiles, he is eager to visit Rome and preach the gospel there.

Paul's statement that he is eager to preach the gospel to those who are at Rome puzzles some commentators since it appears to contradict the missionary principle he states in the closing of the letter: "Thus I have aspired not to preach where Christ is already known, lest I should build on another's foundation, but as it is written, 'Those to whom it has not been proclaimed about him will see, and those who have not heard will understand'" (15:20–21). Paul makes a similar statement in 2 Cor. 10:15–16, in a polemical portion of the letter in which he confronts outside missionaries whom he sarcastically calls "superapostles" (2 Cor. 11:5).

The tension between Rom. 1:15 and 15:20–21, however, is more apparent than real since the letter closing of Romans indicates that Paul will not settle in Rome to establish his own congregation. He will only pass through Rome, on his way to Spain (15:23–24). Consequently, Paul is not coming to build on the foundation that others have laid but to encourage and be encouraged by the Christ-believers at Rome by preaching the gospel there before traveling to Spain.

Most commentators identify 1:16–17 as the theme of the letter. This thematic statement, however, is an integral part of the letter thanksgiving, intimately related to what precedes it. In 1:14–15 Paul has just said that he is under obligation to proclaim the gospel to Gentiles of every social class, the foolish as well as the wise, and thus he is eager to preach the gospel at Rome. Next, he begins with a clause introduced by *gar* (for) that explains why he is eager to preach the gospel: **For I am not embarrassed by the gospel** (1:16a). Following this clause, he uses two other *gar* explanatory clauses to explain why he is not embarrassed by the gospel. First, **for it is God's own power, resulting in salvation for all who believe** (1:16b). Second, **for in it God's righteousness is revealed** (1:17a). The train of thought of this thematic statement and its relationship to the material that precedes it can be displayed in this way:

> Paul is eager to preach the gospel to those in Rome.
>   Why?
> Because he is not embarrassed by the gospel.
>   Why?
> Because the gospel is God's own power resulting in salvation for all.
>   Why?
> Because in the gospel God's own righteousness is revealed.

But why should the gospel be a cause of embarrassment for Paul? Although contemporary Western Christians are no longer scandalized by the gospel, there was good reason for Paul to be ashamed of the gospel since he proclaimed the crucified Christ, "a stumbling block to Jews and foolishness to Gentiles" (1 Cor. 1:23). Paul, however, is not embarrassed by this gospel, which he identifies as the "message about the cross" (1 Cor. 1:18), because he knows from personal experience that the gospel is "God's own power resulting in salvation."

Believers already experience this power in the gift of the Spirit that God bestows on those who embrace the gospel (Gal. 3:5). But there is also a paradoxical dimension to the power of God that cannot be grasped apart from the cross. For example, Paul writes, "For the message about the cross is foolishness to those who are perishing, but to us who are being saved it is the power of God" (1 Cor. 1:18). Fully aware that his proclamation is scandalous to many, Paul writes, "We proclaim Christ crucified, a stumbling block to Jews and foolishness to Gentiles, but to those who are called, both Jews and Greeks, Christ the power of God and the wisdom of God" (1 Cor. 1:23–24).

Paul knows that inasmuch as the gospel is "God's own power" (*dynamis theou*), it results **in salvation for all who believe, for the Jew first and then for the Greek** (1:16b). The salvation that Paul has in view is eschatological and cosmic in scope, as chapter 8 will show. It entails nothing less than the general resurrection from the dead and creation's freedom from its present corruption (8:19–23). In what follows, Paul will show that this salvation is available to all on the basis of faith in what God has accomplished in Christ. But there is a salvation-historical order in God's work of salvation. Because Israel is and remains God's chosen people, this salvation belongs to the Jews first and then to the "Greeks," which should be taken in the broader sense of the Gentiles. Paul will repeat this salvation-historical order in 2:9–10, and throughout this letter he will emphasize the universality of the salvation that God offers in Christ, on the basis of faith, but always with a view to Israel's enduring role in God's salvific plan. To summarize, Paul is not embarrassed by the gospel he preaches because God's salvific power is at work for all in the proclamation of the gospel.

There is another reason why Paul is not embarrassed by the gospel: when the gospel is proclaimed, God's own righteousness is revealed **from faith to faith, as it is written, "The righteous one will live by faith"** (1:17b). Although I have construed *dikaiosynē theou* as a subjective genitive ("God's own righteousness"), it could be taken as a genitive of origin, "the righteousness that comes from God." If the phrase is taken as a genitive of origin, the focus of the letter is on the gift of righteousness that God communicates to the justified. This reading makes good sense of the letter and has been adopted by some of its most significant commentators (Luther, Nygren, Cranfield). But in recent years, since the seminal essay of Ernst Käsemann (1969b), " 'The Righteousness of God' in Paul," commentators have increasingly construed this phrase as a subjective genitive. When the phrase is so understood, the focus is on God's own righteousness. This righteousness, however, is not to be understood in a legal sense as God's retributive justice (*justitia dei*), but as God's saving justice, God's covenant loyalty, God's uprightness and integrity, God's faithfulness to what it means for God to be God. This dimension of God's righteousness, which appears in the Psalms and in the book of the prophet Isaiah, can be seen in Isa. 51:5, 8 LXX, which equates God's "righteousness" (*dikaiosynē*) with God's "salvation" (*sōtēria*):

> My *righteousness* draws near swiftly,
>   my *salvation* will go out, . . .
> but my *righteousness* will be forever,
>   and my *salvation* for generations of generations. (Isa. 51:5, 8 NETS)

The parallel nature of these texts indicates that God's "righteousness" (*dikaiosynē*) is God's "salvation" (*sōtēria*). Righteousness, then, is not a static

35

quality whereby God exercises justice but a dynamic quality whereby God effects salvation. This interpretation of the righteousness of God puts the emphasis where it ought to be (on God's saving justice) without neglecting the righteousness that God grants as a free gift. For when the righteousness of God is revealed, those who respond in faith receive the gift of God's righteousness.

Everything begins and ends with faith. Thus Paul writes that God's righteousness is revealed "from faith to faith." Although commentators have interpreted this phrase in a variety of ways, it seems best to take it as Paul's way of saying that from start to finish, from beginning to end, the revelation of God's righteousness in the gospel is related to faith. Or, as Paul will soon say, it is not a matter of doing the works of the law. To confirm what he means, he quotes Hab. 2:4, "The righteous will live by faith." Once more, Paul confronts us with a number of interpretive decisions. Does he mean that the one who is righteous on the basis of faith will live? Or does he mean that the one who is righteous will live by faith? Although the LXX of Hab. 2:4 reads "But the just shall live by my faith [God's faithfulness]" (NETS), the Hebrew text reads "The righteous man is rewarded with life for his fidelity" (NJPS). Neither the Hebrew nor the LXX, however, understands the text as referring to someone who has been justified on the basis of faith. Consequently, although reliable commentators (Nygren 1949, 89–90) have understood the text to mean that the one who is righteous through faith will live, it is more natural to take the phrase with the verb that follows it ("live") rather than with the noun that precedes it ("righteous"). Accordingly, I interpret the text to mean that the righteous person lives by faith, as Paul will show in his discussion of Abraham in chapter 4.

To summarize, the purpose of Paul's thanksgiving is to broach the subject of his upcoming visit, which he will discuss in greater detail in the letter closing, and to announce the theme of the gospel that he will proclaim in this letter and when he comes to Rome: the righteousness of God.

Theological Issues

Paul sees an intimate relationship between his apostleship and the gospel he proclaims. He preaches the gospel with authority because he knows that he has been called and set apart to be an apostle of Christ Jesus. Having received this grace of apostleship, Paul understands that he must preach the gospel to the Gentiles in order to bring them to the obedience that faith entails. There is a close relationship, then, between Paul's understanding of himself as an apostle of Jesus Christ and the gospel he preaches. He preaches the gospel because he is an apostle, and the gospel he preaches is rooted in the apostleship he has received. To deny Paul's gospel is to deny his apostleship, and to deny his apostleship is to call into question the gospel he preaches. Consequently, although the letter opening of Romans raises a number of theological issues, it will be helpful to focus on this single issue. For unless we understand the relationship that Paul draws between his apostleship and the gospel he preaches, we will never comprehend how and why he speaks with such sublime authority and confident assurance in this letter.

Paul's Apostleship

Paul is consumed with his apostleship. In Gal. 1:1 he defends himself against those who have called his apostleship into question, insisting that he did not receive this apostleship from or through human beings but through Jesus Christ and God the Father. In 1 Cor. 3:5–4:21, he explains the nature of his apostolic ministry in light of the message of the crucified Christ, whom he proclaims. And in 2 Cor. 2:14–7:4 he provides the Corinthians with a careful presentation of what it means to be a minister of the new covenant, an ambassador of Christ who calls people to reconciliation. When Paul writes to the Romans, then, he addresses them with a profound understanding of himself as someone who has been sent to preach the gospel to the nations. Karl Barth captures the significance of Paul's apostleship for the gospel he preaches when he begins his Romans commentary in this way: "The man who is now speaking is an emissary, bound to perform his duty; the minister of his King; a servant, not a master. However great and important a man Paul may have been, the essential theme of his mission is not within him but above him—unapproachably distant and unutterably strange" (Barth 1933, 27). Because he understands himself as someone who has been called and set apart, someone who has received the grace of apostleship, Paul speaks as if he were proclaiming his message from a lofty mountaintop where he sees what nobody else sees, and understands what everybody else has misunderstood. How else can the apostle condemn humanity as being under the power of sin? How else can he say that God's own righteousness has been revealed in Christ? How else can Paul claim to be establishing the law when he says that a person is justified by faith rather than by the works of the law? How else can the apostle reveal the mystery of God's plan for Gentiles and Jews? In a word, Paul dares to speak as he does because he knows that he is a called apostle with a unique ministry to the Gentiles.

This is not to say that Paul views himself as the only apostle or the most important apostle. In 1 Cor. 15:9–10 he calls himself the least of the apostles, although he claims to have worked harder than all of them. And in his greetings to the Romans, he acknowledges Andronicus and Junia as prominent among the apostles, believers in Christ before he was (16:7). Paul knows of other apostles whose names will never be known to us. And there is no reason to think that he considered his apostleship as different in kind from theirs. But apart from the Twelve, whom Paul sees as a distinct group, he is the apostle we know best. And if we are to understand how he can proclaim the gospel from such a lofty height, we must come to grips with his apostleship. For unless we acknowledge Paul's apostolic claims, we will always be offended by the assurance and authority with which he speaks about God, Christ, the Spirit, and the human condition apart from God. Put another way, just as we must accept Jesus as God's messianic Son if we are to embrace his message of the inbreaking kingdom of God, so we must accept Paul's claim to apostleship if we are to embrace the gospel of God's righteousness that he preaches.

The Gospel Paul Preaches

What Paul preaches can be summed up in single word: *euangelion*. Paul proclaims the gospel, the good news of what God has accomplished in Christ's saving death and resurrection. For Paul this gospel is God's power—not a faint reflection of it, not an imitation of it, not a representation of it, but the very power of God. To proclaim the gospel is to make God's salvific power present to all who believe, Gentile as well as Jew. The proclamation of the gospel, then, is an urgent task. For unless people hear the gospel, they will not believe; and if they do not believe, they will not be saved. Consequently, Paul preaches the gospel to bring the Gentiles to the obedience that is faith, confident that when the Gentiles believe in the gospel, they will be obedient to God's will.

The gospel is not a message that Paul or others have devised. When Paul speaks of "my gospel" (2:16) he is not making a claim of authorship, nor is he saying that there is a particular version of the gospel that is distinctively his own. There is only one gospel, the gospel of God, God's own gospel, and the content of this gospel is Jesus Christ. This is why Paul speaks of the gospel of God's Son (1:9) or the gospel of Christ (15:19), by which he means the gospel about Jesus Christ. Thus the gospel of God is the gospel about Christ: God's own good news, which God has entrusted to Paul and other apostolic ministers for the salvation of the world.

For Paul, the proclamation of the gospel is an apocalyptic event because something is revealed: the saving righteousness and covenant loyalty that God manifested in Jesus Christ's death and resurrection. Apart from the proclamation of the gospel, this saving righteousness is hidden. For how else can one "see" the saving righteousness of God in what the world perceives as a crucified criminal? How else can one see God's covenant loyalty in the shameful death of a crucified man, apart from the gospel? Thus the preaching of the gospel reveals the righteousness of God. The preaching of the gospel discloses God's eternal purpose for Gentile and Jew. The preaching of the gospel reveals how God has justified and reconciled humanity to himself. The preaching of the gospel assures the reconciled and justified of the salvation that awaits them and the entire cosmos at the resurrection of the dead.

Apostleship and Gospel

It is little wonder that Paul begins his Letter to the Romans with a summary of his apostolic credentials and the gospel he preaches. For unless the listeners/

readers of this letter understand the relationship between Paul's gospel and his apostleship, they will not accept or comprehend his letter. Romans is written from a lofty mountain, from a higher vantage point, because the one who writes is an apostle of Jesus Christ. He does not preach his own message but the gospel that God has entrusted to him: God's own gospel about his Son, Jesus Christ. To comprehend the relationship between gospel and apostle is to understand the profound significance of this letter, which challenges every attempt of humanity to assert itself before God. To understand the relationship between gospel and apostle is to comprehend that, as offensive as it may sound to secular ears, Paul speaks God's word, a word that condemns and saves, a word that exposes and purifies, those who hear it.

PART 1

Romans 1:18–3:20

Gentiles and Jews in the Light of God's Wrath

The first part of Romans begins with a powerful description of the human predicament apart from God's saving righteousness. Apart from God's righteousness, humanity finds itself under God's wrath, which is God's just judgment in the face of humanity's refusal to acknowledge the truth about God. Paul places this description of the human predicament between two thematic statements in which he proclaims the righteousness of God. This results in the following structure:

A The gospel reveals the *righteousness of God* (1:16–17)
 B The *wrath of God* is being revealed from heaven (1:18–3:20)
A′ The *righteousness of God* has been manifested in Christ's saving death apart from the law (3:21–26)

Paul's description of the human predicament consists of four movements: the failure of Gentiles to acknowledge God (1:18–32), God's impartial judgment of Gentiles and Jews (2:1–16), Jewish failure to observe the law (2:17–29), and the enslavement of Gentiles and Jews to the power of sin (3:1–20).

Paul's purpose in this part of Romans is to show the universal need for the salvation that the gospel brings. To establish his point, he demonstrates that not only the Gentiles but even God's chosen people have sinned and fallen short of the glory for which God intended them. First, Paul explains that God has delivered the Gentile world to the consequences of its sinfulness (1:18–32). Next, he establishes the utter impartiality of God, who judges Gentiles and Jews on the basis of what they have done rather than on the basis of who they are (2:1–16). Having reminded his audience of God's impartiality, Paul points to the failure of God's own people, even though they have had the advantage of the law and circumcision (2:17–29). Finally, in the climax of his argument, Paul explains why the Gentiles (who knew something of God from creation) and the Jews (who had the law and circumcision) have fallen short of God's glory (3:1–20). The reason is that both find themselves under the power of sin, which frustrates every attempt to do God's will (3:9). Consequently no one will be justified before God on the basis of doing the works of the law (3:20), for humanity finds itself under a power from which it cannot free itself (3:9).

Those who read through the first part of Romans will do well to keep the following in mind. First, Paul is describing the human situation from the point of view of the gospel. He sees what others do not see because he views the human predicament from God's perspective. Second, Paul sees no exit from this predicament apart from Christ, for humanity is under a power that frustrates its attempt to do God's will. Finally, in this section Paul has both Gentiles and Jews in view. His primary concern is to show that these two peoples, those who have the benefit of the law and circumcision and those who do not, find themselves in the same predicament, a situation from which they cannot extricate themselves.

Romans 1:18–32

Gentile Failure to Acknowledge God

⌘

Introductory Matters

Before I consider Paul's train of thought in this section, three introductory matters need attention: (1) the background to this text, (2) the subject of this text, and (3) the structure of this text.

The Background to This Text

The consensus among most commentators is that, in this section, Paul employs the kinds of arguments against Gentile idolatry that one finds in the book of Wisdom, especially chapters 13–15, and other Jewish writings such as the *Sibylline Oracles* (3.8–45). For example, Peter Stuhlmacher (1994, 34) writes: "In terms of content, Paul follows closely the way of thinking found in the (Hellenistic) Jewish wisdom tradition, as it is represented, for example, in the Wisdom of Solomon, which the apostle found in his Greek Bible." Christopher Bryan (2000, 79) notes that Paul's language "reminds us of the language with which the LXX in various places speaks of Israel's falls from grace." The examples to which he points are the psalmist's description of the episode of the golden calf (Ps. 105:20 LXX [106:20 Eng.]) and Jeremiah's description of Israel's idolatry in his day (Jer. 2:11). This text also shares some common themes (Gentile idolatry and God's self-revelation in creation) with Paul's missionary sermon at Athens (Acts 17:22–31). Although these common themes have suggested to some that we are hearing echoes of Paul's missionary preaching

God Revealed in Creation

"For all people who were ignorant of God were foolish by nature; and they were unable from the good things that are seen to know the one who exists, nor did they recognize the artisan while paying heed to his works; but they supposed that either fire or wind or swift air, or the circle of the stars, or turbulent water, or the luminaries of heaven were the gods that rule the world. If through delight in the beauty of these things people assumed them to be gods, let them know how much better than these is their Lord, for the author of beauty created them. And if people were amazed at their power and working, let them perceive from them how much more powerful is the one who formed them. For from the greatness and beauty of created things comes a corresponding perception of their Creator." (Wis. 13:1–5)

to Gentiles, William O. Walker (1999) argues that the material in this section is part of a non-Pauline interpolation that consists of 1:18–2:29. The general consensus, however, is that Wis. 13–15 is the primary background for Rom. 1:18–32 and that Paul is the author of this text.

Wisdom 13–15 makes a number of points about Gentile idolatry that Paul echoes in Rom. 1:18–32. First, it argues that those who are ignorant of God are foolish by nature because they do not know or recognize God from creation (Wis. 13:1). Second, it assumes that humanity can perceive something about the Creator from the greatness and beauty of what God has created (13:5). Third, it states that the Gentiles are without excuse because they could have known something about God from the created world (13:8). Fourth, it contends that idolatry is the root cause of fornication and sexual disorder. Indeed, it is the cause of every evil (14:12, 26–27). Fifth, it affirms that idolatry entered the world through human vanity (14:14).

Paul, however, differs from the book of Wisdom's critique of Gentile idolatry in two ways. First, whereas Wisdom supposes that Gentile humanity did not attain a knowledge of God from creation (13:1), Paul assumes that the Gentiles knew something of God from creation. Thus their sin is all the greater. Second, whereas the book of Wisdom boasts that even if the children of Israel sin they belong to God, and then affirms that they will not sin because they know that God acknowledges them (15:2), Paul argues that Israel's special status does not exempt it from the coming judgment, for all are under the power of sin.

The Subject of This Text

Most commentators argue that Paul is speaking of the Gentile world (Rom. 1:18–32), and I agree. But in recent years some have insisted that this reading is too restrictive, maintaining that Paul has the whole of humanity in view, Jews as well as Gentiles. For example, C. E. B. Cranfield (1975, 105–6) acknowledges that Paul primarily has the Gentiles in view in this section. But then he notes that 1:18 begins with the general term for humankind and that nowhere in this section does Paul refer to Gentiles or Greeks. Moreover, when he does describe idolatry, Paul uses the language of Ps. 105:20 LXX (106:20 Eng.) and Jer. 2:11 LXX, both of which concern Israel's fall into idolatry. Cranfield then argues that Paul's critique in Rom. 2:1 (that those who judge others are guilty of the same things) makes better sense if 1:18–32 has all humanity in view. For if all humanity is in view in 1:18–32, then those who judge others are condemning themselves (2:1). Acknowledging the force of these arguments, Douglas Moo (1996, 97) makes two counterpoints. First, "the passage is reminiscent of Jewish apologetic arguments in which Gentile idolatry was derided and the moral sins of the Gentile world were traced to that idolatry." Second, he notes that "the knowledge of God rejected by those depicted in 1:18–32 comes solely through 'natural revelation.'" He concludes that Paul does not have the Jewish world in view in 1:18–32.

In my opinion, the rhetorical goal of Paul's argument is served best if 1:18–32 has the Gentile world in view. Paul's purpose in part one (1:18–3:20) is to demonstrate that Jews as well as Gentiles are in need of God's saving grace. Therefore, he begins with a traditional description of Gentile sinfulness with which a Jewish audience would agree: the Gentile world is filled with idolatry and sexual immorality (1:18–32). Having found common ground with those who might otherwise criticize his gospel as pandering to Gentiles, Paul takes up another Jewish theme that his audience would approve: God will judge everyone on the basis of deeds (2:1–16). Paul can now spring his rhetorical trap and point to Jewish failure to observe the law (2:17–29), concluding that all—Jews as well as Gentiles—are under the power of sin (3:1–20). In light of this line of argument, I interpret 1:18–32 as a description of Gentile failure to recognize God as God and 2:17–29 as a description of Jewish failure to observe the law.

Depending on their approach to this text, scholars understand Paul's purpose in 1:18–32 differently. According to Thomas H. Tobin (1993, 299), who views the text rhetorically, Paul is trying to allay the fears of those who are suspicious of his understanding of faith and the observance of the Mosaic law by showing them that he understands and agrees with traditional Jewish teaching about sin and repentance. For Philip Esler (2003, 135–54), who is concerned with social identity, Paul is trying to provide his "Judean" (Esler's term for Jews) and Greek addressees with a new social identity derived from the righteousness of God through faith. For those like myself who view the text theologically, Paul is describing the reality of the human situation in light of God's righteousness and wrath.

The Structure of the Text

The structure of this text continues to puzzle commentators even though the text is filled with linguistic clues as to its organization. The point of contention

Romans 1:18–32 in the Rhetorical Flow

The letter opening (1:1–17)

Gentiles and Jews in the light of God's wrath (1:18–3:20)

▶ **Gentile failure to acknowledge God (1:18–32)**

The revelation of God's wrath (1:18)

Why God's wrath is being revealed (1:19–23)

Because they are without excuse (1:19–20)

Because something of God is knowable (1:19a)

For God manifested it to them (1:19b)

For God's attributes are manifested in creation (1:20a)

For this reason they are without excuse (1:20b)

Because they did not honor and thank God as God (1:21–23)

Because they did not glorify and thank God (1:21a)

But became vain in their thoughts (1:21b)

And their hearts were darkened (1:21c)

They became foolish (1:22)

They exchanged the glory of God for idols (1:23)

How God's wrath is being revealed (1:24–31)

Deliverance to the *desires of their hearts* (1:24–25)

God delivered them over (1:24)

They exchanged the truth for a lie (1:25a)

They worshiped the creature rather than the Creator (1:25b)

A benediction (1:25c)

Deliverance to their *dishonorable passions* (1:26–27)

God delivered them over (1:26a)

Females and females (1:26b)

Males and males (1:27)

Deliverance to their *undiscerning mind* (1:28–31)

They did not discern God (1:28a)

Therefore God delivered them over (1:28b)

They are filled with . . . (four items) (1:29a)

They are full of . . . (five items) (1:29b)

They are . . . (twelve items) (1:29c–31)

Final condemnation (1:32)

Those doing such things are worthy of death (1:32a)

Not only doing them (1:32b)

But even approving of those who do such things (1:32c)

is how to construe the three phrases in which Paul says that God "delivered" or "handed over" humanity to its own devices (1:24, 26, 28). Some (Byrne 1996, 64) take these phrases with the material that precedes them. Understood in this way, the preceding material provides the reason why God has delivered the Gentiles to their own devices:

> fundamental refusal to acknowledge God (1:21–23)
>> therefore God delivered them up (1:24)
> fundamental refusal to acknowledge God (1:25)
>> therefore God delivered them up (1:26–27)
> fundamental refusal to acknowledge God (1:28a)
>> therefore God delivered them up (1:28b–31)

Although this is an attractive solution, I view 1:19–23 as providing the reasons for the revelation of God's wrath and 1:24–31 as the punishment that God's wrath brings (so Légasse 2002, 113).

Tracing the Train of Thought

Paul begins with a thesis statement that controls the argument he will make in 1:18–32: The wrath of God is being revealed in the present time against all "unrighteousness" (*adikian*) that suppresses the truth about God (1:18). Following this statement, Paul develops his argument in two ways. First, he explains *why* the wrath of God is being revealed in the present time (1:19–23). Second, he describes *how* the wrath of God is being revealed in the present time (1:24–31). The unit concludes with a final condemnation of those who not only practice the unrighteousness that Paul describes but also approve of the conduct of those who do the same things (1:32).

The first subunit provides two reasons for the revelation of God's wrath (1:19–23). First, the Gentiles are without excuse because something of God is knowable from creation. Second, although the Gentiles knew something of God from creation, they did not honor God as God. In the second subunit, Paul draws out the consequence of the Gentiles' refusal to acknowledge God as God: God is delivering them to their own devices (1:24–31). First, God delivers them to the desires of their hearts with the consequence that they exchange the truth of God for a lie (1:24–25). Second, God delivers them to their dishonorable passions with the result that they exchange natural sexual relations for those that are not natural (1:26–27). Third, since they did not deign to know God (1:28a), God delivered them to their undiscerning minds (1:28b). Paul chronicles the result of this undiscerning mind in a list that begins with four cardinal vices, moves to five more vices, and concludes with twelve descriptions of the rebellious Gentile world that no longer discerns God's will (1:29–31). The unit ends with a final condemnation of those who do and approve of the things that Paul lists (1:32).

1:18. This verse functions as Paul's thesis statement: **For God's wrath is being revealed from heaven against every impiety and unrighteousness of human beings who are suppressing the truth by unrighteousness** (1:18). The statement is somewhat surprising since Paul normally employs "wrath" (*orgē*) as an eschatological term for the coming judgment that God will effect at the end of the ages (1 Thess. 1:10; 5:9; Rom. 2:5, 8; 5:9; Eph. 5:6; Col. 3:6; but cf. 1 Thess. 2:16, which speaks of God's wrath as already making its appearance). Paul has not forgotten the eschatological dimension of God's wrath, as is evident from what he writes about "the day of wrath" (Rom. 2:5). But just as he affirms that the gospel reveals God's righteousness, so he declares that God's wrath is being revealed from heaven against those who are suppressing the truth by their wickedness. Although the phrase "from heaven" suggests a spectacular manifestation of God's wrath (see *1 En.* 91.7), the emphasis here is on the divine origin of that wrath, which is being revealed in an unexpected manner.

> ### Sin Provokes God's Wrath
>
> *"When sin, oppression, blasphemy, and injustice increase, crime, iniquity, and uncleanliness shall be committed and increase (likewise). Then a great plague shall take place from heaven upon all of these; the holy Lord shall emerge with wrath and plague in order that he may execute judgment upon the earth."* (1 En. 91.7, OTP 1:72)

God's wrath is not to be identified with an emotion, as if God were overcome with anger. The wrath of God is God's just and necessary response to sin. It is God's judgment upon every kind of *asebeia* (irreverence toward God) and *adikia* (wickedness toward others) that suppresses the truth. These two terms, governed by the adjective "every," form a hendiadys that sums up "the total sinfulness and rampant unrighteousness of pagan humanity" (Fitzmyer 1993, 278). The most insidious aspect of this unrighteousness is its suppression of the truth, by which Paul means the truth about the reality of God. Human "unrighteousness" (*adikia*), which embraces *asebeia*, stands in sharp contrast to God's own "righteousness" (*dikaiosynē*). For whereas God's righteousness results in salvation for all who believe, the unrighteousness of human beings refuses to acknowledge God as God. Consequently, those who suppress the truth about God by their unrighteousness experience God's righteousness as wrath.

1:19–23. Having announced that God's wrath is being revealed against those who are suppressing the truth by their unrighteousness, Paul explains how Gentiles suppress the truth about God (1:19–23). Paul's argument proceeds in two movements, each beginning with the conjunction *dioti* (because). In the first, Paul affirms that the Gentiles are without excuse because God has revealed something of himself in and through the created world (1:19–20). In the second, Paul argues that, although the Gentiles knew something of God, they refused to glorify God as God, exchanging the glory of God, which is already manifested in creation (Ps. 19:1), for idols (Rom. 1:21–23). Therefore, even though the Gentiles knew something of God from the created world, they deliberately suppressed what they knew to worship the creature rather than the Creator. For this reason, God's wrath is being revealed against them at the present time.

The first movement of Paul's argument shows that although the Gentiles did not enjoy the advantage of the oracles of God, as embodied in the law that God graciously gave to Israel, they knew something of God **because what can be known about God is evident to them** (1:19a). Paul then provides two reasons why the Gentiles could know something of God, each introduced by the conjunction *gar* (for). First, they can know something of God, **for God disclosed it to them** (1:19b). Paul does not mean that the Gentiles did or could know everything about God; nor does he suggest that they can know God apart from God's initiative. But something is knowable about God because God has disclosed it. Second, Paul explains how and what God discloses about himself. **For God's invisible attributes—his eternal power and divine nature—can be seen, since they can be understood by God's created works** (1:20a). Here Paul neither establishes nor denies what later theology would call "natural theology." But he does echo the sentiments of Hellenistic Jewish thought such as is found in the book of Wisdom: "For from the greatness and beauty of created things comes a corresponding perception of their Creator" (13:5). But although the book of Wisdom concludes that the Gentiles failed to know the Creator from creation (13:1), Paul affirms that the Gentiles did know something of God from creation (Rom. 1:21). The conclusion to the first movement of Paul's argument is inevitable: **for this reason they are without excuse** (1:20b). The Gentiles are without excuse because God disclosed "his eternal power and divine nature" (*aidios autou dynamis kai theiotēs*) to them through his created works. Therefore, although they did not have the advantage of the revelation that God granted Israel, they knew enough to understand that God is other than his creation and not to be confused with it. And yet they chose to worship the creature rather than the Creator, thereby suppressing the truth of God's eternal power and divine nature. This is why they are presently experiencing the wrath of God, even if they do not fully understand the presence of this wrath.

Having shown that the Gentiles are without excuse since God revealed something of his eternal power and deity to them, Paul in the second movement of his argument brings his indictment against the Gentile world. Beginning with the same conjunction he used earlier (*dioti*), Paul writes: **Because, although** they knew God, they did not glorify or render thanks to God as God, but they were made foolish by their reasoning, and their senseless heart was darkened (1:21). In Paul's view, the Gentile world cannot plead ignorance. The Gentiles knew something of God but refused to thank or praise God as God. More specifically, they refused to acknowledge the truth that God is their Creator. Echoing Jeremiah's indictment against Israel, which "went after worthless things and became worthless themselves" (Jer. 2:5), Paul accuses the Gentiles of preferring their futile speculations to the truth about God. In saying that their senseless heart became darkened, Paul introduces a theme to which he will return in Rom. 1:24 and that he will develop in the rest of the letter: the human heart darkened by its rebellion against God is in need of an inner renewal that only God's Spirit can effect (2:5, 29; 5:5; 6:17; 8:27; 10:9–10).

In 1:22–23 Paul explains what happened to the Gentiles when they engaged in futile speculation instead of acknowledging God as God. First, **claiming to be wise they became foolish** (1:22), a theme Paul had already developed in light of his message about the cross (1 Cor. 1:18–25). The ultimate manifestation of their foolishness was their idolatry, by which they **exchanged the glory of God who is immortal for the likeness of an image of a mortal human being, and of birds, and animals, and reptiles** (Rom. 1:23). Although Paul is speaking of Gentile idolatry, he employs language that evokes Moses's warning to Israel not to make an idol of any kind (Deut. 4:15–19). In doing so, Paul uses the same Greek verb that the LXX employs when it recalls Israel's idolatry in the incident of the golden calf: "They exchanged [*ēllaxanto*] their glory for a likeness of a bull calf that eats grass" (Ps. 105:20 LXX [106:20 Eng.], NETS). Since the reference to "their glory" here most likely refers to God, who is the glory of Israel, Paul implicitly draws a comparison between Israel's idolatry at Sinai and the idolatry of the Gentiles at the present time. In both instances, Israel and the Gentiles foolishly preferred what is mortal and corruptible to the one who alone is immortal and thus incorruptible.

Paul's indictment against the Gentile world can be summarized in this way: Gentile impiety and unrighteousness suppress the truth about God by worshiping the creature rather than the Creator. Although aware of God's eternal power and deity—because God revealed something of himself through his creation—the Gentiles preferred the creature to the Creator because of their futile speculations. Consequently, their darkened hearts were no longer able to comprehend the reality that is God. Having lost their power to understand, they foolishly exchanged what is immortal and incorruptible for what is corruptible and mortal. For Paul, idolatry is the root of all sin, the sin that gives birth to every sin. Thus he affirms what the book of Wisdom says: "For the idea of making idols was the beginning of fornication, and the invention of them was the corruption of life" (14:12).

1:24–31. Having explained *why* God's wrath is being revealed against the Gentiles (1:19–23), Paul proceeds to describe *how* the wrath of God is being revealed (1:24–31). Contrary to the expectations of those who anticipate a dramatic apocalyptic manifestation of God's wrath, Paul proclaims that God's wrath is presently upon the Gentiles, even though they do not realize or understand that they are experiencing it. God is presently manifesting his wrath against the Gentiles by delivering them to their own sinfulness. Thus the Gentiles are experiencing God's wrath by living out the consequences of their refusal to acknowledge God as God. The punishment that God inflicts upon them is to allow them to live according to the futile reasoning of their darkened hearts. Having suppressed the truth about God, they dwell in a world of their own making, which denies the truth about God. As the book of Wisdom already understood, the punishment for sin is sin: "You sent upon them a multitude of irrational creatures to punish them, so that they might learn that one is punished by the very things by which one sins" (Wis. 11:15b–16).

Paul develops this argument in three movements, each beginning with a phrase in which he says that God "handed over" or "delivered" (*paredōken*) the Gentiles to their own devices. The first movement focuses on sexual immorality (1:24–25). The second is more specific, dealing with same-sex relations (1:26–27), while the third contains an extended list of vices that is all-embracing in its scope (1:28–31).

The first of the three movements begins with the conjunction *dio*, which refers to all that Paul has said in 1:19–23 about the refusal of the Gentiles to acknowledge God as God: **For this reason, God delivered them over to their heart's desire to impurity with the result that they dishonored their bodies among themselves** (1:24). Returning to the theme of the senseless and darkened heart that he introduced in 1:21, Paul affirms that God is exercising his wrath against the Gentiles by allowing them to follow the desires of their senseless heart, which has been darkened by its refusal to acknowledge God. This desire or longing (*epithymia*), which the Vulgate translates as *concupiscentia* (concupiscence), has a negative connotation in Romans, which relates it to sin (6:12; 7:7, 8) and to the flesh (13:14). Here it refers to illicit sexual desires that result in "impurity" (*akatharsia*) and the dishonoring of the body. This *akatharsia* is a state of moral corruption that stands in contrast to the holiness to which God has called those who believe in Jesus Christ (1 Thess. 4:7; also see Rom. 6:19, 22).

The relationship of 1:25 to 1:24 is problematic. For some, 1:25 is the beginning of a new section that provides the reason for the next wave of condemnation that begins in 1:26 (Cranfield 1975, 25; Byrne 1996, 64). But since 1:25 is closely related to 1:24 by the relative pronoun (*hoitines*) that begins 1:25, I have construed 1:25 as describing the moral failure of those whom God has handed over to their own desires: **these exchanged the truth of God for a lie and worshiped and served the creature rather than the Creator** (1:25a). What Paul says here echoes 1:23. But whereas there he wrote that they exchanged the glory of the immortal God for the likeness of mortal images, here he says that they exchanged the truth of God for a lie with the result that they worshiped the creature rather than the Creator:

exchanged	the glory of God	for the likeness of an image (1:23)
exchanged	the truth of God	for a lie
worshiped	the creature	rather than the Creator (1:25)

The "truth of God" echoes Paul's thematic statement in 1:18 that God's wrath is being revealed against those who suppress the truth by their unrighteousness. The truth is the truth about God that Gentile unrighteousness suppresses by its idolatrous worship, which results in immorality. Filled with reverence for the God whom the Gentile world does not worship, Paul concludes this first movement with a benediction: **who is blessed forever. Amen** (1:25b).

Paul begins the second movement of his argument in a similar way: **For this reason, God delivered them over to their dishonorable passions** (1:26a). Having delivered the Gentiles to the desires of their hearts, God now delivers them to their dishonorable passions, which in this context, as in Col. 3:5 and 1 Thess. 4:5, are their sexual passions. Writing about the Gentile world from the perspective of the Jewish world, Paul focuses his attention on same-sex relations: **Their women exchanged sexual relations that are in accord with nature for those contrary to nature. Likewise, setting aside relations with women in accord with nature, men were inflamed by their lustful passions for one another, men doing what is shameful with men, receiving in themselves the punishment that is proper for their error** (1:26b–27).

Paul does not speak at length about homosexuality in his letters, this being his most detailed description of such relationships. The other references in the Pauline Letters occur in 1 Cor. 6:9 and 1 Tim. 1:10. For Paul, these relationships are contrary to nature, as he argues here, and contrary to God's law as expressed in Lev. 18:22 and 20:13. Thus Paul would probably have affirmed the sentiments of the first-century Jewish historian Josephus: "What are our marriage laws? The Law recognizes no sexual connexions, except the natural union of man and wife, and that only for the procreation of children. Sodomy [*tēn de pros arrenas arrenōn*] it abhors, and punishes any guilty of such assault with death" (*Ag. Ap.* 2.199, trans. Thackeray 1926). Like his Jewish contemporaries, Paul viewed same-sex relations as a moral failing particularly characteristic of the Gentile world, although such relationships undoubtedly occurred in the Jewish world as well, as the strong prohibition of Leviticus suggests.

This example of same-sex relations in the Gentile world provides Paul with the kind of argument he needs. He views the *exchange* of sexual relations between men and women for relations between members of the same sex as the natural outcome of *exchanging* the glory of God for the likeness of an image (1:23) and for *exchanging* the truth of God for a lie (1:25). Having refused to acknowledge God as God, the Gentiles have lost their sense of the natural order of creation. And since they no longer comprehend the natural order of creation, they violate the use of their sexual capacity as inscribed in creation. Paul views such relations as shameful because men and women no longer exercise their proper sexual roles.

The third movement in Paul's argument begins in a slightly different way. First, he starts with a phrase that summarizes his indictment against the Gentile world: **And inasmuch as they did not see fit to have a true knowledge of God** (1:28a). Next, he introduces the formula that he has employed in the other two movements: **God delivered them over to their undiscerning mind to do what is not proper** (1:28b). Thus God first delivers the Gentiles to their heart's desire, next to their dishonorable passions, and finally to their undiscerning mind. This movement from desire and passion to the undiscerning mind is significant. For whereas in the first two movements of his argument Paul has dealt with sins of passion and desire, here he deals with sins that originate with a cold and calculating mind that no longer distinguishes between good and evil. This emphasis on the undiscerning mind complements what Paul has already said about the body that has been dishonored by impure desires and dishonorable passions. In Paul's view, there must be a renewal of the mind if human beings are to present their bodies (their very selves) as living sacrifices to God (12:1–2).

The extended list of vices that Paul adduces in 1:29–31 has three parts. First, he lists four items that function as cardinal vices: **They are filled with every unrighteousness, wickedness, greed, evil** (1:29a). Next, he lists five more items: **They are full of envy, murder, strife, deceit, meanness** (1:29b). Finally, he identifies those whom he indicts in twelve ways: **They are gossipers, slanderers, God-haters, insolent, arrogant, boasters, evil schemers, disobedient to parents, without understanding, without loyalty, without humanity, without mercy** (1:29c–31).

The first item of the list, "unrighteousness" (*adikia*), echoes Paul's thesis statement that God's wrath is being revealed against all who are suppressing the truth by their *adikia*. The description of the Gentiles as "God-haters, insolent, arrogant, boasters, evil schemers" highlights their rebellion against the truth of God, which Paul has been describing throughout this passage. Their disobedience to parents suggests a further disruption of the natural order of things. The use of "without" before the final four items is my attempt to reproduce something of the Greek in which each item begins with the letter *alpha*. The first of these items, "without understanding" (*asynetous*), echoes Paul's description in 1:21 of the "senseless heart" (*asynetos kardia*).

This list of vices is not complete, nor are Gentiles the only ones who commit such evils. Paul is aware that Jews commit these offenses as well. But in this section, his rhetorical purpose is to show that the Gentile world is in a predicament of its own making, from which it cannot extricate itself. Having suppressed the truth about God, it has condemned itself to live without God.

1:32. The culmination of Gentile unrighteousness is that **although they know God's righteous decree that those who do these things are worthy of death, not only do they do these things, they even approve of those who are doing such things** (1:32). The book of Wisdom makes a similar point when it says of the Gentiles: "Then it was not enough for them to err about the knowledge of God, but through living in great strife due to ignorance they call such great evils peace" (14:22). But while the book of Wisdom assumes that the Gentiles did not know God from the created world (14:1), Paul supposes that they did. Not only did they know something of God, they also knew something of God's righteous "commandment" (*dikaiōma*) about the ethical life. But just as they refused to acknowledge God, so also they refused to acknowledge God's commandment. Not satisfied to do such things themselves, they approve the behavior of those who do the same things, thereby confirming their unrighteousness. For such a rebellion there is only one punishment: death, which Paul identifies as the wages of sin (Rom. 6:23). This death is eternal separation from God. For, having exchanged the glory of the immortal God for the likeness of a mortal image, there is only mortality and corruption for those who have abandoned the Creator.

Theological Issues

Those who read Paul's description of the moral depravity of the Gentile world are often taken aback. Is the situation of the Gentiles really so dire? Did not Greek and Roman philosophy acknowledge the existence of God? Did not the Stoics, Cynics, and Epicureans teach their students to live in a morally appropriate way? There were certainly people in the Gentile world who lived good and upright lives. How, then, can Paul make such a sweeping condemnation of the Gentile world, maintaining that all have practiced idolatry and gone astray?

Cranfield (1975, 104) provides an answer to this question when he observes that if we read this text as if it were "an historian's assessment of the moral condition of his contemporaries, . . . the result will be thoroughly unfair to Paul's contemporaries." For, although there was moral depravity in the Gentile world, there were men and women who led morally upright lives, of whom Paul says nothing. But as Cranfield notes, Paul is not making this kind of moral assessment. This is not Paul's personal judgment on the Gentile world but the gospel's judgment. It is a judgment "which Paul has heard and to which he himself has submitted." Paul's description of the Gentile world is a description of how that world looks in light of God's righteousness. It is how that world appears from the perspective of Christ's death and resurrection.

Paul's sweeping indictment of the Gentile world is off-putting. But it is no more off-putting than the message of the crucified Messiah that he proclaims. It is in light of this gospel that he makes the sweeping judgment he does. Paul knew that there were good Gentiles, and he was aware of the moral philosophy of his day. But he is not speaking of this or that particular individual. In light of the gospel that has been revealed to him, he is speaking of the Gentiles as a group. And in light of that gospel, he views their situation in an entirely new way, for he knows something of their situation—indeed of the entire human situation—that he did not know before. Ernst Käsemann (1980, 35) writes: "Prior to the gospel man does not really know what sin is even though he lives in it. Similarly he does not know about the wrath to which he has fallen victim." Prior to the gospel, Paul did not know the full extent of the human plight, but when the gospel was revealed to him, he realized that the wrath of God is already being revealed against the unrighteousness of those who are suppressing the truth about God.

Paul is not presenting his audience with a scientific or social analysis of the Gentile world that will hold up under the scrutiny of historical investigation. Nor is he providing us with a description of the Gentile world that takes into account what was good in the ancient world. Pressed by his contemporaries, he would have acknowledged that there were morally good Gentiles, as he will indicate in the next chapter. But in light of his gospel about God's own righteousness, Paul proclaims that all are in need of the righteousness that the gospel brings. Thus people find themselves experiencing either the righteousness or the wrath of God.

For Paul, God's righteousness and wrath are two sides of a single coin. Accordingly, when the righteousness of God is revealed in the proclamation of the gospel, the wrath of God is revealed from heaven, placing all who stand outside the gospel under God's wrath. God's wrath, however, is not so much a punishment that God inflicts on humanity as it is the absence of God's presence. Apart from the divine presence, humanity lives in a world of its own making—a world from which it has excluded the truth about God.

But the gospel is ultimately good news intended to save rather than to condemn. Thus the proclamation that the wrath of God is being revealed shows humanity's profound need for God's righteousness. By exposing the real situation of the Gentiles, Paul has prepared the way to proclaim the saving grace of God. For Paul, everything looks different from the perspective of Christ's death and resurrection. From the perspective of the cross, he sees the futility of the human situation from which humanity needs to be redeemed. From the perspective of the resurrection, he sees what it means to stand in the justifying grace of the eschatological Adam.

In his description of the Gentile world, Paul refers to same-sex relations as one, but not the only, example of Gentile failure. Although such relationships were common in the Greco-Roman world, they were not necessarily viewed as depraved, in part because sexual activity was understood in a way that did not always connect it with procreation. David Halperin (*OCD*, 720–21), for example, notes that "Greek and Roman men . . . generally understood sex to be defined in terms of sexual penetration and phallic pleasure, whether the sexual partners were two males, two females, or one male and one female." Sexual activity that "involved the penetration of a social inferior (whether inferior in age, gender, or status) qualified as sexually normal for a male," regardless of the person's sex. But it was deemed shameful for a free male to be penetrated by someone who was socially his inferior. Thus the Greco-Roman world countenanced an older or free male having sexual relations with a youth or with a slave, provided that the older or free male was the dominant partner. But it looked askance upon an adult free male who assumed a subservient position.

Paul's critique of same-sex relationships is different. Schooled in the Mosaic law, he views such relations as not only contrary to the natural order but also contrary to God's will that man and woman should marry and procreate. For Paul, such relations reveal that *exchanging* the truth about God for a lie results in *exchanging* sexual relations in accord with nature for those that are not in accord with nature.

The use that Paul makes of same-sex relations is controversial today. Some have argued that in this text Paul's primary focus is pederasty rather than same-sex relations between adults (Scroggs 1983, 109–18). Others suggest that there is a significant difference between the ancient and contemporary understanding of same-sex relations. While it is true that pederasty was prevalent in the ancient world and that Paul's enigmatic vocabulary in 1 Cor. 6:9–10 and 1 Tim. 1:9–10 may be pointing in that direction, the descriptive language of Romans does not appear to be limited to pederasty. Moreover, Paul's Jewish background, informed by the teaching of Leviticus, seems to have in view same-sex relations between adults. Paul's own attitude toward these sexual relationships, be they between adults and minors or between adults and adults, is clear.

The more difficult question today is the hermeneutical issue: What is the authority of Paul's remarks about such relations? For some, this is not an issue. For others, the text raises questions about a phenomenon whose biological and social origins are not fully understood. In my view, further discussion will do well to recognize the following. First, Paul's own position about same-sex relations is clear. Second, the example of same-sex relations plays a rhetorical role in Paul's argument in Romans, and his discussion of such relations is not the main point of the passage. Third, while Paul opposed such relationships, they do not otherwise play a significant role in his writings. Other forms of behavior such as greed and strife are condemned more regularly. Fourth, Paul's discussion of same-sex relations occurs in a context that emphasizes that all are under the power of sin and have fallen short of God's glory (3:9, 23). Consequently, no one is in a position to condemn others, for all are in need of God's saving grace. The most prudent course of action in the present time, then, is to treat all with compassion, aware that only God is in a position to judge another person.

Romans 2:1–16

God's Impartial Judgment of Gentiles and Jews

Introductory Matters

The transition from the end of chapter 1 to the beginning of chapter 2 has proved to be problematic for commentators. Paul abandons the use of the third person and begins to speak in the second-person singular, addressing an unnamed interlocutor. The usual way of interpreting this shift is to suppose that, after describing the dire situation of the Gentile world, Paul now turns to the Jewish world. According to this reading the unnamed interlocutor is a Jewish person, something that Paul reveals in 2:17, when he explicitly addresses the interlocutor as someone who calls himself a Jew. In recent years, however, scholars have challenged this reading. On the basis of studying the nature and use of the rhetorical form of the diatribe, Stanley Stowers (1981) argues for the unity of chapter 2 with the material in 1:18–32. And, after her study of the theme of divine impartiality in Romans, Jouette Bassler (1982) supports the unity of 1:16–2:16. Both of these studies call into question the traditional approach noted above. They maintain that the central theme of 2:1–16 has to do with God's impartiality toward Gentiles and Jews rather than with a theological assault on Jewish hypocrisy. Therefore, before I trace Paul's train of thought, it will be helpful to say something about his use of diatribe and the theme of God's impartiality.

Paul's Use of Diatribe

David Aune (2003, 127) defines diatribe as "a modern literary term describing an informal rhetorical mode of argumentation principally characterized by a lively dialogical style including the use of imaginary discussion partners (often abruptly addressed), to whom are attributed hypothetical objections and false conclusions." Philosophers employed this rhetorical mode not, as is sometimes thought, to attack their enemies but as a pedagogical technique (Stowers 1981, 175). Noting that this mode of argumentation occurs more frequently in Romans than in any other Pauline letter, Aune (2003, 129) suggests that Paul, as a Christian teacher of both Jews and Gentiles, used the diatribe in Romans "since he knew less about the recipients' situation than he did about communities he himself had founded." Stowers makes a similar suggestion (1981, 183), and Changwon Song (2004, 121) goes so far as to propose that "the main part of Romans (1.16–14.23) was originally the diatribe that was taught in Paul's schoolroom."

Romans 2:1–5 is the first example of Paul's use of diatribe in this letter. Other examples occur in 2:17–24; 9:19–21; 11:17–21; 14:4, 10. In 2:1 and 2:3 Paul addresses an imaginary interlocutor (ō *anthrōpe*), accusing him of doing the very things of which he judges others, and of foolishly believing that he will escape God's judgment. Although Paul portrays the imaginary interlocutor as brash and arrogant, he is not presenting the interlocutor as an opponent or adversary to the gospel, and certainly not as "the typical Jew." Making use of a mode of argumentation that philosophers employed with their students, Paul instructs his Roman audience to beware of being arrogant. While the imaginary interlocutor could be a Jew, a Gentile, or a Christ-believer of Jewish or Gentile origin (Bryan 2000, 92), it is the behavior and attitude of the interlocutor that most concerns Paul. Thus Paul's Roman audience would not be offended by his diatribe, as if he were suddenly turning on them. Nor would they immediately associate the interlocutor of this diatribe with a Jewish person who opposes Paul's teaching on justification. Rather, with the benefit of some of Paul's own associates in their midst, his Roman audience would understand that the apostle is teaching them something, although the full extent of his teaching is not yet apparent.

This diatribe (2:1–5), however, is not isolated from its surrounding context. It is related to the indictment that Paul has leveled against the Gentile world in 1:18–32. Having described the moral morass of that world and condemned those who do such things, Paul teaches the Romans to avoid the arrogant attitude of those who condemn others but do what they condemn, foolishly imagining that they will escape God's judgment (2:1–16). In light of the depravity described in 1:18–32, the proper attitude is repentance rather than arrogant judgment (2:5). There is an intimate relationship, then, between the material we have studied (1:18–32) and the material we are about to consider (2:1–16). The indictment of 1:18–32 leads to the warning of 2:1–16 that God is an impartial judge.

This reading of the material has important implications for a Jewish-Christian dialogue since it shows that Paul's purpose is not to condemn or characterize Jews as hypocritical, although he will have harsh words for them in 2:17–29. His target is the pretentious and arrogant person, no matter who he or she is (Stowers 1981, 177).

God's Impartiality

The climax of 2:1–16 is not the diatribe of 2:1–5 but Paul's statement that God is impartial (2:11). It is this statement more than any other that relates what Paul writes in 1:18–32 about Gentile sinfulness to what he says in 2:17–29 about Jewish failure to observe the law. In 2:1–16, Paul will argue that since God is impartial, God will judge Gentiles and Jews in the same way, namely, on the basis of their actions, whether or not they enjoy the gift of the law.

References to God's impartiality are present in the OT, the intertestamental writings, and the rabbinic literature. The theme also occurs in other Pauline writings. But as Bassler has demonstrated, Paul employs the theme in a radically new way. While there are statements of divine impartiality in the OT, "Impartiality does not annul Israel's special status before God" (Bassler 1982, 186). The same is true for the literature of the intertestamental and rabbinic periods, which speaks of God's impartiality. Paul's contribution to the understanding of God's impartiality is the manner in which he applies God's impartial judgment to Gentiles and Jews. According to Paul's teaching, God does not distinguish between Gentiles and Jews on the basis of their national or ethnic status. God judges all people impartially on the basis of what they do rather than on the basis of who they are.

Paul's radical understanding of God's impartiality raises a number of theological issues. For example, how does his teaching on justification by faith cohere with his teaching on God's divine impartiality and judgment by works? For the moment it is sufficient to note that the movement of Paul's argument is as follows. Having

> **Romans 2:1–16 in the Rhetorical Flow**
>
> **The letter opening (1:1–17)**
>
> **Gentiles and Jews in the light of God's wrath (1:18–3:20)**
>
> > **Gentile failure to acknowledge God (1:18–32)**
> >
> > ▶ **God's impartial judgment of Gentiles and Jews (2:1–16)**
> >
> > > God's just and impartial judgment (2:1–11)
> > >
> > > > First address to one who judges others (2:1–2)
> > > >
> > > > > You are inexcusable (2:1)
> > > > >
> > > > > God's judgment is true (2:2)
> > > >
> > > > Second address to one who judges others (2:3–11)
> > > >
> > > > > Two accusing questions (2:3–4)
> > > > >
> > > > > Warning of God's coming judgment (2:5–11)
> > >
> > > An example of God's impartiality (2:12–16)
> > >
> > > > Thesis: God judges Jews and Gentiles (2:12)
> > > >
> > > > Reason: Doing more important than hearing (2:13)
> > > >
> > > > Example: Gentiles who do the law (2:14–16)

indicted the Gentile world of suppressing the truth about God (1:18–32), Paul argues that God is an impartial judge who judges everyone on the basis of deeds (2:1–16). Having reminded his listeners of God's impartiality, Paul employs another diatribe to indict his Jewish compatriots of failing to observe the law (2:17–29). After this indictment, he introduces another diatribe to ask if there is any benefit in being a Jew, concluding that all are under the power of sin and that no one will be justified in God's presence on the basis of legal observance (3:1–20).

Tracing the Train of Thought

The overall theme of this section is God's impartial judgment of Gentiles and Jews. Having indicted the Gentile world of suppressing the truth about God, Paul adopts the form of the diatribe to warn his Roman audience not to judge others, for God is an impartial judge who judges everyone on the basis of deeds rather than on the basis of social, ethnic, or religious identity. Only after reminding his audience of God's impartiality (2:1–16) will Paul bring an indictment against the Jewish world (2:17–29).

This section consists of two units. In the first, Paul describes God's just judgment (2:1–11). Making use of the diatribal form, he twice addresses an imaginary interlocutor who judges others: first in 2:1–2, then in 2:3–11. The climax of this unit is Paul's statement in 2:11 that God is impartial. In the second unit, Paul provides an example of this impartiality (2:12–16), moving from thesis (2:12) to supporting reason (2:13) to a specific example (2:14–16). The striking aspect of this unit is not Paul's discussion of God's impartiality and just judgment (both of which were traditional Jewish themes) but the manner in which he applies these traditional themes to Jews and Gentiles alike.

2:1–11. There is a change in tone between this unit and Paul's indictment of the Gentile world (1:18–32). Whereas Paul wrote his indictment in the third-person plural, in this unit he employs the second-person singular to address an imaginary interlocutor. Because Paul is using the form of the diatribe, there is no need to speculate about the identity of the interlocutor. Paul is addressing an imaginary interlocutor in the hearing of the Christ-believers at Rome to illustrate the arrogant attitude they must avoid.

Making use of a diatribe, Paul turns to an imaginary interlocutor (ō anthrōpe) who judges others: **Therefore, whoever you are, you are without excuse, you who judge others, for in whatever matter you judge another, you judge yourself, for you who judge do the same things. We know that God's judgment against those who do such things is in accordance with the truth** (2:1–2). Verse 1 begins with the particle *dio* (therefore), which suggests that Paul is drawing a connection between what he has already said and what he is about to say. But what is the connection? After all, Paul's imaginary interlocutor condemns the very behavior that Paul has described in 1:18–32. Why, then, does Paul charge that the one who judges condemns himself?

The linguistic connections between these verses and 1:18–32 provide a partial answer. First, just as Paul has accused the Gentiles of being "without excuse" (1:20), so he accuses his imaginary interlocutor of being "without excuse" (*anapologētos*, 2:1), thereby drawing a relation between the interlocutor and those whom he judges. Second, just as Paul has condemned those who "do" such things and approve of those "who are doing such things" (1:32), so here he condemns his imaginary interlocutor of "doing" or "practicing" (*prasseis*) what he condemns (2:1–3). Finally, just as Paul has accused the Gentiles of suppressing the truth by their unrighteousness (1:18) and exchanging the truth for a lie (1:25), so here he warns his interlocutor that God's judgment is "in accordance with the truth" (2:2) and that God's wrath and fury will come upon all who disobey the truth (2:8). In this first address to his imaginary interlocutor (2:1–2), therefore, Paul draws a close relation between those whom he has indicted in 1:18–32 and the arrogant interlocutor who judges them. That interlocutor may think that he is morally superior but, in the light of the gospel that Paul preaches, Paul knows that such a person is the same as those whom he judges.

Paul's second address to his imaginary interlocutor is longer and more developed, and it becomes apparent that the imaginary interlocutor does far more than judge others (2:3–11). This person has little regard for God's judgment and kindness and does the very things of which he so contemptuously judges others: **You who judge those who practice such things and yet do the same things, do you think that you will escape God's judgment? Or do you have such little regard for his abundant kindness, clemency, and forbearance, ignorant that God's kindness is intended to lead you to repentance? (2:3–4).** Here it appears that Paul is making use of a syllogism. But instead of beginning with his major and minor premises, he states the conclusion first. The reordered syllogism is as follows:

Major premise: God's judgments are true against all who do these things (2:2).

Minor premise: You do what you judge others for doing (2:3).

Conclusion: Therefore, you are without excuse (2:1).

Paul is not merely talking about someone who judges others; he is also speaking of someone who hypocritically does the very things he judges others for doing, and so shows contempt for God's mercy and patience. Accordingly, although Paul's imaginary interlocutor appears to be morally superior to those whom he judges, he is not.

Paul's accusation against his imaginary interlocutor is twofold (2:3–4). First, the interlocutor foolishly supposes that he will escape "God's judgment" (*to krima tou theou*). Second, he has such little regard for God's kindness, clemency, and forbearance that he no longer knows that God's kindness in delaying judgment is meant to bring sinners to "repentance" (*metanoian*, a term that rarely occurs in the Pauline writings, but see 2 Cor. 7:9, 10; 2 Tim. 2:25). In Rom. 1:18–32, Paul spoke of the present manifestation of God's wrath, but here he points to "God's judgment" as a future reality, thereby showing the full dimension of his thought regarding God's judgment. On the one hand, God's judgment is already being revealed insofar as God allows people to suffer the consequences of their sins. On the other hand, there will be a day of reckoning when God will punish sin.

The way in which Paul describes God in these verses is different from the manner in which he spoke of God earlier. In 1:20 he spoke of God's invisible attributes, his eternal power and divine nature, but now he speaks of God's *chrēstotētos* ("goodness, kindness, generosity"; BDAG 1090, def. 2), *anochēs* ("forbearance, clemency, tolerance"; BDAG 86, def. 3), and *makrothymia* ("forbearance, patience toward others"; BDAG 612, def. 2). Although these more traditional Jewish attributes of God might suggest that Paul has a Jewish interlocutor in view, the purpose of Paul's diatribe is to instruct his Roman audience, which is familiar with the themes and language of Israel's scriptures.

Having exposed the hypocrisy of those who present themselves as morally superior to others, Paul issues a harsh warning of what will happen to such people on the day of judgment (2:5–11). The logic of these verses proceeds in four steps. First, Paul warns that **because of the hardness of your unrepentant heart, you are storing up wrath for the day of wrath and the revelation of the just verdict of God** (2:5). This description of their hearts as unrepentant echoes what Paul has already said about the "senseless heart" of the Gentiles (1:21), whom God delivered over to "their heart's desire" (1:24), thereby establishing another relation between the interlocutor and those whom the interlocutor arrogantly judges. The description of the heart as "unrepentant" echoes a similar description of the people of Israel (Deut. 9:27), whereas "the day of wrath" recalls the day of the Lord as described in Israel's scriptures (Zeph. 1:14–18; 2:2–3). On that day, "the just verdict of God" (*dikaiokrisias tou theou*) will be revealed against the sinfulness of humanity (see 2 Thess. 1:5).

Second, Paul quotes from Ps. 61:13 LXX ("because you will repay to each according to his works" [NETS]; 62:12 Eng.): **who will reward each person according to his works** (2:6). The introduction of this text lays the foundation for Paul's argument about the impartiality of God: God is impartial because God judges all—Gentile and Jew alike—on the basis of what they do rather than on the basis of who they are.

Third, making use of an elegant chiasm, Paul shows the double aspect of God's judgment, which will bring eternal life, glory, honor, and peace to those who do good, but wrath, fury, affliction, and anguish to those who do evil. The chiasm can be outlined in this way:

A *Eternal life* to those who, through their perseverance in doing good, are seeking glory, honor, and immortality (2:7).

B *Wrath and fury* to those who, because of selfish ambition and disobedience to the truth, obey the way of unrighteousness (2:8).

B′ *Affliction and anguish* [will come upon] everyone who does evil, the Jew first and then the Greek (2:9).

A′ But *glory and honor and peace* [will come upon] everyone who does good, the Jew first and then the Greek (2:10).

As the outline shows, references to eternal life, glory, honor, and peace enclose the references to wrath, fury, affliction, and anguish. Eternal life, by which Paul means resurrection life, is the outcome of seeking the "glory" (*doxan*), "honor" (*timēn*), and "immortality" (*aphtharsian*) that only God can grant. But as Paul notes, it requires perseverance in doing good to attain such life (2:7). Likewise, God's "glory," "honor," and "peace" (*eirēnē*) come upon "everyone who does good" (2:10). In contrast to this recompense from God, there is only "wrath" (*orgē*) and "fury" (*thymos*) for those who disobey the "truth" (*alētheia*) by their "unrighteousness" (*adikia*, 2:8). And there will be "affliction" (*thlipsis*) and "anguish" (*stenochōria*) for those who do "evil" (*kakon*, 2:9). The mention of "unrighteousness" (*adikia*) and "truth" (*alētheia*) recalls Paul's thesis statement in 1:18 about those who are suppressing the truth by their unrighteousness, while the references to doing good and evil clearly echo the principle of Ps. 62 that God will repay each one according to deeds.

At two points in this chiasm (2:9 and 2:10), Paul introduces the phrase "the Jew first and then the Greek" ("Greek" referring to Gentiles). With this phrase, Paul recalls what he has said about the gospel being the source of salvation for all who believe, "the Jew first and then the Greek" (1:16). Now he employs the same phrase to speak of God's impartial judgment. Punishment will come upon all, the Jews first and then the Gentiles, if they persist in evil. But for those who turn to God, there will be glory, honor, and peace, the Jews first and then the Gentiles. Thus there is a salvation-historical order of precedence in God's impartial judgment.

The fourth and climatic step in Paul's argument is the reason he adduces for this judgment: **for there is no partiality on the part of God** (2:11). In itself, this affirmation of God's impartiality, to which Israel's sacred writings attest (Deut. 10:17–18; cf. Sir. 35:12–16; Wis. 6:7), is not surprising. But, in the context of what Paul has just said, it is unexpected. Paul affirms that since God is not partial, God will treat Gentiles and Jews in the same way. God will judge Gentiles and Jews on the basis of their deeds rather than on the basis of their ethnic heritage. But how does this work out in practice if the Jews possess the gracious gift of God's law and the Gentiles do not?

2:12–16. Having argued that God is an impartial judge who will judge Gentiles and Jews on the basis of what they have done (2:1–11), Paul provides an example that illustrates this impartial judgment (2:12–16). He develops this

---

God Is Impartial

"For the LORD *your God is God of gods and Lord of lords, the great God, mighty and awesome, who is not partial and takes no bribe, who executes justice for the orphan and the widow, and who loves the strangers, providing them food and clothing."* (Deut. 10:17–18)

"Give to the Most High as he has given to you, and as generously as you can afford. For the Lord is the one who repays, and he will repay you sevenfold. Do not offer him a bribe, for he will not accept it; and do not rely on a dishonest sacrifice; for the Lord is the judge, and with him there is no partiality. He will not show partiality to the poor; but he will listen to the prayer of one who is wronged." (Sir. 35:12–16)

"For the Lord of all will not stand in awe of anyone, or show deference to greatness; because he himself made both small and great, and he takes thought for all alike." (Wis. 6:7)

---

example in three steps. First, he presents his thesis in which he explains how God will judge the Gentiles who do not possess the law and the Jews who do possess it (2:12). Second, Paul provides his audience with a supporting reason for his thesis statement: doing the law is more important than possessing it (2:13). Third, Paul provides an example of Gentiles who do the law—even though they do not have the law—in order to illustrate what he has said in 2:13, thereby suggesting that even Gentiles can be justified if they do God's will (2:14–16). Thus Paul establishes the utterly impartial manner in which God judges Gentiles and Jews. This section, which introduces the theme of the law, provides a transition to the next section, in which Paul will deal with Jewish failure to observe the law (2:17–29).

Paul presents his thesis: **For whoever has sinned apart from the law will perish without reference to the law, and whoever sins knowing the law will be judged in reference to the law** (2:12). In this neatly balanced sentence, Paul refers to the law four times, establishing a distinction between the Gentiles, who do not have the law, and the Jews, who do. Since God is impartial, God will not judge the Gentiles as if they were Jews, nor will God judge the Jews as if they were Gentiles; for the law speaks only to those who are under the law (3:19). Therefore, God will not judge the Gentiles by the standards of the Mosaic law. Paul's thesis can be displayed in this way:

Those who sin *anomōs*

will perish *anomōs*.

Those who sin *en nomō*

will be judged *dia nomou*.

The only other occurrence of the adverb *anomōs* in the Greek Bible is in 2 Macc. 8:17, where it refers to lawless behavior. But in our text the adverb clearly indicates the conduct of those who sin apart from the Mosaic law. The phrase *en nomō* refers to the realm of the Mosaic law, whereas *dia nomou* explains that this judgment will be carried out by the criterion of the law. Paul uses similar language in 1 Cor. 9:20–21, where he says that he became "as one under the law" (*hypo nomon*), although he is not under the law, so that he might win those under the law, and "to those outside the law" (*anomois*) he became as one outside the law, although he is not free from God's law but "under Christ's law" (*ennomos Christou*).

Having established this principle of divine impartiality, Paul provides a supporting reason for it: **For it is not the hearers of the law who are righteous before God, but it is those who do the law who will be justified** (2:13). At first it may appear that only the Jews can be "the hearers of the law," but as the argument develops, it becomes apparent that even Gentiles can be "hearers of the law" insofar as something of the law is written on their hearts. Paul's argument, however, is that it is not the "hearers of the law"—be they Jews or Gentiles—who will be justified, but those who "do the law." The Letter of James makes a similar point when it contrasts being "hearers of the word" with being "doers of the word" (1:22–25). Again, since only the Jews have the law, it might appear that only they can do the law, but the following verses show that even the Gentiles can do something of the law. The most striking aspect of this verse is the statement that it is only those who do the law who will be justified, which stands in tension with Paul's affirmation in Rom. 3:20 that no one will be justified on the basis of doing the works of the law.

To illustrate what he means, Paul provides the Romans with an example of Gentile observance of the law. **For when Gentiles, who do not have the law, spontaneously carry out the prescriptions of the law, these who are without a law regulate themselves. They show the reality of the law written on their hearts, as their conscience gives evidence in support of them; and their thoughts, in dialogue with each other, either accuse or excuse them, on the day when, in accord with the gospel I preach, God will judge through Jesus Christ those things people have hidden** (2:14–16). Given Paul's indictment of Gentile sinfulness in 1:18–32, this example is surprising. But it is precisely this example that Paul needs if he is to make his argument that God is an impartial judge. It is not merely the Jews who can do God's law; it is the Gentiles as well. And when they do, God, who is impartial, judges them accordingly. This argument prepares for the next section, in which Paul will describe Jewish failure to keep the law, thereby establishing a striking contrast between Jewish and Gentile behavior (2:17–29).

Paul's line of thought in 2:14–16 proceeds in three steps. First, he recognizes that there are instances of Gentiles who, although they do not have the law, do what the law requires (2:14). These instances show that there is a law, or something of the law, within the Gentiles that allows them to govern themselves. The Gentiles, then, are not completely lawless, and it is evident from what Paul says here that his indictment of the Gentiles in 1:18–32 does not mean that they never do what is right in God's sight. But the fact that they know something of God's will, just as they know something of God, does point to their moral responsibility and failure (Keck 2005, 79–80). Second, building on what he said in 2:14, Paul maintains that something of the law is written on the hearts of the Gentiles, the witness to this being their moral consciousness—their conscience—an inner dialogue within a person that accuses and excuses (2:15). Third, Paul relates this moral consciousness of the Gentiles to the day of judgment, when God will reveal all that is hidden in accordance with the gospel that Paul preaches (2:16). Thus Paul returns to the theme of God's eschatological judgment, which he introduced in 2:3.

But what does Paul mean when he says that the Gentiles observe the law? Is he referring to a natural law that human beings deduce from the nature of things, as many Greek philosophers taught? Or does Paul still have the Mosaic law in view? Paul's use of *physei* (lit., "by nature," which I have translated "spontaneously") in 2:14 could suggest that he is referring to the Greek notion of an unwritten or natural law (D. Moo 1996, 150), the sense being that the Gentiles do what is right by nature. But Paul's reference in 2:15 to "the reality of the law" (lit., "the work of the law") written on the hearts of the Gentiles appears to allude to Jer. 31:33 and Isa. 51:7, texts that speak of the prescriptions of the Mosaic law written in or on the hearts of the people. Paul, of course, is not saying that the Gentiles have internalized the law in the way that Isaiah and Jeremiah envisioned. But he is affirming that something of the Mosaic law is already accessible to them in their hearts. Thus Paul combines something of the Greek understanding of a natural law with his Jewish understanding of God's law as the source of all law inasmuch as "the world is in harmony with the Mosaic law, and the law with the world," as Philo taught (Tobin 2004, 114).

Paul's train of thought in Rom. 2:12–16 can be summarized in this way: God will judge Gentiles as Gentiles and Jews as Jews on the basis of what they do rather than on the basis of who they are. Jews will not be in a more

---

The Law Internalized

"Listen to me, you who know righteousness, you people who have my teaching in your hearts; do not fear the reproach of others, and do not be dismayed when they revile you." (Isa. 51:7, emphasis added)

"But this is the covenant that I will make with the house of Israel after those days, says the LORD: I will put my law within them, and I will write it on their hearts; and I will be their God, and they shall be my people." (Jer. 31:33, emphasis added)

advantageous position, nor will Gentiles be at a disadvantage before this impartial Judge. For although Jews have the advantage of the law, which reveals God's will, it is not the possession of the law but its observance that matters. Observance of the law is even possible for Gentiles, to a certain degree, since something of the law is written in their hearts.

Theological Issues

The central theological theme of this section is God's impartial judgment. God does not discriminate between people on the basis of who they are but judges all impartially on the basis of what they do. As noted above, the distinctive aspect of Paul's teaching is not so much the concept of divine impartiality as it is the manner in which he applies this concept to Gentiles and Jews. He affirms that although there is a fundamental difference in the way Gentiles and Jews are related to God (since only the Jewish people stand in a covenant relationship to God), God remains an impartial judge, who judges both on the basis of what they do rather than on the basis of who they are.

While Paul's Jewish compatriots would have agreed that God is an impartial judge, many would have been taken aback by the manner in which Paul leveled the differences between Gentiles and Jews. If God judges everyone impartially on the basis of their works, not taking into account Israel's distinctive relationship to God, what does Israel's divine election mean?

Paul does not address these questions because his rhetorical goal in 1:18–3:20 is to show that all—Jew as well as Gentile—are in need of the salvation God has revealed in Christ. Consequently he argues that since all are under the power of sin, all are in need of God's saving grace, which God extends impartially. God the impartial judge does not excuse the sins of some because of who they are—be they Gentiles, Jews, or even Christians—but God does treat all impartially. In Paul's words, God rewards each according to works (2:6). Because God is an impartial judge, it is not the hearers of the law who will be justified but those who do the law (2:13).

But if doing plays such a central role in Paul's understanding of God's impartiality, how does Paul's theology of impartiality cohere with his teaching on justification by faith? How can Paul say that the doers of the law will be justified (2:13) and then affirm that no one will be justified before God on the basis of doing the works of the law (3:20)? For some, the solution to this conundrum is that Paul is speaking about Gentiles and Jews who are already Christ-believers. Both groups, which have already been justified by God, will be judged on the basis of what they do rather than on the basis of who they are. But there is no indication that Paul is speaking of Christians here. Therefore, it is better to take the plain meaning of the text: Paul is speaking of Gentiles and Jews in order to show that God is impartial toward both groups: God will judge each on the basis of what they have done (2:6), not on the basis of who they are.

In light of the gospel, Paul has come to a new understanding of the human situation. As he has already shown, the wrath of God is coming upon the Gentiles because, viewed as a group, they have sinned (1:18–32). And as Paul will show, even the Jews, viewed as a group, have failed to keep the law (2:17–29). The profound reason for the failure of both groups, as Paul has yet to explain, is that all are under the power of sin (3:9). Consequently, even though there are instances of people doing what is right, all have sinned; and because all are under the power of sin—Jew as well as Gentile—doing the works of the law will not justify a person before God. For even though there are people who do what is in accordance with the law (Paul says he was blameless; Phil. 3:6), Paul now understands that the power of sin has made it impossible for anyone (himself included) to be justified on the basis of doing the works of the law before the all-holy God of Israel. Therefore God, who is an impartial judge, has revealed his own righteousness in Jesus Christ, a saving righteousness impartially available to Gentiles and Jews on the basis of faith.

Romans 2:17–29

Jewish Failure to Observe the Law

Introductory Matters

In the opening verses of this section, Paul makes use of the diatribe once more by addressing, questioning, and eventually condemning an imaginary interlocutor. Thus there is a parallel between this section and the previous section:

Diatribe: Paul addresses his interlocutor (2:1–5).
    Paul discusses God's impartial judgment (2:6–16).
Diatribe: Paul addresses his interlocutor (2:17–24).
    Paul discusses circumcision and judgment (2:25–29).

However, whereas in 2:1–5 Paul does not reveal the identity of the interlocutor, in 2:17–24 he does: Paul is addressing a Jewish person who has been trained in the law and so views himself as a teacher of others. Some (Fitzmyer 1993, 297; Byrne 1996, 79–80) argue that the interlocutor in 2:1–5 and 2:17–24 are the same person, a Jew; others (Keck 2005, 74; Tobin 2004, 115) maintain that the interlocutor of 2:1–5 is a Gentile, thereby establishing a balance with the Jewish interlocutor of 2:17–24. In my view, there is no need to be so specific about the identity of the interlocutor in 2:1–5, who, in light of the diatribal form, could be a Jew, a Gentile, or a Christ-believer of either Jewish or Gentile origin.

Romans 2:17–29 in the Rhetorical Flow

The letter opening (1:1–17)

Gentiles and Jews in the light of God's wrath (1:18–3:20)

Gentile failure to acknowledge God (1:18–32)

God's impartial judgment of Gentiles and Jews (2:1–16)

▶**Jewish failure to observe the law (2:17–29)**

Reliance on the law is insufficient (2:17–24)

Five points of identity (2:17–18)

Call oneself a Jew (2:17a)

Rely on the law (2:17b)

Boast in God (2:17c)

Know the will (2:18a)

Approve what is excellent because **taught by the law** (2:18b)

Five claims of superiority (2:19–20)

Guide for the blind (2:19a)

Light for those in darkness (2:19b)

Disciplinarian for the foolish (2:20a)

Teacher of the immature (2:20b)

Possesses knowledge and truth **in the law** (2:20c)

Five questions indicating failure (2:21–23)

Do you teach yourself? (2:21a)

Do you steal? (2:21b)

Do you commit adultery? (2:22a)

Do you rob temples? (2:22c)

Do you **dishonor the law**? (2:23)

Condemnation from Scripture (2:24)

Reliance on circumcision is insufficient (2:25–29)

The importance of law observance (2:25)

When circumcision is of value (2:25a)

When circumcision is of no value (2:25b)

Gentiles who keep the law (2:26–27)

How their noncircumcision will be reckoned (2:26)

Whom they will judge (2:27)

Description of the true Jew (2:28–29)

Not the one who is so outwardly (2:28)

But the one who is so inwardly (2:29)

Although Paul launches an unrelenting assault upon his Jewish interlocutor, his diatribe is not a condemnation of Judaism. Paul's rhetorical goal in 1:18–3:20 is to show that all, Jew as well as Gentile, are under the power of sin. Therefore, all are in need of God's saving justice. To arrive at this goal, Paul must convince his audience that even Israel, which has the benefit of God's law and the covenant sign of circumcision, has failed to observe the law. The object of Paul's diatribe is not Judaism as a religion but the ethnic and national pride of those who mistakenly think that their religious status exempts them from God's judgment. Keck (2005, 83) notes that Paul "uses this indictment of the hypocrisy of a particular type of Jew to express the idea that simply being a Jew does not automatically confer privileged status in God's impartial judgment." Similarly, N. T. Wright (2002, 446) states: "The ethnic boast of 'the Jew' is thereby called into question." This section, then, continues the theme of divine impartiality introduced in 2:1–11. Those who stand before an impartial God must do the law on which they rely and boast; otherwise circumcision and the law will be of no avail to them.

The use Paul makes of diatribe in this section indicates that he is teaching and explaining his gospel rather than attacking an opponent or a particular group of people at Rome. His teaching would have caused his listeners to reflect on their own situation, especially those Christ-believers who were Jewish by birth and those who had converted to Judaism prior to becoming believers in Christ. Both groups would have continued to revere circumcision and the law. Paul's purpose, then, is not to attack the law and circumcision but to expose the failure of those who rely on them without doing what they require.

Tracing the Train of Thought

This section consists of two units. In the first, Paul shows that reliance on the law is of no avail for those who do not observe the law (2:17–24). In the second, he argues that circumcision is of no value if one does not keep the law (2:25–29).

The first unit has four subunits. In the first, Paul lists five ways in which his Jewish interlocutor identifies himself (2:17–18). In the second, he catalogs five claims of superiority that the interlocutor makes (2:19–20). In the third, he poses five rhetorical questions that accuse the interlocutor of failing to keep the law (2:21–23). In the fourth, he accuses his interlocutor of causing God's name to be blasphemed among the Gentiles by failing to observe the law (2:24). In each of the three lists of five, the fifth element always refers to the law (2:18b, 20c, 23). The second unit (2:25–29) begins with a thesis statement about the importance of keeping the law (2:25). Next, it opposes the noncircumcised Gentile who keeps the law and the circumcised Jew who does not (2:26–27). Finally, it establishes a contrast between the internal and external Jew (2:28–29).

2:17–24. Paul begins by listing five ways in which his imaginary Jewish interlocutor identifies himself vis-à-vis the Gentile world: **Now if you call yourself a Jew, and rely on the law, and boast in God, and know the will, and approve of what is best since you have been instructed by the law** (2:17–18). The emphatic "you" (*sy*) in 2:17 and the use of verbs in the second-person singular indicate that Paul has embarked upon another diatribe. The identity of the interlocutor as a "Jew" (*Ioudaios*, 2:17) and Paul's contrast between the outward and the inward "Jew" (2:28–29) bracket the entire section, highlighting the central role that Jewish identity plays in this section.

The five items in this first list are related to one another in this way: (1) The one who bears the name "Jew" identifies himself as an adherent to the Mosaic traditions that his ancestors fiercely defended at the time of the Maccabean revolt; (2) because he is a zealous adherent to these traditions, he relies on the law; (3) because he relies on the law, he boasts in God, who is the giver of the law; (4) because he possesses the law, he knows "the will," a pious circumlocution for "the will of God"; (5) because he knows God's will and has been instructed in the law, Paul's interlocutor approves of what is "best" or "superior."

> ### Relying on the Law
>
> "In you we have put our trust, because, behold, your Law is with us, and we know that we do not fall as long as we keep your statutes. We shall always be blessed; at least, we did not mingle with the nations. For we are all a people of the Name; we, who received one Law from the One. And that Law that is among us will help us, and that excellent wisdom which is in us will support us."
> (*2 Bar.* 48.22–24, *OTP* 1:636)

Although Paul will eventually condemn his Jewish interlocutor, he does not disparage or call into question the way in which his interlocutor identifies himself. From the Maccabean period onward—a period in which pious Israelites suffered persecution and death for their religious and ethnic identity as expressed in the law and circumcision—*Ioudaios* became the way in which the people of the covenant identified themselves, replacing, to some extent, the older terms "Hebrews" and "Israelites" (Fitzmyer 1993, 316). This term, which focused on race, birth, and religion, identified those who bore it as adherents to the Mosaic tradition, especially circumcision and the prescriptions of the law. Paul continues to see himself as *Ioudaios* (Gal. 2:15).

Although "relying on the law" can have a negative connotation when it is not accompanied by law observance, it also enjoys a positive connotation, as Sir. 39:8 and *2 Bar.* 48.22–24 testify. Similarly, although boasting normally has a negative connotation in Paul's writings, he quotes Jer. 9:22–23 to exhort believers to boast in the Lord (1 Cor. 1:31; 2 Cor. 10:17). The noncanonical *Pss. of Sol.* 17.1 makes a similar point: "Lord, you are our king forevermore, for in you, O God, does our soul take pride" (*OTP* 2:665). The way in which Paul's interlocutor identifies himself, then, is not the problem.

Next, Paul draws out the implication of how his interlocutor identifies himself. Since the interlocutor prides himself on his Jewish identity and the law, he views himself as capable of instructing others: **and if you are confident that you are a guide for the blind, a light for those in darkness, an instructor for those who are foolish, a teacher of those who are immature, since you have the embodiment of knowledge and the truth in the law** (2:19–20). Once more there is a logic in the way Paul has arranged this list. The interlocutor, who has been instructed by the law, sees what others do not see. Consequently, he fancies himself to be a guide for the blind and a light for those who are in darkness because they do not have the law. Bereft of the law, such people are foolish and immature. Therefore, Paul's interlocutor willingly becomes their instructor since he has the embodiment of knowledge and truth in the law. Paul does not dispute or disparage this missionary outreach to those who dwell in the darkness of ignorance. After all, God called his servant Israel "as a covenant to the people, a light to the nations, to open the eyes that are blind, to bring out the prisoners from the dungeon, from the prison those who sit in darkness" (Isa. 42:6–8). It was Israel's vocation to be "a light to the nations" so that God's salvation might "reach to the end of the earth" (Isa. 49:6). All of this was possible because the law is the "embodiment" (*morphōsin*, Rom. 2:20; the outward manifestation of an inner reality) of "knowledge" and "truth," the very realities that the Gentiles rejected when they refused to acknowledge God as God (1:21, 25). As Sirach affirms, wisdom and the book of the covenant (the law) are one (24:23–27).

The problem is not *who* the interlocutor claims to be or *what* he aspires to do but *what he has failed to do.* Although he is a Jew instructed by the law, and although he aspires to be a teacher because he has the embodiment of truth and knowledge in the law, he fails to do what the law requires. Therefore, instead of concluding the series of conditional clauses that he began in 2:17, Paul springs his rhetorical trap and asks a series of five questions, all of which assume that his interlocutor has failed to keep the very law in which he boasts: **Then do you who teach others, do you not teach yourself? Do you who preach "do not steal," do you steal? Do you who tell others not to commit adultery, do you commit adultery? Do you who detest idols, do you rob temples? Do you who boast in the law, do you dishonor the law of God by transgressing the law?** (2:21–23). The first question ("do you who teach") refers to the interlocutor's desire to be an "instructor of the foolish" and a "teacher of the immature" (2:20). The second and third questions refer to specific commandments of the Decalogue (Exod. 20:14–15), while the fourth question insinuates that the Jewish interlocutor has violated the first commandment (Exod. 20:2–3) by his involvement with pagan temples. Thus Paul draws an implicit relationship between his interlocutor and the idolatrous Gentiles described in chapter 1. Although I have translated the verb *hierosyleis* as "do you rob temples," Paul may have in view the purchase of stolen temple artifacts (D. Moo 1996, 164) or making profits from "assets irrevocably dedicated to an idolatrous purpose" (Derrett 1994, 571) rather than the actual robbery of temples. In the fifth question, Paul returns to the theme of boasting. But now he speaks of boasting in the law rather than of boasting in God so that the fifth item of this list also refers to the law (see 2:18b, 20c). Paul's final question is more general inasmuch as he asks if the one who boasts in the law has dishonored it by transgressing it. This rebuke recalls God's reprimand of the wicked as recorded in Ps. 50:16–21, which begins: "What right have you to recite my statues, or take my covenant on your lips? For you hate discipline and cast my words behind you."

Having described how his Jewish interlocutor identifies himself and his mission, and having shown the disparity between who the interlocutor professes to be and what he does, Paul pronounces his verdict: **As it is written, "because of you, the name of God is blasphemed among the Gentiles"** (2:24). The verdict is not Paul's own but the verdict of the very Scriptures upon which his interlocutor depends. However, although the text of Isa. 52:5 says that the Gentiles blasphemed God's name because they witnessed Israel's suffering, Paul makes use of the Septuagint, which adds "because of you" and "among the nations," and he rereads the text in the light of his people's contemporary situation: the Gentiles are presently blaspheming God's name because of Jewish failure to observe the law (Käsemann 1980, 71).

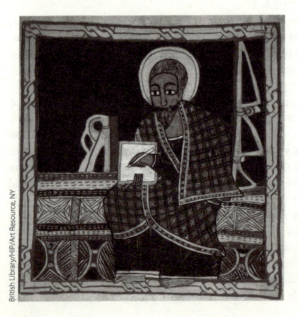

British Library/HIP/Art Resource, NY

Figure 3. Moses Writing the Law, frontispiece to Exodus from a parchment manuscript of the Octateuch, Four Gospels, and Synodicon (late seventeenth century AD), Gondar, Ethiopia. Paul affirms the holiness of the law but says that it was unable to bring about salvation.

Lest Paul's indictment be misunderstood, it is important to recall that he is not criticizing Judaism as corrupt and hypocritical. Nor is he saying that this behavior is representative of each and every Jew. The purpose of his diatribe is to show that Israel has failed to fulfill its vocation to be a light to the nations (Wright 2002, 447). For reasons that Paul has yet to explain, Israel has not observed the very law in which it boasts.

2:25–29. Having made use of a diatribe to expose Jewish failure to observe the law, Paul considers the outstanding mark of Jewish identity: the sign of circumcision. To be sure, Paul's Jewish interlocutor has transgressed the law, but the interlocutor still stands in a privileged relationship to Israel's God. He is a circumcised Israelite, a member of the covenant people. Surely this counts for something; but Paul will not relent. Returning to the topic of God's impartiality (without using the term), Paul argues that just as God judges Gentiles and Jews impartially on the basis of what they do rather than on the basis of who they are, so God treats the uncircumcised and the circumcised impartially. It is not circumcision that counts but observance of the law. Accordingly, there is a further parallel between 2:1–16 and 2:17–29:

A diatribe directed at one who arrogantly judges others (2:1–5).

God's impartial judgment based on what one does (2:6–16).

A diatribe directed at one who boasts in his privileged identity (2:17–24).

God's impartial treatment of circumcised and uncircumcised (2:25–29).

Paul presents a thesis statement that has two parts: (1) Circumcision is of value if you observe the law (2:25a). (2) But if you are a transgressor of the law, your circumcision is nullified (2:25b). These statements affirm and go beyond traditional Jewish teaching. Circumcision was the way in which a Jew entered into the eternal covenant God made with Abraham (Gen. 17), and those who accepted circumcision were required to do all that the law requires, as Paul reminds his Galatian converts (Gal. 5:3). But in saying that transgressions of the law nullify their circumcision, Paul goes beyond the teaching of his contemporaries (Käsemann 1980, 73). The great defender of justification by faith emphasizes that the value of circumcision depends on observing the law, a point he makes in a slightly different way in 1 Cor. 7:19: "Circumcision is nothing, and uncircumcision is nothing; but obeying the commandments of God is everything" (see also Gal. 6:15).

Having presented this thesis statement, Paul illustrates what he means: **Therefore, if the noncircumcised Gentile should observe the just commandments of the law, will not his state of noncircumcision be reckoned as circumcision? Thus the one who by birth is not circumcised but carries out the law will judge you who, in spite of the written letter and circumcision, are a transgressor of the law** (2:26–27). The example Paul employs here is similar to the one that he has presented in 2:14–16, and it makes a similar point: When Gentiles do what the law requires, God, who is impartial, rewards their behavior. But the conclusion Paul draws goes beyond any conclusion his contemporaries would have drawn: the uncircumcised Gentile who observes the law will be reckoned as if he were a Jew. Employing the emphatic second-person singular (*sy*), Paul warns his interlocutor, who has "the written letter" (*grammatos*) and circumcision (but has failed to observe the law), that he will be judged by the Gentile whom he esteems as "blind," "in the darkness," "foolish," and "immature" (2:19–20). By threatening this eschatological reversal of fortunes, Paul points to the utter impartiality of God.

Having shown that God does not show partiality toward others on the basis of circumcision or the lack of it, Paul makes the point toward which he has been moving since the beginning of this section (2:17): being a Jew is not a matter of externals but a matter of internal disposition: **For it is not the one who is a Jew outwardly, nor the one whose circumcision is exteriorly manifested in the flesh but the one who is a Jew inwardly, whose circumcision is of the heart, by the Spirit rather than by the written letter, whose praise does not come from human beings but from God (2:28–29).** These carefully formulated verses establish a contrast between two kinds of people:

The outward Jew	The inward Jew
circumcised in the flesh	circumcised in the heart
by the Spirit	by the written letter (the law)
praise from humans	praise from God

Jeremiah had already urged his contemporaries to circumcise their hearts lest God's wrath come upon them (Jer. 4:4; 9:25). The book of Deuteronomy also warned the Israelites to circumcise their hearts (10:16), adding, "For the LORD your God is God of gods and Lord of lords, the great God, mighty and awesome, *who is not partial and takes no bribe*" (10:17, emphasis added). Recognizing that only God can circumcise the heart, Deuteronomy says that God will circumcise the heart of Israel and its descendants so that they will love the Lord their God with all their heart (30:6). Paul follows this train of thought when he contrasts a circumcision effected by the Spirit with a circumcision effected by "the written letter" of the law. The letter has no power to effect an inner change because it is only a written code, but the Spirit brings such change because it is God's life-giving Spirit.

By the end of the section, Paul has established the following: (1) God is utterly impartial toward people, whether or not they are circumcised; (2) observance of the law is more important than possession of the law or circumcision; (3) Israel has failed to observe the law. Paul has also introduced a theme that he will develop later: the need for the power of God's Spirit.

Theological Issues

Paul's distinction between the "inner" and the "outer" Jew points to his understanding of the Spirit, which lies at the heart of his theology. For Paul, Christ-believers have experienced an inner renewal through the power of the Spirit that changes and transforms them from within. The Spirit of God has renewed their hearts and minds so that they can know and do God's will in a way they previously could not. For Paul, Christ-believers are the recipients of the new covenant that Jeremiah promised (Jer. 31:31–34; see 2 Cor. 3:6), and God has circumcised their hearts, as the book of Deuteronomy commanded (Deut. 10:16). When writing to his Gentile converts at Philippi, therefore, Paul affirms, "For it is we who are the circumcision, who worship in the Spirit of God and boast in Christ Jesus and have no confidence in the flesh" (Phil. 3:3). And in Colossians, Paul speaks of a "spiritual circumcision" by which believers have stripped away "the body of the flesh in the circumcision of Christ," which believers experienced in their baptism (2:11–12). When he distinguishes between the outward and the inward Jew, Paul is anticipating some of the themes that he will develop later in this letter.

However, in this section it is not Paul's purpose to argue that Christ-believers have supplanted those Jews who have not believed in Christ. As Paul will argue in Rom. 9–11, God has not rejected Israel, even though a hardening has come upon a part of Israel. Paul's rhetorical goal has been to show his contemporaries—whether or not they are Christ-believers—that God is utterly impartial and that all have sinned. Consequently, Paul has exposed the failures of his contemporaries in order to convince them of their need for that inner renewal that only the Spirit of God can effect. He is not seeking to supplant them. God is not partial toward one group of people at the expense of another—God is utterly impartial. The criterion of God's judgment remains the same for all: behavior in accordance with God's will. It would be a grave mistake, then, to use this text to denigrate ancient or contemporary Judaism.

Romans 3:1–20

Gentiles and Jews under the Power of Sin

Introductory Matters

This section brings to completion the first part of Romans (1:18–3:20), in which Paul has been discussing the situation of Gentiles and Jews in light of God's wrath/judgment. Thus far, Paul has shown his audience that God is utterly impartial. Consequently, at the last judgment God will judge Gentiles and Jews on the basis of *what* they have done rather than on the basis of *who* they are. This theme of divine impartiality comes to its climax in this section, in which Paul draws the conclusion toward which he has been moving: God is impartial toward Gentiles and Jews since both find themselves under the power of sin, which frustrates every human effort to do God's will.

This section (3:1–20) continues the form of the diatribe, which Paul has employed in 2:1–5 and 2:17–24. But whereas in those diatribes Paul has accused imaginary interlocutors of arrogantly judging others or of failing to obey the law in which they boast, in this diatribe he enters into a dialogue with an interlocutor in which one party poses a series of questions to which the other responds. This dialogue allows Paul to draw his first and most important conclusion: Gentiles and Jews find themselves in the same situation before God because all are under the power of sin (3:9). To convince his Jewish interlocutor that this situation applies to him as well, Paul employs a chain of scriptural quotations (3:10–18) to substantiate what he says in 3:9. Then, having shown that Scripture itself testifies to this situation of human sinfulness, Paul draws a conclusion that is integral to the gospel he preaches: no one will be justified in God's sight on the basis of doing the works of the law (3:20).

This first unit of this section consists of a series of questions and responses (3:1–8). But who is asking the questions, and who is responding to them? Most commentators maintain that Paul is debating an imaginary Jewish interlocutor who questions and refutes what Paul has been saying. According to this reading, Paul's Jewish interlocutor polemically poses the questions in 3:1, 3, 5, 7–8a, and Paul responds to them in 3:2, 4, 6, 8b. Stowers (1984), however, has questioned this reading and argued that the dialogical exchange in this section is pedagogical rather than polemical. Pointing to examples from the ancient world of this pedagogical technique, he maintains that it is Paul who poses the questions in 3:3, 5, 7–8, and the interlocutor who answers them in

---

Romans 3:1–20 in the Rhetorical Flow

The letter opening (1:1–17)

Gentiles and Jews in the light of God's wrath (1:18–3:20)

    Gentile failure to acknowledge God (1:18–32)

    God's impartial judgment of Gentiles and Jews (2:1–16)

    Jewish failure to observe the law (2:17–29)

▶Gentiles and Jews under the power of sin (3:1–20)

    Questions and responses (3:1–8)

      Interlocutor: Is there an advantage to being a Jew? (3:1)

      Paul: Yes, they have been entrusted with the oracles of God (3:2)

      Interlocutor: God's faithfulness will not be nullified, will it? (3:3)

      Paul: Of course not! God's truthfulness is enduring (3:4)

      Interlocutor: God's judgments are not unjust, are they? (3:5)

      Paul: Of course not; God must judge the world (3:6)

      Interlocutor: Why am I being judged? (3:7)

      Paul: Their judgment is just (3:8)

    All under the power of sin (3:9–20)

      Interlocutor: Are the Jews at an advantage/disadvantage? (3:9a)

      Paul: No, for all are under the power of sin (3:9b)

      Confirmation from Scripture (3:10–18)

      Conclusion (3:19–20)

        The law addresses those under the law (3:19a)

        All will be accountable to God (3:19b)

        No one is justified on the basis of doing the works of the law (3:20a)

        The law makes one aware of sin (3:20b)

3:4 and 3:6. It is by these questions, then, that Paul leads the interlocutor to his point of view.

Stowers's construal has found support from Byrne (1996, 107–11) and Keck (2005, 89–94). Although this approach makes a valuable contribution by reading the text as a dialogical exchange that is pedagogical rather than apologetic in nature, it attributes questions that begin with *mē genoito* (of course not) in 3:4 and 3:6 to Paul's dialogical partner, whereas in the rest of Romans, Paul reserves this expression for himself (3:31; 6:2, 15; 7:7, 13; 9:14; 11:1, 11). Consequently, while I agree that Paul is engaged in a process of pedagogy rather than polemics against Judaism, I maintain that it is the interlocutor who is asking the questions and Paul who is responding to them, except in 3:8, where Paul answers the question of 3:7 with a question.

The material of 3:9–20 forms a second unit, which continues the diatribe of 3:1–8. First, Paul's dialogue partner asks a question in 3:9a, to which Paul responds in 3:9b. Next, in 3:10–18 Paul substantiates his response by a series of quotations from Scripture and then draws his conclusion in 3:19–20.

Tracing the Train of Thought

This section consists of two units (3:1–8 and 3:9–20), each beginning with *ti oun*, "what, then?" The first unit is divided into two subunits, the first of which deals with questions about the faithfulness of God to the Jewish people (3:1–4), while the second concerns itself with the righteousness of God's judgments (3:5–8). Although C. H. Dodd (1932, 46) once complained that "the whole argument of iii.1–8 is obscure and feeble," there is an inner logic to this section. Paul begins by assuring his Jewish interlocutor that God remains faithful, even if some of the interlocutor's compatriots have been unfaithful (3:1–4). He then concludes by reminding his interlocutor that God is just in judging those who have sinned, even though their sins have led to the manifestation of God's truth and faithfulness.

The second unit begins with the thematic statement toward which Paul has been driving ever since 1:18: all are under the power of sin. It then concludes with a corollary: no one will be justified before God on the basis of doing the works of the law (3:19–20). The material between these two statements provides the scriptural confirmation for Paul's argument (3:10–18).

3:1–8. Paul's indictment of his imaginary Jewish interlocutor in 2:17–29 leads the interlocutor to pose a two-pronged question: **What then is the advantage of being a Jew, or what is the benefit of circumcision?** (3:1). To be sure, it is Paul who formulates this question. But inasmuch as he is employing the form of the diatribe, he places it on the lips of an imaginary Jewish interlocutor who relies on the law and circumcision. Having been accused by Paul of transgressing the law (2:21–24) and having been told that circumcision is of value only if one observes the law (2:25), the Jewish interlocutor raises a first objection: Doesn't Jewish identity count for anything before God? Has Paul forgotten Israel's unique relationship with God, which distinguishes it from other nations (Deut. 4:7–8)? Did not God deal with Israel in a special way (Ps. 147:19–20)? Paul has not forgotten these privileges. Beginning as if he will list a series of advantages, Paul responds, **Much in every way. First of all, they were entrusted with the oracles of God** (3:2). But the list abruptly ends here (although Paul will give an extended list of such privileges in 9:4–5, when he takes up the question of Israel's role in God's salvific plan). For the moment, Paul only says that the Jews were entrusted with "the oracles of God" (*ta logia tou theou*, an expression that occurs in Num. 24:4 LXX and Ps. 106:11 LXX [107:11 Eng.]; also see Josephus, *J.W.* 6.310–13). Although the expression is open to a range of meanings (the messianic promises, the promises to the patriarchs, the commandments of the law, the whole of Scripture), it seems best to follow C. K. Barrett (1957, 62) and Fitzmyer (1993, 326), who take it as referring to the whole of Scripture. Thus, despite his indictment of his Jewish interlocutor, Paul does not say what the interlocutor might have expected ("there is no advantage to being a Jew or to circumcision"). Instead, he affirms that the Jews are in an advantageous position because they know God's will and purpose as revealed in Scripture.

Paul's use of the verb "entrusted" suggests that those who have received these oracles took a certain responsibility upon themselves. Entrusted with the oracles of God, they were to remain faithful to God, even as God had been faithful to them. Aware of this, the interlocutor picks up on the verb *episteuthēsan* (they were entrusted) and asks: **So what if some were unfaithful? Their unfaithfulness will not nullify God's faithfulness, will it?** (3:3). Aware of the critique that Paul has leveled against him in 2:24–29, the interlocutor acknowledges that not all have been faithful. Posing his questions in a manner that expects a negative answer and playing on the words "faithfulness" and "unfaithfulness," the interlocutor asks if the "unfaithfulness" (*apistia*) of some will annul God's "faithfulness" (*pistis*) toward the Jewish people, who "were entrusted" (*episteuthēsan*) with God's oracles.

Making use of an expression (*mē genoito*) he uses throughout Romans when he wants to deny a blatantly false conclusion, Paul responds, **Of course not!** (3:4a). How could the God who is faithful be unfaithful, even in the face of human unfaithfulness? To affirm such a statement would be to deny who God is. Alluding to Ps. 115:2 LXX (116:11 Eng.), "I said in my alarm, 'Every person is a liar'" (NETS), and making use of a quotation from Ps. 50:6 LXX (51:4 Eng.), Paul explains what he means: **Let God be shown to be true and every human being a liar, as it is written, "So that you may be justified in your words and prevail when you go to court"** (3:4b). Whereas the introduction to the psalm focuses on God's truthfulness (*alētheia*), which, for Paul, is equivalent to God's faithfulness (*pistis*), the psalm text draws upon the imagery of a lawsuit. When God and humans contend, God will always be justified by his words and prevail because, unlike human beings, God is always true. God's truthfulness is the truth that the Gentiles suppress by their unrighteousness (1:18).

Paul and his interlocutor would have known that the implied speaker of this psalm was Israel's great king, David, who uttered these words when the prophet Nathan came to him after David's adultery with Bathsheba (as the superscription of Ps. 51 notes). Barrett (1957, 63) captures the essence of Paul's logic: "The truth, or faithfulness, of God is to be believed, even though maintaining it (in the teeth of human unfaithfulness) leads to the conclusion that all men are liars."

Paul's response that God will always prevail in such lawsuits with human beings (because God is always true) leads the interlocutor to raise a third question: **But if our unrighteousness serves to show the righteousness of God, what shall we say? God is not unjust when he inflicts wrath, is he? (I am speaking in a merely human way)** (3:5). If God will always prevail in the court of justice because God alone is true, it would seem that "our unrighteousness" (*adikia hēmōn*) only serves to show the "righteousness of God" (*theou dikaiosynēn*). Consequently, the interlocutor boldly formulates a daring question, to which he expects a negative answer: Paul, you are not saying that God is unjust when God inflicts wrath, are you? Realizing the blasphemous nature of this statement, which he has put into the mouth of the interlocutor, Paul introduces a parenthetical statement lest he offend his audience—he is speaking in a merely human way. (Similar expressions occur in 6:19; 1 Cor. 9:8; 15:32; Gal. 3:15.)

Employing his *mē genoito* formula again, Paul responds to the question as strongly as he can: **Of course not! Otherwise, how would God be able to judge the world?** (3:6). If Paul were implying that God is unjust to inflict wrath, God would not be able to judge the world. But as Paul and every Jew know, God is a just judge, and judgment belongs to God alone. Thus the psalmist addresses God, "Rise up, O Judge of the earth; give to the proud what they deserve" (Ps. 94:2). Paul knows that God is the judge before whose judgment seat all must stand (Rom. 14:10). Consequently, although human unrighteousness becomes the occasion for God to manifest righteousness, it is not unjust for God to manifest wrath against human unrighteousness.

The interrogator's fourth question is similar to the third but more subtle. Realizing that, in the face of human falsehood, God's truthfulness is all the more apparent, the interlocutor asks, **But if God's truthfulness abounds to his glory because of my falsehood, why am I still being judged as a sinner?** (3:7). This question is more challenging than the previous questions since it is not framed in a way that expects a negative answer: "You are not saying that . . . , are you?" Moreover, the question the interlocutor asks here suggests that he has Paul's teaching on justification in view. Instead of answering the question, Paul alters the pattern of the dialogue and adds a further objection that explicitly has his gospel in view: **And why not (as we are slandered and as some say we say) "let us do evil in order that good may come of it"?** (3:8a). At this point, it is difficult to determine if this is a further objection on the part of the interlocutor or if Paul is responding to the interlocutor's question by posing a more outrageous question that explicitly challenges his gospel. In either case, Paul introduces a parenthetical remark: "as we are slandered and as some say we say." For Paul, the theological implications of the last two questions are so perverse that he only gives a terse response: **Their judgment is well deserved!** (3:8b). Anyone who would adopt such a position is no different from those Gentiles described in 1:18–32, who have forfeited their moral compass by their unrighteous behavior. Stuhlmacher (1994, 51) suggests that this critique has in view the kind of Jewish-Christian missionaries who opposed Paul's teaching at Corinth, Galatia, and Philippi.

Paul's train of thought in this unit can be summarized in this way: Although the Jews have failed to observe the law, they are still in an advantageous position since they were entrusted with the Scriptures. Although some have been unfaithful, God will remain faithful. This does not imply that there is no place for God's judgment, for God, who is the just judge, must judge the world. Nor does the righteousness of God—so clearly manifested in the face of human unrighteousness—exempt anyone from God's judgment. God, the judge of the world, is utterly impartial.

3:9–20. The dialogue between Paul and his interlocutor is not finished. The interlocutor asks one final question (3:9a), to which Paul responds with an extended answer (3:9b–20), bringing the first part of his letter to a conclusion. The precise meaning of the question, however, is not clear since the verb Paul employs (*proechometha*) can be taken as (1) a true middle, (2) a middle voice with an active meaning, or (3) a passive. If it is taken as a true middle, the translation would be, "Are we making excuses?" or "Are we protecting ourselves?" If it is taken as a middle with an active sense, the meaning would be, "Do we have an advantage?" or "Do we excel?" If the mood is construed as passive, the translation would be, "Are we excelled?" or "Are we in a worse position?"

Stuhlmacher (1994, 53) takes the verb as a true middle and translates the 3:9a as follows: "What now? Are we making excuses? For sure, not!" In doing so, he supposes that Paul, rather than the interlocutor, poses the question. The Vulgate construes the verb as a middle with an active sense (*praecellimus eos*, "do we surpass them?"), as do most modern translations. For example, the NRSV reads, "What then? Are we any better off?" Although such a use of the middle voice is possible, "no instance of this use is attested for *proechein*" (Fitzmyer 1993, 331). Moreover, as Jewett (2007, 257) observes, this translation seems to run counter to the logic of Paul's diatribe. Having heard Paul's responses to his questions about the faithfulness of God and the justice of God's judgments—all of which substantiate the utter impartiality of God—the interlocutor might well think that he and his Jewish compatriots are in a disadvantageous position. Accordingly, following Fitzmyer and Jewett, I take the verb as a passive and translate the opening questions, **What then shall we say? Are we at a disadvantage?** (3:9a).

As in his other responses, Paul does not answer in the manner his interlocutor might expect ("yes, you are at a disadvantage"). Instead he responds: **Not at all. For we have already charged that all, Jew and Greek, are under the power of sin** (3:9b). The Jewish interlocutor is not at a disadvantage inasmuch as all, "Jew and Greek," find themselves in the same position before God. This is the fourth time that Paul has used the expression "Jew and Greek." In 1:16 he has described the gospel as the power of salvation for all who believe, for the Jew first and then for the Greek. In 2:9–10 he has used the expression twice when speaking of punishment and reward at the last judgment: for the Jew first and then for the Greek. Now, looking back to all that he has said since 1:18, he reveals that everyone, Jew as well as Greek, is "under the power of sin" (*hyph' hamartian*).

Although Paul has been describing the sinful situation of Gentiles and Jews all along, this is the first time in Romans he has employed the noun "sin" (*hamartia*), a term that will play an increasingly important role as the letter progresses. As is clear from his use of the term here, Paul is not speaking about sin as a transgression or fault but as a power or force that enslaves those under its rule. In chapters 5–7 Paul will personify sin by presenting it as a taskmaster who has (1) ruled over humanity, (2) paid out the wages of death, and (3) frustrated the purpose of God's law. Paul's Jewish interlocutor then is not at a disadvantage, because all find themselves in the same situation. All are under the power of sin, which rules over their lives.

But how can Paul make such a statement about Jews and Gentiles alike? Yes, the Gentiles find themselves in a sinful situation of their own making. But can one say the same for the people of the covenant? After all, did not Paul acknowledge that the Jews had the oracles of God? Did not Israel's cult provide a means to expiate and atone for sins? Paul was surely aware that such objections could be posed, but in the light of the cross, he now understands that the human predicament is more dire than humanity has imagined. Therefore, to teach his interlocutor that even the covenant people find themselves under the power of sin, he presents a catena of passages from Israel's Scripture ("the oracles of God" mentioned in 3:1) to demonstrate that *all* have sinned and that there is *no one* who is righteous (3:10–18).

The texts Paul employs in 3:10–18 come from Ecclesiastes, Psalms, Isaiah, and Proverbs, but Paul does not identify them in this way. He simply begins, **as it is written** (3:10a), thereby indicating that what follows has the full authority of Scripture. Viewed in terms of its thematic content, the catena has two parts. In the first, the quotations emphasize the universal scope of sin:

> No one is righteous, not one.
> There is no one who understands,
> there is not one who seeks God.
> All have turned aside, together they are depraved,
> there is no one who does what is right,
> there is not even one. (3:10b–12)

The repetition of "no one" and "not one" and the statement "all have turned aside" indicate that there are no exceptions. The verdict of Scripture is clear: The power of sin is so all-encompassing that no one is "righteous" (*dikaios*). No one understands or seeks God.

In the second part of the catena, the quotations refer to various parts of the body:

> Their throats are an open grave,
> with their lips they deceive,
> the venom of poisonous serpents is under their tongues,
> their mouths are filled with curses and bitterness,
> their feet are swift at shedding blood.
> Ruin and misery follow in their paths.
> and the way of peace they do not know.
> There is no fear of God before their eyes. (3:13–18)

These references to different parts of the body (throats, lips, tongues, mouths, feet, eyes), indicate that the entire body—the whole person—is involved in sin. Not only has everyone sinned, the entire person has participated in sinning. By focusing on the total involvement of the embodied person in sin, Paul prepares for what he will say in chapter 6 about the need for believers to present the members of their bodies as slaves to righteousness and for his exhortation in chapter 12 that believers should present their bodies as living sacrifices to God. This emphasis on the sinfulness of the body echoes Paul's earlier condemnation of the Gentiles who dishonored their bodies (1:24), thereby drawing a relation between the Gentiles who sinned without knowledge of the law and the Jews who sinned while under the law.

Having employed this catena of scriptural quotations to convince his Jewish interlocutor that all, Jews as well as Greeks, are under the power of sin, Paul reminds his audience that the law applies to those who live under its regime: **We know that whatever the law says, it says to those bound by the law so that every mouth may be shut closed and the whole world be answerable to God** (3:19). Paul's references "to those bound by the law" suggest that even though these scriptural quotations affirm that all have sinned, he has the Jewish world in view. If so, he pronounces a judgment on the Jewish world similar to the judgment he pronounced on the Gentile world (1:29–32).

Beginning with a formula ("we know") that he frequently employs "to express a truth or fact which he believes or hopes is a matter of common ground between himself and those he addresses" (Byrne 1996, 84), Paul reminds his interlocutor that the law applies to those who are under it. Thus when Paul speaks of "the whole world" here, he appears to be referring to the Jewish world (Keck 2005, 99). The law, which is embodied in Israel's scriptures, pronounces judgment on those bound by it.

Next, Paul provides a supporting reason for what he has just said in 3:19. **Because by the works of the law no will be justified before him, for through the law comes an awareness of sin** (3:20). Everyone stands as a sinner before God, as the catena of quotations from Scripture has shown. Doing the works of the law, therefore, will not justify one before God. The law only makes people conscious of their sinfulness.

In saying that no one is justified before God, Paul draws from Ps. 143:2: "Do not enter into judgment with your servant, for no one living is righteous before you." Paul, however, modifies the psalm, adding, "by the works of the law." Consequently, whereas the psalm states that no one is righteous before God (something with which every Jew could agree), Paul surprisingly asserts that no one will be justified/acquitted before God on the basis of doing "the works of the law" (*ex ergōn nomou*).

Paul makes a similar statement in Gal. 2:16, where he contrasts "the works of the law" with faith in (or the faith of) Jesus Christ. The meaning of "the works of the law" here and in Gal. 2:16 has been contested in recent scholarship, with many arguing that it refers to those prescriptions of the law that have to do with Jewish identity: the observance of circumcision, food laws, and Sabbath observance (Dunn 1988, 1:362–64). This is surely part of what Paul means: those works that identify one as a Jew will not justify one before God. But the use of this phrase in a text from Qumran (4QMMT 3.29) and the overall argument of Romans suggest that "the works of the law" has a broader meaning that refers to the prescriptions or commandments of the Mosaic law. If so, Paul is affirming that one will not be justified/acquitted before God on the basis of doing what the law requires. Why? Because, as Scripture testifies, all have sinned, a clear indication that no one is justified before God on the basis of doing the prescriptions of the law. In light of the gospel, Paul affirms that the law only makes one aware of sin. Byrne (1996, 121) calls this last statement "the first of a series of 'throwaway' lines," which point to the negative effects of the law. Other examples to which he points are 4:15b; 5:20a; 6:14; 7:5.

The train of thought in this unit can be summarized in this way: Paul's Jewish interlocutor and his compatriots are not at a disadvantage vis-à-vis the Gentiles because everyone, without exception, is under the power of sin. In the case of God's covenant people, Scripture testifies to this, making plain that all are guilty before God. Consequently, justification/acquittal before God will not and cannot come on the basis of legal observance. There is need for another way, which Paul will now describe.

Theological Issues

The argument that Paul has been developing in the first part of Romans (1:18–3:20) can be summarized in this way: In light of the gospel, Paul perceives the human situation in a way he previously did not and could not. Both Gentiles and Jews are under the power of sin, from which there is no escape apart from the gospel. Consequently, before he can proclaim the righteousness of God, Paul must reveal the predicament in which humanity finds itself—a predicament of which humanity is not fully aware.

Paul begins with the situation of the Gentiles, affirming that the wrath/judgment of God is already being revealed against the Gentiles because they are suppressing the truth about God by their "unrighteousness" (*adikia*), even though they have known something of God from the created world. Although the Gentiles do not realize it, they are experiencing God's wrath inasmuch as God has delivered them to the consequences of their refusal to acknowledge God. The punishment for their sins is their sins.

Before turning to the situation of God's covenant people, Paul reminds his audience of the impartiality of God, who judges people on the basis of what they do rather than on the basis of who they are. Having shown that God is impartial toward Gentiles and Jews alike, Paul highlights the failure of the Jewish world to do God's will, even though it has the sign of circumcision and the gift of God's law. Although the Jewish world would have acknowledged these failures, it would not have viewed itself as being in the same situation as the Gentile world. After all, the Jewish people are God's covenant people, God's elect. Even if they sin, there are means of atonement and forgiveness. But this is not how Paul sees the situation. In light of the gospel, he affirms that all are under the power of sin (3:9). Because all are under this power, all have sinned, an indication that no one will be justified before God on the basis of doing the works of the law. The problem is not that the law is wrong or inadequate, nor is it that the law does not indicate God's will. The problem is more profound. As Paul will explain, the power of sin is so encompassing that it frustrates the goal of the law. Therefore, although he writes that it is the doers of the law rather than the hearers of the law who will be justified (2:13), Paul affirms that no one will be justified before God on the basis of doing the works of the law (3:20), because all are under the power of sin (3:9).

The first part of Romans lays the groundwork for what Paul will say in the rest of the letter. For if the human predicament is not as Paul describes it, then there is no need for Christ. If one can be justified before God on the basis of doing the works of the law, there is no need for the righteousness that God offers in Christ. If Paul is exaggerating, if all that he says is merely a rhetorical ploy, then there is no need for the gospel. To be sure, Paul is employing rhetoric. He is a skillful—some would say a manipulative—writer. But what he writes is not mere rhetoric. It is grounded in his experience of God.

Underlying all that Paul writes in the first part of Romans is a knowledge of God that refuses to limit God in any way. The experience of God to which Paul witnesses can be summarized in this way: God is utterly impartial. Although the Jewish people enjoy a unique relationship with God, God is not partial in his judgment toward them to the disadvantage of the Gentiles. Conversely, God is not partial toward the Gentiles to the disadvantage of the covenant people. God does not judge on the basis of who people are but on the basis of what people do.

The God whom Paul proclaims is the judge of the world. It is this aspect of God—God as judge—that is most difficult for the contemporary world to understand. Why does God judge at all? If the situation is as dire as Paul describes it, if all are under the power of sin, why does God judge the world? Paul is aware of this objection, but it does not dissuade him from affirming that God is the judge of all. In light of the gospel, Paul knows that God's judgments are inscrutable. Not only is God an impartial judge; God also judges in hidden and unexpected ways. For example, God judges the Gentiles by allowing them to live out the consequences of their sinful rebellion. And as we shall see, God judges the world by the death of his Son, thereby revealing that God's saving righteousness is the other side of God's judgment. Consequently, for those who believe, God's judgment is God's saving righteousness, whereas for those who refuse to believe, God's saving righteousness is God's judgment.

Third, for Paul, God is utterly true and faithful; God can be relied upon because God is always faithful to his promises. God's word is always true. It is unthinkable that God's ways have changed. God has not unexpectedly favored the Gentiles to the exclusion of the covenant people. God has not introduced a new plan of salvation or inaugurated a new salvation history at the expense of Israel. God is faithful to the covenant promises; God is true to himself. This is why the wrath of God is coming upon those who suppress the truth about God by their *adikia*. This is why not even the covenant people can presume that they will escape God's wrath. God's faithfulness is God's truthfulness, and God's truthfulness is God's faithfulness. The God whom Paul discloses is the impartial judge who is faithful and true, the God who transcends national and ethnic boundaries and every human attempt to contain and control God.

PART 2

Romans 3:21–4:25

*Gentiles and Jews in the Light of
God's Righteousness*

The second part of Romans provides a powerful response to Paul's description of the plight in which Gentiles and Jews find themselves. If all have sinned so that no one can be justified before God on the basis of doing the works of the law, then both Gentiles and Jews are in need of a salvation they cannot effect for themselves if they hope to escape the eschatological wrath/judgment of God. In the second part of Romans (3:21–4:25), Paul describes this salvation as the saving righteousness of God that has been manifested in Jesus Christ, thereby returning to the theme of God's righteousness that he introduced in 1:16–17.

In this part of Romans, Paul's purpose is to show that the manifestation of God's righteousness in Jesus Christ has justified and redeemed Gentiles and Jews alike, and that this justification/redemption is available to all on the basis of the kind of faith that Abraham manifested when God credited Abraham's faith as righteousness. Thus Paul continues the theme of God's impartiality. Just as God judges Gentiles and Jews impartially on the basis of what they do rather than on the basis of who they are, so God justifies Jews and Gentiles impartially on the basis of their faith rather than on the basis of who they are.

This second part of Romans has two sections. In the first, Paul explains that God has now manifested his saving righteousness in Christ for Gentile and Jew apart from the law, thereby excluding every occasion for human boasting before God (3:21–31). In the second section, Paul provides a homiletical exegesis of Gen. 15:6 to demonstrate that faith establishes rather than abrogates the law (Rom. 4:1–25). Paul's decision to focus on Abraham in this section makes eminent sense. On the one hand, Abraham is the father of Israel, the one through whom God gave Israel the covenant of circumcision that identifies the Jewish people as God's covenant people. On the other hand, God declared Abraham righteous while he was in the uncircumcised condition of a Gentile. Thus the second part of Romans argues that God has manifested his saving righteousness in Jesus Christ and the result of this righteousness (justification and redemption) is now available to all—Gentile as well as Jew—on the basis of trusting faith in what God has done in Christ.

Romans 3:21–31

A Righteousness Accessible to All through Faith

Introductory Matters

All commentators recognize that this section marks a turning point in Paul's argument. Up to this point he has described the dire situation of Gentiles and Jews. Viewing their predicament from the point of view of the gospel, Paul declares that all are under the power of sin so that no one will be justified before God by doing the works of the law. Now he turns from his description of God's wrath to the manifestation of God's saving righteousness in Jesus Christ, a righteousness available to Gentiles as well as to Jews on the basis of faith. In doing so, Paul provides his audience with an exposition of what he means by justification by faith apart from doing the works of the law, much as he did in Gal. 2:15–21 for his Galatian converts. But while the thematic statement of Galatians focuses on how a person is justified on the basis of faith rather than on the basis of doing the works of the law, the thematic statement of Rom. 3:21–26 highlights God's saving righteousness.

Paul's summary of his gospel, however, is fraught with exegetical issues, and there is hardly a phrase over which commentators do not argue. Four of these issues are important for our discussion: (1) the meaning of *dikaiosynē theou* in 3:21, 22; (2) the meaning of *dia pisteōs Iēsou Christou* in 3:22 and *ton ek pisteōs Iēsou* in 3:26; (3) the meaning of *hilastērion* in 3:25; and (4) the meaning of *paresin* in 3:25. These are not the only exegetical issues in 3:21–26, and as we shall see, there are others in 3:27–31, but they are the most important.

The Meaning of "the Righteousness of God"

Although we discussed the phrase "the righteousness of God" when treating 1:16–17, it is necessary to return to it once more since it occurs once in 3:21 and again in 3:22. As was the case in 1:16, *dikaiosynē theou* can be construed as a genitive of origin ("the righteousness that comes from God") or as a subjective genitive ("God's own righteousness"). Taken as a genitive of origin, the focus is on the gift of righteousness that God communicates to those who believe in Christ. Rudolf Bultmann (1951, 285) summarizes this interpretation: "The reason why 'righteousness' is called '*God's righteousness*' is just this: Its one and only foundation is God's grace—it is God-given, God-adjudicated righteousness, . . . so 'God's righteousness' means the righteousness from God which is conferred upon him [the believer] as a gift by God's free grace alone." Taken as a subjective genitive, the focus shifts to God's own righteousness. Fitzmyer (1993, 344) defines this righteousness as "God's bounteous and powerful uprightness whereby he acquits his sinful people in a just judgment." Arland Hultgren (1985, 13) provides a more expansive definition: "The phrase expresses God's dynamic, saving action toward the world, which has been manifested already in the cross of Christ and is operative still in the gospel." Thus the genitive of origin provides an anthropological interpretation of the phrase that focuses on the redemptive effects of Christ's death and resurrection, and the subjective genitive offers a more theological interpretation that emphasizes God's activity.

These two interpretations do not exclude each other. In Phil. 3:9 Paul clearly refers to a righteousness that is not his own but "the righteousness from God based on faith." Similarly, in 1 Cor. 1:30 he speaks of Christ as the one "who became for us wisdom from God, and righteousness and sanctification and redemption." And in 2 Cor. 5:21 Paul affirms that Christ stood in our human situation so that "we might become the righteousness of God." In these three instances, Paul speaks of God's conferring righteousness upon the believer through Christ's redemptive death and resurrection.

Although it is possible to interpret *dikaiosynē theou* in Rom. 3:21, 22 as "a status of righteousness before God which is God's gift" (Cranfield 1975, 202), the manner in which Paul has been arguing since 1:18 suggests that he has God's activity in view, God's saving righteousness. Throughout 1:18–3:20 the emphasis has been on God's activity: God's wrath (1:18), God's righteous judgment (2:5), God's impartiality (2:11), and God's righteousness in the face of human unrighteousness (3:5). In light of this emphasis on God's activity, it would be surprising if Paul were not referring to God's own righteousness in 3:21, 22. Moreover, since Paul speaks of God's putting forth Christ as a *hilastērion* (see below) in order to show his own righteousness (3:25), it would appear that this is the same righteousness to which Paul refers in 3:21, 22.

God's righteousness and the righteousness that comes from God are not mutually exclusive. The righteousness that comes from God presupposes

God's own righteousness, a saving activity manifested in Jesus Christ. Inasmuch as Romans focuses so forcefully on what God has done in Christ, I have construed *dikaiosynē theou* here, and throughout Romans, as God's own righteousness, always keeping in mind that God's righteousness effects the gift of righteousness for those who believe in Christ.

Faith in Jesus or Faith of Jesus?

The second issue in 3:21–26 is akin to the first. Is the phrase *dia pisteōs Iēsou Christou* in 3:22 to be taken as an objective or a subjective genitive? Taken as an objective genitive, the translation would be, "the righteousness of God through faith in Jesus Christ" (NRSV). Taken as a subjective genitive, the translation would be, "the righteousness of God through the faithfulness of Jesus Christ" (NET). The first translation is the more traditional, emphasizing the faith that believers put in what God has accomplished in Christ. So understood, Christ is the object of faith. The second translation is grammatically possible, and a growing number of scholars have argued for its use, not only here but in Gal. 2:16, 20; 3:22; Phil. 3:9; and Eph. 3:12 as well. Understood as a subjective genitive, the phrase emphasizes Christ's faithfulness toward God throughout his earthly life, particularly at the moment of his passion and death. Christ has manifested this faithfulness in and through his obedience as the eschatological Adam (Rom. 5:12–21).

As is the case with "the righteousness of God," the "faithfulness of Christ" and "faith in Christ" are not mutually exclusive. To argue for "the faithfulness of Christ" does not exclude "faith in Christ." Those who believe in Christ do so because they know that Christ was the faithful Son of God who died for their sins. Moreover, if the subjective genitive is the correct reading in *dikaiosynē theou*, then both concepts are present in 3:22. Paul would be saying that God has now manifested his own saving righteousness through the faithfulness of his Son Jesus Christ for all who believe in Jesus Christ. Understood in this way, the faithfulness of Christ is the concrete manifestation of God's own faithfulness.

Although it is true that the faithfulness of Christ does not occur frequently in Paul's writings (some would say never), it is also true that this is the only place where Paul speaks of Christ as a *hilastērion* (see below), a concept that plays a central role here in his understanding of Christ's death. Accordingly, while the issue remains disputed, it is possible that Paul has in view "the faithfulness of Christ" in 3:22. If he does, then it is probable that the same concept lies behind the difficult phrase *ton ek pisteōs Iēsou* at the conclusion of 3:26. A literal translation of this phrase would be, "from the faith of Jesus." Taken as an objective genitive, the phrase would mean, "the one who has faith in Jesus" (NRSV). Construed as a subjective genitive, it could be, "the one who lives because of Jesus' faithfulness" (NET) or "the one who has the faith of Jesus" (NRSV margin). Thus 3:26 can be taken in several ways:

God justifies those who believe in Jesus; God justifies those who rely on the faithfulness of Jesus; God justifies those who manifest the faithfulness of Jesus in their lives. While the first interpretation (faith in Jesus) is the way in which Paul normally speaks of faith, it is possible that here Paul has Jesus's own faithfulness in view.

The Meaning of Hilastērion

In 3:21–26 Paul employs three metaphors to explain the significance of Christ's death: the juridical metaphor of justification or acquittal, the social metaphor of redemption, and the cultic metaphor evoked by the term *hilastērion*. The first two occur somewhat frequently in Paul's writings, but this is the only instance of the third metaphor. Moreover, it appears that Paul employs this metaphor to explain in greater depth the first two metaphors. Thus in 3:24–25 Paul says that believers have been freely *justified* through the *redemption* in Christ that God effected when God publicly displayed or set forth Christ as a *hilastērion* to show his (God's) righteousness. For the moment, I refrain from translating the term since a translation would be an interpretation.

Hultgren (1985, 47–81) notes that there are three principal ways in which the text has been interpreted throughout the history of exegesis. First, the LXX employs *hilastērion* to translate Hebrew *kappōret* (mercy seat), the cover of the ark of the covenant that the high priest sprinkled with blood on the Day of Atonement to make atonement for himself, for the sins of the community, and for the holy place itself (Lev. 16). Origen and other early church writers interpreted the term typologically: Christ is the new "mercy seat," his cross being the new place of atonement. Second, Hultgren (1985, 49–50) notes, "The Vulgate breaks rank with the typological correlation," rendering *hilastērion* as *propitiationem* ("propitiation" rather than *propitiatorium*, "propitiatory" or "place of propitiation"). Accordingly, the emphasis shifts from Christ viewed as the new mercy seat, the place of atonement, to Christ as the victim who is a propitiatory sacrifice. Third, hesitant to view Christ's death as a propitiatory sacrifice that appeases God's wrath, the modern period introduced the notion of expiation: Christ's death is an expiatory sacrifice that deals with sin. Thus Dodd (1932, 55) writes: "The rendering *propitiation* is therefore misleading, for it suggests the placating of an angry God, and although this would be in accord with pagan usage, it is foreign to biblical usage." The term *hilastērion*, then, has been construed in three ways: (1) mercy seat: a place where God effects atonement; (2) propitiation: a propitiatory sacrifice that appeases God's wrath; (3) expiation: an expiatory sacrifice that deals with sin.

The phrase that precedes *hilastērion* ("whom God publicly displayed," *hon proetheto ho theos*) suggests that Paul has the imagery of the Day of Atonement in view: God publicly displayed the crucified Christ as a new mercy seat, the place where God effected atonement for sinful humanity through the blood of his own Son. Unlike the rituals of the Day of Atonement, which were carried out in the holy of holies, behind the curtain, where the people could not see what was happening, the new Day of Atonement happens in a public way on the cross. There, in the view of all, God has dealt with sin in a definitive way.

The Meaning of Paresin

The noun *paresin* in 3:25 presents another problem since this is its only occurrence in the entire Greek Bible (the LXX as well as the NT). On the one hand, it could mean "passing over" or "letting go unpunished." On the other hand, it might mean "forgiveness," inasmuch as it is "used of 'remitting' debts and other obligations" in ancient Greek literature (see BDAG 776, s.v. *paresis*). The latter is the way in which the Vulgate (and most writers in the ancient church) understood it, translating *paresin* as *remissionem* (forgiveness). It is difficult to make a choice here, given the limited lexical data. If the word is taken in the first sense, the meaning would be that God has put forth Christ as the new mercy seat to show his (God's) righteousness because, in his clemency, God had passed over sins committed in the past. If the word is taken in the second sense, the meaning would be that God has put forth Christ as the new mercy seat to show his righteousness for the forgiveness of sins committed in the past. On the whole, the first sense ("passing over," "letting go unpunished") seems to make more sense of Paul's thought. In the past God passed over or left unpunished certain sins because of his clemency, but now, to show his righteousness/uprightness, God deals with those sins by presenting Christ as the new place of atonement.

Romans 3:21–31 in the Rhetorical Flow

The letter opening (1:1–17)

Gentiles and Jews in the light of God's wrath (1:18–3:20)

Gentiles and Jews in the light of God's righteousness (3:21–4:25)

▶ **A righteousness accessible to all through faith (3:21–31)**

The manifestation of God's righteousness (3:21–26)

Independently of the law (3:21–22b)

Need for God's saving righteousness (3:22c–23)

God's response (3:24–26)

All freely **justified** by his favor (3:24a)

Through the **redemption** in Jesus Christ (3:24b)

Whom God put forth as a **hilastērion** (3:25–26)

Boasting excluded (3:27–31)

Question and response (3:27a–b)

Room for boasting? (3:27a)

Boasting excluded (3:27b)

Questions and response (3:27c–28)

By what kind of law? The law of works? (3:27c)

By the law of faith, supporting reason (3:27d–28)

Questions and response (3:29–30)

God of the Jews only? God of the Gentiles also? (3:29a–b)

Response and supporting reason (3:29c–30)

Question and response (3:31)

Faith nullifies the law? (3:31a)

Faith establishes the law (3:31b)

Although 3:21–26 functions as an important summary of Pauline soteriology, this passage is open to several translations and interpretations. These interpretations are not always mutually exclusive, but they do represent different ways of approaching this passage. On the one hand, the passage can be understood from an anthropological perspective: the believer's justification. On the other, it can be read from a theological perspective: God's saving activity as manifested in the faithfulness of his Christ. It is from this second perspective that I will trace Paul's train of thought.

Tracing the Train of Thought

This section consists of two units. In the first, Paul states his thesis regarding the righteousness of God and its significance for all who believe (3:21–26). In the second, he argues that the appearance of God's righteousness, apart from the law, excludes all boasting before God (3:27–31). In both units, Paul insists that (1) the saving effects of God's righteousness are available to Gentiles as well as to Jews, (2) faith plays an indispensable role in the appropriation of the saving effects of God's righteousness, and (3) there is continuity between the law and the manifestation of God's righteousness.

The first unit has three subunits. In the first subunit, Paul announces the new situation occasioned by the appearance of God's righteousness (3:21–22b). In the second, he explains the universal need for what God has done in Christ (3:22c–23). And in the third, he employs three metaphors (justification, redemption, atonement) to explain God's response to this need (3:24–26). The second unit resumes the form of the diatribe and proceeds in four steps by a series of questions and responses: (1) boasting is excluded; (2) faith excludes boasting; (3) God belongs to Gentiles and Jews alike; (4) faith establishes the law.

3:21–26. The opening verses of this unit stand in stark contrast to what Paul has just said: no one will be justified before God by doing the works of the law. With those words still ringing in the ears of his audience, Paul begins: **But now, independently of the law, God's righteousness has been manifested** (3:21a). Paul's opening words, *nyni de* (but now), signal a new stage in his argument. More important, they indicate that a new era of salvation has begun. Since no one will be justified before God on the basis of doing the works of the law, God has intervened in a decisively new way, manifesting his saving righteousness "independently of the law." Thus Paul affirms that God's saving righteousness does not depend on the law nor is it the outcome of human observance of the law. But lest Paul's audience mistakenly suppose that his gospel portrays God's righteousness as standing in opposition to the law, Paul quickly adds, **although witnessed to by the law and the prophets** (3:21b). With this phrase the apostle introduces an important qualification to which he will return throughout this letter: Although the new way in which God has acted in Christ does not depend on the law, it finds a prophetic witness in the law and the prophets. This is why Paul will insist that the faith that the gospel proposes does not nullify the law but confirms it (3:31).

Since this saving righteousness has been manifested in Jesus Christ, Paul writes: **God's righteousness manifested through the faithfulness of Jesus Christ** (3:22a). While many commentators take *pisteōs Iēsou Christou* as an objective genitive ("through faith in Jesus Christ"), the subjective genitive makes good sense in this context. God has revealed his saving righteousness in and through the faithfulness of his Son, Jesus Christ. This faithfulness was Jesus's complete obedience to God, and it stands in sharp contrast to Adam's disobedience (5:12–21). God's saving activity, however, requires a response, and so Paul adds, **for all who believe** (3:22b). Thus God has manifested his saving righteousness in and through the faithfulness of Christ, and the saving effects of that righteousness are available to all who entrust themselves to what God has done in Christ.

Next, Paul explains why God acted in this way: **For there is no distinction. For all have sinned and are in need of God's glory** (3:22c–23). With these words, Paul summarizes the essential content of 1:18–3:20. His insistence that there is no distinction (*diastolē*; see also 10:12) echoes the theme of God's divine impartiality developed in 2:1–16, and his affirmation that all are in need of "God's glory" (*tēs doxēs tou theou*) recalls his remarks about glory in 1:23; 2:7, 10. While "God's glory" could refer to the praise that comes from God, the logic of Romans suggests that it refers to God's own glory, which believers will share at the resurrection of the dead (8:18–23).

It is now evident why Paul spent so much time in 1:18–3:20 describing the human predicament. Before he could say that all are in need of God's saving righteousness, he had to establish that all have sinned and fallen short of God's glory. Were this not the case, there would be no need for God's saving righteousness in Christ. For Paul, God's new and decisive intervention in Christ reveals the true plight of humanity and its need for salvation.

Verses 25–26 form a theologically rich but complex subunit in which Paul explains God's response to the universal need for salvation described in 3:22c–23, thereby detailing what Paul means by "God's righteousness" (3:21–22b). Paul employs three metaphors to describe the benefits of God's righteousness: the legal metaphor of justification, the social metaphor of redemption, and the cultic metaphor of atonement. Having said that all have sinned and are in need of God's glory, Paul writes: **Therefore, all are graciously justified by God's favor through the redemption effected in Jesus Christ** (3:24). This statement, which contains two different metaphors, indicates that God "acquitted" (*dikaioumenoi*) humanity through the "redemption" (*apolytrōseōs*) that has been brought about in Christ. Throughout 1:18–3:20 Paul has insisted that God is an impartial judge who judges on the basis of what people do rather than on the basis of who they are. But now, having shown that humanity cannot be justified before God by doing the works of the law, Paul proclaims that this

Judge has "graciously" (*dōrean*) justified humanity by his "favor" (*chariti*). Since humanity is unable to declare itself innocent before God, God has graciously acquitted humanity on the basis of the redemption effected in Christ.

This metaphor of redemption derives from a social world in which prisoners and slaves were set free when someone paid a price or ransom for their freedom. It recalls God's redemption of Israel from Egypt (Exod. 6:6; Deut. 7:8) and Babylon (Isa. 51:11), as Bryan (2000, 104) notes. The metaphor plays a central role in Jesus's description of his own death (Mark 10:45) and Paul's understanding of the significance of that death. Believers were "bought" at a price (1 Cor. 6:20; 7:23), and they now proclaim that Christ is their redemption (1 Cor. 1:30) as they await the final redemption of their bodies—their resurrection from the dead (Rom. 8:23). The acquittal/justification that those in Christ enjoy, then, is the result of a redemptive act whereby they were ransomed and set free from the power of sin that enslaved them.

Employing a further metaphor to explain this one, Paul turns to the cultic imagery of the Day of Atonement to show how God has effected this redemption: **whom God publicly displayed as a mercy seat—appropriated through faith—by his blood** (3:25a). Applying the metaphor of the *hilastērion* (the gold-plated lid that covered the ark of the covenant) to Christ, Paul indicates that Christ's death on the cross (indicated by the phrase "by his blood") effected atonement for humanity in a manner analogous to the way in which the high priest expiated or atoned for his sins and those of the people when he entered the holy of holies on the Day of Atonement and sprinkled the "mercy seat" of the ark with the blood of goats and bulls (Lev. 16). Paul, however, employs the metaphor in another way. The subject of the metaphor is God, who "publicly displayed" (*proetheto*) Christ as a "mercy seat" (*hilastērion*) when Christ died on

Figure 4. Ark of the covenant. The cover of the ark, seen here in this replica, is the "mercy seat" on which the high priest sprinkled the blood of a goat on the Day of Atonement.

the cross. The significance of the metaphor is threefold: (1) God is the primary actor in the drama of salvation, the one who has effected atonement, thereby dealing with sin and reconciling humanity to himself; (2) this atonement took place on the cross in Christ's death so that, in terms of the metaphor, Christ is the new mercy seat; (3) believers appropriate the benefits of this atoning death by faith in what God has effected in Christ. Since God is the one who has displayed Christ as a new mercy seat, the emphasis is on the way in which God brings about atonement/reconciliation through the death of his Son rather than on Christ's death as a sacrifice that appeases or propitiates God's wrath.

Next, Paul explains why God acted in this manner. Returning to the theme of God's righteousness that began this unit, Paul writes that God put Christ forth as the new mercy seat or place of atonement **to show his [God's] righteousness on account of previously committed sins that had been left unpunished because of God's clemency, in order to show his righteousness at the present time so that he [God] might be just and justify the one who has the faithfulness of Jesus** (3:25b–26). Here Paul employs two purpose clauses, and in each of them he refers to God's righteousness. The first purpose clause explains that God put forth Christ as a mercy seat to show God's righteousness since in the past, because of his "clemency" (*anochē*, the same word used in 2:4), God had left certain sins unpunished. Although Paul does not explain what he means here, he may be thinking of the sins of the Gentiles, who did not have access to the cult of the temple (Jewett 2007, 291). Repeating this theme of God's righteousness in the second purpose clause, Paul says that God presented Christ as a *hilastērion*, the mercy seat where God shows his righteousness in the present time—the time of the gospel—so that all might see that God does deal with sin, but in a startling new way that shows how God is "just" (*dikaion*) and "justifies" (*dikaiounta*) the one who manifests the "faithfulness" (*pisteōs*) of Jesus, or perhaps, "the one who believes in Jesus."

The train of thought in this unit can be summarized in this way: No one can be justified by doing the works of the law. Therefore, God has revealed his saving righteousness in Christ, whom God put forth as a mercy seat to effect atonement and show his righteousness, thereby justifying humanity by Christ's redemptive death.

3:27–31. After the dense exposition of 3:21–26, in which he summarizes the soteriological content of the gospel, Paul returns to the form of the diatribe to deal with real or perceived objections to his teaching. I divide this unit into four subunits: the issue of boasting (3:27a–b); why boasting has been excluded (3:27c–28); God is the God of Gentiles and Jews alike (3:29–30); and faith establishes rather than nullifies the law (3:31). Bryan (2000, 105) suggests that it is Paul who is asking the questions, thereby leading his interlocutor to the correct answers, whereas Song (2004, 96–97) contends that the interlocutor raises these questions to which Paul, the teacher, responds. In my view, Paul is simply raising questions about what he said and responding to them.

Having affirmed that God has graciously justified all on the basis of faith since all have sinned and fallen short of God's glory (3:23–24), Paul raises a question that an ardent Jewish person (or a Jewish Christ-believer) might ask: **Where, then, is there any room for boasting?** (3:27a). Doesn't ethnic identity count for anything? Doesn't the observance of the law count at all? Is it permissible, in light of what Paul has said in 3:21–26, for humans to stand before God and affirm what they have done? Paul's response is terse and emphatic, a single word in Greek (*exekleisthē*): **It is excluded** (3:27b). Because it is God who has effected justification, redemption, and atonement in Christ, human beings are not in a position to boast before God.

Continuing the theme of boasting, Paul asks a double question: First, he wants to know **through what kind of law** (3:27c) such boasting is excluded. Paul's initial response is to raise another question: **The law of works?** This "law of works" refers to the Mosaic law, with its prescriptions and commandments. On first hearing it might appear to be the correct answer since Paul has said that no one will be justified before God by doing the works of the law (3:20), for all have sinned. Thus the Mosaic law excludes boasting before God because no one is justified by it. But Paul dismisses this answer since the law involves human striving to attain righteousness, and he replies: **No, rather through the law of faith** (3:27d). Commentators dispute the meaning of this strange and jarring phrase, *dia nomou pisteōs*. Some (Keck, Stuhlmacher, Wright) argue that Paul has in view the Mosaic law understood from the perspective of faith. Others (Byrne, Fitzmyer, Haacker) maintain that Paul is not referring to the Mosaic law but using *nomos* in the sense of "principle." Whatever the precise nuance of the text, its fundamental meaning should be evident. Faith acknowledges that God has effected justification, redemption, and atonement in Christ. By confessing what God has done, such faith excludes all boasting before God.

Next, Paul presents a supporting reason for his answer that "the law of faith" excludes all boasting: **For we are of the opinion that a person is justified by faith apart from doing the works of the law** (3:28). With this simple sentence, he provides the Romans with a concise statement of his teaching on justification. A similar phrase occurs in Gal. 2:16. A person is "rectified," "acquitted," "declared innocent," "put in the right relationship to God" (*dikaiōthēsetai*) "by faith" (*pistei*), "apart from the works of the law" (*chōris ergōn nomou*). It is now clear why there is no room for boasting before God: God has effected justification apart from any works of the law, which everyone has failed to do. But inasmuch as Paul has already affirmed that God has graciously justified humanity on the basis of what God has done, it should be evident that justification *by faith* does not mean that the believer's faith brings about this new situation; otherwise faith would be a work in which believers could boast. A more precise statement of Paul's teaching is that a person is justified by God's grace in Jesus Christ on the basis of faith and apart from doing the works of the law.

In 3:29–30 Paul provides further support for his teaching on justification by faith. If one disputes what Paul has just said and argues that justification depends on doing the works of the law, then one implies that God belongs to the Jews alone since only the Jewish people have the gift of God's law (Byrne 1996, 139). Paul formulates this argument with the double question: **Or does God belong only to the Jews? Isn't he also the God of the Gentiles?** (3:29a). Then he provides the correct answer and a supporting reason for it: **Yes, even of the Gentiles. Since God is one, he will justify the circumcised on the basis of faith and the uncircumcised through faith** (3:29b–30). Here Paul alludes to Israel's central teaching as found in the Shema: God is one (Deut. 6:4). In doing so, he employs this traditional teaching of monotheism in a surprisingly new way. Instead of contrasting Jewish monotheism with Gentile idolatry in order to point to the superiority of his own people, Paul employs Jewish monotheism to support his teaching of justification by faith. If God is one— and impartial—God will justify the circumcised and the uncircumcised in the same way, on the basis of faith. Paul's use of two different prepositional phrases in 3:30 (*ek pisteōs* and *dia tēs pisteōs*) is probably stylistic rather than substantive since his purpose is to show that God deals with Gentiles and Jews in the same way, on the basis of faith (Byrne 1996, 140).

Having responded to a series of questions about his teaching on justification, in 3:31 Paul raises and responds to a final issue. If Gentiles and Jews are justified on the basis of faith, apart from doing the works of the law, doesn't this imply that Paul's teaching subverts the law? Aware of this, Paul asks: **Are we nullifying the law, then, through this faith?** (3:31a). The question makes perfect sense, and the answer Paul gives must eventually cohere with what he will say in 10:4, where he proclaims that Christ is the *telos* ("end" or "goal") of the law. Paul responds, **Of course not! Rather, we are confirming the law** (3:31b). The verb he employs (*histanomen*) means "to establish," "to confirm," "to make valid," "to bring into force." To understand what Paul means by this verb, it is necessary to hear his exegesis of Gen. 15:3 (the subject of Rom. 4), that Abraham was justified by faith.

Paul's train of thought in 3:27–31 can be summarized in this way: There is no place for boasting before God. Because no one will be justified before God on the basis of doing the works of the law, God has justified humanity on the basis of faith. And since God is one, God justifies Gentiles and Jews in the same way, on the basis of faith. This teaching about faith establishes the true meaning of the law.

Theological Issues

Every student of Romans readily acknowledges the theological importance of what Paul writes in 3:21–31. In these eleven verses the apostle summarizes

The Ignominy of Crucifixion

"For they proclaim our madness to consist in this, that we give to a crucified man a place second to the unchangeable and eternal God, the Creator of all; for they do not discern the mystery that is herein." (Justin Martyr, 1 Apol. 13.4, ANF 1:167)

"How grievous a thing it is to be disgraced by a public court; how grievous to suffer a fine, how grievous to suffer banishment; and yet in the midst of any such disaster some trace of our liberty is left to us. Even if we are threatened with death, we may die free men. But the executioner, the veiling of the head, and the very word 'cross' should be far removed not only from the person of a Roman citizen but from his thoughts, his eyes and his ears. For it is not only the actual occurrence of these things or the endurance of them, but liability to them, the expectation, nay the mere mention of them, that is unworthy of a Roman citizen and a free man." (Cicero, Rab. Perd. 16, trans. Hodge 1927)

what is essential about his understanding of God and Christ: God has manifested his saving righteousness in Christ's death and resurrection, a righteousness effected apart from, but not in opposition to, the law. To be sure, these verses do not summarize the whole of Paul's theology, but there is little doubt that this section of Romans provides one of Paul's most powerful statements of what God has done in Christ. Through Christ, God justified, redeemed, and reconciled humanity to himself. To appreciate the significance of Paul's soteriology, however, it is important to recall where it begins—at the cross, with the crucified Christ.

Although the cross has become a sacred symbol of Christian faith, it was not always so. As Paul eloquently explains in 1 Corinthians, the message about a crucified messiah was a "stumbling block" to Jews and "foolishness" to Gentiles (1:23). And with good reason. In the Roman world, crucifixion was normally reserved for slaves, violent criminals, and political rebels, whereas according to Deut. 21:23, "anyone hung on a tree is under God's curse." Crucifixion, then, was a shameful death, an act of capital punishment. Yet Paul and other early Christians saw in this utterly secular event the manifestation of God's saving righteousness. In 3:21–31, then, Paul attributes religious significance to a secular event that some saw as a miscarriage of justice and others as the just punishment of a political rebel.

Paul came to this new understanding of Christ's death through his encounter with the risen Christ. At that moment, he saw the crucified Christ bathed in God's own glory and understood that the one whom he had persecuted as a messianic pretender was none other than God's Son. But if Christ was God's Son, then his death was not merely a miscarriage of justice; it was also a death in and through which God manifested himself to the world. In 3:21–26 Paul expresses the significance of

Figure 5. *Crucified Slaves*, by Fjodor Andrejevitch (1827–1902). In the Roman world, crucifixion was normally reserved for slaves, violent criminals, and political rebels. The intent was not only to kill but also to shame. Decapitation (by sword) was seen as a more humane and honorable form of execution.

Christ's death as the manifestation of God's righteousness. In this death, God manifested his covenant loyalty to Israel. In this death, God dealt with sin. But how? To answer this question, Paul employs three metaphors: justification, redemption, atonement. By the first, he proclaims that God's eschatological (final) judgment against sin has already occurred in Christ. Sin has been judged, and humanity has been acquitted because of what God has accomplished in Christ, not because of anything humanity has done. With the second metaphor, Paul draws an analogy between God's redemptive work on behalf of Israel and God's redemptive work in Christ. As God had redeemed Israel from slavery and exile, so God has redeemed Israel—and with Israel the Gentiles—from slavery once more. In this act of redemption, God redeems Israel and the nations from the slavery of sin, under whose power all find themselves.

Paul's third and most striking metaphor comes from Israel's cult, the Day of Atonement. Like the author of the Letter to the Hebrews, Paul draws an analogy between what happened on the Day of Atonement and what occurred on Good Friday. Although the author of Hebrews is intent on presenting Jesus as the great high priest according to the order of Melchizedek who has entered into the heavenly sanctuary, Paul focuses his attention on God's saving action in Christ. God publicly displayed the crucified Christ as the place of atonement, a mercy seat sprinkled with Christ's blood, where God manifested his righteousness. Thus, whereas the author of Hebrews focuses on Christ's proactive role in the drama of salvation, Paul presents Christ as the agent of God's activity in the drama of salvation.

In light of Christ's shameful death on the cross, it is apparent why Paul insists that there is no place for boasting before God. If God has justified humanity on the basis of Christ's death, in which all of humanity was complicit because of sin, then no one can boast before God. Paul's affirmation that there is no place for boasting, then, becomes the way in which he affirms that redemption is God's work. But if redemption is God's work, and if there is no room for boasting, is there any need to live a morally good life? Paul will deal with this question later. Before he deals with it, however, he must establish that redemption is God's free and gracious gift. Only then will he be able to present the moral life as an act of worship, which is the response of a grateful people for what God has accomplished in Christ.

Much of what Paul has said thus far appears to contradict the plain sense of Israel's scriptures. If God established a covenant with Israel at Sinai, and if observance of the law was the way in which Israel maintained its status within that covenant, how can Paul affirm that the notion of faith he proposes does not nullify the law? Paul answers this question by rereading Israel's scriptures in light of what God has done in Christ. When Paul reads Israel's scriptures in this way, it becomes apparent to him that God has always required such faith and that the promises God made through Abraham had the Gentiles in view, as the story of Abraham will show.

Romans 4:1–25

Abraham, the Father of All Who Believe

Introductory Matters

At the end of chapter 3, Paul insisted that he was confirming rather than nullifying the law through the faith that his gospel proposes. In chapter 4, to explain what he means, Paul employs the story of Abraham to show that the great progenitor of the covenant people was justified on the basis of faith. This chapter is crucial for Paul's argument; for if Paul can show that Abraham was justified because of his faith, then he will have substantiated his claim that faith confirms the law. Moreover, he will be able to say that Abraham is not only the ancestor of those who are circumcised but also of all who are justified on the basis of faith, even if they are uncircumcised, as was Abraham when God credited Abraham's faith as righteousness.

But it will not be easy for Paul to make this argument to his contemporaries. For, although Jewish tradition recognized the importance of Abraham's faith, it never argued that Abraham was justified by faith. Jewish tradition was more inclined to view Abraham as righteous because he was obedient to God, especially when God commanded him to sacrifice his only son, Isaac (Gen. 22). For example, 1 Maccabees refers to this incident and interprets it in reference to Gen. 15:6 (the same text that will play a central role in Rom. 4): "Was not Abraham found faithful when tested, *and it was reckoned to him as righteousness*?" (1 Macc. 2:52, emphasis added). Aware of this tradition, and building upon it, the Letter of James argues

Erich Lessing/Art Resource, NY

Figure 6. *The Sacrifice of Abraham (Isaac)*, by Andrea Mantegna (1431–1506). Jewish tradition viewed Abraham's willingness to sacrifice Isaac as the supreme example of his obedience, but Paul grounds Abraham's justification not in his obedience but in his prior trust in God's promise.

that Abraham was "justified by works when he offered Isaac on the altar" (2:21). James concludes that in Abraham's case "faith was active along with works, and faith was brought to completion by the works" (2:22). For James, Abraham's faith, which was accompanied by his works, is the fulfillment of the Scripture: "Abraham believed God, and it was reckoned to him as righteousness" (2:23). Finally, in its great hymn in praise of Israel's ancestors, Sirach extols Abraham. It notes that "he kept the law of the Most High, and entered into a covenant with him; he certified the covenant in his flesh, and when he was tested he proved faithful" (44:20). Although Jewish tradition (and the Letter of James) acknowledged Abraham's faith, it tended to view Abraham's righteousness in terms of his obedience to God, and as Sirach shows, it supposed that Abraham observed the law before God had given the law at Sinai. In its concluding remarks about Abraham, *Jubilees*, an intertestamental work written in the second century before Christ, makes this assessment of the patriarch: "For Abraham was perfect in all of his actions with the LORD and was pleasing through righteousness all of the days of his life" (*Jub.* 23.10, OTP 2:100).

The traditions about Abraham in *Jubilees*, the *Biblical Antiquities* of Pseudo-Philo, the *Apocalypse of Abraham*, and in the writings of Philo and Josephus tend to present Abraham as the first monotheist, the one who rejected idolatry. Nancy Calvert-Koyzis (2004, 142–43) has reviewed these traditions and draws the following conclusion:

Thus what we have found in these examples of the portrayal of Abraham in Jewish literature is that Abraham functions as the prototype of one who rejects idolatry for faith in the one God and, in many cases, expresses that faith in obedience to the law. Even in the differing historical and political circumstances in which each of these texts was written, Abraham functioned to identify primary characteristics of the people of God.

Abraham's most outstanding characteristic was his monotheism, which distinguished him from the idolatrous Gentiles. Rather than being the father of Gentiles and Jews, as Paul portrays him in Rom. 4, Abraham "announces separation from Gentiles because of their idolatry and because of the sin that is a consequence of this idolatry" (Calvert-Koyzis 2004, 17). Although these traditions about Abraham have the potential for presenting him as a unifying figure if Gentiles abandon idolatry and follow his example of monotheism, Calvert-Koyzis has shown that the traditions about Abraham were employed in another way: to shore up Jewish identity, which was distinguished by its monotheism.

William Campbell (2006, 62) notes that "Paul's linking his gentile communities to Abraham as their father could, however, lead in two diverse directions." Either Paul's Gentile converts should accept circumcision as Abraham did, or Abraham was "the prototype of the believing individual demonstrating that faith alone is what counts before God." Whereas Paul defended the latter position, others adopted the former. In his Letter to the Galatians, for example, Paul responds to Jewish Christ-believers who have argued that his Galatian converts must have themselves circumcised and practice the works of the law if they wish to be counted as Abraham's descendants. Otherwise they will not enjoy the benefits of Israel's Messiah. In response to these intruders, Paul interprets the promise that God made to Abraham in Gen. 12:7 christologically ("To your offspring I will give this land"). Paul argues that God's promise to Abraham had a singular "offspring" or "seed" in view, namely, the Christ (Gal. 3:16). This allows Paul to conclude that his uncircumcised Galatian converts are Abraham's descendants because at their baptism they have been incorporated into Abraham's singular "offspring" or "seed," the Christ (Gal. 3:27–29).

Paul's argument in Gal. 3, however, is not adequate for his needs in Rom. 4. On the one hand, although Gal. 3 does explain why Gentiles need not have themselves circumcised, it tends to portray the Mosaic law as an interloper and latecomer in God's salvific plan. On the other hand, although Paul employs Gen. 15:6 in Gal. 3:6, he never explains *how* Abraham was justified by faith. Since he must show how Abraham was justified by faith in order to support his argument that faith confirms the law, and since he must avoid presenting the law in the negative light that he did in Gal. 3, Paul adopts another approach in Romans: he engages in a creative exegesis or midrash of Gen. 15:6, a text

---

Romans 4:1–25 in the Rhetorical Flow

The letter opening (1:1–17)

Gentiles and Jews in the light of God's wrath (1:18–3:20)

Gentiles and Jews in the light of God's righteousness (3:21–4:25)

   A righteousness accessible to all through faith (3:21–31)

►**Abraham, the father of all who believe (4:1–25)**

    "It was credited to him as righteousness" (4:1–12)

      Why Abraham's faith was credited as righteousness (4:1–8)

        Question (4:1)

        Response (4:2)

        Scriptural support (4:3)

        Explanation of "credited" (4:4–5)

        Scriptural confirmation (4:6–8)

      When Abraham was credited with righteous (4:9–12)

        Question (4:9)

        Two further questions and a response (4:10)

        The significance of Abraham's circumcision (4:11–12)

    "Abraham believed" (4:13–22)

      Why the promise to Abraham is based on faith (4:13–17)

        Promise fulfilled through faith rather than the law (4:13)

        First supporting reason (4:14)

        Second supporting reason (4:15)

        Why the promise is based on faith (4:16)

        God's promise and Abraham's response (4:17)

      What kind of faith Abraham exhibited (4:18–22)

        Abraham's faith in the promise (4:18)

        The quality of Abraham's faith (4:19–21)

        Abraham's faith credited as righteousness (4:22)

    Conclusion (4:23–25)

      Not only for Abraham (4:23)

      But for all who believe (4:24–25)

---

that explicitly affirms that God credited Abraham's faith as righteousness. In the first half of the chapter (Rom. 4:1–12), Paul focuses on the second part of the text ("It was credited to him as righteousness"; 4:3) in order to explain the significance of the verb "to credit." In the second half of the chapter (4:13–22) he turns his attention to the first half of the verse ("Abraham believed") in order to describe the quality of Abraham's faith. The entire chapter reads like a homily that Paul has delivered on other occasions and now incorporates into Romans.

Tracing the Train of Thought

The first half of this chapter consists of two units (4:1–8, 9–12). In the first, Paul employs a quotation from Gen. 15:6 that he exegetes in light of Ps. 31:1–2 LXX (32:1–2 Eng.) to show that the verb "credit" takes on a specific meaning in relation to faith and righteousness (Rom. 4:1–8). He argues that in Gen. 15:6 the verb does not refer to something that is due because of work that has been done but to the gracious way in which God credits faith as righteousness. In the second unit, Paul makes an important hermeneutical move. He points out that Abraham was still uncircumcised when God declared that the great father of the nation was righteous (4:9–12). This allows Paul to argue that Abraham is the father of all who believe, even if they are uncircumcised.

The second half of this chapter (4:13–22) also consists of two units. In the first, Paul explains why the promise God made to Abraham is based on faith rather than on the law: so that it can apply to all of Abraham's descendants and not just to those who were under the law (4:13–17). In the second unit, Paul presents Abraham's faith in terms of resurrection faith since Abraham believed in the God who raises the dead (4:18–22).

The conclusion of this chapter applies Paul's exegesis of Gen. 15:6 to believers (Rom. 4:23–25). All who believe in God who raised Jesus will have their faith credited as righteousness as well.

4:1–8. Paul begins with a question (4:1) and answer (4:2) that continue the form of the diatribe. There is a close connection, then, between what he has just said (3:27–31) and what he will say in chapter 4. Having argued that the law of faith excludes boasting before God, and having insisted that he is confirming rather than annulling the law by this faith, Paul introduces Abraham into the discussion for the first time. Posing the kind of question that a Jewish interlocutor might raise, he asks: **What then shall we say our forefather in the flesh, Abraham, attained?** (4:1). Commentators differ in their interpretation of this text, some maintaining that the phrase *kata sarka* should be taken with the verb "attained" (*heurēkenai*), giving the translation "What then shall we say that our forefather Abraham attained *according to the flesh*?" This reading is also supported by some manuscripts. The best textual witnesses and the more natural reading of that text, however, supports my translation. Thus Paul asks if Abraham, the progenitor of the covenant people, could boast before God on the basis of achievement, the implication being that if anyone could boast in God's sight, it was certainly Abraham.

Paul responds with a simple conditional sentence followed by a strong adversative clause: **For if Abraham was justified on the basis of works, he can** boast—**but not before God** (4:2). Aware that his contemporaries and Scripture extolled Abraham's obedience to God's law (Gen. 26:5; Sir. 44:20), Paul acknowledges that Abraham had reason to boast if, as many of Paul's contemporaries thought, he was justified on the basis of what he did. But then, having conceded this, Paul introduces an important qualification. Although Abraham has a boast before human beings, he does not have a boast before God. Origen (*Comm. Rom.* 4.1.5, trans Scheck 2001–2, 1:239) puts it well: "Therefore, he says, even Abraham, if he was justified by works, indeed has a boast coming from the works, but not that [boast] which is before God alone."

To support his contention that not even Abraham can boast before God, Paul quotes the text of Gen. 15:6, which he will exegete in the rest of the chapter: **For what does Scripture say? "Abraham believed God, and it was credited to him as righteousness"** (4:3). The quotation comes from the narrative that recounts the first covenant that God established with Abraham, before his name was changed from Abram to Abraham (Gen. 17:5). The account begins with God's promise that Abraham's reward will be very great (15:1). When Abraham responds that he is still without progeny and his slave Eliezer will be his heir (15:2), God promises that one of Abraham's own offspring will be his heir and that Abraham's descendants will be as countless as the stars (15:4–5). Although childless, Abraham believes the promise, and the narrator of Genesis remarks, "the LORD reckoned it to him as righteousness" (15:6).

Since Gen. 15:6 can be read as God rewarding Abraham for a righteous act, as the NJPS translation suggests ("And because he put his trust in the LORD, He reckoned it to his merit"), Paul must explain how Gen. 15:6 supports his teaching on justification by faith. To do so, he focuses on the meaning of the verb *logizomai* (to credit), which occurs eight times in the first half of Rom. 4 (4:3, 4, 5, 6, 8, 9, 10, 11) and three times toward the end of this chapter (4:22, 23, 25). A commercial term used in bookkeeping, its meaning in commercial transactions is "to reckon," "to calculate," "to credit" something to another's account. Focusing on this meaning, Paul reminds his audience how this term is used in relation to wages: **To the one who works, payment is not credited as something freely given but as something due** (4:4). Establishing a contrast between what is due to a person and what is freely and graciously given to a person apart from any merit or work, Paul notes that a worker's wages fall into the first category. Employers "reckon," "calculate," "credit" wages on the basis of work done. Wages are never a gift. Employing the verb "to credit" yet again, Paul draws a contrast between the one who works and the one who believes: **But to the one who does not work but believes in the one who justifies the ungodly, his faith is credited as righteousness** (4:5). Here the verb "to credit" takes on another sense. Since the believer is not a worker, faith is not "credited" to an account as something due but as "righteousness." Thus Paul establishes the following comparison:

Worker	wages	credited	as due
Believer	faith	credited	as righteousness

The comparison shows that the verb "credited" can be used in two ways. In the case of a worker, wages are credited as something due because of work done, but in the case of the believer, faith is not credited as something due but is credited as righteousness.

But what kind of faith is Paul speaking of? Employing the unexpected term *asebē* (godless), Paul describes Abraham's faith as "faith in the one who justifies the ungodly." On first hearing, the concept of God justifying the ungodly appears to contradict the very law that Paul says he is confirming (see Exod. 23:7). Moreover, did not Paul say that it is those who do the law who will be justified or acquitted (Rom. 2:13)? But Paul has also affirmed that all are under the power of sin (3:9) and that no one will be justified before God on the basis of doing the works of the law (3:20). The true believer, then, is the one who trusts that God will acquit the ungodly on the basis of Christ's saving death.

In 4:6–8 Paul employs the Jewish exegetical principle *gezerah shawah*, whereby texts that contain an identical word or words are allowed to interpret each other (Fitzmyer 1993, 376). Since both Gen. 15:6 and Ps. 31:1–2 LXX (32:1–2 Eng.) employ the verb *logizomai*, Paul presses the text of the psalm into service to explain the significance of the righteousness that God credited to Abraham according to Gen. 15:6. Beginning with the assumption that David is the author of the psalm, Paul writes: **Just so, David speaks of the blessedness of the one to whom God credits righteousness apart from works** (4:6). Then Paul employs the psalm to explain the nature of the righteousness credited to Abraham according to Gen. 15:6: **"Blessed are those whose lawless deeds have been forgiven, whose sins have been covered over. Blessed is the man to whom the Lord does not credit sin"** (Rom. 4:7–8). Although the psalm text does not mention "righteousness," it does speak of the "blessedness" of the one (1) whose "lawless deeds" (*anomiai*) have been forgiven, (2) whose sin has been covered over, and (3) to whom God does not *credit* sin. Such a person is "blessed" (*makarios*). This allows Paul to explain the "righteousness" mentioned in Gen. 15:6 in terms of the "blessedness" of the person whose sins have been forgiven, as described in Ps. 31:1–2 LXX. On the basis of the verb "credit," then, Paul has been able to draw the following relation between these two texts: God *credited* Abraham's faith as righteousness (Gen. 15:6); this righteousness is the blessedness of the person whose sins God has not *credited* (Ps. 31:1–2 LXX).

To summarize, not even Abraham has a boast before God because Abraham's faith was graciously *credited* as righteousness, which is the *blessedness* of someone whose sins have not been *credited* to his account because they have been graciously forgiven and covered over.

4:9–12. Like the first unit, this unit begins with a question: **When, then, did this blessedness occur, when he was circumcised or still uncircumcised?** (4:9a). By using the word "blessedness" (*makarismos*), Paul relates this unit to the previous one in which the same word (4:6) or related words occur (4:7, 8). But instead of asking how this "righteousness" occurred, Paul inquires when this "blessedness" occurred, thereby indicating that he equates the blessedness mentioned in Ps. 31:1–2 LXX with the righteousness noted in the text of Gen. 15:6. Paul explains why he has asked this question: **For we have said, "Faith was credited to Abraham as righteousness"** (4:9b). Since his readers would have assumed that this "blessedness" occurred when Abraham was circumcised, Paul repeats the quotation he introduced in 4:3, a quotation that comes from Gen. 15, when Abraham was not yet circumcised.

Using the verb "credited" to relate this verse to the quotation, Paul repeats the question of 4:9a by asking two other questions: **How then was it credited? While he was in a state of circumcision or uncircumcision?** (4:10a). But whereas he asked the question of 4:9a in relation to "blessedness," he asks these questions in relation to the verb "credited." In effect, Paul is asking, When was righteousness/blessedness credited to Abraham? Finally, Paul answers all of the questions he has raised: **It was not when he was circumcised but when he was uncircumcised** (4:10b). Paul does not explain his response. He simply assumes that his audience knows that the text of Gen. 15:6 comes from a period prior to Abraham's circumcision, which is narrated later, in Gen. 17. In that chapter, God makes a covenant with Abraham and promises that Abraham will be "exceedingly numerous," the "ancestor of a multitude of nations" (17:2, 5). The sign of this everlasting covenant is circumcision (17:11). In terms of narrative time, then, Abraham was not yet circumcised when God "credited" Abraham's faith as righteousness.

Having made the most important point of his argument—that God credited righteousness to Abraham when he was still uncircumcised—Paul draws out the implication of his argument for Gentile and Jewish believers in Christ: Abraham is their common father. But why was Abraham circumcised if he was already declared righteous when he was uncircumcised? What was the need for circumcision if he was already righteous in God's sight? Paul responds: **He received the sign of circumcision as confirmation of his righteousness that came from faith when he was still uncircumcised** (4:11a). The use of *sēmeion* (sign) is an allusion to the same word in Gen. 17:11. But whereas Gen. 17 speaks of circumcision as "the sign of the covenant," Paul speaks of "the sign of circumcision," which he interprets as the "seal" or the "confirmation" (*sphragida*) of the righteousness credited to Abraham when he was still uncircumcised. With this remark, Paul breaks ranks with his Jewish contemporaries, finding a new meaning for Abraham's circumcision. It was the confirmation of something that had already occurred when he was uncircumcised.

But Paul does not arbitrarily reinterpret the story of Abraham in Genesis. Reading the narrative in light of the gospel, he understands the christological significance of the Abraham story. These events happened in this way so that Abraham could become the father of Gentiles and Jews alike. Paul explains that Abraham's faith was credited as righteousness before he was circumcised **in order that he might be the father of all those who believe while uncircumcised, so that it might be credited to them as righteousness** (4:11b). On the basis of his reading, Paul can argue that his Gentile converts are in the same situation as was uncircumcised Abraham, when his faith was credited as righteousness. Recognizing that Abraham remains the father of the covenant people, Paul adds: **and he might be the father of the circumcised, not only for those who are circumcised but also for those who walk in the way of faith of our father Abraham while he was uncircumcised** (4:12). In making this statement, Paul adds a provision: Abraham is the father of the circumcised who exhibit the same kind of faith that Abraham did when he was uncircumcised. Since this faith is faith in the God who justifies the ungodly (4:5), it is apparent that Paul has faith in Christ in view. Thus Paul seems to be pointing to a division in Israel, which he will discuss in chapter 9, between those who believe as Abraham did and those who do not. In Paul's view, the first group makes up the true spiritual descendants of Abraham, and the second group does not, even though its members are Abraham's physical offspring.

Paul's argument can be summarized in this way: Since righteousness was credited to Abraham on the basis of faith before he was circumcised, Abraham is the father of Christ-believing Gentiles and Jews alike, apart from circumcision. Relating this argument to Paul's argument in the first unit, the first half of Rom. 4 makes the following point: faith upholds rather than nullifies the law because the faith the gospel proclaims is the kind of faith that was credited as righteousness to uncircumcised Abraham.

4:13–17. Having interpreted the second part of the quotation from Gen. 15:6 ("and it was credited to him as righteousness)" in the second half of Rom. 4:1–12, Paul turns his attention to the first part of that quotation ("Abraham believed"). Before describing the quality of Abraham's faith, however, he must explain why the promise is based on faith rather than on the law. The answer he gives in this unit strengthens what he has argued in the second unit: just as Abraham's faith was credited as righteousness when he was uncircumcised in order that he might be the father of Gentiles and Jews, so the promise is based on faith in order that it might be effective for all, Gentiles and Jews.

Paul begins with a negative statement that serves as his thesis: **The promise to Abraham and his descendants that he would inherit the world is not through the law but through the righteousness that comes from faith** (4:13). This is the first time in Romans that Paul has referred to the "promise" (*epangelia*) God made to Abraham, a topic with which Paul deals extensively in Gal. 3. Although he employs the singular ("the promise"), Paul has in view the accounts of the

113

promises that God made to Abraham and the other patriarchs. For example, in Gen. 15 God promises Abraham numerous descendants (15:5), to whom he will give the land (15:18). Genesis 17 records a similar promise, but now Abraham will be "the ancestor of a multitude of nations," and his name is changed to reflect this (17:4–5). In 18:18 God says, "Abraham shall become a great and mighty nation, and all the nations of the earth shall be blessed in him." In 22:17–18 the promise is renewed and proclaims that Abraham's offspring "shall possess the gate of their enemies," and by Abraham's offspring "shall all the nations of the earth gain blessing for themselves." The promise is most expansive in Sir. 44:21, which notes that God assured Abraham that he would "exalt his offspring like the stars, and give them an inheritance from sea to sea, and from the Euphrates to the ends of the earth." Paul's own description of the promise (that Abraham would inherit the world) is part of this ever-expanding tradition of the promise. In light of this tradition and his own conviction that Abraham is the father of Gentiles as well as Jews, Paul affirms that the promise is not "through law" (*dia nomou*) but "through the righteousness that comes from faith" (*dia dikaiosynēs pisteōs*). This expression sums up what Paul has just said about Abraham, and it reminds Paul's audience that when Abraham believed in God's promise, his faith was credited as righteousness. Thus the promise is made effective through the righteousness that comes from faith.

Next, Paul begins to explain why the promise is made effective through faith: **For if the heirs are those who belong to the law, faith is deprived of its power and the promise is void** (4:14). To understand the force of this argument, we must grant its premise: the priority of faith over the law. For Paul, faith is prior to the law since God made the promise to Abraham before the Mosaic law was given (Gal. 3:17). Consequently, if the heirs of the promise are those "who belong to the law" (*hoi ek nomou*), then faith is deprived of its power; for faith relies on God whereas the law requires one to do its works. Likewise, the promise will be nullified if it is based on the law. For whereas the promise requires the kind of faith that Abraham exhibited, the law calls on its adherents to do the works of the law.

Focusing on the nature of the law, Paul provides further support for his argument: **For the law effects wrath. But where there is no law, there is no transgression** (4:15). Alluding to his earlier statement that the law makes people conscious of sin (3:20), and recalling the theme of God's wrath that he has developed in the first part of this letter, Paul affirms that there can be no explicit trespass against the law when there is no law, since people are ignorant of God's will. But when the law makes its appearance, those who are aware of its commandments knowingly transgress them (5:13, 20; 7:7), thus bringing about wrath.

Having shown why the promise that God made to Abraham does not come through the law, Paul explains why it is based on faith: **This is why it is based** on faith: **so that it might be in conformity with grace in order that the promise might be firmly established for all the descendants, not only those who belong to the law but even those who have the faith of Abraham, who is the father of us all** (4:16). Paul's argument can be rephrased in this way: Since Abraham is the father of all, the promise must be based on faith, which is intimately related to God's "grace" or "favor" (*charis*). For if the promise were based on the law, then it would exclude all who are not under the law. Paul makes his point in the following way: First, he argues that since the promise is based on faith, it is in accordance with God's grace. Behind this affirmation stands Paul's conviction that the only response to the gracious gift of God's promise is the kind of trusting faith that Abraham exhibited. Second, since the promise is based on faith, then it is available to all who believe in the way Abraham believed.

Having identified Abraham as "the father of us all," Paul introduces a quotation from Gen. 17:5 to support what he has just said about Abraham: **as it is written, "I will make you the father of many nations"** (4:17a). This quotation, which finds an echo in Sir. 44:19, comes from Gen. 17, the chapter in which God establishes the everlasting covenant of circumcision with Abraham and his descendants. But instead of calling attention to the covenant of circumcision, Paul emphasizes the universal paternity of Abraham. Abraham is not merely the father of the covenant people; he will also be the father of a multitude of nations. In asserting this, Paul does not mean that Abraham will be the physical progenitor of these nations but that he will be the father of all who follow his example of faith.

At the end of the quotation from Gen. 17:5, Paul adds a description of Abraham's faith: **in the sight of God in whom he believed, who gives life to the dead and calls that which does not exist into being** (4:17b). Anticipating what he will say in the next unit, Paul presents Abraham's faith as a kind of resurrection faith. For even though he lived before Christ, Abraham already believed in the God who gives life to the dead and calls into existence what does not exist. In others words, Abraham believed in the God who raises the dead, a description of God that summarizes Paul's understanding of God (see 2 Cor. 1:9).

Paul's train of though in this unit is difficult to follow because he writes in a compact manner that requires us to fill in the gaps. His main argument, however, is consistent: God's promise to Abraham must be based on faith rather than on the law because the law excludes those who do not belong to the covenant people whereas faith includes all who believe, even if they are not circumcised. Inasmuch as God's promise to Abraham has a universal horizon, it requires the response of a faith that is available to all. But what kind of faith is this? Paul addresses this question in the next unit.

4:18–22. Having explained why the promise depends on faith rather than on the law, Paul in this unit describes the specific nature of Abraham's faith, a theme he introduced at the end of the last unit (4:17b). The opening verse functions as a thesis statement: **Contrary to hope, in hope he believed that he would become the father of many nations in accordance with what was spoken, "Thus will your descendants be"** (4:18). Here Paul alludes to the promise that God made to Abraham as recorded in Gen. 15:5: "He brought him outside and said, 'Look toward heaven and count the stars, if you are able to count them.' Then he said to him, '*So shall your descendants be*'" (emphasis added). Since Abraham and Sarah were childless, Paul emphasizes the radical nature of Abraham's trust. At a moment in his life when there was no reason to hope, Abraham hoped that he would become "the father of many nations" (*patera pollōn ethnōn*), a phrase that echoes the promise of Gen. 17:5, which Paul quoted in Rom. 4:17.

The manner in which Paul juxtaposes hope and faith in 4:18 provides an important insight to his understanding of faith. Faith is hope and trust in the one who promises; it is a faith that hopes even when there is no reason to hope.

Next, Paul specifies the qualities that characterized Abraham's faith. Drawing from the account of Gen. 17, which notes that Abraham would be a hundred years old and Sarah ninety if God's promise of offspring is fulfilled (Gen. 17:17), Paul writes: **And without growing weak in respect to faith, he considered his own body as already dead, since he was about a hundred years old, and the deadness of Sarah's womb, but he did not doubt God's promise by unbelief, but strengthened by faith he glorified God, and he was convinced that God was able to do what he promised** (4:19–21). In his retelling of the story of Abraham, Paul does not mention that when God made the promise "Abraham fell on his face and laughed," asking himself if a child can be born to a man who is a hundred years old and a woman who is ninety, and insisting that Ishmael be his heir (Gen. 17:17–18). Instead, weaving the accounts of Gen. 15 and 17 together in order to interpret the latter half of Gen. 15:6, Paul focuses the attention of his audience on a single statement: *Abraham believed*. Then, in light of his understanding of Christ, Paul embellishes the text and draws out its christological meaning.

In 4:19 Paul emphasizes that Abraham's faith did not falter even when he considered his own body "as dead" (*nenekrōmenon*) and the "deadness" (*nekrōsin*) of Sarah's womb. At this point, some manuscripts (D et al.) read, "he did *not* consider," giving the sense that Abraham's faith was so strong that he did *not* consider his body as dead. The reading followed here emphasizes the extraordinary quality of Abraham's faith: Abraham believed even when he knew his body was "dead" in respect to fathering children. The adverb "already" (*ēdē*), which is absent from some manuscripts, highlights the urgency of the situation that Abraham faced. Paul's use of *nekrōsis*, a rare word whose only other occurrence in the Greek Bible (OT and NT) is in 2 Cor. 4:10, echoes his description of Abraham's body as "dead." From a purely human perspective, there could be no hope for new life; for despite the promise, Abraham could see only death. Yet he did not grow weak in faith. Such was the extraordinary nature of his faith.

In 4:20 Paul enhances his description of Abraham's faith in two ways. First, drawing a contrast between unbelief and faith, he notes that instead of doubting the promise by "unbelief" (*apistia*), Abraham was strengthened by "faith" (*pistei*). Second, the result of this renewed faith in the face of death was that Abraham gave "praise" or "glory" (*doxan*) to God. The word "glory" recalls Paul's earlier indictment of the Gentile world that refused to glorify God (1:21) and exchanged the glory of God for idols (1:23). Thus, whereas all sinned and fell short of God's glory (3:23), Abraham glorified God by believing in the promise, even when there was no human reason to hope.

In 4:21 Paul explains why Abraham did not falter in faith but gave glory to God by continuing to hope against all hope: he was fully convinced that God was able to do what God promised. The basis for Abraham's faith in the face of death, then, was the God in whom he believed. Because he believed in the God who gives life to the dead and brings into being what does not exist (4:17), Abraham trusted that God could fulfill the promise of progeny, even though his body and Sarah's womb were dead. From Paul's perspective, Abraham did not merely believe in God; he believed in the God who raises the dead.

Having completed his description of Abraham's faith, Paul draws out the conclusion of the argument: **Therefore, "it was credited to him as righteousness" (4:22).** Quoting the second half of Gen. 15:6, Paul concludes that God credited righteousness (as a gift) to Abraham because he believed (even in the face of death) in the God who was able to fulfill the promise. In effect, Abraham believed in the God who raised Jesus from the dead. The new element in Paul's exegesis of Gen. 15:6 is his understanding of Abraham's faith as a faith in the God who raises the dead. Whereas Paul's contemporaries understood this text to mean that God credited an act of righteousness to Abraham's account as a good deed, Paul interprets it in terms of his teaching on justification by faith. By believing in the promise, Abraham exhibited faith in the God who raises the dead. On the basis of that faith, Abraham was justified in God's sight.

4:23–25. Having explained the text of Gen. 15:6 in relation to Abraham, Paul applies his new reading of this text to his audience. He insists that the text of Genesis does not apply to Abraham alone but to all Christ-believers to whom righteousness will be credited because of their faith in the God who raised Jesus: **But it was not written for his sake only that "it was credited to him" but even for us to whom it will be credited, who believe in the one who raised Jesus our Lord from the dead (4:23–24).** With these words Paul draws a comparison between Abraham's faith and the faith of believers in Christ. As Abraham believed in the God who was able to fulfill the promise, so Christ-followers believe in the God who raised Jesus from the dead:

Abraham	believed	in God who fulfills the promise.
Christ-followers	believe	in God who raised Jesus.

By establishing this relationship, Paul shows that Abraham and all who believe in Christ believe in the same God: the God who fulfills promises and raises the dead. Because faith establishes the law, the God of those who believe in Christ is the God of Abraham, the God who fulfills promises. The God of Abraham is the God of Christ-believers, the God who brings life out of death.

Next, Paul provides a brief soteriological description of God's work in Christ: the one whom God raised from the dead is the one **who was handed over because of our trespasses and raised for our justification** (4:25). This formula has two parts. On the one hand, Jesus was "handed over" (*paredothē*) for our "transgressions" (*paraptōmata*). The use of the passive voice points to God's initiative in the work of redemption. God is the one who "handed over" his Son for our transgressions. This emphasis on the divine initiative in the work of salvation echoes Paul's statement in 3:25 that God put forth Christ as a *hilastērion*. On the other hand, "he was raised" (*ēgerthē*) for our justification (*dikaiōsin*). Although Paul's teaching on justification plays an important role in his theology, this is one of the few times that he uses the abstract noun to describe this teaching (see 5:18 for the other occurrence of this word in Romans). The sense of Paul's formula is that when God raised Jesus from the dead, God vindicated and justified us just as he justified and vindicated the crucified Jesus from the false judgment of the world that condemned him.

The distinction that Paul makes between the effects of Christ's death and resurrection is more rhetorical than real. There would be no justification without Christ's death, just as there would be no forgiveness of transgressions without Christ's resurrection. It is the total work of Christ—his death and resurrection—that effects the forgiveness of transgressions and the justification of sinners.

Theological Issues

Romans 4 is a remarkable theological achievement. By providing a new and insightful interpretation of Gen. 15:6, Paul has redefined the significance of Abraham in light of the saving righteousness that God has manifested in Jesus Christ. It is this new reading that allows Paul to say that faith confirms the law.

There are two dimensions to Paul's understanding of Abraham. First, whereas his Jewish compatriots focused on Abraham as a model of righteousness because he obeyed and worshiped the one God, Paul highlights Abraham's faith in God's promises, presenting him as the model believer.

But Paul is not content to show that Abraham believed in God. Probing the quality of Abraham's faith, he presents him as one who believed in the God who justifies the ungodly (4:5), the God who gives life to the dead and calls into being what does not exist (4:17), the God who is powerful to do what he promises (4:21), even when there is no earthly reason for hope. In a word, Paul describes Abraham as someone who already believed in the God who raises the dead. In doing so, he makes Abraham a model of faith for all Christ-believers, and he forever defines the nature of Christian faith as faith in the God who raises the dead.

Second, whereas his Jewish contemporaries employed the example of Abraham's obedience to God in the face of adversity to strengthen Jewish identity, Paul employs the example of Abraham's faith to show that he is the ancestor of all who believe. This understanding of Abraham allows Paul to make him a figure who embraces Gentile as well as Jew. Because he understands Abraham in this way, Paul emphasizes the promise of Gen. 17:4, which speaks of "a multitude of nations" rather than numerous "descendants" (Gen. 15:5).

It is this christological reading of the Abraham story, especially the text of Gen. 15:6, that allows Paul to say that faith confirms the law (Rom. 3:31). Faith confirms the law because, when the law is read in the light of Christ, one sees that God justified the uncircumcised Abraham on the basis of his faith in the God who raises the dead. In affirming that faith confirms the law, then, Paul asserts that his gospel of justification by faith is already found in the law. More specifically, it is present in the story of Abraham when read from the point of view of the gospel. It is this narrative that testifies to Paul's teaching on justification by faith, to the inclusion of the Gentiles in the blessings that God promised to Abraham, and to the meaning of faith as faith in the God who raises the dead.

Despite Paul's affirmation that the faith he proclaims confirms the law, it is evident that he understands this statement in a nuanced way. Paul is not referring to the law in terms of doing "the works of the law." Such an understanding of the law, in Paul's view, establishes a division between Gentile and Jew, whereas the promise, which depends on faith, is universal in scope and unifies Gentile and Jew. The law (understood as commandment) makes people aware of their transgressions, and their transgressions make them liable to God's wrath, but trusting faith leads to justification. Consequently, when Paul says that faith confirms the law, he means that when Scripture is read in light of Christ, it becomes apparent to all who believe that God graciously effects salvation on the basis of faith.

Paul's presentation of Abraham as the model of faith, the common ancestor of Gentile and Jew, raises a problem. If Abraham is the father of those who believe in Christ, does this mean that those Jews who do not believe in Christ have been disinherited from their patrimony? Are they no longer descendants of Abraham because they do not believe in the Christ? This is a problem with

PART 3

Romans 5:1–8:39

The Experience of Salvation
in the Light of God's Righteousness

The third part of Romans marks a decisive turn in Paul's argument and rhetoric. In the first two parts of this letter, Paul has been arguing that both Gentiles and Jews find themselves under the power of sin (1:18–3:20), so that God has graciously manifested his saving righteousness in Christ (3:21–4:25). In the third part of Romans, Paul turns his attention to the community of those who have embraced this saving righteousness and describes the experience of salvation that the justified already enjoy in Christ (5:1–8:39). Themes that were prominent in the first four chapters (faith, the relationship between Gentiles and Jews, the works of the law) recede to the background. Other themes that have played an important role in chapters 1–4 (sin, justification, boasting) are developed in new ways in chapters 5–8. Finally, new themes emerge (God's love, the eschatological hope of Christ-believers, solidarity with the new Adam, the power of God's Spirit).

In addition to this change of topics and themes, there is a change in Paul's rhetoric. In the first two parts of Romans, he made extensive use of scriptural quotations and diatribe to persuade his audience that the situation of Gentiles and Jews is essentially the same (all have sinned and are in need of God's saving grace). In this part (especially 5:1–11), Paul establishes "a rhetorical bridge" with his audience by drawing "repeated attention to the *de facto* unity that exists between himself and those to whom he is writing" (McDonald 1990, 81). To be sure, Paul continues to persuade and exhort his readers, but the overall purpose of his rhetoric is to celebrate the experience of salvation that the justified already enjoy and to assure them that they can be confident of their hope for salvation. Viewed rhetorically, chapters 5–8 are epideictic in nature.

In addition to this change of rhetorical tone, the rhetoric of these chapters highlights the role of Christ and the Spirit in God's work of salvation. For example, at several points in chapters 5–8 Paul employs phrases such as "through our Lord Jesus Christ" (5:1, 11, 17, 21; 6:23; 7:25; 8:39). The regular occurrence of these phrases, especially at the end of chapters 5, 6, 7, and 8, binds these chapters together and highlights the role that Christ plays in God's plan of salvation. References to the Spirit throughout these chapters, but especially in chapter 8, point to what later theology would call the trinitarian nature of God's work of salvation.

Paul's train of thought in Rom. 5–8 can be summarized in this way: In 5:1–11 he describes the new situation in which the justified find themselves, and he articulates the final or eschatological hope in which Christ-believers boast. Next, in 5:12–21 he draws a comparison between Adam and Christ that explains why believers can be so confident about their future salvation. Since Christ has become the head of a new creation, those who are in Christ belong to this new creation. This comparison between Adam and Christ, which is at the heart of Paul's theology, provides the occasion for him to raise a number of rhetorical questions that structure the material of chapters 6–7. Should believers continue to live in the realm of sin so that grace may abound all the more (6:1)? Should believers persist in sin since they are no longer under the law but under grace (6:15)? Is the law sinful (7:7)? These questions, which pose objections to Paul's gospel, enable the apostle to present a careful reflection on the relation between sin and law in light of his presentation of Christ as the eschatological Adam. Toward the close of chapter 7, Paul raises the cry of sinful humanity. Who can rescue humanity from its hopeless situation (7:24)? Chapter 8, with its careful exposition of the Spirit, responds to this cry. The only antidote to sin is the Spirit. After explaining this, in 8:18–39 Paul returns to the theme of the believer's eschatological hope that he introduced in 5:1–11.

Thus 5:1–11 and 8:18–39 celebrate the believer's eschatological hope, thereby creating a bracket around the material of 5:12–8:17, which deals with humanity's solidarity with either sinful Adam or the life-giving Christ. The material is arranged in this way:

The eschatological hope of the justified (5:1–11)
    Solidarity with Adam or with Christ (5:12–8:17)
The eschatological hope of the justified (8:18–39)

Romans 5:1–21

Transferred from the Realm of Sin to the Realm of Grace

Introductory Matters

Although nearly all commentators recognize that chapter 5 plays a crucial role in the argument of Romans, there has been an ongoing debate about its relation to the material that precedes and follows it. While the majority of commentators view it as the beginning of a new movement in Paul's argument, a minority argue that it concludes the material that precedes it. James Dunn (1988, 1:242), for example, views chapter 5 "as a conclusion to the argument so far," maintaining that "the backward links are too many and deliberate." Accordingly, he sees chapter 5 as the conclusion of a section that begins with 3:21. Peter Stuhlmacher (1994, 78) has a similar view, noting that 5:1–11 is "tightly bound thematically to 3:21–4:25" through the catchwords "justified," "glory of God," and the "the theme of atonement and reconciliation through Christ."

While Dunn and Stuhlmacher are correct to highlight the links that chapter 5 has with what has preceded, chapter 5 has a different rhetorical goal than the chapters that precede it. Although the opening verses of chapter 5 do summarize what Paul has said, the chapter as a whole is the beginning of a new movement in Paul's argument whereby he joins himself with the community of believers to celebrate the experience of salvation that the justified presently enjoy. Accordingly, the language of "we" and "us," introduced at the end of the preceding chapter (4:25), predominates in 5:1–11. To be sure, it quickly gives way to the third-person singular in 5:12–21, but the inclusive language of "we" and "us" soon reappears, and this is the way Paul tends to speak throughout chapters 5–8. Moreover, it is clear that the second half of chapter 5 sets the stage for Paul's discussion of sin and law in chapters 6–8. Although this might suggest that there is a major break between 5:1–11 and 5:12–21, these two units belong together, the latter (5:12–21) providing the theological ground for the hope that the former celebrates (5:1–11). Chapter 5, then, is the beginning of a new movement in Paul's argument rather than the conclusion to what he has been saying thus far. Before discussing the structure of this chapter and tracing Paul's train of thought, we must deal with three introductory matters: a textual question, a grammatical problem, and the background to Paul's Adam-Christ comparison.

A Textual Question

In the opening verse of chapter 5, there is a textual problem whose resolution influences the interpretation of the text. While some textual witnesses read "we have" (*echomen*, present indicative), others read "let us have" (*echōmen*, present hortatory subjunctive). The first reading states a fact: since believers have been justified, they are at peace with God ("Therefore, since we have been justified, . . . *we are at peace* with God"). In contrast to this, the second reading is an exhortation: since believers have been justified, they should seek to be at peace with God ("Therefore, since we have been justified, . . . *let us be at peace* with God"). The choice one makes here also affects the interpretation of the verb *kauchōmetha* in 5:2, which can be construed as either first-person plural indicative ("we boast") or first-person plural subjunctive ("let us boast"). If the hortatory subjunctive ("let us have peace") is the correct reading in 5:1, then one should take *kauchōmetha* as a hortatory subjunctive ("let us boast"). Thus one can read the opening verses of chapter 5 either as a statement of fact ("we are at peace with God, . . . we boast") or as the beginning of a moral exhortation ("let us be at peace with God, . . . let us boast").

While there are good textual witnesses for the indicative *echomen* (א[1] B[2] 1739, et al.), the witnesses for the subjunctive *echōmen* (א* A B* C D K L 33 81, et al.) are stronger. Consequently Jewett (2007, 344) urges that "the more strongly attested subjunctive form should be accepted." In his view this reading also coheres with the social situation that Paul was addressing in Romans (2007, 348). Now that God has provided the Romans with the opportunity "to be in a right relationship with God," they should take advantage of it. Thus Paul would be encouraging the factious community to be at peace.

Bruce Metzger (1994, 452) and most contemporary commentators, however, argue for the indicative ("we have peace") on the basis of context and theology. Since the rest of chapter 5 is an exposition of what God has done for believers, commentators maintain that it is more likely that Paul is describing the situation of the justified rather than exhorting the justified to be at peace with God. Moreover, since the peace to which Paul refers in 5:1 is the reconciliation that he describes in 5:10–11, it appears to me that the context favors the indicative. For, as we shall see, reconciliation is something that God effects for humanity; it is not something that humanity does for itself. Furthermore, if Paul is encouraging the members of his audience to be at peace with one another, it seems strange that he exhorts them to be at peace with God rather than with one another. This is not to deny the role that moral exhortation plays in Romans (see 12:1–15:13). But if "peace" is equated with "reconciliation," the context argues for the indicative reading, which states that believers are already at peace (reconciled) with God. The reading that witnesses to the subjunctive has a venerable history, to which the Vulgate (*habeamus*) witnesses. But, in my view, it misses the significance of what Paul is affirming here: the peace/reconciliation that results from justification.

A Grammatical Problem

The grammatical problem posed by the contraction *eph' hō* in 5:12 is more complicated and theologically significant, and it will be best to deal with it here before proceeding to an analysis of Paul's train of thought. The problem is whether *eph' hō* should be taken as a relative clause or as a conjunction. On the one hand, if it is taken as a relative clause, is *hō* to be construed as masculine or neuter, and to what does it refer? Does it refer to the one man, the world, or death? On the other hand, if *eph' hō* is taken as a conjunction, what is the meaning of the conjunction, and what does it say about the relationship between the sin of Adam and the sins that other humans commit? Does the phrase mean "because," as most commentators and translations suggest? If so, is there any relation between Adam's sin and the sins of his descendants? Or does it mean, as Fitzmyer (1993, 416–17) suggests, "as a result," thereby drawing a connection between the sin of Adam and those who follow him? The choices one makes here are crucial for the interpretation of this passage.

The Vulgate construes *eph' hō* as a relative clause, translating it *in quo* (in whom/what). Augustine, in an interpretation that has had a massive influence on later theology, understood the referent to *quo* to be "the one man," meaning Adam. Understood in this way, the sense of the relative clause is that *in Adam* all sinned because all of humanity was already present in Adam. With this reading, Augustine laid the biblical foundations for the doctrine of original sin. The personal pronoun (*hō* in Greek; *quo* in Latin), however, could also refer either to "death" (*thanatos*) or, if taken as neuter, to "the world" (*ton kosmon*), giving the following senses: "death spread to all so that all sinned in the sphere of death," or "death spread to all so that all sinned in the sphere of the world." Jewett (2007, 376) has recently championed the last of these interpretations. Although Augustine's interpretation offers a profound understanding of the text, grammatically it faces the greatest difficulty since the purported referent, "the one man," is so far removed. The other two suggestions, while grammatically possible, seem banal. What does Paul mean by saying that humans sinned *in the sphere of death*? Why is it necessary to add that they sinned *in the sphere of the world*?

Another line of interpretation is to construe *eph' hō* as a conjunction with the sense "because," or "inasmuch as." In this instance the phrase explains why death spread to all (*because* all sinned). While this line of interpretation has found support among most translations and commentators, it is not without difficulties. First, Fitzmyer (1993, 415) notes "that there are almost no certain instances in early Greek literature wherein *eph' hō* is used as the equivalent of *dioti*." Second, while this translation explains *why* death spread to all (because all sinned), it breaks the nexus between Adam's sin and the sin of his descendants that Paul clearly affirms in 5:18–19. Consequently, commentators often introduce this nexus in another way. For example, all sinned, but their sin was the result of the corrupt nature they inherited from Adam (Cranfield 1975, 275).

Given these difficulties, Fitzmyer's suggestion (though not widely accepted) is worth considering anew. Fitzmyer (1993, 416–17) proposes that *eph' hō* be construed as a consecutive conjunction such as *hōste*, with the meaning "with the result that," "so that." Thus the sense of 5:12 would be that death spread to all "with the result that" all sinned. Byrne (1996, 183) objects that this interpretation "makes little sense in the context: the nub of Paul's argument is that sin causes death, not vice versa." But if one reads this phrase as the conclusion to the *whole* of 5:12, as Bryan (2000, 129) suggests, the sense is that sin entered the world through Adam's sin. As a consequence of this sin, death spread to all human beings. The result of this is that all sinned as a consequence of Adam's sin, which introduced sin and death into the world. Fitzmyer's suggestion appears to make the best sense of what Paul says throughout 5:12–21.

Paul's Understanding of Adam

Just as Paul introduced a new understanding of Abraham so that he could present Abraham as the ancestor of all who believe in Christ, so here he presents a new understanding of Adam so that he can contrast the baleful effects of Adam's transgression with the salvific benefits of Christ's obedience. Arguing that Adam introduced sin as well as death into the world, Paul makes Adam the antitype of Christ, the one whose transgression inaugurated a sinful predicament that only Christ could reverse.

There were two tendencies in the expansion of the Adam tradition (Childs 1962, 43). On the one hand, since Adam was the first human whom God created, there was a tendency to exalt his person. For example, in a hymn in honor of Israel's ancestors (Sir. 44:1–50:21), Sirach affirms: "Shem and Seth and Enosh were honored, but above every other created living being was Adam" (49:16). Similarly, 2 *Enoch* (a writing from the late first century AD) records God as saying of Adam: "And on the earth I assigned him to be a second angel, honored and great and glorious. And I assigned him to be a king, to reign [on] the earth, [and] to have my wisdom. And there was nothing comparable to him on the earth, even among my creatures that exist" (30.11–12, OTP 1:152).

On the other hand, there was also a tendency to expand upon the sin of Adam, often placing the blame on Eve. For example, Sirach, who exalts Adam, says of Eve: "From a woman sin had its beginning, and because of her we all die" (25:24). Similarly, in the *Life of Adam and Eve* (a writing of the first century AD, the Greek text of which is also called *The Apocalypse of Moses*), Adam reprimands Eve: "Why have you wrought destruction among us and brought upon us great wrath, which is death gaining rule over all our race?" (*L.A.E.* 14.2–3, OTP 2:277). Adam then instructs his wife to gather their children and grandchildren and "tell them how we transgressed." Accordingly, Eve recounts the fall in great detail, saying at one point: "And at that very moment my eyes were opened and I knew that I was naked of the righteousness with which I had been clothed" (*L.A.E.* 20.1, OTP 2:281). She then recounts what Adam said to her at the fall: "O evil woman! Why have you wrought destruction among us? You have estranged me from the glory of God" (*L.A.E.* 21.6, OTP 2:281). These references to "righteousness" and "the glory of God" are reminiscent of Paul's language in Romans.

The author of *2 Baruch* laments, "O Adam, what did you do to all who were born after you? And what will be said of the first Eve who obeyed the serpent, so that this whole multitude is going to corruption?" (48.42, OTP 1:637). Similarly, *4 Ezra* (a writing of the late first century AD, which appears as 2 Esd. 3–14 in the OT Apocrypha) says of Adam: "And you laid upon him one commandment of

Figure 7. *Christ Liberating Adam and Eve and All of the Righteous from Limbo*, by Cristoforo de Predis (1440–86). Christ's leading humanity from death to life illustrates his role as the new Adam.

Allinari/Art Resource, NY

yours; but he transgressed it, and immediately you appointed death for him and for his descendants" (3.7, *OTP* 1:528). Drawing an analogy between Adam and his descendants, *4 Ezra* 3.21–22 notes: "For the first Adam, burdened with an evil heart, transgressed and was overcome, as were also all who were descended from him. Thus the disease became permanent; the law was in the people's heart along with the evil root, but what was good departed, and the evil remained" (*OTP* 1:529). *Second Baruch* 54.19, however, insists that Adam did not cause the sins of his descendants: "Adam is, therefore, not the cause, except only for himself, but each of us has become our own Adam" (*OTP* 1:640).

These examples show that Paul was not the only one reflecting on Adam's transgression and its effects on his descendants. In their attempt to understand the presence of sin and death in the world, others were also mining the Adam tradition. But whereas many of them placed the blame on Eve, Paul makes no mention of Eve in Romans (although he does in 2 Cor. 11:3; also see 1 Tim. 2:13). Moreover, while there is general agreement that Adam's transgression introduced death into the world, as Gen. 3:19 already noted, Paul focuses his attention on sin. Adam's transgression introduced sin into the world, and it was *through sin* that death spread to all.

Paul does not introduce Eve into the discussion of Rom. 5 because he wants to establish a contrast between two human beings: one who is the progenitor of the old humanity, and one who is the progenitor of a new humanity. Accordingly, he does not present Adam as a royal or angelic figure filled with all wisdom. Nor does he allude to Eve's role in Adam's transgression. For Paul, all history is summarized in the lives of two men: one disobedient, the other obedient. Thus, just as Paul identifies Abraham as the ancestor of all who believe in Christ, so he identifies Adam as the ancestor of a sinful humanity that only a new Adam can redeem.

The Structure of the Text

The chapter consists of two units. The first unit (5:1–11) employs the first-person plural, thereby uniting Paul and his audience; the second (5:12–21) gives way to the third-person singular because Paul wishes to show the universal implications of what God has done in Christ. Although it may appear that these two units are unrelated to each other, the manner in which the second unit begins, *dia touto* (for this reason), indicates that Paul sees an intimate connection between what he said in 5:1–11 and what he is about to say in 5:12–21: Christ's singular act of obedience described in 5:12–21 is the basis for the hope that Paul celebrates in 5:1–11.

Tracing the Train of Thought

In the first unit, Paul explains the new relationship that believers enjoy with God because they have been justified and reconciled to God (5:1–11). This unit

Romans 5:1–21 in the Rhetorical Flow

The letter opening (1:1–17)

Gentiles and Jews in the light of God's wrath (1:18–3:20)

Gentiles and Jews in the light of God's righteousness (3:21–4:25)

The experience of salvation in the light of God's righteousness (5:1–8:39)

▶**Transferred from the realm of sin to the realm of grace (5:1–21)**

    Humanity's new relationship to God as its ground for hope (5:1–11)

        The believer's new relationship with God (5:1–5)

            Justified and at peace with God (5:1–2)

            Able to boast (5:3–5)

        The assurance of God's love (5:6–8)

        The assurance of final salvation (5:9–11)

    The reason for this new relationship and hope (5:12–21)

        How sin and death entered the world (5:12–14)

        The difference between the trespass and the gift (5:15–17)

            Many died . . . a gracious gift for many (5:15)

            Condemnation . . . acquittal (5:16)

            The rule of death . . . the rule of the righteous (5:17)

        Adam's disobedience and Christ's obedience (5:18–19)

            One trespass . . . judgment . . . one righteous deed . . . righteousness (5:18)

            Many made sinners . . . many made righteous (5:19)

        Law, sin, and grace (5:20–21)

            Law entered . . . sin increased (5:20a)

            Sin increased . . . grace increased the more (5:20b)

            Sin ruled by death . . . grace rules through righteousness to life (5:21)

has three subunits. First, believers are at peace with God. This peace allows them to boast of their afflictions because they know that their hope for God's glory will not disappoint them (5:1–5). Second, believers can be assured of God's love, which was manifested in the death of Christ (5:6–8). Third, because believers have been justified and reconciled to God, they can be all the more confident that they will be saved from the coming wrath (5:9–11).

The second unit draws a comparison between Adam and Christ (5:12–21). In doing so, it prepares for the discussion of sin and law that Paul will take up in chapters 6–7. These verses explain the reason for the new relationship that believers enjoy with God: the obedience of "the one man," Christ, has countered the disobedience of "the one man," Adam. This unit also explains the deeper significance of Paul's statement in 3:9 that all are under the power of sin. The unit has four subunits. In the first, Paul begins a comparison but does not complete it (5:12–14). In the second, he describes the difference between the consequences of Adam's disobedience and Christ's obedience (5:15–17). In the third, he completes the comparison begun earlier (5:18–19). In the final subunit, Paul describes the relationship between sin, law, death, grace, righteousness, and life (5:20–21).

5:1–5. The first subunit summarizes the new relationship that believers enjoy with God, which enables them to boast of the hope they have for God's glory. This subunit consists of two parts. The first begins with a statement of this new relationship (5:1–2); the second expands upon the theme of boasting (5:3–5). The rhetorical effect of these verses is to establish a bond between Paul and the Romans that celebrates their new relationship with God.

Paul begins by summarizing the major themes that he developed in 3:21–4:25: **Therefore, since we have been justified on the basis of faith** (5:1a). But whereas the focus of 3:21–4:25 was on God's saving righteousness manifested in Jesus Christ, here it is on the result of that saving righteousness: the justification of the believer. Those who exhibit the kind of faith that Abraham manifested have been "justified" (*dikaiōthentes*) on the basis of their faith in Christ rather than on the basis of doing the works of the law. This justification, which is not the result of something they have done, means that the justified stand in a correct and proper relationship to God. They are no longer under the wrath of God, for God has graciously acquitted them. Because the justified stand in a positive relationship to God, they can affirm with Paul, **we are at peace with God** (5:1b). This peace is not merely an interior serenity (although this is not excluded) but the objective state of peace that follows after a period of long hostility is ended (Légasse 2002, 239). It is the reconciliation that Paul mentions in 5:10–11. Thus references to peace and reconciliation bracket the entire unit.

Klaus Haacker (2006, 126) notes that the concept of peace would have resonated with Paul's Roman audience since peace is precisely what the Roman Empire promised and provided for its citizens (Pax Romana). Paul, however, envisions another kind of peace that goes beyond this political concept. God has established peace with humanity by reconciling humanity to himself. This is why Paul begins his letters with a greeting of "grace and peace" (1:7), defines the kingdom of God in terms of "righteousness and peace" (14:17), and calls God "the God of peace" (16:20). Peace, which is reconciliation with God, is the immediate effect and experience of justification. The book of Isaiah draws a similar relation between peace and righteousness: "The effect of righteousness will be peace, and the result of righteousness, quietness and trust forever" (Isa. 32:17). This experience of peace, which the justified enjoy, comes **through our Lord Jesus Christ** (Rom. 5:1c), a phrase that begins and ends this unit (5:1, 11; note also the similar phrases "through him" in 5:2, 9, and "through the death of his Son" in 5:10).

Next, Paul specifies Christ's role as the mediator of God's salvific work. Christ is the one **through whom we even have access by faith to this grace in which we stand** (5:2a). This means that the justified stand in the sphere of God's "grace" or "favor" (*charis*) because Christ has given them "access" (*prosagōgēn*) to a realm or state of affairs that they could not otherwise attain (see Eph. 2:18; 3:12, which employ the same noun). The use of the perfect tense, *hestēkamen* (we stand), emphasizes that this is an ongoing experience of peace. Because believers stand in the sphere of God's favor, they can boast in their hope of what God is yet to accomplish for them. Thus Paul writes: **and boast in hope of the glory of God** (Rom. 5:2b). This glory (*doxa*) is God's own glory, which has already been bestowed upon the risen Christ and will be bestowed upon believers at the general resurrection of the dead, when they will be transformed according to the image of the risen Lord. In its rebellion against the Creator, humanity exchanged God's glory, the source of immortality, for the likeness of mortal images (1:23). And by sinning, all found themselves in need of God's grace. But because of God's redemptive work in Christ, the justified can now boast of the future, eschatological glory that God will bestow on them at the end of the ages (see 6:4; 8:18, 21).

Having spoken of boasting in God's glory, in 5:3–5 Paul develops the theme of boasting in another way: **Not only that, but we even boast in afflictions** (5:3a). By "afflictions" Paul means the troubles, trials, and distresses that beset believers precisely because they are believers. Paul has experienced such afflictions throughout his ministry, and he eventually developed a theological understanding of their role in the life of Christ-believers. This understanding of affliction is apparent in 2 Corinthians (1:4, 8; 2:4; 4:17; 6:4; 7:4; 8:2). Boasting in affliction, then, means that Christ-believers boast in the very afflictions that beset them as believers.

The human understanding of boasting in one's self, which Paul excludes because no one can boast before God (Rom. 3:27), gives way to a new kind of boasting that only believers comprehend: boasting in the sufferings that inevitably afflict those who live according to the gospel. But why would anyone boast in the things that highlight suffering and weakness? Paul answers this question by developing something akin to an ethical ladder, whereby each step of the ladder enables a person to progress higher in the ethical life: **knowing that affliction produces patient endurance, patient endurance produces character, and character produces hope** (5:3b–4). Those who endure their afflictions grow in patience, and the patience they learn from enduring their afflictions contributes to the growth of their character. It is the last step of the ladder ("and character produces hope"), however, that distinguishes Paul from the moral philosophers of his day (Wright 2002, 516–17). Instead of ending with "patient endurance produces character," Paul goes on to say that "character produces hope." The hope (*elpis*) that Paul has in view is the eschatological hope that he has already mentioned in 5:2 and will develop further in chapter 8 (see 8:20, 24). For Paul, afflictions are the birth pangs of a new age, which will be revealed at the resurrection of the dead. People who endure, then, will grow not only in character but in hope as well. What Paul writes in 2 Cor. 4:17 draws a similar relation between the present experience of affliction and the glory to come: "For this slight momentary affliction is preparing us for an eternal weight of glory beyond all measure."

The ordinary human experience of hope, however, is that it often ends in disappointment and embarrassment. Accordingly, Paul explains why the eschatological hope of the believer will not end this way: **And hope does not lead to disappointment, because God's own love has been poured into our hearts through the Holy Spirit that has been given to us** (5:5). The eschatological hope of those who believe differs from the hope of others because believers already experience something for which they hope: the love of God. Introducing the concept of "the love of God" (*hē agapē tou theou*) for the first time—which my translation ("God's own love") construes as a subjective genitive—Paul draws a relation between God's love (presumably for the justified) and the gift of the Holy Spirit. Without identifying the Spirit with God's own love, Paul views God's love as being poured in the heart of the believer "through" (*dia*) the mediation of the Spirit. Although Paul's precise meaning may not be clear, it is apparent that he draws a relation between the gift of the Spirit, which is the "first installment" or "pledge" (*arrabōn*) of the salvation that is yet to come (2 Cor. 1:22; 5:5; Eph. 1:14), and God's love. Those who possess this first installment experience God's love. This is why their eschatological hope will not disappoint them, for their hearts have already been transformed. Thus, whereas earlier Paul spoke of the human heart as overpowered by sin (Rom. 1:21, 24; 2:5), now he speaks of it as being filled with God's own love.

5:6–8. Having assured his audience that their eschatological hope will not disappoint them because God's love has been poured into their hearts, in 5:6–8 Paul explains why Christ-believers can be so confident of this love. This subunit has three movements. First, Paul reminds the Romans of what they already know: that Christ died for them (5:6). Second, he explains the extraordinary nature of this love (5:7). Finally, he equates Christ's death for them with God's love for them (5:8).

The opening verse summarizes the essence of the gospel that Paul preaches: **For while we were still weak, at the right time, Christ died on behalf of the ungodly** (5:6). Although "at the right time" can be taken with what precedes, giving the sense that the right time was when we were weak (D. Moo 1996, 307), it can also be taken with what follows, giving the meaning that Christ died at the right moment, the time appointed by God (Cranfield 1975, 264). Given Paul's statement in Gal. 4:4 about the fullness of time, this seems the better choice. Paul highlights the significance of Christ's death in two other ways. First, humanity was weak and unable to do anything for itself. Second, Christ died "for the ungodly" (*hyper asebōn*). In writing this, Paul draws a relation between God, who justifies the ungodly (Rom. 4:5), and Christ, who died for the ungodly.

To emphasize the significance of Christ's death for the ungodly, Paul reminds his audience how difficult it is to die for one who is *dikaios*: **One will hardly die for the sake of a righteous person** (5:7a). Then, as if to correct himself, he adds: **for a truly good person perhaps someone might dare die** (5:7b). Commentators have not been able to explain the distinction that Paul makes here between a good and a righteous person. This suggests to me that this distinction is primarily for rhetorical effect.

Having highlighted the significance of Christ's death as a death for the ungodly, Paul relates the death of Christ to God's love, replacing "the ungodly" with "sinners": **But God demonstrated his own love for us, because while we were still sinners, Christ died for us** (5:8). It is now apparent that the death of Christ was a demonstration of God's love "for us," whom Paul unequivocally identifies as "the ungodly" and "sinners." Those who are justified were once among the ungodly because they were sinners. But now they can be confident of their eschatological hope because it is grounded in the love of God that God demonstrated in and through the death of Christ.

5:9–11. Having assured the Roman Christ-believers that they can be confident of God's love, in 5:9–11 Paul returns to the theme of eschatological hope, which he has introduced in 5:1–5, to assure them that they can also be confident of the final salvation that God has in store for them. Paul argues from the greater to the lesser, employing a type of argumentation that would have been familiar to Jewish and Gentile audiences. His train of thought proceeds in three steps. In the first two, he employs two arguments that move from the lesser to the greater, the first focusing on justification, the second on reconciliation. Then in 5:11, repeating the same phrase he employed in 5:3 ("not only that," *ou monon de*), he resumes the theme of boasting that he developed in 5:3–5. But whereas he spoke of boasting in affliction in those verses, in 5:11 he talks of boasting in God through the Lord Jesus Christ, through whom believers have received reconciliation. These verses are structured in the following way:

> Having been *justified* by his blood,
> > *how much more* will we be saved from the wrath.
> Having been *reconciled* through the death of his Son,
> > *how much more* will we be saved by his life.
> *Not only that*,
> > we boast in God
> > > through our Lord Jesus Christ
> > > > through whom we have received *reconciliation*.

First, Paul draws a conclusion from what he has just said: **Therefore, all the more, now that we have been justified by his blood, will we be saved through him from the wrath** (5:9). Having just argued that God manifested his love in Christ's death, Paul returns to the language of justification with which he began this unit (5:1) to show that since believers are now justified by Christ's blood, it is all the more certain that they will be saved "from the wrath," an unmistakable allusion to Paul's topic sentence in 1:18. The salvation to which Paul refers will occur at the general resurrection of the dead, when creation will be renewed, a topic that Paul will develop toward the end of chapter 8. Consequently, while believers are *already* justified and experience the peace that justification brings, they are *not yet* saved.

Making use of the same kind of argument he employed in 5:9, Paul writes: **For if, when we were enemies, we were reconciled to God through the death of his Son, how much more, since we have been reconciled, will we be saved by his life** (5:10). But the argument here is stronger since Paul highlights the former condition of the justified. Previous to their reconciliation with God, they were God's enemies because humanity had rebelled against the Creator (see Paul's use of "God-haters" in the list of 1:29–31). Since Paul speaks of God's wrath, many commentators think that this enmity "includes God's hostility toward human beings as well as human beings' hostility toward God" (D. Moo 1996, 312), but Paul's description of God's love suggests that the hostility Paul has in view is humanity's hostility toward the Creator (Légasse 2002, 346).

Verse 10 alters 5:9 in a number of ways. The phrase "through the death of his Son" replaces "by his blood," and the phrase "will we be saved by his life" replaces "will we be saved from the wrath." The most important change, however, is Paul's use of "reconciliation" rather than "justification." This reconciliation is the "peace with God" to which Paul has referred in 5:1. Despite these changes, the point of the two verses is similar: if God dealt graciously with humanity when it was weak, it is all the more certain that God will deal more graciously with humanity now that it stands in God's grace. In the case of 5:10, this is expressed in this way: if God reconciled those who were his enemies, it is all the more certain that God will save those who have been reconciled. As in 5:9, Paul maintains the "already–not yet" pattern. Believers are *already* reconciled, but they are *not yet* saved. They will only be saved "by his life," that is, by the life of the risen Lord, to whom they will be conformed at the general resurrection of the dead.

Having assured the justified and reconciled that they can be utterly confident of their eschatological hope, Paul returns to the theme of boasting: **Not only that, we even boast in God, through our Lord Jesus Christ, through whom we have now received this reconciliation** (5:11). Throughout this letter, Paul has referred to boasting: the Jewish person boasts in the law (2:17, 23), there is no room for boasting before God (3:27), not even Abraham has a boast before God (4:1–2), and believers boast in their hope of God's glory (5:2) and even in their affliction (5:3). But now he speaks of boasting in God. Yet, instead of simply saying "boasting in God," he adds "through our Lord Jesus Christ." He then qualifies this by explaining, "through whom we have now received this reconciliation." In this way, Paul develops another theme that has appeared throughout this unit: Christ's role as the agent of God's salvific work. Christ-believers do not simply boast in God any more than they simply believe in God; they boast in God *through Jesus Christ*, and they believe in the God *who raised him from the dead*.

Paul's train of thought in 5:1–11 can be summarized in this way: The justified and reconciled are already at peace with God, fully confident of God's love for them in Christ. Because of their new relationship with God, they can boast of their afflictions and be confident of the final salvation that God has prepared for them.

5:12–14. In 5:12–21 Paul sets aside the first-person plural and returns to the third-person singular in order to draw a comparison between the effects of Adam's transgression and Christ's obedience. Despite this shift in tone, the manner in which he begins, **For this reason** (5:12a), indicates that there is a profound relationship between what Paul has just said (5:1–11) and what he is about to say (5:12–21). The connection, however, is not what we might expect. Paul is not implying that the Adam-Christ comparison is the result of what he has just said. Rather, it is *the ground* for what he has said. In other words, it is because Christ's obedience has countered Adam's transgression that believers can boast in God, through Jesus Christ, through whom they have received reconciliation (5:11). It is not without reason that Joseph Fitzmyer (1993, 406) says, "This paragraph constitutes the second most important passage in the letter, the first being 3:21–26," and Douglas Moo (1996, 314) writes that it "rivals 3:21–26 for theological importance."

Paul's purpose in this subunit is to establish this comparison between Christ and Adam (5:12–14). But instead of completing the comparison he begins in 5:12, he introduces an excursus in 5:13–14 to explain the status of sin and death in the period between Adam and Moses, when there was no law. Then, lest his Adam-Christ comparison be misunderstood, he provides a series of qualifications in 5:15–17 to show that there is no equivalence between the results of Adam's transgression and the effects of Christ's obedience. It is only in 5:18 that Paul completes the comparison begun in 5:12. But aware that his audience may have forgotten the initial comparison begun several verses earlier, he starts anew. The text reads more clearly, then, if one moves from 5:12 to 5:18–21.

Paul's initial statement of the comparison has several elements: **just as sin entered the world through one man, and through sin death, and so death spread to all with the result that all sinned** (5:12b). First, Paul affirms that sin entered the world through one man, whom he will identify as Adam. Second, he says that it was *through* sin that death also entered the world. Third, he states that death then spread to all. Finally, he concludes that the result of this (*eph' hō*; see the discussion above) was that all sinned. This verse manifests a chiastic pattern: sin, death, death, sin:

> *Sin* entered the world through one man.
> *Death* entered the world through sin.
> *Death* spread to all.
> Consequently, all *sinned*.

Several points should be noted here. First, Paul is drawing from the story of Gen. 2–3, which recounts the creation and transgression of Adam and Eve. But he is interested only in Adam, because he wants to compare Adam and Christ. Thus he speaks of the "one man" or "the one" several times in 5:12–21, sometimes in reference to Adam, sometimes in reference to Christ. Second, he assumes that Adam was a historical figure. Third, he presents "sin" and "death" as powers or forces that have invaded the world because of Adam's transgression. Thus these verses explain (a) what Paul meant when he wrote that all are under the power of sin (3:9) and (b) why he speaks of death as "ruling." Sin and death are cosmic forces, actors on the stage of the world, that have power and control over those who live in the world. Fourth, if the translation of *eph' hō* proposed here is correct, Paul sees a double causality for the woeful situation in which humanity finds itself: (a) Adam introduced sin and death into the world, and the result of what he did is that all sinned; (b) in addition to Adam's transgression, all of his descendants sinned as well. Paul does not explain the precise relation between Adam's transgression and the sins of his descendants. But it is clear from what Paul writes in 5:18–19 that there is a connection.

Having said that "all sinned" (5:12), Paul must explain how human beings could sin in the period between Adam and Moses since the Mosaic law had not yet been promulgated. Accordingly, Paul writes: **For up to the period of the law, sin was in the world, but sin was not reckoned as such, there being no law** (5:13). Here Paul makes two points. First, the power of sin, which Adam unleashed by his transgression, was already in the world in the period before the giving of the law at Sinai. Second, although humans sinned, their sins were not reckoned as sins against the Mosaic law since that law did not yet exist. Nonetheless, what they did was sinful.

Next, Paul turns to the status of death during this period: **But death ruled in the period from Adam to Moses even over those who did not sin in the same manner as the trespass of Adam, who is the type of the one who was to come** (5:14). Although the law had not yet been given in the period before Moses, death (understood as a power or force) ruled over humanity. More than the physical destruction of life, death is a power that separates humanity from God. This is why Paul says that it "ruled." For its part, humanity did sin, but not in the same way that Adam did (by transgressing a specific commandment) since the law had not yet been given. But humanity did rebel against the Creator, as Paul's discussion in 1:18–32 confirms. This is why death ruled over humanity. Paul's final remark, that Adam is the type of the one who is to come, sets the stage for the next movement in his argument.

5:15–17. Paul has concluded the previous subunit with the remark that Adam is "the type of the one who was to come." But since "type" (*typos*) suggests that something is the pattern or example of what will follow, Paul needs to qualify the comparison he wants to make between Adam and Christ. Therefore, before completing the comparison begun in 5:12 and already interrupted by 5:13–14, he introduces a series of qualifications lest his audience mistakenly think that Adam foreshadowed Christ by providing a model for what Christ did. To put it paradoxically, before comparing Adam and Christ, Paul must show that there is no real comparison between these two figures. What follows is one of the most confusing passages in Scripture. For even though Paul has carefully structured these verses, the comparisons he makes within them are not symmetrical. Although this may be the result of poor writing on Paul's part, it may also be the result of Paul's rhetorical strategy, which shows, by these nonsymmetrical comparisons, that there is no real comparison between Adam and Christ. If Adam is the *typos* of Christ, it is only in an inadequate way. These verses are structured in this way:

> *But it is not a case of*, "as the trespass, so the gift."
>> By the trespass of the one man many died,
>>> *how much more*
>> the gracious gift by the one man has abounded for the many (5:15).
> *But it is not a case of*, "as the one man's sin, so the gift."
>> A verdict occasioned by one man sinning led to condemnation;
>> a gift occasioned by many trespasses led to acquittal (5:16).
>> By the trespass of the one man death ruled through the one man,
>>> *how much more*
>> those who receive the gift will rule in life through the one man (5:17).

Two formulas structure these verses. First, Paul introduces 5:15, 16 with the phrase "but it is not a case of," which indicates that what he is about to say is not an ordinary comparison. Second, in 5:15 and 17 Paul employs the formula "how much more" to highlight the superiority of Christ and the effects of his obedience compared to Adam and the results of his disobedience.

The first and most important distinction Paul makes is that there is no real correspondence between the "trespass" (*paraptōma*) of Adam and the "gift" (*charisma*) that results from Christ's obedience. For whereas Adam's trespass introduced sin into the world and death spread to all (5:12), God's "grace" (*charis*) overflowed to all for the sake of life. Thus Paul writes: **But it is not a case of "as the trespass so even the gift." For if by the trespass of the one man the many died, how much more has the grace of God and the gracious gift of the one man, Jesus Christ, abounded for the many** (5:15). While we would have expected Paul to compare Adam's trespass and Christ's obedience, he compares Adam's trespass with the gift of God.

Though lacking symmetry, the comparison makes its point: there is no comparison.

In his second comparison, Paul affirms that there is no comparison between the sinning of the one man and the gift of the other: **And it is not a case of "as through one man's sinning so the gift." For a verdict occasioned by one man sinning led to condemnation, but the gift occasioned by many trespasses led to acquittal** (5:16). Once more, the comparison lacks symmetry. For instead of comparing the sin of Adam and the obedience of Christ, Paul compares the sin of Adam and the gift of Christ. In effect, Paul makes the same comparison twice: the trespass and the gift (5:15), one man's sin and the gift (5:16). But here Paul contrasts the difference between the two more sharply. Whereas the sin of the one man brought condemnation, the gift of the other man—which was occasioned by many transgressions in addition to Adam's sin—led to acquittal. In effect, Paul affirms the surpassing greatness of Christ's gift, which was a response not only to Adam's sin but also to the sins of his descendants.

In his third comparison, Paul compares the result of the trespass with what *will* eventually result from the gift: **For if by the trespass of the one man death ruled through the one man, how much more will those who receive the superabundance of grace and the gift of righteousness rule in life through the one man, Jesus Christ** (5:17). Returning to the theme of the reign of death, which he first mentioned in 5:14, Paul contrasts the reign of death that Adam's trespass inaugurated with the future reign of those who have received the gift of righteousness. Although one might have expected Paul to compare the rule of death with the rule of life, he compares the rule that the one man inaugurated with the future rule of the righteous. All three comparisons lack symmetry, but the point they make is clear: there is no real comparison between Adam and Christ. Having established this, Paul is ready to complete the comparison he began in 5:12, confident that it will not be misunderstood to mean that Adam and Christ are similar figures.

5:18–19. After so many qualifications, first in 5:13–14 and then in 5:15–17, Paul is ready to complete the comparison he began in 5:12. But aware that his audience may have forgotten how that comparison began, he reformulates the beginning of the comparison in a new way. Instead of repeating what he said earlier, "just as sin entered the world through one man," and then concluding "so life entered the world through one man," he writes, **So then, just as through one trespass there was judgment for all, so through one righteous deed there is righteousness that brings life for all** (5:18). This new comparison exhibits the kind of symmetry that the comparisons of 5:15–17 lack:

one trespass	judgment for all
one righteous deed	righteousness that brings life for all

The righteous deed, of course, refers to Christ's faithful obedience to God, which found its fulfillment at the cross. Just as Adam's trespass brought judgment for all because it introduced sin and death into the world, so Christ's "righteous deed" (*dikaiōmatos*) led "to righteousness that brings life" (*eis dikaiōsin zōēs*). For Paul, righteousness is not merely a legal status before God; it is entry into the eternal life with God that Adam forfeited.

Having completed this comparison, Paul introduces a second that builds upon what he has just written: **For just as through the disobedience of the one man many were made sinners, so through the obedience of the one man many will be made righteous** (5:19). Once more, the comparison exhibits the symmetry lacking in the comparisons of 5:15–17:

the disobedience of the one man	many made sinners
the obedience of the one man	many made righteous

The most striking aspect of both comparisons is the nexus Paul draws between the transgression and disobedience of Adam and its effects on the one hand, and the righteous deed and obedience of Christ and its effects on the other. In both instances, the deed of one man affects the many. Adam's disobedience makes his descendants sinners, and Christ's righteous deed makes people righteous. Consequently, even if one translates *eph' hō* in 5:12 as "because" and then insists that there is no connection between the transgression of Adam and the sins of his descendants, one must still deal with these verses. Although he never explains *how* Adam's sin makes all sinners, he suggests that Adam's transgression had a baleful effect on his descendants. In light of Christ's obedience, which has made the many righteous, Paul concludes that Adam's transgression made the many sinners.

5:20–21. Having completed his comparison of Adam and Christ, Paul returns to the theme of the law that he introduced in 5:14–15, where he noted that sin was in the world and that death ruled in the period from Adam to the giving of the law. In doing so, Paul provides his Roman audience with a further understanding of the Mosaic law and its role in God's salvific plan. Paul has already said (a) that no one will be justified before God on the basis of doing the works of the law, for through the law comes an awareness of sin (3:20), and (b) that the law effects wrath since there is no transgression where there is no law (4:15). Now he affirms that **the law entered in with the result that wrongdoing increased** (5:20a). In other words, the appearance of the law made God's will known, and for the first time, people violated specific commandments of God's law, just as Adam did. Thus sin increased. But the increase of sin only led to an increase of God's grace, and so Paul writes, **but where sin increased, grace increased all the more** (5:20b). This superabundance of grace, to which Paul refers, is the appearance of the eschatological Adam, the Christ.

Finally, Paul employs a purpose clause to explain that God countered this increase of sin with a superabundance of grace in order that the rule of sin might be replaced by the rule of grace: **in order that just as sin ruled by the agency of death, so grace might rule through righteousness that leads to eternal life through Jesus Christ our Lord** (5:21). In the period before Christ, sin ruled over humanity by means of death, which prevented humanity from standing in God's presence. But in the period of Christ, grace rules through the power of righteousness, which leads to eternal life through Jesus Christ, the agent of God's salvific plan. This relationship of law, sin, and grace can be summarized as follows: The law results in an increase of sin insofar as people explicitly violate God's commandments. As a result of this, sin rules over sinful humanity, employing death to enforce its rule. But just as the law paradoxically leads to an increase of sin, sin paradoxically leads to an increase of grace that rules over redeemed humanity, employing righteousness to lead people to life. This startlingly new understanding of law, sin, and grace introduces the major themes with which Paul will deal in chapters 6–7.

Theological Issues

Of the many theological issues that Rom. 5 raises, two are especially important. The first is Paul's soteriology, expressions of which occur throughout this chapter; the second is the doctrine of original sin, which later theology developed in light of Paul's Adam-Christ comparison.

Paul's Soteriology

In chapter 5 Paul employs four concepts to explain the benefits of Christ's redemptive work: justification, reconciliation, salvation, and eternal life. By justification, Paul means that God has acquitted humanity of its sinfulness on the basis of Christ's righteous act of obedience on the cross (5:18). Thus Paul insists that Christ-believers are justified on the basis of faith (5:1) by the blood of Christ (5:9), that is, by Christ's death. Although justification is a forensic concept, Paul does not view it as a fiction, as if God declares that the sinner is innocent without any real change in the status of the sinner. In 5:19 Paul affirms that just as many were made sinners by Adam's disobedience, so also many were made righteous through Christ's obedience. Thus the starting point of Paul's soteriology is justification: God's declaration that Christ-believers are truly righteous because they now stand in the correct and proper relationship to God.

Paul's understanding of reconciliation is closely related to his teaching on justification, as is apparent from the way in which he speaks of the relationship between justification and reconciliation on the one hand and salvation on the other (5:9–10). But whereas justification is a forensic concept, reconciliation is a social concept, which Paul employs to describe the restoration of a broken relationship in which two parties are at enmity with each other because of something that one or the other has done. But whereas in human relationships either party can initiate the process of reconciliation, this is not so in the relationship between God and humanity. Humanity cannot reconcile itself to God, nor does God need to be reconciled to humanity. Rather, it is humanity that needs to be reconciled to God, but it is only God who can effect this reconciliation. This is precisely what God does in and through Christ's death. Having been justified, believers now stand in the correct and proper relationship to God. Because God acquitted them, they enjoy a new relationship with God that Paul describes as peace and reconciliation (5:1, 11). God, then, has effected what humanity was powerless to do: God has reconciled humanity to himself. This concept of reconciliation is also found in 2 Cor. 5:15–21, where Paul employs the metaphor of a new creation to clarify the effects of reconciliation. Colossians and Ephesians develop the concept in still other ways, describing the cosmic reconciliation that Christ has effected (Col. 1:15–20) and the new humanity that this reconciliation has inaugurated in the church, which is the cosmic body of Christ, the place where the hostility between Jew and Gentile has been overcome (Eph. 2:11–22). Paul's understanding of reconciliation, then, complements and fills out his understanding of justification.

Justification and reconciliation, however, are not the whole of Paul's soteriology. For even though believers are justified and reconciled, they are not yet saved, as is evident from what Paul writes in Rom. 5:9–10. To be sure, Paul can affirm that "we were saved in hope" (8:24). But he does not say that believers are saved (although the expression does occur in Eph. 2:8). The justified will not experience the fullness of salvation until they have been raised from the dead and share the fullness of Christ's resurrection life. Thus the fourth soteriological concept of this chapter—eternal life—is closely related to the third.

For Paul, salvation is eternal life, the reversal of the death that Adam's sin introduced into the world. As Paul sees the human situation in the light of Christ, death began its rule over humanity through Adam's transgression (5:17a), and sin ruled over humanity by means of death (5:21a). But because of Christ's singular act of obedience, life has come to all (5:18b), and God's grace reigns through righteousness, which leads to eternal life (5:21b). While believers already experience something of eternal life inasmuch as they are justified and reconciled, they will not enjoy the fullness of life until they have been raised from the dead.

The soteriology of Rom. 5 can be summarized in this way: Justified and made righteous, believers are reconciled and at peace with God. Consequently, they can hope for the fullness of salvation, which is the eternal life that the resurrection of the dead brings.

Original Sin

Paul's Adam-Christ comparison had an immense impact on later theology, which employed this text to develop the doctrine of original sin. Prior to Paul, however, Adam and his trespass played a surprisingly minor role in Scripture, with only the apocryphal/deuterocanonical books of Wisdom and Sirach making any reference to what later theology would call "the fall." But even in these works, there is no attempt to develop a comprehensive understanding of the fall to account for the human predicament. For Wisdom and Sirach, human beings are free to choose what is good or evil, and the choices they make determine their destiny. Regarding "the fall," the book of Wisdom says that God created humanity for incorruption and that death entered the world "through the devil's envy" (2:23–24) rather than through Adam's sin. When it does mention Adam's transgression, the book of Wisdom notes that wisdom delivered him from this transgression (10:1–2). For its part, Sirach attributes the beginning of sin to Eve rather than to Adam, but it does not draw a nexus between her sin and the sin of her descendants (25:24).

The Primeval History (Gen. 1–11) describes the progressive deterioration of the human community that followed the transgression of Adam and Eve, but it does not explicitly link this deterioration to their sin. When God sees how corrupt humanity has become, God determines to destroy all flesh and inaugurate a new beginning with righteous Noah and his family. Then, after the flood, God promises, "I will never again curse the ground, *because of humankind, for the inclination of the human heart is evil from youth*" (Gen. 8:21, emphasis added). Despite this negative view of humanity, Israel's sacred writings did not view the transgression of Adam and Eve as a fall from grace that resulted in the corruption of human nature. While Israel's sacred writers acknowledged the presence of sin, they remained confident that Israel could do what the Lord required. Paul's understanding of Adam's trespass and its consequences, then, is unique in some ways.

To appreciate how Paul came to his understanding of Adam and the human condition, it is helpful to recall the Adam-Christ comparison he establishes in 1 Cor. 15. Having encountered the risen Lord, Paul was fully convinced that the resurrection of the dead had already begun in God's Son. Consequently, he concludes that "since death came through a human being, the resurrection of the dead has also come through a human being; for as all die in Adam, so all will be made alive in Christ" (15:21–22). The starting point for Paul's Adam-Christ comparison in 1 Cor. 15 is Christ's resurrection. On the basis of that event, to which he can testify, Paul now understands that Christ is the perfect counterpoint to Adam: for whereas one man introduced death into the world (Gen. 2:17; 3:19), the other introduced life. But when Paul takes up this comparison in Romans, the starting point for the comparison becomes the obedience of Christ, manifested in his death, which becomes the counterpoint to Adam's disobedience, which introduced sin and death into the world. It is in light of Christ's death and resurrection, then, that Paul comes to a new understanding of Adam's transgression as an act of disobedience that affected not only Adam but his descendants as well.

Unlike later theology, Paul does not try to explain how the effects of Adam's transgression were transmitted to his descendants, but there is no doubt that he sees a connection between the trespass of Adam, whom Paul views as a historical individual, and the sins of his descendants. For even if one sets aside the disputed text of 5:12, it is apparent from what Paul says in 5:18–19 that Adam's transgression affected his progeny, bringing judgment upon them and constituting them as sinners in God's sight. Why Paul reasons in this way can only be understood in light of Christ: for if the risen Christ is the progenitor of a new humanity destined for life, then Adam must have been the progenitor of a sinful humanity destined for death. It is only because he begins with Christ's death and resurrection, then, that Paul makes the claims that he does about Christ.

Paul's purpose in Rom. 5 is not to develop a doctrine of "original sin" but to contrast the obedience of Christ with the disobedience of Adam in order to highlight the significance of Christ's saving death. The church's teaching on original sin, especially as developed by Augustine, was forged in the crucible of its debates with Pelagianism, "which denied the necessity of grace . . . and the reality of original sin" (Neuner and Dupuis 1996, 183). Consequently, the doctrine of original sin as developed by later theology and church teaching focused on topics that Paul did not develop, such as the original state of Adam and Eve and how Adam's sin was transmitted to his descendants. Nonetheless, that doctrine is deeply rooted in Paul's theology, providing the church with a fuller reading, a *sensus plenior*, of Rom. 5. There is something radically amiss in the human situation that can be remedied only when people are transferred from the realm of Adam to the realm of Christ. So long as they remain "in Adam," they are infected by and subject to the power of his sin. Only when they are "in Christ" are they free from the power of sin, which introduced death into the world.

Romans 6:1–23

No Longer Slaves of Sin and Death

Introductory Matters

Chapter 6 marks a shift in the tone and nature of Paul's discourse. Whereas in 5:12–21 he employed the impersonal third person to compare the historical consequences of Adam's and Christ's deeds, in chapter 6 he returns to the more inclusive first-person plural that he used in 5:1–11 to draw out the moral implications of Christ's death for the believer. In doing so, the apostle moves from the discourse of theological history in chapter 5 to the more personal and practical discourse of the life of the Christ-believer in chapter 6 (Haacker 2006, 140). Elements of the diatribe style, so prominent in the earlier parts of the letter, reappear in 6:1 and 6:15 as Paul raises objections to his teaching in order to persuade his listeners that, far from undermining their moral life, his gospel enables them to live a life that accords with the demands of God's righteousness.

To show the relation between the objective reality of what Christ has done and how those who believe in him must live, Paul reminds the Romans of their incorporation into Christ's death through their baptism into his death. Although commentators note "that baptism is not the subject of the passage" (Dunn 1988, 1:308), this chapter, particularly 6:1–11, has become the locus classicus for Paul's baptismal theology. At this point, it is sufficient to note that the apostle assumes that the members of his audience have been baptized,

---

Romans 6:1–23 in the Rhetorical Flow

The letter opening (1:1–17)

Gentiles and Jews in the light of God's wrath (1:18–3:20)

Gentiles and Jews in the light of God's righteousness (3:21–4:25)

The experience of salvation in the light of God's righteousness (5:1–8:39)

   Transferred from the realm of sin to the realm of God's grace (5:1–21)

▶**No longer slaves of sin and death (6:1–23)**

     Why believers should not remain in sin (6:1–14)

       A first objection (6:1)

       Paul's response (6:2–14)

         An initial response (6:2)

         A detailed response (6:3–11)

           The implications of baptism into Christ (6:3–4)

           The implications of union with Christ's death (6:5–7)

           The implications of Christ's death (6:8–11)

         An exhortation not to subject oneself to sin (6:12–14)

           Negative imperative (6:12)

           Negative imperative (6:13)

           Why sin will not rule over the believer (6:14)

    A change of allegiance from sin to righteousness (6:15–23)

       A second objection (6:15)

       Paul's response (6:16–18)

         A rhetorical question regarding obedience (6:16)

         Thanksgiving for their change of behavior (6:17)

         The outcome of freedom from sin (6:18)

       An exhortation to give themselves to righteousness (6:19–23)

         Presenting oneself to a new master (6:19)

         A reminder of their former status (6:20)

         A question regarding the benefit of their former allegiance (6:21)

         A reminder of their new status (6:22)

         Supporting reason: wages of sin versus the free gift of God (6:23)

---

and so they will understand and accept the relation he draws between their baptism and their participation in Christ's death.

Although an earlier generation nurtured in a history-of-religions approach to biblical studies was more inclined to relate the rite of Christian baptism to the initiatory rites of the mystery religions, contemporary scholarship argues for the distinctive nature of Christian baptism, which is rooted in the unrepeatable historical act of Jesus's death (G. Wagner 1967; Wedderburn 1983). There is less agreement, however, about how innovative or traditional Paul's baptismal theology is. Some maintain that these remarks about baptism belong "to the common primitive Christian teaching" (Cranfield 1975, 300); others urge that Paul should be credited with "the interpretation of baptism in terms of dying (and rising) with Christ" (Schnackenburg 1964, 33).

Just as Paul could presuppose that his audience was familiar with baptism, so he could assume it was familiar with the metaphor of slavery that controls 6:15–23. Robert Jewett (2007, 416) notes that "somewhere between one- and two-thirds of the population were either slaves or former slaves, and that among the significant avenues of replenishing the supply of slaves . . . were the enslavement of debtors and voluntary selling of oneself as a slave." Since many of the Roman Christians were or had been slaves, as the list of names in chapter 16 reveals, Paul's use of slavery as a metaphor for the moral life would have had a powerful impact on his audience.

This chapter, in which Paul takes up the topic of the moral life for the first time, begins with a response to a problem that he causes for himself when he writes, "Where sin increased, grace increased all the more" (5:20b), thereby occasioning the question of 6:1. Paul frequently employs this technique of questioning statements he has made in order to move the discussion forward. Thus the statement of 6:14a evokes the question of 6:15, the statement of 7:6 raises the question of 7:7, and the question of 7:11 leads to the question of 7:13—each question introducing a new discussion.

Tracing the Train of Thought

This chapter consists of two units (6:1–14 and 6:15–23), each beginning with an objection that Paul raises to something he has just said. His first response occurs in 6:2–11 and his second in 6:16–18. After each response, he exhorts his listeners to act in a way that corresponds to his response (6:12–14, 19–23). Thus each unit has three parts: objection, response, exhortation.

The first unit begins with an objection (6:1) that arises from what Paul said in 5:20b: where sin increased, grace increased all the more. Reminding the Romans of their baptism into Christ, he explains that they should not persist in sin, since they have died to sin through their baptismal union with Christ (6:2–11). Paul's response has two parts: an initial response in 6:2 and a detailed response in 6:3–11, which consists of three subunits. In the first he draws out the implication of baptism as an entrance into Christ's death (6:3–4). In the second he draws out the implications of their union with Christ (6:5–7), and in the third he considers the implications of Christ's death for them (6:8–11). Paul then exhorts his audience not to let sin rule over their lives or to present themselves as slaves to sin, because they are no longer under the regime of sin but under the regime of grace (6:12–14).

Paul's statement that the believer is no longer under the law but under grace (6:14b) leads to a second objection, which suggests that believers should continue to sin since they are not under the law (6:15). In response to this, he explains that believers should not sin, since they are no longer slaves of sin but slaves of righteousness (6:16–18). As in the first unit, an exhortation follows this explanation. As believers formerly gave themselves to sin, so they should now give themselves to righteousness (6:19–23).

6:1–14. In light of what he has just written in 5:20b ("where sin increased, grace increased all the more"), Paul raises an objection to his gospel: **Then what shall we say? Shall we remain in sin so that grace may increase?** (6:1). The form of the question employed here, "Then what shall we say?" (*ti oun eroumen*), occurs frequently in Romans (3:5; 4:1; 7:7; 8:31; 9:14, 30), often posing an objection to some aspect of Paul's gospel. In this instance it introduces an objection similar to the one in 3:8, "And why not say—as we are slandered and as some say we say—'Let us do evil in order that good may come of it?' " Both objections impugn Paul's gospel of grace by insinuating that he preaches that God's gracious favor does not require believers to live in a morally upright way. The objection suggests that if, as Paul claims, God has countered Adam's sin with the superabundant grace of Christ, then Christ-believers should remain in the realm of sin since the logic of Paul's gospel appears to imply that sinning will lead to more grace.

As he often does when he responds to an objection that perverts his gospel, Paul replies, **Of course not!** (6:2a). He then answers the objection with a question that outlines the fundamental reason why Christ-believers should not remain in the realm of sin: **How shall we who have died to sin continue to live in it?** (6:2b). Here Paul is not simply talking about sinning (although that is included) but about remaining in and submitting oneself to the dominion of sin, which he personifies as a cosmic power that Adam released into the world by his transgression. If Christ-believers have died to that power, they can no longer remain in it. For all practical purposes they are dead to sin. But what does it mean to say that believers have died to sin? Paul provides a threefold answer in 6:3–11.

First, Paul draws from the experience of baptism that he and the Romans share in order to explain how they have died to sin through their baptism. This subunit begins with a question implying that they know (or should know) the significance of their baptism: **Or are you ignorant of the fact that we who have been baptized into Christ Jesus have been baptized into his death?** (6:3). Although some commentators argue that "baptized into Christ" is equivalent to "baptized into the name of Christ/Christ Jesus" (Cranfield 1975, 301), the parallelism that Paul establishes between "being baptized into Christ Jesus" and "baptized into his death" suggests that he is employing this expression in another way. Drawing from the church's kerygma, which proclaims that Christ died, was buried, and was raised on the third day (1 Cor. 15:3b–4), Paul introduces his distinctive understanding of baptism as the means by which believers enter into the mystery of Christ's death. To understand why and how Paul can make such a statement, it is important to recall what he writes to the Corinthians: "we are convinced that one has died for all; *therefore all have died*" (2 Cor. 5:14, emphasis added). In Paul's view, Christ's death was not the death of just another individual; it was the death of the eschatological Adam, who represented the whole of humanity in his death. Consequently when Christ died, humanity died with him. In light of this understanding of Christ's death as a representative death for all, Paul affirms that those who have been baptized into Christ have been baptized into his death. Thus the baptized belong to the new creation that Christ, the eschatological Adam, inaugurated by his saving death and resurrection (2 Cor. 5:17). Incorporated into Christ by their baptism, they have entered into his saving death.

Taking his cue from the structure of the church's kerygma, Paul associates the baptized with Christ's burial (6:4). This complex verse has two parts. In the first, Paul introduces the concept of being buried *with* Christ through baptism: **We have been buried with him, then, through baptism into death** (6:4a). In the second part, he explains the purpose of having been buried with Christ into his death through baptism: **in order that as Christ was raised from the dead through the Father's glory, so we might walk in newness of life** (6:4b). The verb Paul uses, *synetaphēmen* (we have been buried with), is the first of several compound verbs he employs in this chapter to emphasize how believers are associated *with* Christ. While the verb could suggest submersion into the waters of baptism, Paul's purpose is not to describe the rite of baptism but to highlight the intimate relationship between Christ and the believer. Just as Christ died and was buried (1 Cor. 15:3b–4), so believers have died and were buried *with* him through their baptism into his death. The repetition of the

© H. Richard Rutherford, CSC

Figure 8. A cruciform baptismal font. Located in the baptistery at the early Byzantine pilgrimage shrine at Alahan, Turkey (late fifth to early sixth century), this baptismal font illustrates Paul's understanding of baptism as participation in Christ's death.

phrase "into death" (*eis ton thanaton*) indicates that this is the central notion Paul is trying to communicate. Baptism associates the believer with a historical event, the death and burial of Jesus the Christ.

The believer's participation in Christ's death and burial is not the end of the process. As the purpose clause in the second part of 6:4 indicates, believers have died and been buried with Christ in order that "as" (*hōsper*) Christ was raised from the dead, "so" (*houtōs*) they might walk in newness of life. Here one would have expected Paul to draw a parallel between Christ's resurrection and the believer's resurrection ("just as Christ was raised from the dead, so we will be raised from the dead"). Colossians 2:12 draws just such a parallel, and Paul will draw a comparison between the resurrection of Christ and the resurrection of believers in Rom. 8:11. But he does not do so here since his purpose is to explain why believers should not remain in the realm of sin (6:1). Therefore, he concludes 6:5 in a manner that draws out the implications that their participation in Christ's death has for their moral life. Just as Christ was raised from the dead by the glory of the Father and so entered into resurrection life, so Christ-believers walk in the newness of life that anticipates their resurrection. Whereas the verb "to walk" (*peripatēsōmen*) in 6:4 is a metaphor for conduct (13:13; 14:15; 1 Thess. 4:12), the noun "newness" (*kainotēti*) refers to the newness of life that comes from the Spirit (Rom. 7:6). Believers have entered into Christ's death so that they can live in the newness of life that comes from the gift of God's Spirit—a life that will be perfected at the general resurrection of the dead. Therefore, although believers have not yet been raised from the dead, they ought to live in a way that comports with the resurrection life that they will inherit at the general resurrection of the dead.

In the second subunit, Paul provides another reason why believers should not remain in the realm of sin: since their old self has been "crucified with" Christ, they have been "set free" from sin (6:5–7). The argument is essentially the same as the one Paul made in his discussion of baptism (6:2–4) inasmuch as it focuses on the manner in which the believer has been identified with Christ's death. But here Paul introduces new imagery: the old self, crucifixion with Christ, the body of sin. Although some commentators maintain that "baptism is not the subject of the pericope" (Jewett 2007, 400), Paul's references to the death of the believer suggest that his baptismal theology is close at hand.

Next Paul develops the kind of comparison between Christ's death and resurrection on the one hand and the believer's participation in these salvific events on the other that one expected him to make in 6:4b: **For if we have been identified with him in the likeness of his death, then certainly we will be united with him in the likeness of his resurrection** (6:5). This identification with the likeness of Christ's death took place when the believer entered into the mystery of Christ's death through baptism, and it is this participation in Christ's death that grounds the moral life of the believer. This identification with Christ's death assures believers they will participate in the likeness of

Christ's resurrection at the general resurrection of the dead. In this verse, Paul's use of *homoiōmati* (likeness) can be understood as a pattern or form to which believers already are, and are yet to be, conformed. On the one hand, they have already been conformed to Christ's death by their baptism into his death. On the other, they will be conformed to the pattern or form of Christ's resurrection at the general resurrection of the dead. Unlike Colossians and Ephesians, then, which speak of believers as raised up with Christ (Col. 2:12; 3:1; Eph. 2:6), Romans remains focused on the future dimension of the believer's resurrection. Cranfield (1975, 308) interprets this verse in a moral sense: if believers have been conformed to Christ's death, they will certainly be conformed to his resurrection *in their moral life*. According to this construal, 6:5 repeats the thought of 6:4b. But in my view, Paul is referring to the resurrection of believers, thereby recalling the basic pattern of the Christian life: present conformity to Christ's death leads to future conformity with his resurrection.

Paul presupposes that his audience understands what he means by identification with Christ's death: **This we know, that our old self was crucified with Christ so that the sin-dominated self might be destroyed in order that we might no longer serve sin** (6:6). Introducing another compound verb, Paul affirms that "our old self" (*ho palaios hēmōn anthrōpos*, the old human) has been "cocrucified" (*synestaurōthē*; Christ is understood as the one with whom the believer is crucified). A similar expression occurs in Gal. 2:19. The "old self" refers to unredeemed humanity, which has not been incorporated into Christ. The purpose of this cocrucifixion was to destroy *to sōma tēs hamartias* (lit., "the body of sin"), which I have rendered as "the sin-dominated self" in order to show that Paul is referring not merely to the material body but to "the whole person considered as earth-oriented, not open to God or his Spirit, and prone to sin" (Fitzmyer 1993, 436). Thus 6:6 explains what Paul means by being identified with the form of Christ's death: it involves a death that participates in Christ's death, but this time Paul describes that death as being crucified *with* Christ. Although there is no explicit reference to baptism, I suggest that Paul still has baptism in view. Baptism is an entrance into Christ's death, which Christians make the pattern of their lives by crucifying "the flesh with its passions and desires" (Gal. 5:24). When this kind of death occurs—initially at baptism and repeatedly in the Christian life—the believer is no longer enslaved to the power of sin.

Paul summarizes the point he has made in this second subunit: **For the one who has died has been freed from sin** (6:7). Here it should be apparent that Paul is not talking about the physical death of the believer but the death that the believer has experienced by incorporation into Christ's death through baptism. Although believers are physically alive, they have truly died to an old way of life by their incorporation into Christ's death. Consequently, there is a way of life that is no longer open to them because, through Christ, they have died to it. They have died to the power of sin that Adam's transgression introduced into the world.

The third subunit (6:8–11) is remarkably similar to the second. As in the second subunit, Paul begins by drawing out the implications of Christ's death and resurrection for the believer (cf. 6:5, 8). Next, he reminds his audience of something they should already know (cf. 6:6, 9). Then he draws out the implications of what he has said (cf. 6:7, 10). Finally, in 6:11 Paul concludes with a statement that summarizes his thought and echoes what he said in 6:2: believers have died to sin.

First, Paul associates the believer with Christ by the use of another compound verb (*syzēsomen*): **If we have died with Christ, we believe that we will also live with him** (6:8). Although I have translated this verse as a conditional sentence, there is no doubt in Paul's mind that believers have really died with Christ. Consequently, they can be confident that they will live with him at the general resurrection of the dead. As in the previous unit, there is no reference to baptism here, but the language of dying *with* Christ points to the death that believers have experienced at the moment of their baptism into Christ. If they have entered Christ's death through baptism and make that death the pattern of their lives, they will live *with* Christ. A similar pattern is found in 2 Tim. 2:11.

Next, Paul presupposes that the Roman Christians know what he is about to say, much as he did in 6:6: **For we know that Christ, having been raised from the dead, no longer dies; death no longer rules over him** (6:9). But whereas in 6:6 he focused on the death of the Christ-believer, here he highlights Christ's own death in order to emphasize that Christ can no longer die since he has been raised to the sphere of resurrection life, over which death has no power. Death momentarily ruled over the crucified Christ, but when God raised him from the dead, its lordship ceased since Christ entered into the realm of immortal and incorruptible life.

Having explained Christ's victory over the power of death, Paul draws out the consequences of this victory over sin: **For in regard to the death he died, he died once and for all to sin; and in regard to the life he lives, he lives for God** (6:10). Here Paul explains the nature of Christ's death: by dying he died "once and for all" (*ephapax*) to sin. This does not imply that Christ sinned and so had to die to the pattern of sin in his own life. Rather, having borne the sins of humanity (having died *for us*), he completed the work of redemption once and for all by condemning sin in the flesh of his own body (8:3). Consequently, the resurrection life that Christ now lives, he lives for and in the presence of God. Byrne (1996, 192) puts it succinctly: "He died because he took upon himself the sins of others, . . . and he bore this burden of sin unto death. . . . But, once risen from the dead, any connection with sin, even in this innocent, sin-bearing sense, has come to an end."

Finally, Paul draws the conclusion toward which his argument has been moving since the initial question of 6:1: **So even you must consider yourselves**

as being dead to sin but alive for God in Christ Jesus (6:11). In other words, if death has no power over Christ because he has been raised from the dead (6:9), and if Christ died to sin once and for all by giving his life in order to redeem humanity and now lives to God (6:10), then believers (who have been baptized into Christ's death) should consider themselves as dead to sin and alive to God in Christ Jesus. The verb "consider" (*logizesthe*) is significant because it indicates that there is a difference between Christ's death and resurrection on the one hand, and the death and resurrection of the believer on the other. Christ physically died and has already entered into the sphere of resurrection life; believers have died in Christ and have not yet fully entered the realm of resurrection life. Consequently, they are still prone to the power of sin and will sin unless they remain united with Christ, in whom they died through their baptism.

To summarize, Paul has presented three reasons why believers should not remain in sin: (1) they have been baptized into Christ's death; (2) their old self has been crucified with Christ so that their sin-dominated self has been destroyed; (3) Christ, the pattern of their life, has died once and for all to death and sin.

Having explained why believers are not to remain in sin, Paul introduces a brief moral exhortation that draws out the practical implications of what he has said about their new situation (6:12–14). The exhortation begins with two negative imperatives (6:12–13) and concludes with a statement that explains why sin will not rule over their lives (6:14).

In the first negative imperative, Paul focuses his attention on the body, which is the outward manifestation of the self: **Therefore do not let sin continue to rule in your mortal body with the consequence that you are obedient to its desires** (6:12). Paul has already personified sin as a power that rules over Adamic humanity (3:9; 5:20; 6:6). Now he exhorts believers not to let this power exert its dominion over them, since they died to sin when they were baptized into Christ's death. A supreme realist, Paul is aware that sin can still exercise an influence over believers (what later theology would call concupiscence) if they allow it to do so; for their bodies are still mortal and corruptible. Consequently, he employs the present imperative to highlight the ongoing struggle that believers undergo. They must no longer allow sin to exercise its dominion over them lest they succumb to the desires and cravings of the mortal body, which has not yet been glorified, and in which sin and death still have a foothold. Only at the resurrection of the dead will believers be completely free from the power of sin.

Having focused on the body in the first imperative, in the second negative imperative Paul turns his attention to the parts of the body, all of which can be used as instruments for good or for evil: **and do not continue to present the members of your body as instruments for wickedness in the service of sin, but present yourselves to God as alive from the dead and your members as**

instruments of righteousness in the service of God (6:13). The first imperative in this verse is in the present tense, *mēde paristanete* (do not continue
to present), which suggests an ongoing process; the second is in the aorist,
parastēsate, which indicates the need for a decisive turn. When sin rules in
the body, every part of the body becomes an effective instrument or tool in
bringing about *adikias* ("wickedness" or "unrighteousness"). In this way the
entire body serves sin (see 3:13–18). But when believers have died to sin, they
are to present the parts of their body as instruments or tools that belong to
God's own righteousness, for they are in God's service. Aware that believers are
still confined by their mortal body, Paul encourages them to view themselves
"as alive from the dead," thereby echoing his statement in 6:11, "Consider
yourselves as being dead to sin but alive for God in Christ Jesus."

Although what follows is not an exhortation, it is an indispensable part of
this section since it grounds these negative imperatives. For if believers are still
in the mortal body, how can Paul make these exhortations? Paul's response is as
follows: **For sin will no longer rule over you since you are no longer under the
rule of the law but under the rule of grace** (6:14). Paul reminds those whom he
has been exhorting that they have been transferred from one realm to another.
Formerly, they were under the tutelage of the Mosaic law, which provided
them with a knowledge of good and evil. But, as Paul will explain in chapter
7, the power of sin frustrated their attempts to do the prescriptions of the law
since those under the law were still subservient to the power of sin. But now
the believer has been transferred to the realm of grace, which rules through
righteousness and leads to eternal life (5:21). Although they are still confined
to the mortal body, they are no longer under the law or the power of sin. They
are under the rule of grace, which allows them to live in a new way.

6:15–23. Having explained why believers should not remain in sin (6:1–14),
Paul takes up anew the question he raised in 6:1 from a slightly different vantage point. If it is true that believers are no longer under the law but under the
rule of grace, as Paul stated in 6:14b, this would seem to imply that believers
are "lawless" (*anomoi*), since they are no longer constrained by the Mosaic
law. Consequently, Paul must explain why being under grace does not result
in an antinomian way of life. The argument proceeds in the following way: an
objection (6:15) followed by a response that consists of a rhetorical question
(6:16), a thanksgiving statement (6:17), and a summary of the new situation
in which believers find themselves (6:18).

Paul raises an objection that one could raise in light of his statement that
believers are no longer under the regime of the Mosaic law: **What then? Should
we sin because we are no longer under the law but under grace? Of course
not!** (6:15). Here Paul appears to have the situation of Jewish believers in view.
Formerly they were under the Mosaic law, but now they are *hypo charin*, by
which Paul means they find themselves under the "favor" (*charis*) that God
has manifested in Jesus Christ. But if this is the case, it appears that believers

can do whatever they wish since their lives are no longer determined by the law. This objection, however, misunderstands the nature of the gospel, and Paul immediately dismisses it as groundless.

As he did in 6:3, Paul begins with a rhetorical question that implies his audience knows, or should know, the answer to the objection he has raised: **Do you not know that the one to whom you present yourselves as slaves for the purpose of obedience, you are slaves of that one whom you obey, whether it be sin that leads to death or obedience that leads to righteousness?** (6:16). Making use of the example of slavery, which would have been all too familiar to his audience, Paul employs it as a metaphor for their lives. Life is ultimately a matter of obedience to one lord or another, and the one whom they obey is the one whom they serve as slaves. Drawing a contrast between sin, which leads to death because it separates one from God, and obedience, which leads to "righteousness" (*dikaiosynē*), Paul affirms that people are either slaves of sin or of righteousness, depending on whom they obey. As he so often does in this letter, Paul personifies sin as a power to which people become enslaved by obeying what this taskmaster requires. The phrase, the "obedience that leads to righteousness" (*hypakoēs eis dikaiosynēn*), should be read in the light of Paul's earlier expression, "the obedience that consists in faith" (*hypakoēn pisteōs*, 1:5). So read, it appears that Paul has in view the obedience that is faith and so leads to the righteousness that God reveals in Christ. It is this righteousness that those who are under grace obey, with the result that obedience to sin is excluded.

Confident that the Roman Christ-believers have transferred their allegiance from sin to righteousness, Paul writes: **But thanks be to God because, although you were slaves of sin, you have become obedient from the depths of your heart to the pattern of teaching to which you were handed over** (6:17). "The pattern of teaching" to which they were delivered refers to the teaching of the gospel that they received at baptism (Byrne 1996, 206; Stuhlmacher 1994, 95), a baptismal catechesis summarized in 10:9–10. But instead of writing that this teaching was handed over to them, Paul writes that *they* were handed over to it. In doing so, he suggests that they were formerly slaves to sin, but at their baptism they were handed over to another lord, God's righteousness, to whom they now give themselves as obedient slaves (Dunn 1988, 1:344).

Finally, Paul draws out the paradoxical implication of what he has been saying: **Freed from sin, you have become enslaved to righteousness** (6:18). For Paul, there is no absolute freedom. Human beings live in a cosmos of competing lords, who demand their allegiance. True wisdom is to align oneself with the lord who makes one truly free. So Käsemann (1980, 179) writes that Christ "is the free one who became obedient, whereas we receive our freedom in allegiance to him and as a result of the right of lordship which God has graciously established over us." Being under grace rather than under the law, then, does not lead to sin because those under grace have transferred their allegiance to Christ.

Having explained that believers should not sin because they are no longer slaves of sin but slaves of righteousness (6:15–18), in the remaining verses of this chapter Paul exhorts the Romans to surrender themselves in service to their new master, righteousness, which brings them to eternal life (6:19–23). The exhortation has three parts. First, it encourages them to present the members of their body to their new master just as they formerly presented the members of their body to their old master (6:19–20). Second, it asks what benefit they obtained from their former service (6:21). Finally, it reminds them of their new situation and contrasts the wages of sin with the free gift of God (6:22–23).

Aware that he is employing a metaphor that might be offensive to many of the Romans, some of whom were slaves or former slaves, Paul begins somewhat apologetically: **I am speaking in a merely human way on account of the weakness of your flesh** (6:19a). He has employed the example of slavery because, even though it may be offensive to them, it is an example that they readily understand. In referring to the weakness of their flesh, Paul is not so much criticizing them as he is stating a fact with which, upon reflection, they would readily agree. For having so recently been transferred from the lordship of sin to the lordship of righteousness, the Romans still do not comprehend the full significance of their existence in Christ. Therefore, Paul employs examples from everyday life to explain the implications of living in and for Christ.

Having apologized for the metaphor he will use throughout his exhortation, Paul employs the formula "just as [*hōsper*] . . . so [*houtōs*]" to illustrate how they should conduct themselves: **For just as you presented the members of your body as slaves to impurity and lawlessness for lawlessness, so now present the members of your body as slaves to righteousness for holiness** (6:19b). With this neatly balanced phrase, Paul employs the example of their former slavery to show how they should conduct themselves as slaves of righteousness. Just as they surrendered every member of their body as willing slaves of "impurity" (*akatharsia*) and "lawlessness" (*anomia*), which led to further lawlessness on their part, so they should now surrender every part of their body as slaves of "righteousness" (*dikaiosynē*), which results in "holiness" (*hagiasmos*). Paul arranges these four terms in a pattern whereby the first and fourth terms and the second and third terms stand in contrast to each other: (1) impurity, (2) lawlessness, (3) righteousness, and (4) holiness.

The first term, "impurity," refers to immorality, especially sexual immorality. Such immorality stands in sharp contrast to the fourth term, "holiness," which ought to characterize the life of those who have been consecrated and set apart for service to God in Jesus Christ. For example, Paul tells the Thessalonians that God's will for them is their "holiness" (1 Thess. 4:3 NAB), for they were not called to "impurity" but to "holiness" (4:7 NAB). The second term, "lawless," which means a wanton disregard for law, stands in contrast to the third term, "righteousness," by which Paul means the righteousness that God made possible through Christ, a righteousness that leads to the holiness of life that is pleasing to God. Although there is an ethical dimension to this holiness inasmuch as it requires one to lead a morally good life, the term primarily refers to the holiness that God communicates to believers through Christ whereby they are consecrated and set aside for service to God.

Next, Paul provides a supporting reason for what he has just said: **For when you were sin's slaves, you were free from righteousness** (6:20). When the Romans were still "in Adam" and slaves of sin, they were "free" from the demands of righteousness since they belonged to another lord: sin. To be sure, they were still obligated to do God's will, but inasmuch as they were slaves of sin, they could not do God's will. Their "freedom" from the demands of righteousness, then, was the freedom of slaves who could not serve another master because they were already obligated to a master who controlled every aspect of their lives.

Building upon what he has just said, Paul asks his audience what "benefit" (*karpon*; lit., "fruit") they derived from their former slavery: **What benefit did you have then from those things of which you are now ashamed?** (6:21a). The things of which they are now ashamed are the *akatharsia* and *anomia* that characterized their former life when they were under the lordship of sin. At that time they lived an immoral life, without regard for God's law. Responding to his own question, Paul writes: **For the final end of those things is death** (6:21b). The death that Paul has in view here is more than the end of life; it is a final and unalterable separation from God. For those who remain in the sphere of the old Adam as servants of sin cannot stand in the realm of the eschatological Adam, who has conquered the powers of sin and death.

Having recounted their former situation, when they were enslaved to sin, Paul describes their new situation: **But now, having been freed from sin and enslaved to God, you have your benefit that leads to holiness, and the final goal is eternal life** (6:22). Employing the same adverb (*nyni*) he used in 3:21, when he spoke of the decisive change in the human condition that came about with the manifestation of God's righteousness, Paul reminds his audience how this change has affected their lives. Formerly they were free from righteousness, and the benefit they received was death. Now they have been freed from sin and enslaved to God, and the benefit they enjoy is holiness, which leads to eternal life. The elaborate contrast that Paul establishes can be outlined in this way:

slaves of sin	free from righteousness	benefit		death
slaves of God	free from sin	benefit	holiness	eternal life

The lack of symmetry in this outline highlights the importance of "holiness" (*hagiasmos*), which Paul first introduced in 6:19. By saying that freedom from sin leads to holiness, with eternal life as its goal, Paul emphasizes the moral dimension that should characterize the Christian life in the present. The immediate benefit of being freed from sin is that it allows believers to live a sanctified life because of the holiness that God has graciously bestowed on them. While eternal life is not a reward for living such a life, it is the outcome of such a life inasmuch as God is the source of this holiness.

In the next verse, Paul provides a supporting argument for what he has just said: **For death is the wages sin pays out, whereas God's gracious gift is eternal life in Christ Jesus our Lord** (6:23). Again, the symmetry is not perfect. Whereas Paul writes that the "wages" (*opsōnia*) of sin is death, he does not say that the "wages" of righteousness is eternal life. Rather, he speaks of eternal life as God's "gracious gift" (*charisma*). *Opsōnia* often refers to the wages paid to a soldier; *charisma* highlights the free gift of God, something graciously and freely bestowed on the believer. The vocabulary that Paul employs here is significant, for while one earns death by living a life of immorality and lawlessness, eternal life is a gift that cannot be earned.

The main lines of Paul's argument in chapter 6 can be summarized in this way: Believers are not to remain in the sphere of sin because they died to sin when they were baptized into Christ's death. Buried with and crucified with Christ in this baptismal union, they now live a life in conformity with Christ's death in the hope that they will share in his resurrection. Because they have died to sin, they are no longer slaves of sin. Having been freed from sin, they are slaves of righteousness and thus enslaved to God. Their enslavement to righteousness, however, is paradoxically the source of their freedom, which allows them to live a life of holiness that results in the gracious gift of eternal life.

Theological Issues

Chapter 6 raises two theological issues. The first is Paul's understanding of baptism; the second is the relation he draws between the indicative of salvation and the moral imperative. Although distinct, these issues are closely related; for it is on the basis of the new life that believers already experience through baptism (the indicative) that Paul exhorts them to live in a particular manner (the imperative).

The Pauline Understanding of Baptism

Although it is the Pauline Letters more than any other writings of the NT that have contributed to our understanding of baptism, Paul received this rite and his initial understanding of it from the early church. According to the Acts of the Apostles, Peter summoned his audience at Pentecost to repent and be baptized "in the name of Jesus Christ" so that their sins might be forgiven, and they might receive the gift of the Holy Spirit (2:38). Shortly after his encounter with the risen Christ, Paul was baptized (9:18). The apostle's theology of baptism, then, is rooted in a personal experience of this rite as well as in the traditions he received from the early church, especially from the congregation at Antioch in Syria.

We can suppose that Paul instructed his Gentile converts about the meaning and importance of baptism, but the Pauline Letters do not contain extensive teaching about baptism. Since all of his converts were baptized, Paul assumes that they already possess a basic understanding about this rite by which they entered into the community of those who believe in Christ. Therefore, on several occasions he refers to their baptism (without explaining its meaning) in order to support some point of his argument. It is from such remarks that we must try to construct what will inevitably be an imperfect Pauline theology of baptism. Building upon the work of Schnackenburg (1964) and Ferdinand Hahn (2002, 2:511–21), I organize my comments around five themes: (1) baptism into Christ's name, (2) baptism as cleansing, (3) baptism as an anticipation of the general resurrection, (4) baptism as an entrance into the body of Christ, (5) baptism as an entrance into the salvific event of Christ's death and resurrection.

1. Paul understands that believers have been baptized "into the name of Christ," an expression signifying that the baptized belong to Christ. Consequently, when responding to the divisions threatening the church at Corinth, he writes, "I thank God that I baptized none of you except Crispus and Gaius, so that no one can say that you were baptized in my name" (1 Cor. 1:14–15). Similarly, when he employs the story of Israel in the wilderness to warn the Corinthians against being presumptuous, he tells them that Israel had been "baptized into Moses" (10:1–2) when it passed through the sea. Both of these texts indicate that baptism binds one to the person into whose name one is baptized, be it Christ or Moses, although Paul never explains the precise nature of this binding.

2. Because baptism involves water, it evokes the imagery of washing. Consequently, Paul reminds the Corinthians, "You were washed, you were sanctified, you were justified in the name of the Lord Jesus and in the Spirit of our God" (1 Cor. 6:11). The text, however, appears rather unexpectedly after a list of vices that Paul uses to warn the Corinthians that those who are "unrighteous" (*adikoi*) will not enter the kingdom of God (6:9). This reference to baptism, consisting of a rhythmic threefold formula ("you were washed, you were sanctified, you were justified"), which Paul introduces without further explanation, suggests that the apostle may have been drawing from a baptismal tradition with which the Corinthians were already familiar, a tradition that focused on baptism as a washing that effects sanctification and justification.

3. In another unexpected Pauline reference to baptism, in the midst of his discussion about the general resurrection of the dead (1 Cor. 15), Paul asks the Corinthians, "Otherwise, what will those people do who receive baptism on behalf of the dead? If the dead are not raised at all, why are people baptized on their behalf?" (15:29). Even if Paul is referring to a rite of proxy baptism

on behalf of those who have already died without being baptized, it is clear that Paul draws a connection between baptism and hope for the resurrection of the dead. People are baptized on behalf of the dead because they believe that those who have been joined with Christ in baptism will be raised from the dead as he was. By being baptized, or having themselves baptized for the deceased relatives, then, believers confess their faith and hope in the general resurrection of the dead.

4. At the conclusion of his complex discussion in Gal. 3, where he argues that uncircumcised Gentile believers are Abraham's descendants because they have been incorporated into his singular descendant, the Christ, Paul explains the significance of their incorporation into Christ by referring to baptism: "As many of you as were baptized into Christ have clothed yourselves with Christ. There is no longer Jew or Greek, there is no longer slave or free, there is no longer male or female; for all of you are one in Christ Jesus. And if you belong to Christ, then you are Abraham's offspring, heirs according to the promise" (3:27–29). They are Abraham's children, then, because they have been incorporated into Abraham's singular descendant, the Christ, through baptism. While Paul employs the imagery of being clothed with Christ, it is apparent that his baptismal theology is moving in a new direction here. Believers are baptized *eis Christon*, which suggests that they have been baptized into his person. A more explicit statement of this is found in 1 Cor. 12:13: "For in the one Spirit we were all baptized into the one body—Jews or Greeks, slaves or free—and we were all made to drink of one Spirit." The body to which Paul refers is "the body of Christ," as is apparent from what he writes a few verses later: "Now you are the body of Christ and individually members of it" (12:27).

5. While the texts of Gal. 3:27–28 and 1 Cor. 12:13 speak of the believer being baptized into Christ, which appears to refer to the body of Christ, the text of Rom. 6 goes further. In light of his discussion of Adam and Christ, the progenitors of the old and the new humanity, respectively, Paul writes that believers have been baptized into Christ's death (6:3), buried with him (6:4), and crucified with him (6:6). Thus in Romans the believer's incorporation into Christ is more explicit. When believers are baptized into Christ, they are baptized into the historical event of his death and thus can say that they have been crucified with and buried with him. This, it seems to me, is Paul's distinctive contribution to the church's understanding of baptism, a contribution indebted to his appreciation for Christ as the progenitor of a new creation. Consequently, while Paul inherited a theology of baptism that spoke of believers being baptized into Christ's name and of being washed, justified, and sanctified, his appreciation of Christ as a corporate person, the new human being, led him to present baptism as an incorporation into the saving mystery of Christ's death, with a promise of future resurrection.

Colossians and Ephesians develop this baptismal theology further. Colossians affirms that not only were believers buried with Christ in their baptism;

they were also "raised with him through faith in the power of God" (Col. 2:12). Colossians, however, remains within the orbit of Paul's baptismal thought. For though it says that believers have been raised with Christ (3:1), it also affirms that their life is still hidden in Christ and that Christ is yet to be revealed (3:3–4). Ephesians goes further and speaks of believers as not only being raised up with Christ but also being seated with him in the heavenly places (2:6). Despite these strong statements, neither Colossians nor Ephesians claims that the resurrection from the dead has already occurred in baptism. Rather, developing a line of thought that Paul begins in Rom. 6, they affirm that baptism is a participation in the salvific event of Christ's death and resurrection. In a way that believers will never fully comprehend, their baptism unites them with Christ's unrepeatable death and resurrection. This sacramental union with Christ is, for believers, the foundation of the believer's ethical life, the point to which I now turn.

The Indicative and the Imperative

Although Paul will present an extensive paraenesis in 12:1–15:13, he does not divide his letter into neatly defined sections of theology and ethics. Already in chapter 6, in the midst of a theological discussion, he exhorts his audience to live in a particular way. Theology and ethics are intimately related to each other for Paul.

Neither a systematic theologian nor an ethicist, Paul is the herald of a gospel in which theological and ethical issues are so closely related that it is difficult for the apostle to proclaim this gospel without pointing to its ethical implications or to speak of its ethical demands without proclaiming the gospel. So Victor Furnish (1968, 110) writes, "Neither 'theology' nor 'ethics' nor a combination of the two is to be equated with 'the gospel.' Rather, the good news Paul preaches finds expression now in theological statements, now in ethical exhortations."

Pauline students refer to this intimate relationship between theology and ethics, proclamation and exhortation, in terms of the indicative of salvation, what God has done for the believer, and the moral imperative, the believer's response to God's gift in Christ (see the essays of Bultmann and Parsons in Rosner 1995). The problem, however, has always been how to relate these two concepts to each other. In what sense does the indicative of salvation guide, motivate, interpret, determine, or make the moral life possible?

In an appendix to his monograph on Paul's moral teaching, T. J. Deidun (1981, 239–43) reviews several attempts that he deems inadequate to explain the relationship between the indicative and the imperative. For example, he argues that "to interpret the imperative as a call to the realization of an *ideal*" (239) is to misunderstand the relationship between the indicative and the imperative, since the Pauline indicative of salvation is not an ideal but a reality that requires an appropriate response on the part of the believer. Conversely, it is a mistake to downplay the relationship between the indicative and the imperative "by making the indicative in some way *conditional* upon subsequent realization of the imperative" (240), as if the moral life of the believer somehow actualizes the indicative of salvation. Even the popular expression "become what you are" is inadequate since it "overlooks precisely what is most characteristic of Pauline ethics: that what God demands, he also effects" (241). Similarly, Deidun maintains that those who explain the imperative as "the 'subjective' appropriation of what has been given 'objectively' in Baptism" (241) misunderstand the reality of the indicative of salvation. In a word, difficulties arise whenever one draws a sharp distinction between the indicative and the imperative to the detriment of one or the other.

For Paul, there is an intimate relationship between what God has already done in Christ for the believer (the indicative) and the way in which the believer is to live (the imperative). On the one hand, the indicative of salvation is an existential reality, not an ideal toward which believers are striving. In and through Christ, believers have entered into a new creation because they have been incorporated into Christ, the new human being, through baptism. On the other hand, the imperative to live in a particular way is a summons to an existentially new way of life made possible by what God has done in Christ. The imperative, then, is not an ethical ideal by which Paul challenges believers to do what is ultimately impossible. Nor is it his way of motivating them or making them more conscious of their new existence in Christ. Just as the indicative of salvation points to a new reality, so the imperative points to a new behavior that is possible because believers live in the realm of a new humanity that God has created in Christ.

By emphasizing the reality of the indicative and the imperative, I am not suggesting that those who are in Christ are incapable of sin. A realist, Paul understands the ongoing problem of sin, which threatens his communities. The justified must continually crucify their flesh with its passions and desires (Gal. 5:24) in order to fulfill the imperative of the gospel. Paul says of his own life, "I have been crucified with Christ; and it is no longer I who live, but it is Christ who lives in me. And the life I now live in the flesh I live by faith in the Son of God" (Gal. 2:19b–20). Here the distinction between the indicative of salvation and the moral imperative has almost disappeared. Christ lives in Paul (the indicative), and this enables Paul to live a life characterized by faith in the Son of God (the imperative).

In Rom. 6 Paul expresses the relationship between the indicative and the imperative in terms of baptism. Believers are no longer under the power of sin because they have truly entered into the mystery of Christ's death by their baptism. Their baptism was a real death to sin because they entered into Christ's death, which conquered sin. On the basis of their participation in Christ's death (the indicative), Paul exhorts them not to let sin reign over them (the imperative). His exhortation is not a moral ideal, nor is it an attempt to motivate his audience. It is a real imperative grounded in an existential reality. Because they have died with Christ, the power of sin over their lives has been broken, and it is this new reality (the indicative) that enables them to live in the way Paul commands them (the imperative).

To summarize, the Pauline moral imperative is rooted in an indicative of salvation that has truly altered the life of believers so that they are empowered to live in a way pleasing to God. The gift makes the imperative possible, and faithful fulfillment of the imperative witnesses to the creative power of the gift.

Romans 7:1–25

Released from a Law Frustrated by Sin

Introductory Matters

In chapter 6 Paul showed that his gospel does not imply that believers should persist in sin. Sin should no longer play a role in their lives because they have died to it through their baptism into Christ's death. Since believers are now under the regime of grace rather than the regime of the law, they are no longer slaves to sin, which leads to death, but slaves of righteousness, which leads to life.

Having argued that believers are no longer under the domination of sin, in this chapter Paul takes up the question of the Mosaic law. As in chapter 6, he proceeds by raising and answering objections to the gospel he preaches. Accordingly, after explaining the role the law plays in arousing sinful desires (7:5), he asks if this means that the law is to be equated with sin (7:7). Then, after stating that sin took the occasion of the commandment to deceive and kill its adherents (7:11), he asks if what is good—the law—has become death for its adherents (7:13). In response to the questions he raises in 7:7 and 7:13, Paul provides a vigorous defense of the law by arguing that the culprit is not the law but sin, which takes advantage of the law to deceive those under the law in order to bring them to death.

Paul's exposition of the law in Rom. 7 is a necessary counterbalance to his other great exposition of the law in Gal. 3. There he presents a less-flattering view of the law, suggesting that it was a latecomer on the stage of salvation history, functioning as humanity's "disciplinarian" (*paidagōgos*; Gal. 3:24–25) until Christ should appear. Seemingly aware that the argument of Gal. 3 could be, or had been, misinterpreted, Paul presents a more nuanced and positive view of the law in Rom. 7. Rather than a critique of the law, Rom. 7 provides a vigorous defense of the law. This defense involves a complicated discussion of the relationship between sin, death, and the law, all of which converge in the human person and bring about the conflicted self.

The manner in which Paul explains the conflict that the human person experiences in trying to do what the law requires has played a central role in how Christian theology has understood the human person, making Rom. 7 a classic text for Christian anthropology. Consequently, even though the chapter functions as Paul's defense of the law, Pauline exegetes have repeatedly struggled to identify the conflicted *egō* that Paul describes in 7:7–25. The work of Werner Georg Kümmel (1974) remains the starting point for most scholarly discussions on this topic, and the recent work of Mark Reasoner (2005) provides a helpful historical overview of how this text has been approached by some of its most significant commentators: Origen, Augustine, Abelard, Aquinas, Luther, Erasmus, Wesley, and Barth. Although they interpret the text differently, Cranfield (1975, 342–47) and Fitzmyer (1993, 462–66) also summarize the major positions that commentators have espoused in the history of exegesis.

Those who seek to identify the conflicted self described in Rom. 7 must address the following questions: (1) Is Paul speaking of the same person throughout 7:7–25, or does the change from the past (7:7–13) to the present tense (7:14–25) signal a change of subjects? (2) Is Paul speaking autobiographically when he refers to the conflicted *egō* in 7:7–25, or is he employing a rhetorical form whereby he speaks in the person of a larger group of which he is a part? If Paul is speaking autobiographically, is he referring to his past when he was not in Christ or to his present experience in Christ? (3) If Paul is speaking in the person of a larger group, is he referring to Adamic humanity or to those who are in Christ?

Is Paul Speaking of the Same Person?

While Cranfield (1975, 341) has argued that the change from the past tense in 7:7–13 to the present tense in 7:14–25 indicates that Paul is referring to himself as representing humankind generally in 7:7–13 and Christians in 7:14–25, most exegetes (rightly in my judgment) maintain that Paul has the same subject in view in both sections. In the first section, he deals with the self's first encounter with the law; in the second, he considers the self's ongoing struggle to maintain the law in the present.

Is Paul Speaking of Himself?

There is certainly a sense in which Paul is speaking autobiographically, even if he is employing the *egō* to describe the experience of a larger group. But is

Paul speaking merely autobiographically? Is he primarily concerned with his own experience, past and present? And if he is speaking merely autobiographically, is he referring to his experience before or after his call to be Christ's apostle? In either case, an autobiographical approach presents problems. If Paul is referring to his pre-Christian experience, how are we to interpret his statement in 7:9 that there was a time when he lived apart from the law since Paul was circumcised on the eighth day (Phil. 3:5)? And if Paul is speaking of his Pharisaic past, how are we to construe his self-description in Phil. 3:6 that "as to righteousness under the law" he was "blameless"? Finally, how are we to assess his words in Gal. 1:14 that he advanced in Judaism beyond many of his contemporaries since he was more zealous for the traditions of the ancestors than they were?

Perhaps, then, Paul is speaking of his Christian experience. But if he is, when did he live apart from the law? How are we to balance this description of the conflicted self with what he writes in Gal. 2:19b–20: "I have been crucified with Christ; and it is no longer I who live, but it is Christ who lives in me. And the life I now live in the flesh I live by faith in the Son of God, who loved me and gave himself for me"? Furthermore, how are we to balance this description of the conflicted self with Paul's statement in 2 Cor. 5:17, "If anyone is in Christ, there is a new creation: everything old has passed away; see, everything has become new"? Does such a conflicted person dare say to others, "Be imitators of me, as I am of Christ" (1 Cor. 11:1), or "Join in imitating me, and observe those who live according to the example you have in us" (Phil. 3:17)?

Is Paul Speaking in the Person of Another?

If Paul is not writing autobiographically, perhaps he is speaking in the person of a wider group, a rhetorical technique that Origen noticed centuries ago when he argued that Paul was speaking in the person of weaker Christians (*Comm. Rom.* 6.9.4, trans. Scheck 2001–2, 2:37–38), an opinion many contemporary scholars espouse today, employing the rhetorical term "speech in character" (Tobin 2004, 225–44). But who is this person? Is Paul speaking in the person of Adam, Israel, unredeemed humanity? Or is he speaking in the character of redeemed humanity, in the voice of every believer in Christ? Although the early Augustine maintained that Paul was speaking in the person of unredeemed humanity, he later retracted this view and argued that Paul was speaking in the person of redeemed humanity, himself included (Reasoner 2005, 70–73). Throughout the centuries, Augustine's position has persuaded some of the greatest commentators on Romans (Abelard, Aquinas, Luther, Calvin, and Barth). More important, it persuades everyday readers of Romans since they readily associate themselves with the struggle Paul describes here.

But if Paul is speaking about the conflicted experience of the redeemed person, what did he mean when he wrote, "This we know, that our old self was crucified with Christ so that the sin-dominated self might be destroyed in order that we might no longer serve sin" (6:6)? And why does he describe the redeemed as sold under or indentured to sin (7:14)? And why does he ask who will rescue him from this body of death (7:24) when he has affirmed in chapter 5 that Christ has already done this? Moreover, if Paul is speaking of the present conflict of the Christian, why does he continue to refer to the observance of the law in this section when believers are no longer under the law but under grace? In my view, Paul is not speaking of the present experience of the Christian but describing the experience of those who are not in Christ *as seen from the perspective of one who is in Christ*. The unredeemed may not think of themselves in this way, and Paul certainly did not view himself in this way when he persecuted Christ's followers; but in the light of Christ he sees that this is the real situation of all who are not in Christ, even if they are not aware it.

I have structured the chapter as appears on the next page.

Tracing the Train of Thought

Paul has spoken of the law and sin several times in Romans (3:20; 4:15; 5:20). These remarks have been unsettling, and Paul must now deal with the question of the law in a comprehensive way if he hopes to persuade his audience of the gospel he preaches. Such is the burden of this chapter, which consists of four units: an example drawn from the law to show the limited jurisdiction of the law (7:1–6), Paul's response to an objection that his gospel implies that the law is sinful (7:7–12), Paul's response to a further objection that his gospel equates the law with death (7:13–23), a brief conclusion (7:24–25).

In the first unit, Paul begins with a question regarding the law (7:1). He then draws an analogy between a married woman who is released from the law of marriage when her husband dies (7:2–3) and believers who are released from the law through their participation in Christ's death (7:4–6). In the second unit Paul begins with another question (7:7a), this one occasioned by his statement that the sinful desires of the flesh are at work in the body through the law (7:5). In response to the question he poses (Is the law to be equated with sin?), he explains how sin took advantage of the law in order to arouse sinful desires (7:7b–12). In the third unit, Paul begins with another question (7:13), this one occasioned by his statement in 7:11 that the commandment of the law resulted in death, to which he responds in two ways. First, the problem is not the law, which is spiritual, but the human person who is carnal so that the *egō* does not understand what it does (7:14–17). Second, the problem is not the law but the human person in whose flesh nothing good lives so that the *egō* does not do the good it wants but the evil it hates (7:18–23). Paul then concludes with a desperate cry (7:24), to which he responds with a statement of victory (7:25). As one reads this section, it is striking that in 7:7–12 Paul employs the

Romans 7:1–25 in the Rhetorical Flow

The letter opening (1:1–17)

Gentiles and Jews in the light of God's wrath (1:18–3:20)

Gentiles and Jews in the light of God's righteousness (3:21–4:25)

The experience of salvation in the light of God's righteousness (5:1–8:39)

  Transferred from the realm of sin to the realm of grace (5:1–21)

  No longer slaves of sin and death (6:1–23)

▶**Released from a law frustrated by sin (7:1–25)**

  An example from the law (7:1–6)

    A question regarding the rule of the law (7:1)

    An example to illustrate Paul's point (7:2–3)

    Application to believers (7:4–6)

  The law is not sinful (7:7–12)

    Objection and initial response (7:7a)

    A fuller explanation (7:7b–12)

      Knowledge of sin through the law (7:7b)

      How sin took advantage of the commandment (7:7c–8)

      Living once without the law (7:9a)

      The appearance of the law and the revival of sin (7:9b)

      The death of the *egō* (7:10)

      How sin took advantage of the commandment (7:11)

      Conclusion: the holiness of the law (7:12)

  The law did not bring death (7:13–23)

    Objection and initial response (7:13)

    The carnal self in conflict (7:14–17)

      A spiritual law and the carnal self (7:14)

      The plight of the carnal self (7:15)

      The power of indwelling sin (7:16–17)

    A further description of the carnal self in conflict (7:18–20)

      Nothing good in the carnal self (7:18a)

      The plight of the carnal self (7:18b–19)

      The power of indwelling sin (7:20)

    The conflict of the carnal self (7:21–23)

      What the carnal self discovers about itself (7:21)

      The inner self's agreement with the law (7:22)

      The presence of another law (7:23)

  Conclusion (7:24–25)

past tense to describe the situation of the *egō*, but in 7:13–23 he reverts to the present tense to portray the anguished predicament of the divided self.

7:1–6. Paul begins with an example from the law that illustrates the temporal limits of the law's jurisdiction. Before presenting this example, however, he poses a rhetorical question. Employing the same introductory formula (*hē agnoeite*) he did in 6:3, he asks, **Do you not know, brothers and sisters (for I am speaking to those who are acquainted with the law), that the law rules over a person as long as one lives?** (7:1). The question assumes that Paul's audience is familiar with the law and agrees with his premise that the law has a limited temporal jurisdiction. While Paul's allusion to the audience's acquaintance with the law might suggest that he is addressing Jewish Christians, there were undoubtedly Gentile Christians at Rome who knew and cherished the Mosaic law, especially those who had been Jewish proselytes before being baptized into Christ. But whether the members of Paul's audience were Jewish or Gentile Christians, they would have been surprised by the way in which he applied the law's temporal jurisdiction to their lives.

Beginning with a case with which his audience would agree, Paul presents his example: **For the married woman is bound to her husband by the law so long as her husband is alive. But if her husband should die, she is released from the law binding her to her husband** (7:2). Paul makes a similar statement in 1 Cor. 7:39 when discussing marriage and virginity ("A wife is bound as long as her husband lives. But if the husband dies, she is free to marry anyone she wishes, only in the Lord"). Here, however, he employs the statement to argue that the law's temporal jurisdiction is limited by death since a married woman is released from the law that binds her to her husband when he dies. Paul expands upon his example by describing the different ways in which a woman will be viewed if she marries before or after her husband's death: **Consequently, while her husband is alive, she will be called an adulteress should she marry another man. But if her husband dies, she is released from the law; she will not be an adulteress if she should marry another** (7:3). Everything, then, depends on whether her husband is alive or dead. If he is alive when she marries, she is an adulteress because she is still under the jurisdiction of the law; but if her husband dies, she is free to marry because the death of her husband marks the end of the law's jurisdiction over her. At this point, some manuscripts (33, 629, et al.) add the words "of the husband," so that Paul's statement reads, "she is released from the law *of the husband*." But since Paul is concerned with the law's limited temporal jurisdiction, the reading "she is released from the law" is preferable because it prepares the audience for the point Paul will make about the entire law, not just its marriage legislation.

Having taken one example from the law with which his audience would have agreed, Paul applies that example to the whole law in a way that would surely have surprised those unfamiliar with his understanding of the law (7:4–6). The Greek words that begin these three verses structure the argument Paul will make in this unit: *hōste* (therefore) in 7:4, *hote* (when) in 7:5, and *nyni* (now) in 7:6. First, Paul applies the example he has just proposed to the situation of his Roman audience, whose members have died with Christ through their baptism into his death: **Therefore [*hōste*], my brothers and sisters, you also have died to the law through the body of Christ so that you might belong to another, to the one who has been raised from the dead, so that we might bear fruit for God (7:4).** The analogy Paul draws between the married woman and the Christ-believer, however, is not as precise as we might like it to be. For, in Paul's example, it is the husband who dies and the woman who is released from the law, but in Paul's application of the example, it is the Christian who dies to the law in order to belong to another. This analogy is as follows:

7:2	the husband dies	the woman is released from the law
7:3	the believer dies to the law	in order to belong to another

Note, however, that Paul writes that the believer has died to the law "through the body of Christ" (*dia tou sōmatos tou Christou*), thereby reminding believers that they died to the law when they entered into the mystery of Christ's death through their baptism (6:3; see also 2 Cor. 5:14, where Paul reminds his audience that all died through Christ's representative death). Accordingly, by the phrase "through the body of Christ," Paul shows that he still has the death of Christ in view, a death that makes it possible for the believer to die to the law. In light of this understanding of the believer's participation in Christ's death, we can state the analogy in yet another way: Just as the husband dies so that the woman will be free to marry, so the Christian dies—in Christ—to the law to be united with another. The analogy is as follows:

7:2	The husband dies	so the woman is free to marry.
7:3	The believer dies *in Christ* to the law	to be united with another.

The other to whom the believer is now free to belong is "the one who has been raised from the dead," the risen Lord. Accordingly, just as a married woman is not free to marry another until she is released from the law that binds her to her husband, so Christians are not free to belong to the risen Christ until they have passed from the lordship of the law to the lordship of Christ, a transference that involves death to one way of life in order to be born into a new way of life. However, lest Paul be misunderstood as advocating an antinomian way of life, he immediately explains the purpose of this transference: so that "we might bear fruit" (*karpophorēsōmen*) to God. This reference to bearing fruit recalls Paul's statement, "But now, having been freed from sin and enslaved to God, you have your benefit [*karpon*] that leads to holiness, and eternal life is the final goal" (6:22). Dying to the law through baptism into Christ's death, then, does not lead to an antinomian way of life but allows believers to bear the fruit of holiness precisely because, having been released from the law, they are united with the one who has been raised from the dead.

Having applied his example to the situation of the Roman believers to show that they have been released from the law in order to be joined to another, Paul establishes a contrast between the former situation of the Romans, when they were not in Christ (7:5), and their present situation now that they are in Christ (7:6). Paul begins with the temporal marker *hote* (when) to indicate that he is referring to their pre-Christian situation: **For when [*hote*] we were in the realm of the flesh, our sinful passions were at work through the law in our members to bear fruit that led to death** (7:5). Before they were in Christ, then, they were "in the realm of the flesh" (*en tē sarki*). While "flesh" can refer to that which covers one's bones, here Paul employs the term in a metaphorical sense. Understood metaphorically, "flesh" (*sarx*), which is corruptible and mortal, stands in stark contrast to "spirit" (*pneuma*), which is incorruptible and immortal. Human beings belong to the realm of the flesh, and their destiny is corruption and mortality unless the Spirit of God intervenes. In addition to being corruptible, the flesh is susceptible to the power of sin, which dominates and enslaves it. Understood metaphorically, then, "to be in the flesh" means to live in a purely human way, apart from the power of God's Spirit, under the power of sin. To be in the flesh is the condition of unredeemed humanity; it is the situation of those who are "in Adam" as opposed to those who are "in Christ."

In light of his understanding of being "in the flesh," Paul explains the interaction between humanity's "sinful passions" (*ta pathēmata tōn hamartiōn*) and the law. Alluding to themes he has already introduced—that the law makes people aware of sin (3:20; 4:15) and increases sin (5:20)—Paul states that it was precisely "through the law" (*dia tou nomou*) that our sinful passions were at work in the members of our bodies for the purpose of bearing fruit that would lead to death. Paul is not saying that the law is sinful, nor is he affirming that the law in and of itself leads to death. But he is affirming that the sinful passions at work in our body were aroused through the law for the purpose of bearing fruit that leads to death. Thus, although believers have been released from the law to bear fruit to God, humanity's sinful passions were at work in unredeemed humanity, through the law, to bear fruit that leads to death. Although Paul will explain what he means by the phrase "through the law" in the next unit, it is apparent that he is making a statement that many in his Roman audience will find difficult to comprehend.

Having recalled the situation of unredeemed humanity in 7:5, Paul begins with the temporal marker *nyni* (now) to describe the situation of the redeemed: **But now [*nyni*], we have been released from the law, having died to what restrained us, so that we might serve in the newness that is the Spirit and not the obsolescence that is the written code** (7:6). Paul's argument progresses in four steps. First, as he did in 3:21 when he spoke of the manifestation of God's righteousness, he employs the expression *nyni de* (but now) to highlight the profound change that has occurred through Christ's death and resurrection. Second, using the same phrase as he did in his example of the married woman, he writes that "we have been released from the law" (*katērgēthēmen apo tou nomou*). Third, Paul returns to the theme of dying to the law to explain how believers have been released from the law—"having died to what [*en hō*] restrained us." Although the *en hō* could be masculine or neuter, Paul's train of thought indicates that he has the law in view. It was the law that restrained those under its rule before they were in Christ (Gal. 3:23), and it was only by dying (in Christ) to the law that they were released from it.

Finally, lest he be misunderstood as advocating an antinomian way of life, Paul concludes with a clause revealing that believers have died to the law so that they might serve "in the newness that is the Spirit and not the obsolescence that is the written code." Accordingly, just as Paul said that Christians were buried with Christ through their baptism into his death so that they might walk in newness of life (6:4), so he writes that they have died to the law in order to serve God in the newness that is the Spirit (7:6). This "newness" (*kainotēti*) is the new life of the Spirit in which the baptized walk. For Paul, the opposite of this "newness" is the "obsolescence" (*palaiotēti*) that characterizes "the written code," by which Paul means the law bereft of the Spirit (2:27, 29; 2 Cor. 3:6, 7). The believer has not died to the law to escape the moral life but to live the moral life in a new way, the way of the Spirit that Paul will describe in chapter 8.

7:7–12. Making use of a technique he has already employed in this letter (3:5; 6:1), Paul asks a rhetorical question that he immediately dismisses as a distortion of his gospel: **What then shall we say? Is the law to be equated with sin? Of course not!** (7:7a). Paul raises the question because of the statement he has just made in 7:5. Having said "our sinful passions were at work through the law [*dia tou nomou*] in the members of our body to bear fruit that led to death," Paul is aware that his audience might conclude that he is suggesting that the law is sinful. Consequently, he must explain what he means by the phrase *dia tou nomou*. What is the relation between the law, by which Paul means the Mosaic law, and sin?

First, Paul explains the baleful interaction between the law, which proclaims God's will, and sin, which entices people to rebel against God's will. After affirming that the law is not sinful, Paul qualifies his response. Employing the strong adversative *alla* (but), he writes, **but I did not know sin except through the law** (7:7b). This remark echoes what he has already written in 3:20 (that the law makes people aware of sin) and 5:13 (that in the period before the law, sin was not reckoned as sin because there was no law). Before the appearance of the Mosaic law, then, human beings were not aware that they were violating God's will. With the appearance of the law, however, those under its rule knew that they were violating a specific commandment of the all-holy God.

Jim Yancey

Figure 9. Column of a Torah scroll written on parchment. The earliest extant copies of the Christian scriptures are already in book (codex) form, but Paul would have known the books of Moses as scrolls. As this photograph taken at the Western Wall in contemporary Jerusalem illustrates, the books of the Law are still used in scroll form today.

Next, Paul explains how the law made people aware of sin: **for I would not have experienced desire if the law did not say, "You shall not covet." But sin, seizing an opportunity through the commandment, produced all kinds of desire in me** (7:7c–8a). Paul begins by focusing on the concept of "desire" (*epithymia*). Desire can be a positive emotion, as in Prov. 10:24 ("the desire of the righteous will be granted") and Phil. 1:23 ("having the desire to depart and be with Christ"), but here Paul portrays it negatively, as he did when he spoke of God's handing humanity over to the desires of its heart (Rom. 1:24), and when he referred to the sinful desire that sin incites (6:12). Personifying sin as a deadly power that enslaves those under its dominion, the apostle maintains that sin was able to find a foothold or "opportunity" (*aphormēn*; lit., a starting point or a base of operations) through the commandment (*dia tēs entolēs*). The specific commandment to which Paul refers is from the Decalogue: "You shall not *covet* your neighbor's house; you shall not *covet* your neighbor's wife, or male, or female slave, or ox, or donkey, or anything that belongs to your neighbor" (Exod. 20:17, emphasis added; Deut. 5:21). Focusing on the negative aspect of desire as the craving and longing for something one does not possess, Paul suggests that when the law forbade those under its rule to covet something, sin found the opportunity it needed to arouse every kind of desire, since what is forbidden becomes desirable. Imagine the scene in this way: The law says, "You shall not covet," but sin whispers, "Why not? Isn't the law restricting your freedom?"

Paul concludes this portion of his argument with the phrase **for apart from the law sin is dead** (7:8b). Once more, he assumes that sin is in the world, even when there is no law. In the absence of a specific law, however, sin did not have the opportunity it needed to assert itself. And because sin is a violation of God's law, human beings do not fully comprehend the gravity of their evil when there is no law. When Paul affirms that sin is dead apart from the law, then, he means that it lacks the occasion it needs to arouse its sinful desires in humanity.

Paul now introduces the pronoun *egō* (I), and with this pronoun his argument takes a new turn: **I was once living apart from the law** (7:9a). To be sure, the apostle has already employed the first-person singular in 7:7 (*ouk egnōn*, "I did not know"; *ouk ēdein*, "I would not have experienced"). But here he uses the personal pronoun in conjunction with the verb *ezōn* (I was living). Although Greek often employs the pronoun to emphasize the subject of the verb, that is not the case here. For if Paul is speaking of himself, what does he mean when he affirms that he once lived without the law? Although some have suggested that he is speaking of the period of his adolescence before he took on the yoke of the law, this argument is hardly convincing given what the apostle writes elsewhere (Phil. 3:4–6) and what he will say in the next verse. Here, then, the *egō* signals that Paul is speaking in the person of another: the voice of unredeemed humanity, of which sinful Adam was the progenitor and to which Paul belonged before he was incorporated into Christ. In the period before the Mosaic law, Adamic humanity lived in ignorance of God's will as expressed in the law.

Having alluded to the situation of Adamic humanity, Paul writes, **but when the commandment came, sin sprang to life** (7:9b). With this phrase, the apostle completes the thought he introduced at the close of 7:8, where he said that apart from the law, sin is dead. Sin was indeed dead in that it was dormant when there was no law, but once the law appeared, sin revived and took advantage of the opportunity the law afforded it to arouse desires contrary to God's law.

The next verse begins with *egō*: **I died, and I discovered that the commandment, which was intended to bring about life for me, this same commandment led to death** (7:10). With this verse, it is evident that Paul is not speaking autobiographically but in the person of Adamic humanity when it is confronted with God's law. With the appearance of the law, humanity became aware of God's will for the first time, and sin took the opportunity occasioned by the law to arouse its sinful desires. The result was that Adamic humanity died, by which Paul means it came under the power of sin and so died to God. The law revived the power of sin, which previously had been dead, and it resulted in death for those under its rule because it became the occasion for sin to arouse its sinful desires in humanity. The great irony that Paul sees *in the light of Christ* is that the law, which was intended to bring life, led to death because it revived sin and afforded sin the opportunity to do what it previously could not do.

Paul employs a clause beginning with *gar* (for) to explain what he means. Echoing what he said in 7:8, he writes: **For sin, taking the opportunity occasioned through the commandment, deceived me and through it killed me** (7:11). But whereas in 7:8 he said that sin "produced all kinds of desire in me," here he writes that sin "deceived me" (*exēpatēsen me*). The word Paul employs here is the same verb that occurs in the Greek text of Gen. 3:13, when Eve explains why she ate the forbidden fruit: "The serpent deceived me [*ho ophis ēpatēsen me*], and I ate" (my translation). Paul's use of the identical verb in 2 Cor. 11:3 ("But I am afraid that as the serpent *deceived* Eve by its cunning . . ."), an explicit reference to Gen. 3:13, confirms that he is alluding to the story of Genesis here as well. It is also another indication that he is speaking in the voice of Adamic humanity. For just as the serpent deceived Eve, and so Adam, with the result that both would die as God had warned ("for in the day that you eat of it you shall die"; Gen. 2:17), so the *egō* discovers that sin has deceived it "through the commandment," with the result that sin killed the *egō* through the commandment. Thus Paul acknowledges that the law had a role in consigning humanity "to the domination of sin" (Fitzmyer 1993, 469) inasmuch as sin employed the law to deceive those under the law.

Finally, Paul comes to the conclusion toward which he has been driving since the opening of this unit when he refused to equate the law with sin: **So the law is holy and the commandment is holy, righteous, and good** (7:12). Although Paul spoke somewhat negatively of the law in his Letter to the Galatians, there is no critique of the law here. How could there be? If the law comes from God, then it is holy as God is holy; and if the law is holy, all of its commandments are holy, righteous, and good. No, the law is not to be equated with sin, even though sin uses the occasion of the law to arouse desire and deceive those under its regime. The culprit is not the law but sin that makes use of the law to deceive those under the law to transgress its commandments.

7:13–23. Having explained that the law is holy and not to be equated with sin, in this unit Paul examines the relation between sin and law from the vantage point of the conflicted or divided self. As in the previous unit, he insists that the culprit is not the law itself but the power of sin that dwells in the carnal self, so that even though the self knows and wants to do God's law, it cannot because it is merely carnal and overcome by the power of indwelling sin.

In the previous unit, Paul has employed the past tense to explain Adamic humanity's initial encounter with sin; in this unit, he uses the present tense to describe the ongoing struggle that Adamic humanity encounters as it tries to observe the law. Written from the perspective of one who is in Christ, these verses describe the inner conflict that Adamic humanity encounters when it tries to observe God's spiritual law. After an initial question (7:13), the unit consists of three subunits (7:14–17, 18–20, 21–23), each of which describes a particular aspect of the conflict that the carnal self encounters when it tries to observe the law.

As he did in the previous unit, Paul begins with an objection to something he has said. Having just stated that sin took the opportunity of the law to "deceive me" and "to kill me" through the commandment (7:11), he raises an objection: **Then did what is good become death for me?** (7:13a). Since Paul has just praised the commandment as "holy, righteous, and good," it is clear that he is referring to the law here and asking if the law brings its adherents to the death that is eternal separation from God. Employing the same technique he used in the previous unit, Paul immediately dismisses this objection and responds: **Of course not! But sin, in order that it might be shown to be sin, brought about death for me through what is good so that through the commandment sin might be shown to be exceedingly sinful** (7:13b). Since the law is holy, it is unthinkable that it should become the cause of death. Reiterating what he has already said, Paul insists that the real culprit was sin, not the law. So that sin might be shown for what it truly is—a complete and total rebellion against God—it effected death "through what is good" (*dia tou agathou*). Thus sin worked through what was most holy, God's own law, to deceive and kill. As a result, it was "through the commandment" that sin became even more sinful! By employing the expression *dia tēs entolēs* (through the commandment) here, as he did in 7:8, 11, Paul shows that it was not the law but sin working *through the commandment* that resulted in death. And by saying that this happened so that sin might be exposed for what it truly was, Paul affirms that the full evil of sin is only apparent in the light of God's law.

Next, Paul introduces the first of three subunits that deal with the carnal self, the *egō* (7:14–17). Still asserting the essential goodness of the law, he draws a powerful contrast between the acting subject, the *egō*, and God's law: **We know that the law is spiritual, but I am carnal, indentured to sin** (7:14). With this statement, Paul assumes that he and his audience agree on two points. First, the law is "spiritual" (*pneumatikos*) because it belongs to the realm of God, who is holy. Second, the *egō* is "carnal" (*sarkinos*) because it belongs to the realm of what is mortal and perishable. Not only is it carnal, it is also "indentured to sin" (*pepramenos hypo tēn hamartian*; lit., "sold under sin," as though one were sin's slave). Accordingly, there is a chasm between the commandments of the law, which belongs to the realm of God, and the unredeemed *egō*, which belongs to the realm of what is mortal and destined to perish. Whereas the law expresses God's will because it is spiritual, the unredeemed *egō*, whether it is aware of it or not, is indentured to sin.

Having introduced the carnal self, Paul shows how this self is revealed as a divided self: **For I do not understand what I am doing; for it is not what I intend that I do, but the very thing that I hate that I do** (7:15). Speaking from the perspective of redeemed humanity, Paul looks back and understands the conflict of the unredeemed self better than the unredeemed self understands itself. The proof that the *egō* is indentured to sin is its inability to comprehend itself, as is apparent from the inner conflict it experiences between what it wants to do and what it actually does because it is under the power of sin. The presence of this conflict in the carnal self of unredeemed humanity paradoxically testifies to the goodness of the law. For if the self does what it does not want to do, then it acknowledges that God's law is good. Accordingly, Paul writes, **But if I do what I do not want, I am in agreement with the law that it is good** (7:16). The conflicted self, then, knows what is right, but it cannot do what is right because it is carnal; it is indentured to sin.

Paul concludes this unit by describing the real situation of unredeemed humanity as seen from the perspective of one who is in Christ: **Now it is no longer I who am doing this but sin dwelling in me** (7:17). Once more the culprit is sin, which is so deeply embedded in the *egō* that the *egō* no longer makes its own decisions. Because it is indentured to sin, the unredeemed *egō* has lost its power to make its own decisions. To understand this situation, it is helpful to contrast what Paul writes here about unredeemed humanity with what he says of himself in Gal. 2:19b–20a: "I have been crucified with Christ; and it is no longer I [*egō*] who live, but it is Christ who lives in me." The contrast could not be greater. Whereas in Rom. 7 it is the power of indwelling sin that controls the *egō* so that the self cannot do what it wills, in Gal. 2 it is Christ who controls the *egō* so that the self does God's will.

The second subunit of Paul's argument (7:18–20) manifests a striking structural similarity with the first (7:14–17). It begins with a statement about the human condition (7:18a; cf. 7:14). Next, it describes the plight of the conflicted self (7:18b–19; cf. 7:15). Finally, it draws the same conclusion as the first subunit did: the real culprit is not the law but indwelling sin (7:20; cf. 7:16–17). With this second subunit, Paul employs repetition to reinforce and strengthen his argument.

Paul begins with a statement about the human condition: **For I know that nothing that is good dwells in me, that is, in my flesh** (7:18a). Although Paul's initial assessment of the human condition is utterly pessimistic, we must recall that he is speaking in the persona of Adamic humanity *from the perspective of one who has been redeemed in Christ*. It is from this perspective, and only from this perspective, that Paul is able to make such a statement. For just as it is the light that makes one aware of the darkness, so it is God's grace that makes one aware of one's sinfulness. Paul's qualification that nothing good dwells *in my flesh* indicates that the *egō* of whom he speaks is the self defined by what is merely mortal and perishable. Nothing good dwells in such a self.

Having defined the carnal human condition in 7:18a as deprived of all that is good, Paul provides another description of the divided self: **For the intention is there, but doing what is good is not. For I do not do the good I intend; instead, I do the evil I do not intend** (7:18b–19). Here Paul makes use of two clauses, each beginning with *gar* (for), to support his argument. In the first he draws a contrast between the self's willingness to do what is good and its inability to do so, thereby supporting what he has said about the human situation (7:18b). In the second he makes a statement similar to the one he made in 7:15—that the self does not understand its own actions (7:19). Although the self wants to do what it good, it does the very evil it does not want to do. Thus it is apparent that nothing good resides in the self that is determined by what is merely mortal and perishable. When controlled by the flesh, the *egō* cannot do the good it wills.

Beginning with a conditional clause, Paul draws out the inevitable conclusion of this situation: **But if I do what I do not intend, it is no longer I who am doing it but sin dwelling within me** (7:20). There is something else at work in the *egō*, which can only be perceived from the perspective of God's grace. Still speaking in the voice of unredeemed humanity, but always from the vantage point of redemption, the apostle draws the only conclusion that can explain the situation of the conflicted self: the *egō* of Adamic humanity is not in control of itself. There is something else at work, the power of indwelling sin, which opposes the *egō*'s effort to do what is good.

Having described the situation of the carnal self in the first two subunits (7:14–17 and 7:18–20), in the third Paul will draw a conclusion from what he has said (7:21–23). Still speaking in the person of unredeemed humanity, but always from the perspective of one who has been redeemed, he enunciates the principle that characterizes the life of the carnal self (7:21) and then illustrates that principle in two ways (7:22–23). This subunit, which I have titled "the conflict of the carnal self," is complicated because Paul employs *nomos* (law) in different ways.

First, Paul draws a conclusion from his description of the conflicted self. Employing *nomos* in the sense of "principle," he writes, **Therefore, I discover the following law: that when I intend to do what is good, evil lies close at hand** (7:21). The *nomos* that structures the life of unredeemed humanity is such that no matter how much the *egō* wills to do what is good, evil is always at hand to disrupt its good intentions. The conflict that Paul has been describing, then, is built into the very structure of Adamic humanity. To describe what he means, in 7:22–23 Paul contrasts two "laws" that are at war with each other: (1) the law of God, which the inner self and the mind acknowledge, and (2) the law of sin, which is lodged in the members of the carnal body. Paul relates the law of God and the inner self in this way: **For I delight in God's law in my inner self** (7:22). This law is the Mosaic law, which Paul has already identified as holy in 7:12. By "the inner self" (*ton esō anthrōpon*), Paul means the aspect of the person that recognizes what is right and good, the aspect of the conflicted self that knows what is good and wants to do what is good. This is the person that delights in the Mosaic law.

Although the inner self delights in the Mosaic law (God's law), it is frustrated by another law that Paul calls the law of sin: **But I see another law in the members** of my body at war with the law of my intellect, making me a prisoner to the law of sin that dwells in the members of my body (7:23). This other law is not the Mosaic law. It is lodged in the carnal members of the body, and Paul identifies it as "the law of sin" (*tō nomō tēs hamartias*), by which he means the power of sin. Thus sin is a "law" inasmuch as it is a principle that determines how those under its power act. This "law" of sin is at war with "the law of my intellect" (*tō nomō tou noos mou*), by which Paul means the Mosaic law. The intellect, like the inner self, delights in God's law, but it cannot do God's law because "the law of sin"—sin itself—has taken it captive. The self of unredeemed humanity is divided and conflicted, then, because it finds itself in the middle of a battlefield between two opposing armies: the law of God and the law of sin. Still in the realm of the flesh and not yet in the realm of the Spirit, the unredeemed person is unable to do the law in which its inner self delights.

7:24–25. Having described unredeemed humanity's inability to do the law in which the mind and the inner self delight, Paul concludes his discussion of the law with the desperate cry of the conflicted self, to which he immediately responds with an expression of thanksgiving (7:24–25). Frustrated that it cannot do the good it wills, and assaulted by the law of sin that has taken it captive, the conflicted and divided self cries, **Miserable one that I am, who will rescue me from this body doomed to death?** (7:24). The "miserable one" (*talaipōros egō anthrōpos*) is not the Christ-believer but the one who is still in Adam. The self that Paul describes here needs to be rescued "from this body doomed to death" (*ek tou sōmatos tou thanatou toutou*), by which Paul means a body destined to death and separation from God because it is merely mortal and dominated by sin.

Although this is the desperate cry of the conflicted self, Paul makes this cry in light of his own redemption in Christ. Aware that Christ has already rescued him from this situation, Paul responds to his own question with the words, **but thanks be to God through Jesus Christ our Lord** (7:25a). With this thanksgiving, the apostle recalls the victory he has already described in chapter 5, and he anticipates his discussion of life in the Spirit, which he will present in chapter 8.

Having responded to the desperate cry of the unredeemed, Paul summarizes the situation of the conflicted self: **Therefore, with my intellect I myself serve the law of God, but in the flesh I serve the law of sin** (7:25b). The carnal *egō* recognizes God's law with its intellect, but inasmuch as the unredeemed self is in the flesh, it serves the law of sin because it does not have the inner power to observe God's law, the power of God's Spirit, which Paul will describe in chapter 8.

Theological Issues

Although the law plays a central role in Paul's theology, it is one of the most disputed aspects of his writings. Referring to the law as "an enigma in Paul's thought," J. Christiaan Beker (1980, 235) writes, "Paul maintains that the law is the instrument of God, but he asserts at the same time that it is the servant of sin. The law is God's holy will, obedience to which is the condition for life; but God also gave the law to increase sin in order to indicate its deadly character." Writing in a similar vein, Udo Schnelle (2005, 333) speaks of "an almost unsolvable problem of Pauline thought: How is the election of Israel and the gift of the law/Torah related to the new, final, unsurpassed revelation of God in Jesus Christ?"

Paul's comments about the law are puzzling and enigmatic, some would say self-contradictory. To make sense of them, we must recall that Paul wrote in response to questions and issues that arose in the communities he founded or, in the case of Romans, a community he was about to visit. Consequently, instead of developing a systematic treatise on the law, he discusses the law in relation to specific issues and problems that arose in the local community. For example, in Galatians he portrays the law in a rather unflattering manner because he must defend his Torah-free gospel from intruding missionaries who are teaching the Galatians that they must be circumcised and do the works of the Mosaic law in order to be numbered among Abraham's descendants. Faced with this crisis, Paul draws a sharp contrast between the promises that God made to Abraham and the law given to Moses through angels 430 years later (Gal. 3:17). Reminding the Galatians that they are already Abraham's descendants because they have been baptized into his singular offspring, the Christ (Gal. 3:27–29), Paul emphasizes the priority of God's promises to the law that 430 years later came to deal with transgressions until the promised offspring—the Christ—should appear (Gal. 3:19). Seeking to persuade his Gentile converts that they need not be circumcised and adopt a Jewish way of life characterized by doing the works of the law, Paul emphasizes the temporary role of the law. Its function in the period before Christ was akin to that of the *paidagōgos*, the household slave who watched over the heir of the family until the heir attained maturity and received the inheritance. Thus Paul writes, "The law was our disciplinarian [*paidagōgos*] until Christ came, so that we might be justified by faith" (Gal. 3:24).

Although he does not explicitly denigrate the law, Paul insists that it belonged to the period of humanity's minority: "Now before faith came, we were imprisoned and guarded under the law until faith would be revealed" (Gal. 3:23). But now that the Christ has come, that period is over, as is the salvation-historical role that the law played. Accordingly, Paul exhorts his converts to give their allegiance to Christ rather than to the law. The key to understanding Paul's treatment of the law in Galatians, then, is to appreciate the situation to which he was responding. Pointing to this contingent aspect of Paul's thought, Beker (1980, 240) writes, "The main pitch of the argument in Galatians is the meaning of the new lordship of Christ for the Gentiles: The law is an outmoded and unnecessary reality for Gentiles, because it was not meant for them (3:6–14) and because it represents their former bondage to 'the elemental spirits of the universe' (Gal. 4:3)."

In Romans, Paul writes in a more irenic fashion about the law because he is not facing the polemical situation that occasioned Galatians. Seeking to present his gospel to a community he did not establish and has not visited, but which undoubtedly has heard of his Torah-free gospel, Paul's remarks are more nuanced. Aware that many at Rome are disturbed or misinformed about his preaching among the Gentiles, in Romans he discusses the law in several contexts, sometimes in an unflattering way, other times in a more positive manner.

The Law and God's Impartiality

In Rom. 2:12–24 Paul refers to the law as he discusses God's impartiality. He argues that God does not judge people on the basis of whether they possess the law but on the basis of what they do. Consequently, it is not the hearers of the law who are righteous in God's sight but those who do God's law (2:13). The law is of great value if one observes its prescriptions. But if one merely listens to it without doing it, the law has no value. It leads to condemnation.

The Law as Condemnatory

After showing that all, Jew and Gentile alike, are under the power of sin (3:9–18), Paul highlights in 3:19–20 the condemning aspect of the law. Employing an extended list of scriptural quotations (3:10–18), he shows that all have sinned. From this description of the human situation, Paul concludes that since all have sinned, no one will be justified by doing the works of the law. What the law does is make people conscious of sin, for those who know the law understand that their transgressions violate God's will.

The Law as Prophetic

Having spoken of the human predicament, Paul returns to the theme of God's righteousness (3:21–31). In doing so, he makes two important statements about the law. First, although God has manifested his saving righteousness apart from the law, the law and the prophets witness to God's righteousness (3:21). Second, the faith that the gospel requires does not nullify the law but upholds it (3:31). Thus Paul attributes a prophetic function to the law insofar as it points to the saving righteousness of God revealed in Christ.

To explain how he upholds the law, in chapter 4 Paul turns to a narrative from the Torah to show that Abraham was justified on the basis of faith in God's promises rather than on the basis of works. By employing a story about Abraham from the Torah, Paul supports his claim that he upholds the law since the Abraham narrative proclaims that righteousness comes from faith in God's promises rather than from doing the works of the law. In light of this Torah narrative, Paul writes that the law brings wrath since it is only when human beings know God's law that they explicitly violate it (4:15) and so are liable to judgment. The law then is both prophetic and condemnatory. On the one hand, it heralds the gospel's teaching of justification by faith. On the other, it places sinful humanity under God's judgment by making it aware that its transgressions violate God's will.

The Law and the Human Situation

In chapters 5–6, the law plays an important role in Paul's understanding of the human situation. Paul begins his description of the human predicament by noting that sin entered the world by Adam's transgression, and through sin, death made its appearance, spreading to all (5:12). According to Paul's understanding of history, sin was in the world before the Mosaic law made its appearance. In the period before the law, however, people sinned unaware that they were transgressing a specific commandment of God's law (5:13). Consequently, although the purpose of the law was to make them aware of God's will, the law multiplied transgressions by making people conscious that they were sinning against God's law (5:20).

The appearance of Christ marks a decisive shift in humanity's relationship to the law. Prior to Christ, humanity was under the power of sin and the law (although sin and law are not to be equated with each other, as Paul explains in chap. 7). With the appearance of Christ, however, those who have been baptized into his death are no longer under the law but under grace. Having been incorporated into Christ, they have transferred their allegiance from one lord to another. Formerly slaves of sin, they are now slaves of righteousness. Consequently, they are under the rule of grace rather than under the rule of the law. Thus Paul portrays the law as belonging to humanity's former condition, when it was in the old Adam. But when the plight of Adamic humanity is overcome, there is no further need for the regime of the law.

Paul's Defense of the Law

What Paul says in chapters 5–6 leads to his defense of the law in chapter 7. Having related the law so closely to sin, Paul appears to be saying that the law is sinful. To counter this, he insists that the law is holy and spiritual (7:12, 14). It is not the law that causes people to sin; it is sin working through the law that deceives and causes them to transgress God's commandments. Analyzing the human situation in the light of Christ, Paul sees something he previously could not see: Because humanity was in the old Adam, it was carnal and sold under the power of sin, which insidiously worked through the law to deceive people and lead them to death. So long as people are in the realm of the flesh, under the domination of sin, sin will frustrate their efforts to do the law, no matter how well-intentioned they are. Chapter 7 then is Paul's most positive statement about the law.

What the Law Could Not Do

In 8:2–4 Paul affirms that what the law could not do (because its adherents were under the powers of sin and death), God has accomplished through his Son, who conquered the powers of sin and death on their own battleground. Assuming human flesh in order to enter the realm of all that is human, the Spirit-endowed Son of God did what Adamic humanity could not do: he was perfectly obedient to God. Through this obedience, God's Son overcame the powers of sin and death and made it possible for humanity to do what the law requires. As a result of God's work in Christ, those who are in Christ can do what the carnal self wanted to do but could not do.

Christ, the Terminus of the Law

For Paul, the salvation-historical role of the law, which began with Moses, ended with the coming of Christ; for the appearance of Christ marked the goal and terminus of the law (10:4). Now that the Messiah has come, it is futile to strive for a righteousness based on the law when the righteousness based on faith has been revealed in Christ. To pursue a righteousness based on the law is to stumble on what Paul calls "the stumbling stone," namely, the Christ (9:32).

Fulfilling the Law

Is the law irrelevant for those who are in Christ so that they may ignore its prescriptions? Hardly! Paul continues to call upon and make use of the law,

---

The Mosaic Law in Paul's Theology

- The law is holy and spiritual. It is an authentic expression of God's will.
- The law played a prophetic role in the period between Moses and the Messiah by preparing Israel for, and pointing to, the Christ.
- The law's role was temporary and destined to end with the appearance of the Christ.
- Sin worked through the law to deceive and lead people to death.
- The law made people aware that their transgressions violated God's will.
- The carnal self's inability to do God's law, which the inner person recognizes as good, reveals the depth of the human predicament.
- The law continues to play an educative role for those who are in Christ, but its observance is not the source of their righteousness.
- Those in Christ "fulfill" the law's just demands through the love commandment.

especially the Decalogue. He insists that those who are in Christ fulfill the law through the love commandment (13:8–10). In the light of Christ, however, he now understands that legal observance did not lead to righteousness, because sin frustrated humanity's ability to do the law. Those who are in Christ find their righteousness in him. They continue to honor and revere the law as an expression of God's will, but they do not view it as the source of their righteousness since the righteousness that counts before God depends upon faith in Jesus Christ.

Romans 8:1–39

Life and Hope in the Realm of the Spirit

⌐⌐

Introductory Matters

Chapter 8 is a climactic moment in Paul's Letter to the Romans, even if it is not *the* climax, as many commentators once maintained. Having dealt with the plight of unredeemed humanity (1:18–3:20), the origin of that plight (5:12–21), and the inability of those in solidarity with Adam to do the prescriptions of the law (7:7–25), in chapter 8 Paul presents the new life and hope for final or eschatological glory that belongs to those who are in solidarity with Christ. To be sure, Paul has already proclaimed God's saving righteousness in 3:21–26 and celebrated the hope of the justified and reconciled in 5:1–11. In chapter 8, however, he provides his audience with an extended discourse of the new life and hope for glory that the justified enjoy because they dwell in the sphere of God's life-giving Spirit. Accordingly, whereas Paul has proclaimed God's own righteousness in 3:21–26 and the eschatological hope of the justified in 5:1–11, in chapter 8 he celebrates the power of God's indwelling Spirit, which empowers believers with the inner dynamism to *fulfill* a law they could not *do* because of the overriding power of sin. The conclusion to Paul's discussion of Israel's destiny in chapters 9–11 will provide another climactic moment in his argument, and 12:1–15:13 will offer an extended exposition of how the justified should live their new life in Christ. Yet it is chapter 8 that provides the soteriological grounding for the ethical life of the justified that Paul will describe in 12:1–15:13 and the hope for the eschatological restoration of Israel that he will present in chapters 9–11.

In addition to being a climactic moment in Romans, chapter 8 plays an important role in the argument that Paul has been developing since the beginning of chapter 5, bringing closure to what he has been saying about sin, death, and the law. It is not surprising, then, that Nils Dahl (1977), Richard Dillon (1998), and others have highlighted the coherence of chapters 5–8 by showing how chapter 8 alludes to and develops the central themes presented in chapters 5–7. For example, Dahl has cataloged the numerous literary relationships between 5:1–11 and chapter 8, and Dillon has shown how Paul's exposition of life in the Spirit corresponds to his ethical discussion in chapters 6–7. Nygren (1949, 305) says that in chapter 8 Paul turns back to his starting point in 5:12–21, and D. Moo (1996, 469) notes the close relationship between 8:18–39 and 5:1–11, concluding that there is a ring composition in chapters 5–8, whereby the second part of chapter 8 (8:18–39) returns to the themes of the first part of chapter 5 (5:1–11), and the first part of chapter 8 (8:1–17) recalls the second part of chapter 5 (5:12–21). Before I discuss Paul's train of thought in chapter 8, then, it will be helpful to explain how this chapter brings closure to several themes that Paul has been developing in chapters 5–7.

First, in 8:1–4 Paul provides a response to the plight of unredeemed humanity that he described in chapter 7. There he showed that as long as humanity was in solidarity with Adam, it was unable do what God's law required because of the power of indwelling sin (7:7–25). Accordingly, God dealt with sin by sending his own Son into the realm of the flesh so that humanity could fulfill the just requirement of the law through the power of God's life-giving Spirit.

Second, in 8:5–17 Paul describes the new life that believers enjoy when they live according to the Spirit rather than according to the flesh. In doing so, he provides another response to the objection he raised against his own gospel, that it encourages people to persist in sin (6:1, 15). In response to this objection against his Torah-free gospel, Paul shows that those who are no longer under the law, because they are under grace, can live an ethically good life through the power of God's Spirit, which dwells in them. Not only have believers died to sin by their baptismal participation in Christ's death, they have also entered into the realm of God's Spirit, which empowers them to live in a way pleasing to God.

Finally, in 8:18–39 Paul returns to the theme of hope for eschatological glory that he introduced in 5:1–11 and to which he alludes at the end of his Adam/Christ comparison when he speaks of the reign of grace (5:21). But whereas in 5:1–11 and 5:12–21 Paul grounded the believer's hope for future glory in the present experience of justification and reconciliation, in chapter 8—without neglecting God's salvific work in Christ—he grounds the believer's final hope in the present experience of the Spirit, which is the firstfruits of salvation. Moreover, he highlights the cosmic scope of salvation, which embraces the whole of creation as well as the justified. In chapter 8, then, Paul enhances and develops the vision of hope that he presents in chapter 5.

Romans 8:1–39 in the Rhetorical Flow

The letter opening (1:1–17)

Gentiles and Jews in the light of God's wrath (1:18–3:20)

Gentiles and Jews in the light of God's righteousness (3:21–4:25)

The experience of salvation in the light of God's righteousness (5:1–8:39)

  Transferred from the realm of sin to the realm of God's grace (5:1–21)

  No longer slaves of sin and death (6:1–23)

  Released from a law frustrated by sin (7:1–25)

▶ **Life and hope in the realm of the Spirit (8:1–39)**

  The Spirit as the source of life (8:1–17)

    God's resolution to the human predicament (8:1–4)

      No condemnation for those in Christ (8:1–2)

      The sending of God's Son (8:3–4)

    The mind-set of the flesh and the mind-set of the Spirit (8:5–8)

    The new situation of those in Christ (8:9–11)

    The consequences of this new situation (8:12–17)

      Either death or life (8:12–13)

      A Spirit of adoption (8:14–15)

      Children, heirs, coheirs with Christ (8:16–17)

  The Spirit as the source of hope (8:18–30)

    The glory to be revealed (8:18–25)

      Thematic statement (8:18)

      The longing of creation (8:19–22)

      The longing of believers (8:23–25)

    The Spirit's assistance (8:26–27)

    The consummation of God's plan (8:28–30)

  The irrevocable character of God's love (8:31–39)

    Rhetorical questions and responses (8:31–36)

      First question and response (8:31–32)

      Second question and response (8:33)

      Third question and response (8:34)

      Fourth question and response (8:35–37)

    Paul's confidence in God's love (8:38–39)

      Why believers are victorious (8:38)

      Nothing stronger than God's love (8:39)

Thus at several points chapter 8 returns to and develops themes found in chapters 5–7. The relationship between these two blocks of material can be viewed in this way:

8:1–4: The Spirit is the antidote
to the power of indwelling sin described in 7:7–25.

8:5–17: The Spirit is the enabler
of the ethical life described in 6:1–23.

8:18–39: The Spirit is the firstfruits
of the eschatological hope described in 5:1–11.

As this outline shows, chapter 8 recalls and develops the major themes of chapters 5–7. But instead of treating those themes in the order in which they occur (the eschatological hope of the justified, the ethical life of the justified, the inability of those in the flesh to do the law), chapter 8 begins with the last of these themes and ends with the first. In this way Paul brackets his discussion of the ethical life of the justified and the plight of the unredeemed with expositions of the eschatological hope that the justified enjoy. The theological themes of chapters 5–8 unfold as follows:

Eschatological hope grounded in justification and reconciliation (Rom. 5)
The ethical life of the justified (Rom. 6)
The plight of the unredeemed (Rom. 7)
Eschatological hope grounded in the Spirit (Rom. 8)

From the way in which Paul has arranged his argument, it is apparent that chapter 8 plays a pivotal role in Romans for several reasons, not the least of which is the central place it ascribes to the Spirit. Previous to chapter 8, there were only four references to the Spirit in Romans (1:9; 2:29; 5:5; 7:6), and after this chapter there will be only eight more (9:1; 11:8; 12:11; 14:17; 15:13, 16, 19, 30). But in this chapter there are nineteen references to the Spirit. While chapter 8 is not a systematic exposition of the Spirit, it is one of Paul's most important statements about the role of the Spirit in the Christian life, a topic to which I will return after I have traced Paul's train of thought.

Tracing the Train of Thought

Chapter 8 consists of three parts. In the first, Paul presents the Spirit as the source and dynamism of the believer's new life (8:1–17). In the second, he shows that the Spirit grounds the believer's hope for final or eschatological glory (8:18–30). In the third, he affirms the irrevocable character of God's love (8:31–39), thereby echoing the chapter's thematic statement that there is no condemnation for those who are in Christ (8:1).

The first part (8:1–17) consists of four units. The first looks back to the desperate predicament of humanity described in 7:7–25, and it explains how God has resolved this situation (8:1–4). In addition to looking back, this unit anticipates what Paul will say about the Spirit in the rest of the chapter. On the basis of the contrast that Paul draws in 8:1–4 between the law of the Spirit of life and the law of sin and death, the second unit establishes a sharp distinction between two contrasting ways of life, life according to the Spirit and life according to the flesh (8:5–8). By arguing that believers are not to walk according to the flesh but according to the Spirit, Paul provides further support for the ethical argument he made in chapter 6 that believers are not to persist in sin, because they have died with Christ. In the third unit, Paul directly addresses the Romans, assuring them that they are no longer in the realm of the flesh because they belong to the realm of the Spirit (8:9–11). Finally, in the fourth unit, Paul draws out the consequences of the believer's new life. Contrasting the Spirit of adoption with a spirit of slavery, he assures the Christ-believers at Rome that they are God's sons and daughters, coheirs with Christ (8:12–17). Paul's reference to the Romans as coheirs who will be glorified with Christ echoes what he has said about their hope for God's glory in 5:2 and provides a transition to the next stage of his argument, which deals with the believer's hope for final glory.

In the second part of the chapter (8:18–30), Paul returns to the theme of hope for eschatological glory that he introduced in 5:1–11. This part consists of three units. In the first, he describes the longing of creation and humanity for this eschatological hope (8:18–25). In the second, he points to the assistance that the Spirit brings to the believer (8:26–27). In the third, he celebrates the consummation of God's plan (8:28–30).

The third part of the chapter (8:31–39) is a rhetorical tour de force that celebrates the irrevocable character of God's love and recalls the themes of affliction and endurance that Paul introduced in 5:1–11. It consists of two units. In the first, Paul asks a series of rhetorical questions (8:31–36). In the second, he affirms his confidence in God's love (8:37–29).

8:1–4. In chapter 7 Paul described the plight of Adamic humanity: although the inner self knew God's law and desired to do what it commanded, it could not do the good it wanted because of the power of indwelling sin. In 7:24 Paul brought his description of humanity's predicament to a climax with the anguished cry of the conflicted self: "Who will rescue me from this body doomed to death?" Having concluded his exposition of the human condition apart from Christ, Paul announces God's response to the predicament of unredeemed humanity (8:1–4). This theologically rich unit consists of two subunits. In the first, Paul announces his theme that there is no condemnation for those who are in Christ because the law of the Spirit has freed them from the law of sin and death (8:1–2). In the second, he explains that God sent his own Son into the realm of the flesh to condemn sin in the flesh so that the requirement of the law is now fulfilled in those who belong to Christ (8:3–4).

The first verse of this chapter functions as a thematic statement that signals a decisive turning point in Paul's argument, similar to those announced in 3:21 and 5:1. Having spoken of the "condemnation" or "judgment" that Adam's trespass brought upon humanity (5:16, 18), and having described the predicament of Adamic humanity (7:7–25), Paul announces the new situation in which believers find themselves: **Consequently, now there is no condemnation for those who are in Christ Jesus** (8:1). The "condemnation" (*katakrima*) of which Paul speaks is God's just judgment upon Adamic humanity, which stands in solidarity with the old Adam and transgresses God's commandments. So long as Adamic humanity dwells in the realm of the flesh, under the power of sin, there is only one verdict: the "death sentence" of eternal separation from God. In 8:3 Paul will explain how God has condemned sin in the flesh by sending his own Son into the realm of sinful flesh, and at the end of this chapter he will ask who can "condemn" the justified (8:34). But that question will be merely rhetorical. For there is no condemnation for those who are "in Christ" since they have been transferred from the realm of sin and death to the realm of grace and life.

Some manuscripts (A, D¹, et al.) emphasize the moral requirements of this new life by reading, "there is no condemnation for those in Christ *who do not walk according to the flesh*." Others (ℵ², D³, et al.) are more expansive: "There is no condemnation for those in Christ *who do not walk according to the flesh but according the Spirit*." Although Paul will highlight the need to walk according to the Spirit rather than according to the flesh in 8:5–8, these longer readings appear to be secondary additions intended to emphasize the ethical dimension of what Paul says.

Having announced his theme, Paul provides a supporting reason for what he has just said: **For the law that is the life-giving Spirit has freed you in Christ Jesus from the law that is sin and death** (8:2). This verse is fraught with exegetical problems, not the least of which is the meaning of the two laws to which Paul refers here. Stuhlmacher (1994, 118) and Wright (2002, 576–77) maintain that both expressions refer to the Torah but from different vantage points: the Torah empowered by God's Spirit, and the Torah debilitated by the powers of sin and death. Others argue that Paul is employing *nomos* in the sense of "principle" or "rule" (Fitzmyer 1993, 482; Fee 1994, 521–27).

As is evident from my translation, I support the second position. The NRSV offers a more literal translation of the Greek: "the law of the Spirit of life" and "the law of sin and of death." If *nomos* refers to the Mosaic law in both instances, Paul is saying that the Mosaic law as now exercised in the realm of God's Spirit has set us free from what the Mosaic law could not do when we were under the powers of sin and death. Although this is an attractive interpretation that coheres with Paul's description of the law as holy and spiritual (7:12, 14), it does not cohere with his overall argument that *God*, not the law, has freed humanity from sin and death through the saving death of Christ. But if Paul is not speaking of the Mosaic law, why does he use the word *nomos*? Why doesn't he simply contrast the Spirit with sin and death?

Here we must recall the different ways in which Paul employs "law" in 7:22–25: "God's law" (*tō nomō tou theou; nomō theou*), "another law" (*heteron nomon*), "the law of sin" (*tō nomō tēs hamartias; nomō hamartias*). While "the law of God" in 7:22 and 25 does refer to the Mosaic law, we have already seen that "another law" (7:23) and "the law of sin" (7:23, 25) refer to the power of sin that frustrates the divided self rather than to the Mosaic law. When Paul refers to the "the law of sin and death" in 8:2, then, he is referring to the "law of sin" mentioned in 7:25. This is the reason for my translation, "the law *that is* sin and death." As for the expression, "the law of the Spirit of life," if Paul still had the Mosaic law in view, one would have expected him to write, "the law of God," as he did in 7:22 and 25. But instead he introduces a new expression that plays on *nomos*. Employing *nomos* in the sense of principle, he refers to the "law" that is God's own life-giving Spirit. Thus "law" is used as a metaphor for the Spirit, which frees humanity from another "law," the rule of sin and death. In effect, Paul plays on the word *nomos* to contrast two opposing "laws" (the Spirit and sin/death), thereby reminding his audience that the "law" that is God's own Spirit has done what the Mosaic law could not do.

Before we ask how God's life-giving Spirit has freed humanity from sin and death, we must deal with two subsidiary issues. First, although the text I have followed (e.g., ℵ, B, F, G) reads "freed you," other witnesses (e.g., A, D, 1739ᶜ) read "freed me," and still others (e.g., Ψ) "freed us." The first of these variants makes eminent sense, since the conflicted self has asked, "Who will rescue *me* from this body doomed to death." The second also makes sense since Paul is addressing this letter to a community of believers. The reading adopted here is the more difficult one since Paul unexpectedly switches from the first to the second person. But it also makes good rhetorical sense. Having addressed an imaginary interlocutor in the second-person singular earlier in the letter (2:1), he addresses that interlocutor again, thereby highlighting how God's work in Christ has redeemed the interlocutor.

Second, how is one to construe the phrase *en Christō* in 8:2? Should the phrase be read with the noun that precedes it ("the life-giving Spirit in Christ") or with the verb that follows it ("has freed you in Christ")? My translation reads the phrase with what follows, thereby emphasizing the role of Christ.

Having proclaimed that there is no condemnation for those who are in Christ Jesus because the "law that is the life-giving Spirit" has freed them "from the law that is sin and death," in 8:3–4 Paul provides further support for his thesis: There is no condemnation for those who are in Christ because God sent his Son into the realm of human flesh to condemn sin in order that the just requirement of the law might be fulfilled in those who are in Christ.

Paul establishes a contrast between what the law could not do and what God has done in Christ: **For what was impossible for the law because it was weakened through the flesh, God accomplished. Sending his own Son in the likeness of sinful flesh and for sin, he condemned sin in the flesh** (8:3). The precise meaning of the phrase Paul employs here, "in the likeness of sinful flesh" (*en homoiōmati sarkos hamartias*), is elusive for two reasons. First, as Florence Morgan Gillman notes (1987, 599), the noun *homoiōma* could imply "similarity but not full identity" as it does in 1:23; 5:14; 6:5; or "full identity" as it does in Phil. 2:7. Second, as Vincent Branick (1985) has argued, *sarkos hamartias* can be taken in either an ethical or a cosmic sense. Taken in an ethical sense, it suggests that Christ became human to the point of sinning. Taken in a cosmic sense, it means that Christ entered into the cosmic situation of sin and death that afflicted Adam's descendants. Given Paul's insistence on Jesus's humanity (Rom. 1:3; Gal. 4:4), it is unlikely that Paul employs "likeness" in the sense of similarity but not full identity. And since Paul has already spoken of sin and death as cosmic forces and affirms Christ's sinlessness in 2 Cor. 5:21, the phrase "sinful humanity" is best taken as a description of the cosmic condition into which Christ entered rather than his sinfulness. In a word, Paul affirms that the preexistent Son, whom the Father "sent" into the world, possessed the very "form," "image," and "likeness" that defines the human condition. Accordingly, the Son entered the realm of sinful flesh—a realm determined by the cosmic powers of sin and death—as one totally human, but not as a sinner. For had the Son of God sinned, he would have been no different than those whom he came to redeem. Instead of defeating sin in the realm of sinful flesh, he would have been defeated by sin.

To explain why the Father sent the Son into the realm of the flesh, a realm under the cosmic powers of sin and death, Paul employs another enigmatic phrase: "for sin" (*peri hamartias*). Here the commentators disagree once more. Some (Byrne 1996, 243; D. Moo 1996, 480) argue that Paul has the OT imagery of the sin offering in view. Thus God sent the Son as an offering for sin. Others (Cranfield 1975, 382; Fitzmyer 1993, 485–86) maintain that the phrase specifies the purpose for which God sent the Son: to deal with sin. While both interpretations make good sense, Paul's train of thought in this verse seems to favor the latter. God sent his own Son, who fully entered into the sphere controlled by sin and death, for the sake of sin; that is, to deal with sin. Thus, through the Son, God condemned sin in its own realm. Paul does not use the language of preexistence or incarnation, but what he writes in this remarkably rich verse provides the seeds for those doctrines.

Second, having explained *how* God did what the law could not do, Paul explains *why* God condemned sin in the flesh: **so that the requirement of the law might be fulfilled in us who walk not according to the flesh but according to the Spirit** (8:4). Employing the first-person plural rather than the third person, Paul focuses on the outcome of God's salvific work in the Son. Through the Son, God condemned sin in the flesh so that the singular requirement of the

Pauline Texts That Intimate the Preexistence of Christ

"Yet for us there is one God, the Father, from whom are all things and for whom we exist, and <u>one Lord, Jesus Christ, through whom are all things and through whom we exist.</u>" (1 Cor. 8:6)

"I do not want you to be unaware, brothers and sisters, that our ancestors were all under the cloud, and all passed through the sea, and all were baptized into Moses in the cloud and in the sea, and all ate the same spiritual food, and all drank the same spiritual drink. For they drank from the spiritual rock that followed them, <u>and the rock was Christ.</u>" (1 Cor. 10:1–4)

"For you know the generous act of our Lord Jesus Christ, that <u>though he was rich, yet for your sakes he became poor,</u> so that by his poverty you might become rich." (2 Cor. 8:9)

"But <u>when the fullness of time had come, God sent his Son,</u> born of a woman, born under the law, in order to redeem those who were under the law, so that we might receive adoption as children." (Gal. 4:4–5)

"Who, <u>though he was in the form of God, did not regard equality with God as something to be exploited, but emptied himself,</u> taking the form of a slave, being born in human likeness. And being found in human form, he humbled himself and became obedient to the point of death—even death on a cross." (Phil. 2:6–8)

"He is <u>the image of the invisible God,</u> the firstborn of all creation; <u>for in him all things in heaven and on earth were created,</u> things visible and invisible, whether thrones or dominions or rulers or powers—<u>all things have been created through him and for him.</u> He himself is <u>before all things,</u> and in him all things hold together." (Col. 1:15–17)

law might be fulfilled "in us." Here it is important to pay attention to Paul's language. The apostle does not say that "we might *do* the just *requirement* of the law" but that "the *requirement* of the law might be *fulfilled* in us." For Paul, the law has been perfectly fulfilled through Christ's singular act of obedience. Consequently, he does not speak of believers "doing" the many prescriptions of the law. Instead, he writes that the singular requirement of the law is now fulfilled in those who no longer walk according to the flesh but according to the Spirit because they are in the Christ, the new Adam. Paul makes a similar semantic distinction in Galatians when he distinguishes between the obligation to do the entire law with its many prescriptions (5:3) and the fulfillment of the whole law through the love commandment (5:14).

The train of thought in Rom. 8:1–4 can be summarized in this way: There is no condemnation for those in Christ. Why? Because the law that is the Spirit has overcome the law that is sin and death. How did this come about? God sent his own Son into the realm of the flesh. Why? To condemn sin. For what purpose? So that the just requirement of the law might be fulfilled in those who are in Christ. Although Paul is not explicitly developing a trinitarian theology here, there is an implicit trinitarian logic to his thought that highlights the Spirit's work in 8:1–2 and the Father's work in the Son in 8:2–4.

8:5–8. At the end of the previous unit, Paul affirmed that the law's singular requirement is fulfilled in those who walk according to the Spirit rather than according to the flesh. In this unit, he explains what he means by comparing these two divergent ways of life—life according to the Spirit and life according to the flesh.

Paul's first comparison is general, one could even say redundant: **For those who are aligned with the flesh are intent on the things of the flesh, while those who are aligned with the Spirit are intent on the things of the Spirit** (8:5). "Those aligned with the flesh" (*hoi kata sarka*) are those who orient their lives according to what is mortal and perishable. They are intent on what belongs to the realm of the flesh, for they view reality from the perspective of what is merely perishable and mortal. In contrast to them, "those who are aligned with the Spirit" (*hoi kata pneuma*) are intent on what pertains to the realm of God's Spirit, and so they orient their lives according to God's imperishable and immortal Spirit. Those aligned with the flesh are in the sphere of the old Adam, where the powers of sin and death still reign, whereas those who are aligned with the Spirit are in the eschatological Adam, where the power of God's Spirit and grace reign.

Having established this contrast between life according to the flesh and life according to God's Spirit, Paul describes the difference between these two ways of life in terms of death, life, and peace: **For the mind-set of the flesh is death, whereas the mind-set of the Spirit is life and peace** (8:6). By the "mind-set" (*phronēma*) of the flesh, Paul means the flesh's fundamental orientation. Since flesh represents all that is mortal and perishing, its mind-set is directed toward death understood as physical death and eternal separation from God. In contrast to the flesh, God's life-giving Spirit is oriented toward eternal life with God, life that transcends death.

At the end of 8:6 Paul notes that in addition to "life," the mind-set of the Spirit focuses on "peace," by which Paul means the reconciliation God has effected through Jesus Christ (5:1). This reference to "peace" leads to the next verse, in which Paul explains why those aligned with the flesh cannot do what God requires. **Because the mind-set of the flesh is at enmity with God, it is not obedient to the law of God, nor can it be** (8:7). Echoing his description of Adamic humanity in 7:7–25, Paul explains that those aligned with the flesh are not able to submit to God's law because they are still at enmity with God. On the basis of this statement, Paul can now make his assessment of those aligned with the flesh: **Those who are in the realm of the flesh cannot please God** (8:8). In saying that those who are *en sarki* cannot please God, Paul has more in view than the physical condition of flesh and blood. He is referring to a sphere of existence determined by the cosmic forces of sin and death; thus my translation, "Those who are in the realm of the flesh."

The contrast that Paul has established in the unit can be summarized in this way: Whereas life according to the flesh results in death, enmity, and the inability to please God, life according to the Spirit results in life and peace with God. This is why the just requirement of the law can only be fulfilled in those who walk according to the Spirit rather than according to the flesh, and why even the justified must be careful to walk according to the Spirit rather than according to the flesh.

8:9–11. At the end of the last unit, Paul wrote that those who are *en sarki* cannot please God. In this unit, characterized by the use of the second-person plural, Paul reminds the Romans of their new situation: they are not *en sarki* but *en pneumati*, so long as the Spirit of God dwells in them. Consequently, although their mortal bodies are presently doomed to death, the Spirit is their assurance of the life they will receive at the resurrection of the dead. Although brief, the unit is rich and complex.

Paul begins with a thematic statement that includes a condition: **But you are not in the realm of the flesh but in the realm of the Spirit if indeed the Spirit of God dwells in you** (8:9a). If the Spirit truly dwells in the Romans (as Paul surely believes it does), they are not in the realm of the flesh. To reinforce what he has just said, Paul states his thesis in a negative way. This time, however, he speaks of the Spirit of Christ rather than the Spirit of God, and he employs the third person rather than the second person: **But if someone does not possess the Spirit of Christ, this one does not belong to him** (8:9b). The Spirit of Christ is not different from the Spirit of God. It is the Spirit that God bestowed upon Christ during his earthly ministry and preeminently at the resurrection, when Christ became "a life-giving spirit" (1 Cor. 15:45). Those who possess the Spirit of Christ belong to Christ, whereas those who do not possess this Spirit do not belong to Christ.

Having spoken of the consequences of being indwelt by the Spirit of God, which is the Spirit of Christ, Paul speaks of the consequences of being indwelt by Christ: **But if Christ is in you, although the body is dead on account of sin, the Spirit is life-giving for the sake of righteousness** (8:10). This verse begins with a conditional clause followed by two neatly balanced clauses indicated by the Greek markers *to men* and *to de*:

> If Christ is in you,
> > (*to men*) although the body is dead "on account of" (*dia*) sin,
> > (*to de*) the Spirit is life-giving "for the sake of" (*dia*) righteousness.

Although the mention of the body in the first couplet might suggest that Paul is speaking of the human spirit in the second couplet (Fitzmyer, Lagrange, Haacker), I am inclined to agree with those (Byrne, Cranfield, Dunn, Fee,

Jewett, Käsemann, Légasse, D. Moo) who argue that Paul is referring to God's Spirit in the second couplet. For even though interpreting *pneuma* as God's Spirit rather than the human spirit disrupts the symmetry of this couplet, it makes excellence sense of what Paul has been saying thus far. The believer's mortal body is destined for death because of the sin that Adam introduced into the world. Nevertheless, God's Spirit, which now dwells in believers for the sake of their justification, is the source of life and the pledge of a future resurrection from the dead (Cranfield 1975, 390), the very point Paul will develop in the next verse.

Having assured the Romans that even though their mortal bodies are destined for death, they already possess the promise of life because they have been justified, Paul draws a comparison between Christ's resurrection and the future resurrection of those who belong to him: **And if the Spirit of the one who raised Jesus from the dead dwells in you, the one who raised Christ from the dead will give life even to your mortal bodies through his Spirit dwelling in you** (8:11). Again, it is important to pay attention to Paul's language. He does not say that the Spirit raised Christ from the dead (Fee 1994, 553), nor does he write that the Spirit will raise believers from the dead. It is God the Father who raised Jesus from the dead, the very God who will raise believers from the dead through the life-giving Spirit that dwells in them. Rather than saying that the Spirit raised Christ and will raise those who believe in him, then, Paul affirms that the Spirit who presently dwells in believers is the Spirit of God, the very God who raised Jesus from the dead. It is the presence of this Spirit, which dwells in them, that assures believers that God will revivify their mortal bodies destined for death.

Paul's train of thought can be summarized in this way: The Romans are no longer in the realm of the flesh, because God's Spirit/Christ's Spirit dwells in them. Their bodies may be destined for death because of sin, but the presence of the Spirit that they received when they were justified is the promise of life that will be fulfilled when God raises them from the dead, just as God raised Christ from the dead.

8:12–17. In the previous subunit, Paul described the new situation in which believers find themselves, reminding them that God will raise them from the dead just as God raised Christ from the dead, provided that the Spirit dwells in them. In this subunit, Paul draws out the consequences of this new situation in which believers find themselves. Building upon their hope for the general resurrection of the dead, which he introduced in 8:11, the apostle now focuses on the final or eschatological inheritance that awaits those led by the Spirit. This subunit unfolds in three steps. First, like Moses in Deuteronomy (30:19), Paul places a stark choice before the Romans: living according to the flesh, which leads to death, or living according to the Spirit, which leads to life (8:12–13). Second, he draws out the consequences of living according to the Spirit: the gift of a Spirit of adoption that allows them to address God as Father (8:14–15). Third, he draws out the eschatological consequences of their adoption: an inheritance that results in being glorified *with* the glorified Christ (8:16–17). This subunit, which begins to shift the argument of chapter 8 from ethics to eschatology, functions as the bridge to the second part of this chapter (8:18–30), in which Paul will describe the cosmic scope of the hope that belongs to those who live according to the Spirit.

Paul begins with the strong inferential particle *ara* and the conjunction *oun*, both of which indicate that he is about to draw out the consequences of what he has been saying: **So then, brothers and sisters, we are not indebted to the flesh to live according to the flesh** (8:12). Believers are no longer obligated to live in the way they formerly did when they were "in Adam," in a realm controlled by the power of the flesh; for they have been transferred to another realm, the sphere of God's life-giving Spirit. To be sure, it is still possible for believers to live according to the flesh, but having been freed from the cosmic powers of sin and death that once controlled their lives, they are no longer indebted to the realm of the flesh. They have been set free to live in a new way.

Aware that even Christ-believers can revert to their old way of life, Paul places a stark choice before his audience: **For if you live according to the flesh, you are going to die. But if, by means of the Spirit, you put to death the disgraceful deeds of the body, you will live** (8:13). Believers are no longer indentured to the sinful realm of the flesh, but if they return to that old way of life, the consequence will be death. However, if they continue to live according to the Spirit, the consequence will be life. The life and death that Paul has in view here is more than physical life and death. If believers revert to their old way of life, they will experience eternal separation from God, but if they continue to live in the Spirit, they will enjoy imperishable and immortal life with God. The new life that believers have embraced then requires a daily reaffirmation on their part. Having embraced a new way of life, they must put to death the "deeds of the body" (*tas praxeis tou sōmatos*), which I have translated as "the *disgraceful* deeds of the body" (following BDAG 860, s.v. *praxis*, def. 4) since Paul is thinking of the body as dominated by sin. For example, in Rom. 6:6 he wrote, "Our old self was crucified with Christ so that the sin-dominated self might be destroyed in order that we might no longer serve sin." And in Gal. 5:24 he said, "And those who belong to Christ Jesus have crucified the flesh with its sinful passions." Here, however, he refers to the "body" rather than to the "flesh" because he has in view the body controlled and overpowered by sin.

Having set before his audience life and death, Paul draws out the eschatological consequences of living according to the Spirit: **For those who are led by God's Spirit are God's sons and daughters. For you did not receive a spirit that enslaves, leading to fear once more. Rather, you received a Spirit that leads to adoption, by which we cry out, "Abba, Father"** (8:14–15). Paul begins with a thematic statement in 8:14: those led by the Spirit are God's sons and daughters (*huioi theou*). Then he explains why this is so: the Spirit they have received has made them God's adopted sons and daughters, and the Spirit enables them to address God as Father (8:15). Paul makes a similar statement in Gal. 4:6–7, but whereas in Galatians he suggests that God has granted the Spirit to believers because they are his children, here he suggests that it is the Spirit that makes believers into God's adopted children, enabling them to address God, "Abba, Father."

When Paul affirms that those led by the Spirit are *huioi theou*, he is drawing an intimate connection between God's unique Son, Jesus, whom God sent into the world (8:14), and believers, who are God's sons and daughters by adoption because the indwelling Spirit of God has made them God's adopted children. In contrasting a Spirit of adoption with a spirit of slavery, Paul is emphasizing the distinctive nature of the Spirit that believers have received rather than implying that there is another Spirit. God's Spirit does not result in slavery to sin or fear of death but in adoption that allows those who were formerly alienated from God to address God as Jesus did (Mark 14:36): "Abba, Father" ("Father" added for emphasis rather than as a translation of "Abba"; Cranfield 1975, 400).

Having explained that the indwelling of God's Spirit leads to adoption, in the third step of this argument (8:16–17) Paul draws out the eschatological consequences of adoption. First, he assures the Romans that because the Spirit dwells in them, they have a reliable witness that they are "God's children" (*tekna theou*): **The Spirit itself testifies with our spirit that we are God's children** (8:16). Some translations read, "The Spirit himself witnesses *to* our spirit" (NET), thereby highlighting the priority and importance of the Spirit's testimony, but I have rendered the Greek verb *symmartyrei* as "testifies with" because Paul seems to imply that there is an inner dialogue between the believer's spirit, which has been transformed by God's Spirit, and the transforming Spirit of God, both jointly testifying that believers are truly God's children.

But if believers are God's children, there are important eschatological consequences, as Paul notes: **And if we are children, then we are heirs—God's heirs and coheirs with Christ, if indeed we suffer with him in order that we may be glorified with him** (8:17). Free children are heirs who can hope for an inheritance. In the case of God's children, the inheritance is eschatological in nature—an inheritance they will acquire at the end of the ages. As God's heirs (God's children), they are "coheirs" (*synklēronomoi*) with Christ, and if they are coheirs with Christ, they will be "glorified *with* him" (*syndoxasthōmen*), provided they "suffer *with* him" (*sympaschomen*). Christ, the unique Son of God, has already received his Father's inheritance, the eschatological glory of resurrection life. Believers, however, have not. In the Spirit, they have received the down payment and assurance of that glory, but they have not yet received their inheritance, which will be revealed only at the general resurrection of the dead. In the meantime they must suffer *with* the one *with* whom they are coheirs if they hope to be glorified *with* him.

8:18–25. This is the first of three units that make up the second part of this chapter (8:18–30), which presents the Spirit as the foundation of the believer's eschatological hope. The unit consists of three subunits. In the first, Paul states his thesis that there is no comparison between the sufferings that believers are enduring and the glory that will be revealed to them (8:18). In the second, he substantiates his thesis by noting that even creation longs for the revelation of this glory since creation itself will be freed from its servitude to corruption when God's children are glorified (8:19–22). Finally, in the third subunit, Paul speaks of the longing of believers as they wait for the redemption of their bodies (8:23–25). The vision of this unit is cosmic in scope (8:18–25). Not only will God's sons and daughters be saved, but creation itself will also be saved. It is not surprising, then, that Dunn (1988, 1:467) calls 8:18–30 the climax of the first eight chapters of Romans, for in these verses Paul reveals "the final reversal of man's failure and climax of his restoration."

The first subunit begins with a strong verb (*logizomai*), which introduces a thematic statement signaling the beginning of a new unit: **For I am fully convinced that the sufferings of the present time are unworthy to be compared with the glory that is going to be revealed to us** (8:18). The "sufferings" (*pathēmata*) are the afflictions (see 5:3) that believers presently endure on account of their faith in Christ. As such, they are participating in Christ's sufferings (Dunn 1988, 1:468). As burdensome as they may be, there is no comparison between these sufferings and the "glory" (*doxan*) to be revealed. Although Paul does not specify what that glory will be, the context of Rom. 8 does. In 8:11 Paul spoke of the believer's future resurrection, and in 8:17 he identified believers as Christ's coheirs, who will be glorified *with* him if they suffer *with* him. Since Christ has already been glorified, the glory to which Paul refers is their participation in Christ's resurrection, the glory that will be bestowed on them at the general resurrection of the dead as described in 1 Cor. 15:42–55.

In 2 Cor. 4:17–18 Paul draws a similar comparison between his present apostolic sufferings and the resurrection glory he hopes to attain. Confident that he is living in the last age because the general resurrection of the dead has already begun in Christ, Paul knows that there is no comparison between "this slight momentary affliction" and "an eternal weight of glory beyond all measure," which will be revealed at the resurrection of the dead (2 Cor. 4:17).

In the second unit, Paul provides his thesis with a supporting argument that gives a cosmic dimension to his understanding of salvation (8:19–22). In order to show the surpassing glory of what is to be revealed to believers, he argues that creation itself eagerly anticipates the revelation of this glory: **For with eager expectation creation awaits the revelation of God's sons and daughters** (8:19). Although some have argued that "creation" (*ktisis*) refers to humankind or that it includes humankind as well as the created world, the contrast Paul establishes between creation and the believer in 8:23 indicates that here he is personifying "creation," just as he has personified sin and death in chapters 5–7. In this passage, then, creation refers to the inanimate and animate world apart from humankind. Personifying that world, Paul portrays it as filled with "eager expectation" (*apokaradokia*), a word he also uses in Phil. 1:20 to describe his "eager expectation and hope" that he will not be put to shame. Applying the same word to creation, he portrays the created world as consciously waiting for the general resurrection of the dead, when believers—finally raised from the dead—will be revealed for who they truly are: God's sons and daughters.

Beginning with a *gar* (for) explanatory clause, Paul explains the reason for creation's eager longing: **For creation was made subject to futility, not of its own will but because of the one who subjected it—in hope** (8:20). Alluding to the punishment that came upon Adam and Eve after they transgressed God's commandment (Gen. 3:17–19), Paul presents creation as being in a state of "futility" or "purposelessness" (*mataiotēti*), not because of anything it did ("not of its own will") but because of what humanity did. For when humanity rebelled against its Creator—the theme Paul develops in Rom. 1—its rebellion affected creation as well. Having disrupted the original order of creation, humanity finds itself at enmity with creation as well as with God. Instead of being the crown of creation, with all things subjected to it, as envisioned in Ps. 8, humanity is out of sorts with the animate and inanimate world in which it lives. And because human beings did not "render thanks to God as God, but . . . were made foolish by their reasoning" (*emataiōthēsan en tois dialogismois*, 1:21), the created world itself was subject to "futility" (*mataiotēti*).

But who subjected the created world to futility? While some argue that it was Adam or Satan, the phrase "in hope" suggests that God subjected it. In cursing the ground that was originally intended to be a source of blessing for Adam (Gen. 3:17–19), God subjected creation, as well as Adam and his

The Glory of the Human Person in God's Plan

"When I look at your heavens, the work of your fingers,
   the moon and the stars that you have established;
what are human beings that you are mindful of them,
   mortals that you care for them?"

"Yet you have made them a little lower than God,
   and crowned them with glory and honor.
You have given them dominion over the works of your hands;
   you have put all things under their feet." (Ps. 8:3–6)

descendants, to futility—but not without hope. Creation's eager expectation for the revelation of God's sons and daughters is rooted in this hope.

Paul describes this hope: **because creation itself will be set free from the slavery of corruption to the glorious freedom of the children of God** (8:21). In writing that creation will be set free "from the slavery of corruption" (*apo tēs douleias tēs phthoras*), Paul employs the same language he used to describe the resurrection body of believers in 1 Cor. 15:42, 50, thereby implying that creation will participate in God's final victory over death at the general resurrection of the dead, when all things will be subjected to Christ, and Christ to God, so "that God may be all in all" (1 Cor. 15:28). At the present time, however, creation is subjected to the slavery that is corruption. For, like humanity, the animate and inanimate world will pass away. But when God's sons and daughters are revealed at the general resurrection of the dead for who they truly are, then creation will be freed from its servitude as well.

In this extraordinary passage, Paul envisions the restoration of creation as inseparable from the resurrection of the dead. When humanity is restored to its original state in the new Adam, the rest of creation will be restored as well. For just as humanity does not exist apart from creation, neither does creation exist apart from humanity. The fate of each is intimately related to the other.

Once more personifying creation, Paul writes: **For we know that the whole creation groans together and suffers great pain together to this very moment** (8:22). The use of the compound verbs *systenazei* (groans together) and *synōdinei* (suffers great pain together)—the only occurrences of these compounds in the LXX and NT—portrays the whole of creation as participating in a common agony as it awaits the birth of a new age. The final phrase of this verse, "to this very moment," suggests that this agony and groaning have been under way for some time. Now, however, with Christ's resurrection, which is the beginning of the general resurrection of the dead, the groaning and agony have reached a critical moment.

Paul's description of the creation's birth pangs and groaning (8:22) provides a transition to his third subunit (8:23–25), in which he describes the groaning of believers, who are waiting in hope for the resurrection of the dead. Paul establishes a relationship between the groaning of the created world and the groaning of believers: **Not only creation, but we ourselves who possess the firstfruits of the Spirit, even we groan among ourselves as we long for our adoption, the redemption of our bodies** (8:23). It is not only creation that groans for this new age, then, but also those who possess the *aparchēn* (firstfruits) of the Spirit. Paul employs this noun several times in his letters (Rom. 11:16; 16:5; 1 Cor. 15:20, 23; 16:15; 2 Thess. 2:13), but this is the only place where he describes the Spirit as the "firstfruits." But the meaning here is undoubtedly similar to the image he employs when he speaks of the Spirit as the *arrabōn* ("first installment," "down payment," "pledge") of the believer's final inheritance (2 Cor. 1:22; 5:5; Eph. 1:14). In and through the gift of the Spirit, believers possess the beginning of the resurrection life, which will come to fruition at the general resurrection of the dead. Consequently, just as the animate and inanimate creation groans for the appearance of the new age, so those who enjoy the gift of the Spirit groan among themselves—perhaps in the worshiping assemblies of the churches—as they wait for their "adoption" (*huiothesian*), which Paul identifies as the redemption of their bodies.

Whereas in Rom. 8:15 Paul wrote that believers have *already* received a "Spirit of adoption," which allows them to address God as "Abba, Father," in 8:23 he speaks of adoption as something that believers have *not yet* attained, leading some manuscripts ($\mathfrak{P}^{46\text{vid}}$, D, F, G, et al.) to omit *huiothesian*. The tension caused by this verse, however, is not irreconcilable. For whereas in 8:15 Paul has affirmed that believers have received a Spirit of adoption, in 8:23 he presents the life of the Spirit as the "firstfruits" of a future harvest. The "adoption" that believers already experience, thanks to the gift of the Spirit, will not be complete then until they experience the "redemption" (*apolytrōsin*) of their bodies at the general resurrection of the dead, when the harvest assured by the firstfruits of the Spirit will occur.

In a text that ought to be read in conjunction with 5:9–11, Paul explains why those who possess the Spirit are groaning with creation for the birth of the new age: **For we were saved in hope. Now hope that is seen is not hope. For who hopes for what one sees? But if we hope for what we do not see, we wait with patient endurance** (8:24–25). Those who belong to Christ have *already* been justified and reconciled, but they have not yet been saved (5:9–10). Final salvation will be attained only at the general resurrection of the dead, when the last enemy, Death, will be destroyed (1 Cor. 15:26). Believers, then, have been saved "in hope" (*tē elpidi*). Having received the firstfruits of the Spirit, they can be confident of the fullness of adoption, when their bodies will be redeemed from death. At the present time, however, they live in hope of what will be rather than in possession of the reality. At the present time, they do not see the final reality, for if they did there would be no need for hope. Accordingly, they wait with "patient endurance" for what they cannot see, an unmistakable echo of what Paul wrote in Rom. 5:3–5 and 2 Cor. 4:18.

8:26–27. These verses make up the second part of Paul's discussion about the Spirit as the source of the believer's hope (8:18–30). Having described how creation (8:22) and the justified (8:23) are groaning for the revelation of the glory to be revealed, Paul explains in this unit how the Spirit assists believers as they wait and hope for the revelation of this glory and the redemption of their bodies. Aware that believers find themselves in a "vulnerable position" because they are caught between two ages (Jewett 2007, 522), Paul assures them that God's Spirit is presently assisting them in their prayers. Consequently, in addition to being the firstfruits of their future glory, the Spirit is their intercessor as well.

Paul begins with an adverb (*hōsautōs*) that establishes a comparison between what he has just written in 8:18–25 and what he will write about the intercession of the Spirit in these verses: **In the same way, the Spirit comes to our assistance in our weakness; for we do not know what we should pray for as we ought, but the Spirit itself intercedes for us with inexpressible sighs** (8:26). Just as creation "groans" as it awaits the revelation of God's sons and daughters, and just as believers "groan" as they hope for their final adoption and the redemption of their bodies, so the Spirit intercedes for believers "with inexpressible sighs" or "groaning" (*stenagmois alalētois*). But whereas the groaning of creation and of believers is a longing for something they hope to attain, the groaning or sighs of which Paul speaks here refer to the Spirit's intercession on behalf of the justified. For even though the justified and redeemed address God as Jesus did ("Abba, Father"), they are still weak, and so they do not know what they are to pray for. To be more precise, although they know *how* to pray, they do not know *what* fully conforms to God's plan. It is for this reason that the Spirit comes to their assistance "with inexpressible sighs." The inexpressible sighs/groaning to which Paul refers is not the gift of tongues, as Käsemann (1980, 240–41) contends, but the Spirit's intercession on behalf of believers, who do not know the full scope of God's plan, and so do not know for what they ought to pray. Because he is speaking of how the Spirit addresses God, Paul describes the Spirit's "sighs" as *alalētois*, sighs that cannot be expressed in human words.

Although human beings cannot comprehend the sighs of the Spirit on their behalf, God does. Accordingly, Paul writes, **the Searcher of hearts knows the mind of the Spirit because he intercedes for the holy ones according to God's will** (8:27). The "Searcher of hearts" is a metaphor for God, rooted in Israel's understanding of God as the one who knows and searches the heart. Thus God says to Samuel, "The LORD does not see as mortals see; for they look on the outward appearance, but the LORD looks on the heart" (1 Sam. 16:7). And the psalmist cries out, "Search me, O God, and know my heart" (Ps. 139:23). God is the Searcher of hearts because God penetrates the most profound mysteries; God is the one from whom nothing is hidden. Paul makes a similar statement in his discussion of the Spirit in 1 Cor. 2. But whereas in Romans he presents God as the one who understands the Spirit's inexpressible sighs and groaning, in 1 Corinthians he writes that "no one comprehends what is truly God's except the Spirit of God" (1 Cor. 2:11).

Although the idea of the Spirit as intercessor does not occur "in the OT or in pre-Christian Jewish writings" (Fitzmyer 1993, 518), the Gospel of John develops a similar notion in Jesus's farewell discourse (especially John 16:7–15).

8:28–30. Having begun this part of his argument (8:18–30) by expressing his confidence that there is no comparison between the sufferings that the justified presently endure and the glory that will be revealed to them (8:18), Paul describes in this unit the full sweep of God's plan, which starts with God's foreknowledge and leads to election, justification, and glorification. Paul begins with a statement of confidence about the final outcome of this plan: **We know that all things work toward what is good for those who love God—for those called in accordance with God's purpose** (8:28). Whereas in chapter 5 the apostle spoke of God's love for the justified (5:5, 8), now he speaks of the love that the justified have for God, a love made possible because God's love has been poured into their hearts through the Holy Spirit (5:5). Although believers presently endure suffering and affliction, if they love God, who first loved them, they can be confident that their sufferings and afflictions are part of God's plan, which is at work for their good.

The manner in which Paul phrases this verse highlights the relation between the believer's love for God and God's election. Since those who love God have been called according to a divine plan, their confidence is rooted in more than their personal love for God; it is grounded in God's election, a call that enables them to love God.

Developing the theme of election, which he introduced at the end of 8:28, Paul describes the full sweep of God's plan in 8:29–30. This description proceeds in two steps. First, Paul provides an initial summary of the divine plan: **since those whom he foreknew he predetermined to be conformed to the image of his Son so that the Son might be the firstborn among many siblings** (8:29). Making use of a number of words that begin with the prefix *pro*, Paul affirms that those whom God "foreknew" (*proegnō*) God "predetermined" (*proōrisen*) to be conformed to the image of his Son so that the Son might be the "firstborn" (*prōtotokon*) among many siblings. With this statement, Paul indicates that the outcome of the divine plan is the general resurrection of the dead, when the justified will be conformed to the image of the risen Christ, who is the firstborn of the dead (Col. 1:18; Rev. 1:5). Paul makes a similar point in Phil. 3:21: "He will transform the body of our humiliation that it may be *conformed* to the body of his glory, by the power that also enables him to make all things subject to himself."

Second, beginning with the concept of predetermination, which he introduced in the previous verse, Paul outlines the divine plan in another way: **Whom he predetermined, these he also called; and whom he called, these he also justified; and whom he justified, these he also glorified** (8:30). According to this verse, then, there are four movements in the divine economy: (1) predetermination, which leads to (2) election, which results in (3) justification, which effects (4) glorification. Contemporary readers might be inclined to think of predetermination in terms of a doctrine of double predestination, whereby God elects some and rejects others, but Paul employs the concept to assure his audience that all things will work for their good. For inasmuch as they have been justified, they can be confident that they belong to God's elect. Put another way, all who accept the gospel—which excludes none who do so—will be justified and glorified. And if they are justified and glorified, they can be confident that they are among God's elect. Paul, then, is not so much developing a doctrine of double predestination as he is assuring the justified of their role in God's plan.

Although Paul normally speaks of glorification as occurring at the general resurrection of the dead, when the justified will be glorified with Christ (8:17), the use of the aorist tense here (*edoxasen*) suggests that believers already enjoy something of that future glorification because they possess the gift of the Spirit, the firstfruits of the final glorification that they will experience at the general resurrection of the dead.

8:31–39. Having assured his audience that all things work for the good of those who love God (8:28–30), Paul in this unit celebrates the irrevocable character of God's love for the justified. The unit is a rhetorical tour de force that provides a fitting conclusion not only to the third part of Romans (chaps. 5–8) but to all that Paul has written thus far. The confidence he displays in this section also provides a transition to the fourth part of Romans (chaps. 9–11), in which the apostle will affirm God's irrevocable call and faithfulness to Israel.

In addressing the irrevocable character of God's love, Paul returns to a theme he has introduced in 5:1–11. There he identified God's love for the justified as the foundation of their hope (5:4). Then he pointed to the death of the Son as the proof of God's love and the assurance of future salvation (5:6–11). Returning to these themes, Paul now proclaims that given the irrevocable character of God's love displayed in Christ, there is nothing that can separate the justified from God.

Although the central message of this unit is clear, there is a great deal of disagreement about its genre, structure, and how it should be punctuated. For example, older translations tended to treat 8:33b and 8:34b as questions ("God who justifies?" "Christ who died?"); more recent translations are inclined to interpret these verses as statements of fact. Although distinguished commentators such as Joseph Fitzmyer and Robert Jewett still translate these verses as questions, I have chosen to interpret them as statements that respond to Paul's questions. Moreover, building upon a structure proposed by N. T. Wright (2002, 610), I have divided the unit into two subunits. The first (8:31–37) contains four rhetorical questions that begin with the Greek interrogative *tis* (who) followed by Paul's response: (1) Who can stand against us? (2) Who will accuse God's elect? (3) Who will condemn? (4) Who will separate us from Christ's love? After responding to these four questions, Paul expresses in the second subunit (8:38–39) his confidence that nothing can separate believers from God's love, which is manifested in Christ Jesus.

Paul begins with a retrospective question signaling that he is bringing the argument he has developed thus far to a conclusion: **What then shall we say about these matters?** (8:31a). Although "these matters" (*tauta*) finds an immediate referent in what Paul has just written (8:28–30), it could also refer to what he wrote about the hope that the justified have for eschatological glory (8:18–30), as well as to the whole of Rom. 5–8 (Fitzmyer 1993, 530; D. Moo 1996, 539). In response to this question, Paul asks the first of the four rhetorical questions that structure his discourse: **Since God is on our side, who can stand against us?** (8:31b). Paul makes this statement in light of all that he has said thus far, especially what he has written in chapters 5–8. For Paul, Christ's redemptive death on behalf of sinners (5:6–8) is the irrefutable proof that God stands for, rather than against, the justified.

In response to this rhetorical question, whose answer is already implied in the question, Paul asks a further question that highlights the quality of God's love and provides assurance that God will grant the eschatological gifts Paul has described in 8:18–30: **How will he, who did not spare his own Son but handed him over for our sake, not give us, along with his Son, everything else?** (8:32). Alluding to the example of Abraham, who did not spare his own son (see Gen. 22:16 LXX, which employs the same verb), Paul describes the God "who is on our side" (*hyper hēmōn*) as the one who did not spare his own Son, thereby echoing what he said in 5:8 that the death of Christ was the demonstration of God's love for humanity. If God gave his own Son for believers when they were still godless (5:6), they can be all the more confident that they will inherit the eschatological blessings, with the Son, that Paul described in 8:18–30.

Having established that no one can stand against those for whom God did not even spare his own Son, Paul raises the second of the four rhetorical questions that control this subunit: **Who will accuse God's elect?** (8:33a). With the verb "accuse," Paul returns to the imagery of the lawcourt, and with the noun "elect" he recalls his statement that those whom God has "called" he has also "justified" (8:30). Again, the answer to the question is embedded in the question itself: no one can accuse God's elect since those whom God has elected, God has acquitted. Nonetheless, Paul provides a brief response that I have construed as a statement: **God is the one who justifies.** Whether Paul intended these words to be read as a statement or a question ("God who justified?")— there is no punctuation in the Greek—the force of the argument is essentially the same: no one can accuse God's elect since God has justified them.

Next, Paul raises the third of the four rhetorical questions that structure the material. Maintaining the imagery of the lawcourt, he asks, **Who will condemn?** (8:34a). The question recalls the opening of this chapter, in which Paul proclaims that there is no condemnation for those who are in Christ (8:1). Those who have been justified and reconciled to God are no longer threatened by God's wrath, which Paul described in 1:18–3:20. Paul answered the second rhetorical question with a terse statement that it is God who has acquitted us, but he responds to this question with a more elaborate statement that begins by recalling Christ's redemptive death and then describes his resurrection, enthronement, and intercession on behalf of God's elect: **It** is Christ Jesus who died—more than that, who was raised up, who is at the right hand of God, and who intercedes for us (8:34b). Paul's train of thought can be stated in this way: No one can condemn those for whom Christ died, rose, and intercedes at God's right hand. This description of the risen Christ interceding for the justified draws an interesting relation between the Spirit, which dwells within believers and intercedes for them "with inexpressible sighs" (8:26), and the Son, who intercedes for them from his exalted position at God's right hand.

Finally, Paul asks the last of the four rhetorical questions that guide this unit: **Who will separate us from Christ's love?** (8:35a). While the *tēs agapēs tou Christou* could be taken as an objective genitive ("our love for Christ"), I have construed it as a subjective genitive so that it refers to Christ's love for believers. Once more the answer to Paul's question is implied in the question. Since Christ has demonstrated his love by dying for the justified when they were still among the ungodly, nothing can separate the justified from Christ's enduring love for them. To illustrate what he means, Paul answers his question with another that enumerates seven hardships that the justified are enduring or will endure for the sake of Christ: **Affliction or distress or persecution or hunger or nakedness or danger or the sword?** (8:35b). The first of these seven hardships, "affliction" (*thlipsis*), recalls Paul's affirmation that the justified now boast in their "afflictions," knowing that affliction leads to endurance, endurance to character, and character to hope (5:3–4). Although these hardships, which Paul regularly endured in his own life (1 Cor. 4:11–13; 2 Cor. 6:4–11; 12:23b–28), threaten to separate believers from their Lord, the reality is that Christ's love conquers all (Rom. 8:37).

Next, Paul employs a text from Ps. 43:23 LXX (44:22 Eng.) to explain the significance of the sufferings that believers are presently enduring: **So it is written: "For your sake we are in danger of death the whole day long; we are reckoned as sheep for slaughter"** (8:36). In the psalm, "we" originally applied to Israel, which was being put to death and accounted as sheep for the slaughter for the sake of Yhwh, but in Paul's christological reading of the psalm, "we" refers to those who are enduring affliction and persecution for the sake of Christ. Returning to the theme of Christ's love, which he introduced in 8:35, Paul explains why persecution and affliction cannot separate believers from Christ: **But in all these things we are surpassingly victorious owing to the one who has loved us** (8:37). The justified, however, are not "surpassingly victorious" (*hypernikōmen*) because of their endurance but because of the one—Christ—who has loved them. For since his love is irrevocable, no amount of suffering or persecution can separate those whom Christ loves from Christ.

Having proclaimed in 8:35–37 that nothing can separate believers from the love that *Christ* has for them, Paul expresses his confidence that nothing can separate believers from the love that *God* has for them in their Lord, Jesus Christ: **For I am convinced that neither death nor life, neither angels nor cosmic** powers, neither what is present nor what will be, not heavenly powers, not the world above nor the world below, nor any other created thing can separate us from God's love, which is present in Christ Jesus our Lord (8:38–39). Whereas in 8:35 Paul listed seven hardships that afflict those who are suffering for the sake of Christ, here he catalogs ten powers or cosmic forces that threaten to separate believers from God's love. Although Paul views these powers as real, and although they continue to exert their influence in the world, they cannot separate believers from the irrevocable love that God has manifested in the death and resurrection of his Son. For Paul, the event of the cross and resurrection was the decisive moment in God's salvific work, an act of divine love that cannot be reversed.

Theological Issues

One of the most distinctive aspects of Paul's theology is the role he attributes to the Spirit. The Spirit plays a major role in all of Paul's writings, especially in his Corinthian and Galatian correspondence. It is in Rom. 8, however, that the apostle presents us with his clearest statement about the role of the Spirit in the Christian life. Having described the human predicament apart from Christ (1:18–3:20), how sin and death entered the world (5:12–21), and the manner in which sin frustrated the purpose of God's law (7:7–25), in chapter 8 Paul celebrates the new life that believers enjoy when they live in the realm of the Spirit. This Spirit is God's own Spirit, which was released into the world through the resurrection of God's Son. Consequently, just as Jesus Christ, the preeminent Son of God, now lives transformed by God's own glory in the realm of the Spirit, so those who believe in him will dwell in the realm of the Spirit of God, which Paul also identifies as the Spirit of Christ (8:9) since the risen Christ has become "a life-giving spirit" (1 Cor. 15:45). As "coheirs" of the resurrection glory that Christ has already attained, those who believe in him enjoy the Spirit as the "firstfruits" of a harvest they will reap at the resurrection of the dead. The Spirit, then, is (1) the identifying mark of the Christ-believer, (2) the norm by which Christ-believers conduct their lives, and (3) the promise of their final glorification.

The Spirit as the Defining Characteristic of the Believer

Human beings are either "in Adam" or "in Christ." If they are "in Adam," they dwell in the realm of sin and death, the realm of the flesh, which frustrates every human attempt to do God's law. If they are "in Christ," however, they have been transferred to the realm of grace and life, the realm of the Spirit, in which the just requirement of God's law is fulfilled through the power of the Spirit at work in them. It is the Spirit, then, that is the defining characteristic of the Christian life. Without the Spirit, there is no life with God; without the Spirit, there is no hope for the general resurrection of the dead. To be a Christian is to be in, and to live by, the Spirit. James Dunn (1988, 1:424) makes this point: "Where Paul the Pharisee might have identified the proselyte as one who has received the law and lived in accordance with it, Paul the apostle identifies the Christian as one who has received the Spirit and lives in accordance with it."

In Rom. 8, after drawing a sharp distinction between those who belong to the realm of the flesh and those who belong to the realm of the Spirit (8:5–8), Paul emphatically says, "But you are not in the realm of the flesh but in the realm of the Spirit if indeed the Spirit of God dwells in you. But if someone does not possess the Spirit of Christ, this one does not belong to him" (8:9). With this remark, Paul explicitly identifies those who belong to Christ as those who possess the Spirit. To be in the realm of the Spirit is to be in Christ, and to be in Christ is to dwell in the realm of the Spirit. Put another way, since the justified live in the realm of the Spirit, those who possess the Spirit are justified (see Gal. 3:1–5). When Paul writes that believers are no longer under the law but under grace (6:14), then, he is not denigrating the law, which he acknowledges as spiritual (7:14), but pointing to the new reality that defines one's identity in Christ. For whereas the law is a written code that expresses God's will but cannot empower people to do what it commands, the Spirit provides the newness of life that empowers people to live in accordance with God's will (7:6). Thus their moral conduct is not merely a matter of their own doing but the manifestation of the Spirit at work within them.

The Spirit as the Norm of the Moral Life

Although Paul's teaching on justification by faith apart from doing the works of the law can be misconstrued as an invitation to an immoral life, Paul's concern for the moral life of the justified is apparent from what he writes in Rom. 6–8. Paul the Pharisee viewed the Mosaic law as the norm for this moral life, but Paul the apostle presents the Spirit as the guiding principle and power by which believers can live a morally good life. Supremely confident that those who follow the Spirit will do God's will, Paul urges those who believe in Christ to walk according to the Spirit (8:4). But what does it mean to walk according to the Spirit? Is not such an optimistic morality naive and misguided?

Paul is optimistic. How could he be otherwise? He firmly believes that in Christ, God has overcome the powers of sin and death that alienated humanity from its Creator. But Paul is not naive. He recognizes that even though the powers of sin and death have been defeated by Christ, they still exercise control over those who allow them to do so. Moreover, he understands that believers need moral guidance, which he continues to find in Israel's scriptures and the Mosaic law. But having experienced the power of the Spirit in his own life and having witnessed the power of the Spirit in the communities he has founded, Paul views the moral life from the perspective of the Spirit rather than from the perspective of the law. The law is a written code that commands and instructs, but it cannot empower people to act as they ought. In contrast to the law, the Spirit is a life-giving force; it is the presence of God in the life of the believer. For this reason, the Spirit is a living and dynamic norm that inspires and illuminates mature believers to live in a way that conforms to the one who lives within them. Accordingly, when Paul writes that God sent his own Son so that "the requirement of the law *might be fulfilled in us* who walk not according to the flesh but according to the Spirit" (8:4), he affirms that the moral life is more than a matter of "doing" the prescriptions of the law. The righteousness that the law requires is "fulfilled" in those who follow the guidance of the Spirit because they live their lives in the realm of Christ, who died for them.

The Spirit as the Firstfruits of Eschatological Glory

In addition to defining the identity of the believer and providing a "living norm" for the moral life, the Spirit assures believers of the final or eschatological glory that will be theirs at the general resurrection of the dead. Paul writes, "And if the Spirit of the one who raised Jesus from the dead dwells in you, the one who raised Christ from the dead will give life even to your mortal bodies through his Spirit dwelling in you" (8:11). For Paul, the Spirit is "the firstfruits" of a harvest that believers will reap when their bodies are redeemed from death at the general resurrection of the dead (8:23). Believers can be confident that they will participate in this harvest because they already experience the Spirit, which enables them to address God in the way that Jesus did: "Abba, Father" (8:15). Thus they know that they are God's adopted children, coheirs of their elder brother, the Son of God, who has already entered into the inheritance of eschatological glory through his resurrection from the dead (8:17). The Spirit, then, is the assurance of this eschatological glory because it confirms that believers are destined to receive an inheritance that Christ has already claimed: the glory of God that will be bestowed on those who are raised from the dead.

To summarize, in Rom. 8 Paul presents the Spirit in three ways: (1) as the defining mark of the believer's identity "in Christ"; (2) as the living and dynamic norm for living a morally good life; (3) and as the firstfruits of the eschatological glory that will be given when God raises believers from the dead. If contemporary believers find this Pauline teaching foreign, the fault does not lie so much with the apostle's theology as it does with *the absence of an experience of the Spirit* that often characterizes contemporary Christianity. For just as this experience of the Spirit accounts for the amazing growth and vitality of the early church, so the absence of this experience accounts for the malaise that afflicts much of contemporary Christianity.

PART 4

Romans 9:1–11:36

God's Righteousness and the Destiny of Israel

⌘

The fourth part of Romans deals with an issue that has been simmering throughout this letter: the destiny of Israel in light of the saving righteousness that God has so recently manifested in the death and resurrection of Jesus Christ. Previous to this part of the letter, Paul has argued that all, Jews as well as Gentiles, were under the power of sin, which Adam introduced by his transgression, and so all were alienated from God. Apart from Christ, humanity was in solidarity with Adam and in servitude to sin, which led to death and eternal separation from God. But God graciously manifested his saving righteousness in Christ, a righteousness available to all on the basis of faith. Those who are in Christ, the eschatological Adam, now find themselves under God's grace rather than under the law; they are in the realm of the Spirit rather than in the realm of the flesh; they are destined for resurrection rather than for death. Consequently, there is no distinction between Gentiles and Jews: all have sinned and are freely justified and reconciled on the basis of God's saving righteousness in Christ.

But if there is no distinction between Gentile and Jew, what does this say about the destiny of Israel in God's redemptive plan? Has God rejected his people? Has historical Israel been superseded by a new Israel? Has there been a midcourse correction in God's redemptive plan? If so, what does this understanding of redemptive history imply about God? To put it another way, Rom. 9–11 is not merely a discussion about Israel's destiny; it is also a profound theological discussion about God's redemptive plan and a probing discussion of God's saving righteousness in Christ. In these chapters, Paul explores the following questions: Has the word of God failed? Has God remained faithful to Israel? Has God rejected Israel? Has the appearance of the Christ changed God's redemptive plan? If it has, it would appear that God has been unfaithful to, and rejected, Israel. It would appear that God's redemptive purpose for Israel has failed.

Romans 9–11 plays a central role in Paul's gospel of God's righteousness. For if the apostle cannot explain the continuity between God's saving righteousness manifested to Israel in the past and God's saving righteousness manifested in Jesus Christ, there is no continuity between what God has done and what God is presently doing. If this is so, Paul's gospel calls into question the faithfulness and reliability of God. In a word, there is a festering wound between synagogue and church.

Paul deeply believed in, and argued for, the continuity of God's saving work in Jesus Christ. Moreover, he clearly affirmed that God did not reject Israel (11:1), for the call of Israel is irrevocable (11:29). Nevertheless, an understanding of Paul as one who opposed his own people has contributed to a tragic history of anti-Semitism that found its culmination in the Holocaust and remains with us to this day. Contemporary Christianity, then, will do well to reflect on what Paul writes in Rom. 9–11 about Israel's destiny in God's redemptive plan in light of God's saving justice.

Although the individual arguments that Paul develops in Rom. 9–11 are subtle and complicated, Jean-Noël Aletti (1998, 167–74) has clarified Paul's overall argument. According to Aletti, Paul develops his argument in the following way: First, he begins with an *exordium*, in which he expresses his concern about the present situation in which historical Israel finds itself (9:1–5). Next, he develops an extended *probatio*, which consists of three parts (9:6–11:32), each part governed by a *propositio*. In the first part, guided by its *propositio* in 9:6a, Paul argues that an examination of how God acted in the past and is presently acting shows that the Word of God has not failed (9:13–29). In the second part, guided by the *propositio* in 10:4, Paul explains that the situation of historical Israel is the result of Israel preferring its own righteousness to the righteousness that comes from Christ, who is the *telos* ("end" and/or "goal") of the law (9:30–10:21). In the third part, guided by the *propositio* in 11:1a, Paul argues that God has not rejected his people. Rather, Israel's refusal to accept God's righteousness has become the occasion for the Gentiles to come to righteousness. When the full number of the Gentiles has entered, then all Israel will be saved (11:1–32). Thus Paul's argument inexorably moves to the surprising conclusion that all Israel will be saved. The argument concludes with a *peroratio* in which Paul celebrates God's inscrutable wisdom manifested in his saving righteousness (11:33–36).

Romans 9:1–29

The Mystery of Divine Election

Introductory Matters

Romans 9:1–29 provides the theological underpinnings for the argument that Paul will develop in Rom. 9–11. Aware that the destiny of Israel is intimately related to the question of God's righteousness, Paul will argue that God's ways have not changed. To the contrary, the manner in which God is presently dealing with Israel and the Gentiles is the way in which God has always dealt with Israel: by divine election. Thus Paul defends God's integrity and consistency by reminding his audience of the mystery of divine election that has characterized the story of Israel from its inception.

To defend God—whom no human need defend, for the Creator is not answerable to the creature—Paul turns to God's own word as found in Israel's scriptures. Thus, after the "long draught of direct citation of the Scriptures in chapters 5–8" (Seifrid 2007, 638), which Paul ended with a quotation from Ps. 43:23 LXX (44:22 Eng.) in Rom. 8:36, the apostle employs a host of scriptural citations in Rom. 9–11 to explain and "defend" God's fidelity to Israel. The number of direct citations from Israel's scriptures that Paul employs in these chapters—not to mention allusions to Scripture—underscores his profound and sustained reflection on Israel's scriptures. Rather than provide his own solution to the question of Israel's destiny, then, Paul turns to God's word to uncover God's eternal plan as inscribed in Israel's scriptures, a plan revealed in Christ.

N. T. Wright (2002), J. Ross Wagner (2003), and Mark Seifrid (2007) have shown how integral Paul's use of Scripture is to the argument he develops in these chapters. Carefully examining the manner in which he employs Scripture, they have chronicled the ways in which the apostle rereads and retells Israel's story through the lens of Scripture in order to show his readers God's enduring purpose in electing Israel and calling Gentiles as well as Jews into the restored people of God. Before tracing Paul's train of thought in 9:1–29, then, it will be helpful to preview how he uses Israel's scriptures in the argument of this chapter.

In 9:6–13, a unit in which Paul reviews God's elective process on behalf of Israel, the apostle employs four quotations. These quotations (three of which come from Genesis) focus on the patriarchal period. Although Paul quotes Israel's scriptures in Greek and tends to follow the Septuagint, for the sake of convenience I will quote from the NRSV, unless otherwise noted. The portions of these quotations that Paul employs are italicized.

In 9:7 Paul quotes from Gen. 21:12:

> But God said to Abraham, "Do not be distressed because of the boy and because of your slave woman; whatever Sarah says to you, do as she tells you, *for it is through Isaac that offspring shall be named for you.*"

Next, in 9:9 Paul quotes from material found in Gen. 18:10, 14. The larger context of the passage (Gen. 18:9–15) reads as follows:

> They said to him, "Where is your wife Sarah?" And he said, "There, in the tent." Then one said, "*I will surely return to you in due season, and* your wife *Sarah shall have a son.*" And Sarah was listening at the tent entrance behind him. Now Abraham and Sarah were old, advanced in age; it had ceased to be with Sarah after the manner of women. So Sarah laughed to herself, saying, "After I have grown old, and my husband is old, shall I have pleasure?" The LORD said to Abraham, "Why did Sarah laugh, and say, 'Shall I indeed bear a child, now that I am old?' Is anything too wonderful for the LORD? *At the set time I will return to you,* in due season, *and Sarah shall have a son.*" But Sarah denied, saying, "I did not laugh"; for she was afraid. He said, "Oh yes, you did laugh."

Then in 9:12 Paul quotes from Gen. 25:23:

> And the LORD said to her [Rebecca], "Two nations are in your womb, and two peoples born of you shall be divided; one shall be stronger than the other, *the elder shall serve the younger.*"

Finally, in 9:13 he draws upon Mal. 1:2–3:

> I have loved you, says the LORD. But you say, "How have you loved us?" Is not Esau Jacob's brother? says the LORD. Yet *I have loved Jacob but I have hated Esau;* I have made his hill country a desolation and his heritage a desert for jackals.

With the help of these four quotations, Paul summarizes the patriarchal period as a time of election whereby God selected, first from Abraham's sons and then from Isaac's sons, the true "offspring" or "seed" (*sperma*) of Abraham in order to create Israel.

In 9:14–19 Paul employs two quotations to show how God's elective love preserved Israel during the period of its exodus from Egypt. First, in Rom. 9:15 he quotes from Exod. 33:19 to highlight God's mercy toward Moses and Israel:

> And he said, "I will make all my goodness pass before you, and will proclaim before you the name, 'The LORD'; and *I will be gracious to whom I will be gracious, and will show mercy on whom I will show mercy.*"

Second, in 9:17 Paul quotes Exod. 9:16 to explain the role that Pharaoh will play in God's elective plan:

> *But this is why* I have let you live: *to show you my power, and to make my name resound through all the earth.*

As in the previous unit (Rom. 9:6–13), Paul quotes Israel's scripture to show that just as God worked on the basis of election during the patriarchal period, so God worked by election during the period of the exodus to save Israel.

In 9:19–21 Paul employs yet another scriptural text in his response to an imaginary interlocutor who objects to the seemingly arbitrary way in which God elects some and rejects others. Responding to the objector, in 9:20 Paul draws upon Isa. 29:16 and 45:9. Other texts also stand in the background (Job 9:12; Jer. 18:6; Wis. 15:7). The text of Isa. 29:16 reads as follows:

> You turn things upside down! Shall the potter be regarded as the clay? *Shall the thing made say of its maker,* "He did not make me"; or the thing formed say of the one who formed it, "He has no understanding"?

The text of Isa. 45:9 is similar:

> Woe to you who strive with your Maker, earthen vessels with the potter! *Does the clay say to the one who fashions it,* "What are you making?" or "Your work has no handles?"

Although the election theme is not mentioned in these texts, Paul employs them to defend God's elective purpose by reminding his interlocutor that it is not the place of the creature to question the Creator.

Paul's final scriptural quotations occur in 9:24–29, a unit in which he describes the people whom God has created from among the Gentiles as well as from among the Jews, a people that is the outcome of God's elective love.

The quotations are explicitly attributed to Hosea and Isaiah. In 9:25 Paul draws from Hosea 2:23:

> And I will sow him for myself in the land. And I will have pity on Lo-ruhamah, and *I will say to Lo-ammi, "You are my people"*; and he shall say, "You are my God."

Then, in 9:26 he quotes from Hosea 1:10:

> Yet the number of the people of Israel shall be like the sand of the sea, which can be neither measured nor numbered; *and in the place where it was said to them, "You are not my people," it shall be said to them, "Children of the living God."*

However, whereas in Hosea the text has the restoration of Israel in view, in Romans it refers to the creation of a people that includes Gentiles as well as Jews.

In 9:27–28 Paul cites Isa. 10:22–23:

> *For though your people Israel were like the sand of the sea, only a remnant of them will return.* Destruction is decreed, overflowing with righteousness. *For the Lord* GOD *of hosts will make a full end, as decreed, in all the earth.*

Next, in 9:29 he quotes from Isa. 1:9:

> *If the* LORD *of hosts had not left us a few survivors, we would have been like Sodom, and become like Gomorrah.*

With this second text from Isaiah, Paul returns to the theme of "descendants"/"seed" (*sperma*), which he introduced in the quotation of Rom. 9:7 from Gen. 21:12. Thus the story of God's elective purpose has come full circle. Just as election was at work in the creation and preservation of Israel, so God's elective purpose is at work in the present time. And since God has left Israel a remnant/seed, Paul's audience can be confident that God's election of the Gentiles will not exclude Israel, a topic that Paul will develop in chapter 11.

In what follows, Paul's use of Scripture in 9:1–29 will reveal the following: First, Paul employs Scripture to retell the story of Israel. Second, Paul's christological reading of Scripture enables him to uncover God's elective purpose for his own time. Third, Paul views Israel's scripture as a living word that finds new meaning in light of God's saving righteousness in Jesus Christ.

Tracing the Train of Thought

The material of 9:1–29 consists of four units. In the first, Paul expresses his profound concern for his people and enumerates Israel's privileges (9:1–5).

Romans 9:1–29 in the Rhetorical Flow

The letter opening (1:1–17)

Gentiles and Jews in the light of God's wrath (1:18–3:20)

Gentiles and Jews in the light of God's righteousness (3:21–4:25)

The experience of salvation in the light of God's righteousness (5:1–8:39)

God's righteousness and the destiny of Israel (9:1–11:36)

▶ **The mystery of divine election (9:1–29)**

> **Paul's concern for Israel (9:1–5)**
>
> > An expression of Paul's concern (9:1–3)
> >
> > The privileges of Israel (9:4–5)
>
> **The principle of election (9:6–13)**
>
> > Thesis: No failure of God's word (9:6a)
> >
> > Abraham's and Isaac's descendants (9:6b–13)
> >
> > > Not all belong to Israel (9:6b)
> > >
> > > Not all belong to Abraham (9:7a)
> > >
> > > Scriptural support and explanation (9:7b–8)
> > >
> > > Scriptural support for the promise (9:9)
> > >
> > > Rebecca's sons and the principle of election (9:10–13)
>
> **A first objection and Paul's response (9:14–18)**
>
> > Objection and initial response (9:14)
> >
> > Scriptural confirmation (9:15)
> >
> > Conclusion: A matter not of effort but of God's mercy (9:16)
> >
> > Scriptural confirmation (9:17)
> >
> > Conclusion: Mercy and hardening (9:18)
>
> **A second objection and Paul's response (9:19–29)**
>
> > Objection (9:19)
> >
> > Response to the objector (9:20)
> >
> > An example from ordinary life (9:21)
> >
> > Application to the present situation (9:22–29)

In the second, he affirms that the word of God has not failed (9:6–13). To support this statement, he reminds his audience that God's elective purpose has always been at work for and on behalf of Israel. Accordingly, Abraham's true descendants are those who belong to the line of Isaac rather than Ishmael, and to the line of Jacob rather than Esau. This does not completely solve the question that Paul is addressing, since one can ask why all of these descendants have not believed in the Christ, but it provides Paul with the hermeneutical key he needs to discern the purpose of God's plan: the principle of election.

In the third unit, Paul employs the rhetoric of the diatribe to raise an objection to this principle of election: God's ways appear arbitrary and unjust (9:14–18). Paul's response is that the principle of election is an expression of God's mercy. To be elected depends on God's mercy, not upon human willing or doing. In the fourth unit, Paul deals with an objection that arises from his answer to the first objection (9:19–29). If God has mercy on whom he wishes, then who can resist God's will? Paul's first response is that the creature is out of order to question the Creator. To support this, he employs the example of a potter. Just as pottery does not question the potter, so humans are not to question God. The potter makes some works for ordinary use and others for special use. Cannot God do the same? Paul concludes his argument with scriptural citations from Hosea and Isaiah that highlight God's elective love and intimates that Israel will be restored through a remnant, which is the seed of a restored Israel.

Throughout 9:1–29 Paul holds two competing concepts together: God's elective love and God's faithfulness to Israel. He proposes that God's word has not failed because God has always worked on the principle of election.

9:1–5. Paul begins his argument with a personal lament that consists of two parts. In the first, he expresses his profound grief that the majority of his Jewish compatriots have not responded to the gospel of God's saving righteousness in Jesus Christ (9:1–3). Identifying them as "Israelites," in the second part he enumerates their privileges as God's chosen people (9:4–5). The pathos with which Paul begins this unit could not be greater. Unlike his discussion of Jewish failure to observe the law (2:17–29), this passage highlights Israel's enduring privileges, thereby dispelling any notion that Paul has forsaken his people.

Paul begins his lament with a carefully crafted statement in which he assures his audience of the truth of what he is about to say. Grounding his truthfulness in his relationship to Christ and in his own moral consciousness, he writes: **I am speaking the truth in Christ, I am not lying. My conscience testifies on my behalf in the Holy Spirit** (9:1). While Paul often emphasizes the truthfulness of what he writes (2 Cor. 11:31; Gal. 1:20), the manner in which he grounds the truth of what he says here ("in Christ" and "in the Holy Spirit") is especially striking. What he is about to say is utterly reliable and should dispel any suspicion that he has abandoned his people.

Completing the sentence he began in 9:1, Paul writes, **that my heart is afflicted with overwhelming sorrow and unrelenting distress** (9:2). Paul has already referred to "the heart" several times in Romans (2:15; 5:5; 6:17), and in 8:27 he has called God the "Searcher of hearts." Now, referring to his own heart, the seat of his emotional life, he describes his state of mind in two ways: he is filled with (1) sorrow because his compatriots have not accepted his gospel and (2) distress because their refusal to do so (which is based on a misguided zeal; 10:2) has deprived them of the righteousness that comes from God.

To explain why he is filled with such sorrow and distress, Paul introduces an explanatory clause that begins with *gar* (for): **For I could wish to be cut off from Christ for the sake of my brothers and sisters, my kindred according to the flesh** (9:3). Despite his statement at the end of chapter 8 that nothing can separate the justified from the love of Christ and the love that God has for them in Christ, here Paul expresses his willingness to be "cut off" (*anathema*, lit., "cursed") from Christ if this could bring about the conversion of his people. By uttering this wish, Paul acts like Moses, who, after the incident of the golden calf (Exod. 32), implored God on Israel's behalf: "Alas, this people has sinned a great sin; they have made for themselves gods of gold. But now, if you will only forgive their sin—*but if not, blot me out of the book that you have written*" (Exod. 32:31–32, emphasis added). But whereas Moses begs to be stricken from the book of life if God will not forgive Israel's sin, Paul asks to be separated from Christ if it will lead to his people's incorporation into Christ. What Paul writes here, however, is merely a hypothetical statement intended to underline the depth of his sorrow and distress since, at the end of chapter 11, he will affirm that all Israel will be saved.

In 9:3 Paul calls his compatriots, literally, "my brothers" (*adelphōn mou*) and "my kindred according to the flesh" (*syngenōn mou kata sarka*). In doing so, he identifies himself as one of their compatriots: a fellow Jew. But next he identifies them as those **who are Israelites** (9:4a). This designation, which Paul uses two other times in his letters (Rom. 11:1; 2 Cor. 11:22), recalls the religious history of his people. In both instances, Paul emphatically affirms that he is an Israelite, a descendant/seed of Abraham. By identifying his compatriots who have not believed in the gospel as "Israelites," he implicitly affirms their enduring status before God. Although they have not believed in Christ, they have not forfeited their status as Israelites; for God's call is irrevocable (11:29).

Next, Paul lists the privileges that belong to his compatriots inasmuch as they are Israelites: **To them belong the adoption, the glory, the covenants, the law, the worship, and the promises. To them belong the patriarchs, from whom comes, in terms of human descent, the Messiah, who is over all, God, forever blessed. Amen** (9:4–5). The Greek pronouns in 9:4, 5, *hōn* (to them), suggest that Paul divides the list into two unequal parts. In 9:4 there are six items that can be divided into two groups:

1. the adoption	4. the law
2. the glory	5. the worship
3. the covenants	6. the promises

In 9:5 there are two related items: (1) the patriarchs, from whom (2) the Messiah is descended.

Paul has already spoken of the "adoption" that Christians have and hope for (8:15, 23). Here he recalls the adoption that Israel enjoys as God's "firstborn son" (Exod. 4:22), the son whom God called out of Egypt (Hosea 11:1). The "glory" refers to God's own glory, which was manifested to Israel throughout its history, especially at the Red Sea, at Sinai, and in the temple of Jerusalem (Fitzmyer 1993, 546). Although Paul tends to focus on the covenants that God made with Abraham and the covenant that God made with Israel at Sinai, Paul may also have in mind the covenants made with Noah, the other patriarchs, and David as well. The "law" or the "legislation" (*nomothesia*) refers to the legislation given at Sinai and recalls Paul's earlier remark that the Jewish people "were entrusted with the oracles of God" (3:2). An essential component of this law, which Israel received at Sinai, was the legislation for the cult, which enabled Israel to worship God and experience the divine glory (Exod. 25–31), first in the tent of meeting in the wilderness, then in the temple of Jerusalem. Somewhat surprisingly, "the promises" that God made to Abraham, Isaac, and Jacob occur last in this list, even though they predate the other items. The presence of the promises at the end of the list, however, provides a transition to the second list, which begins with the patriarchs and concludes with the Messiah.

The "patriarchs" refer to Abraham, Isaac, and Jacob, all of whom will play a prominent role in the next unit (9:6, 13). Here Paul introduces them to establish the continuity between Israel's faith and the gospel he preaches. The Messiah, who is the content of Paul's gospel, is a true Israelite, a human descendant of the patriarchs and, according to Paul's understanding, the fulfillment of the promises that God made to them. Except for the last of these privileges ("the Messiah"), Paul's compatriots continue to possess all of these irrevocable gifts of God (11:29). It is not that these *were* their privileges; they *are and remain their* privileges (Bell 2005, 207). Paul's compatriots, however, must still appropriate the last of them, the Messiah.

The manner in which I have translated 9:5 ("from whom comes, in terms of human descent, the Messiah, who is over all, God, forever blessed. Amen") reflects an exegetical decision on my part since the Greek can be construed in a different way. If a period is placed after "Messiah" ("from whom comes, in terms of human descent according to the flesh, the Messiah"), then the following phrase becomes a benediction ("God who is over all be forever blessed. Amen"). But if one places a comma after Christ, then *theos* (God) functions as a predicate of "the Messiah."

Both translations have their supporters. For example, Dunn, Fitzmyer, and D. Moo argue that Paul predicates *theos* of Christ, whereas Brendan Byrne and Peter Stuhlmacher maintain that Paul is interjecting a benediction here. Although Paul does not otherwise predicate *theos* of Christ (but see Titus 2:13), it is not inconceivable that in this instance he is drawing a distinction between the earthly descent of the Messiah and his exalted status, much as he does in Rom. 1:3–4. In predicating *theos* of Christ, then, Paul is not confusing Christ with God the Father (*ho theos, ho patēr*), but affirming that the one who is *kyrios* (Lord) shares in and enjoys the status of *theos*.

9:6–13. Having introduced his discussion of Israel's destiny with a lament over the failure of his people to accept the gospel, in this unit Paul confronts the issue that underlines all that he writes in Rom. 9–11: the effectiveness of God's word. Has God's redemptive purpose for Israel failed? Paul's response is a resounding affirmation of the effectiveness of God's word. To support this response, however, he must remind his audience that God has always worked on the basis of election. Consequently, even though the majority of his coreligionists have refused to believe in the gospel, Paul affirms that God's word has not failed because now, as in the past, God's elective purpose is a work. The unit begins with a statement of Paul's thesis (9:6a), which he develops by pointing to the example of Abraham's descendants through Isaac (9:6b–9), and Isaac's descendants through Jacob (9:10–13). To appreciate how this unit functions in the whole of 9:1–29, we should note that Paul will establish a relationship between the "descendants"/"seed" (*sperma*) of Abraham (9:6–7) and the "remnant" (*hypoleimma*) and "descendants"/"seed" (*sperma*) of which Isaiah speaks in the quotations of 9:27 and 9:29, respectively.

Despite his distress over the failure of his compatriots to believe, Paul proclaims, **But it is not as though the word of God has failed** (9:6a). By affirming his confidence in the effectiveness of God's word, Paul echoes two texts from the book of the prophet Isaiah: "The grass withers, the flower fades; but the word of our God will stand forever" (Isa. 40:8). And again, "so shall my word be that goes out from my mouth; it shall not return to me empty, but it shall accomplish that which I purpose, and succeed in the thing for which I sent it" (Isa. 55:11). To confirm his thesis, Paul asserts, **For not all who are from Israel belong to Israel** (9:6b). Although "Israel" occurs twice in this phrase, Paul does not use the term the same way both times. In the first instance, he refers to the patriarch Israel, in the second to the nation that has descended from him. Paul's thesis is that not all of the great patriarch's physical descendants belong to the people that bear his name.

To explain what he means, Paul begins with the example of Abraham's "descendants"/"seed." Quoting Gen. 21:12, Paul recalls how, at a crucial moment in the patriarchal narrative, Sarah required Abraham to dismiss his concubine Hagar and Ishmael, the son whom he begot through her. Although Abraham is reluctant to do so, God tells him not to be distressed because his "descendants"/"seed" (*sperma*) will be through Isaac rather than through Ishmael. Accordingly, Paul employs Gen. 21:12 to make the following point: **Nor are all of Abraham's children his descendants. Rather, "your descendants will be designated through Isaac"** (9:7). Consequently, although Ishmael and his children are Abraham's "children" (*tekna*), they are not his *sperma* ("descendants"/"seed") in the sense of belonging to the people of Israel.

Paul explains the reason for this: **That is, it is not the children of the flesh who are God's children but the children of the promise who are counted as descendants** (9:8). Drawing on a distinction he has already made in his allegory of Sarah and Hagar (Gal. 4:21–27), Paul distinguishes between "the children of the flesh" and "the children of the promise" and establishes a relation between the children of the promise and "God's children." This allows him to argue that it is only the children of the promise who are Abraham's seed/descendants. To appreciate the significance of this point, we must remember that Paul has already identified the justified as "God's children" (8:16, 17, 21). Consequently, although they are physically children of Abraham, Ishmael and his descendants are not children of the promise, nor can they be counted as "God's children" in the same way that the children of the promise are. For whereas Ishmael was born of a woman of childbearing age, Isaac was born when Sarah was beyond the age of childbearing; he was marvelously born in virtue of God's promise. To confirm his argument, Paul turns to the story of Gen. 18:1–15, in which the Lord appeared to Abraham at Mamre in the guise of three men who promised that Sarah would have a child within a year's time, causing Sarah to laugh (Gen. 18:13). Drawing from Gen. 18:10, 14, Paul writes: **For this is the word of the promise, "I will come about this time and Sarah will have a son"** (9:9).

The first part of Paul's argument can be summarized in this way: There is a distinction among Abraham's children. While all are his children, not all are counted as his seed/descendants—members of the people of Israel; for the line of descendants is through Isaac, the child of the promise.

Lest someone object that Isaac was preferred to Ishmael because Sarah was Abraham's wife and Hagar his concubine, in 9:10–13 Paul employs a more-powerful example, in which he explicitly introduces the concept of "election" for the first time (D. Moo 1996, 578). Turning to the births of Jacob and Esau, who shared the same mother as well as the same father (Rebecca and Isaac), Paul highlights how God chose Jacob and rejected Esau before either was born or accomplished anything.

Paul argues by noting the difference between this example and the previous one: **Not only that, but even when Rebecca conceived through one man, our father Isaac** (9:10). In the case of the two children that Paul will now discuss—Esau and Jacob—both were conceived by the same mother through the agency of the same father. This is a crucial point for Paul since it highlights that, unlike Isaac and Ishmael, Esau and Jacob were of equal status. To reinforce this point, Paul emphasizes that God's election of Jacob rather than Esau occurred **before they were born or had done anything good or bad** (9:11a). Pointing to this moment before the birth of the children, Paul concludes that this occurred **in order that God's purpose of election might stand not on the basis of works but on the basis of the one who calls** (9:11b–12a). With this statement, Paul explicitly introduces the word "election" (*eklogēn*) for the first time, a term that will reoccur in 11:5, 7, 28. Paul affirms that this election occurred before the children were born so that it would be clear that Jacob's election had nothing to do with any "works" he had done but was completely dependent on God, who called him before he was born. To confirm this, Paul concludes his argument with two scriptural quotations: **it was said to her, "The older will serve the younger." As it is written, "Jacob I have loved, but Esau I have hated"** (9:12b–13). The first comes from Gen. 25:23, which is part of an episode in which Rebecca (OT Rebekah) complains to God when the children in her womb "struggle together within her" (25:22). In response, God reveals that two nations are in her womb, and that "the older will serve the younger." The second quotation comes from the beginning of the book of the prophet Malachi (1:2–3). Although God affirms his love for the people, they ask, "How have you loved us?" leading God to respond, "Is not Esau Jacob's brother? . . . Yet I have loved Jacob [Israel], but I have hated Esau [Edom]." In other words, although Esau and Jacob were brothers, God's elective love preferred Jacob.

The upshot of Paul's argument is this: Israel has come into being by divine election. God selected the descendants of Isaac rather than those of Ishmael, and God chose the descendants of Jacob rather than those of Esau. Not all of Abraham's children are his true descendants. His true descendants are those who belong to the line of Isaac and Jacob. This is why not all of Israel has believed in the gospel. The word of God has not failed, for as Paul will show, God is still working in the same elective/selective way to bring about the fulfillment of the redemptive plan that began with the election of Israel.

9:14–18. In 9:7–13 Paul introduced the principle of election to support his thesis that the word of God has not failed (9:6a) despite the failure of the majority of his compatriots to accept the gospel (9:1–5). He argued that throughout Israel's history, God has always worked on the basis of election. The refusal of the majority of Paul's compatriots to believe the gospel, then, is not a failure of God's word but another example of the mystery of divine election. Aware that this argument has the potential for misunderstanding, in 9:14–29 Paul returns to the style of the diatribe and poses two objections to his thesis about God's elective purpose (9:14, 19). He then returns to the theme of election in 9:24–29 to illustrate how God's elective purpose is at work at the present time.

Paul raises the first of these objections in this unit (9:14–18): Is not God's elective purpose arbitrary and a manifestation of "injustice" (*adikia*) on God's part—an objection that echoes the charge in 3:5? To respond to this objection, Paul turns to the period of Israel's sojourn in Egypt to illustrate how God's elective purpose resulted in mercy and protection for Israel. In doing so, the apostle continues to retell the story of his people from the point of view of divine election. Employing an expression (*ti oun eroumen*) he has already used on numerous occasions (3:5; 4:1; 6:1; 7:7; 8:31), and to which he will return in 9:30, Paul asks, **What then shall we say? Is there injustice on God's part?** (9:14a). He then emphatically responds to his own question, as he does whenever he considers the question a misunderstanding or misrepresentation of his gospel: **Of course not!** (9:14b). To substantiate his response, Paul recalls an episode of Israel's history in which God's elective love preserved and insured the continuation of the nation. Quoting from Exod. 33:19 LXX, he writes: **For he says to Moses, "I will have mercy on whomever I have mercy, and I will have compassion on whomever I have compassion"** (9:15). The context for the quotation is as follows: After the episode of the golden calf (Exod. 32), the Lord instructs Moses to "leave this place" and go to the land that God swore he would give "to Abraham, Isaac, and Jacob" (33:1). But since Israel has broken the covenant, the Lord informs Moses, "but I will not go up among you" (33:3). Distraught, Moses pleads on Israel's behalf, asking God that the divine presence accompany them (33:12–19). At this point, the Lord relents and Moses asks, "Show me your glory, I pray." The Lord replies with the words that Paul quotes in Rom. 9:15.

Employing the formula *ara oun*, Paul draws a conclusion based on God's elective purpose as manifested at the period of the exodus: **Consequently, it is not a matter of willing or striving but of God's exercising mercy** (9:16). With this verse, Paul echoes what he has said in 9:11–12 concerning the gracious nature of God's elective love for Jacob. In 9:11–12 Paul has insisted that it was "not on the basis of works but on the basis of the one who calls," but here he affirms that it is not a matter of "willing or striving" but of "God exercising mercy." The parallelism between the two passages is as follows:

not on the basis of works	but on the basis of the one who calls
not a matter of willing or striving	but of God exercising mercy

The exercise of God's mercy at the time of the exodus, then, was another manifestation of God's calling and electing his people; it was not the outcome of the people's willing or striving, for it did not result from anything they had done. To the contrary, God manifested his elective mercy on behalf of Israel after the people's rebellion as narrated in Exod. 32.

Paul, however, has not finished his response. Having described the gracious and merciful way God treated Israel through Moses, he recalls the manner in which the Lord dealt with Pharaoh at the time of the exodus. Quoting from Exod. 9:16, he writes: **For Scripture says to Pharaoh, "This is why I have raised you up, so that I might show my power by you and thus my name might be proclaimed throughout all the earth"** (Rom. 9:17). This quotation comes from an encounter between Moses and Pharaoh, when Moses warns Pharaoh of the seventh plague of thunder and hail that is about to come upon Egypt (Exod. 9:13–35). Speaking in the name of the Lord, Moses tells Pharaoh what his role is in God's redemptive plan for Israel. But whereas the Hebrew reads "I have *spared* you [Pharaoh] for this purpose" (NJPS), and the LXX reads "for this reason you have been *spared*" (*dietērēthēs*; NETS), Paul alters the LXX to read, "This is why I have raised you up (*exēgeira*)." By "raising up" Pharaoh, God "elected" him to play a role in Israel's redemptive history, of which he was not even aware. For by refusing to obey Moses, the servant of God, Pharaoh enabled the Lord to show his power to redeem Israel. Thus the Lord's name was proclaimed throughout the earth.

As in Rom. 9:16 Paul employs the expression *ara oun* to draw a conclusion about divine election from this scriptural text: **Consequently, he has mercy on whom he wishes, and he hardens whom he wishes** (9:18). Paul's conclusion has two parts; the first part refers to Moses and Israel, the second to Pharaoh. Whereas God's elective purpose resulted in mercy toward Moses for the sake of Israel, it led to the hardening of Pharaoh's heart for the glory of God. Although Paul is not quoting a specific text at this point, he echoes a series of scriptural texts from the book of Exodus that affirm how God hardened Pharaoh's heart (4:21; 9:12; 10:1, 20, 27; 11:10; 14:8). To be sure, other texts speak of Pharaoh's hardening his own heart (7:13–14, 22–23; 8:15, 19, 32; 9:7, 34–35), but Paul does not allude to these. Nor is there any suggestion that the Lord hardened Pharaoh's heart *because* Pharaoh hardened his heart, since Paul's point is to highlight God's elective purpose in Israel's history.

To summarize, in 9:14–18 Paul counters an objection that calls into question God's uprightness by recalling God's elective mercy on behalf of Israel during the period of the exodus. To these objections Paul responds that there was no injustice on God's part in electing Isaac, Jacob, and the people of Israel since God's elective love is not arbitrary, as the objector presupposes, but part of God's redemptive plan, which Paul will soon explain. Before doing so, however, he must deal with another objection.

9:19–29. Having highlighted how God has shown mercy to some and hardened others, Paul anticipates a second objection. If Paul's gospel of election is correct, then who can resist God's redemptive plan of election, which inexorably moves forward despite human resistance? Put more concretely, if not even mighty Pharaoh could resist the Lord, who can? Aware of this difficulty, in 9:19 Paul anticipates the objection of an imaginary interlocutor to which he will respond in the rest of this unit (9:18–29). In the previous units, Paul has focused on clearly defined periods in Israel's history (the time of the patriarchs and the exodus), but the period to which he refers here is not explicitly defined. Paul's quotations from Isaiah and Hosea, however, suggest that he may have in view a later period in Israel's history, characterized by disobedience, punishment, and restoration.

Paul begins with a question in which he anticipates the objection of an imaginary interlocutor: **Accordingly, you will say to me, "Then why does he still find fault, for who can oppose his will?"** (9:19). This objection is similar in form to the question raised in 3:7, when the interlocutor asked why he was still being condemned as a sinner when his falsehood served to highlight God's truthfulness. In other words, if God is so completely in charge, what room is there for human initiative? The book of Wisdom echoes a similar sentiment: "For who will say, 'What have you done?' or will resist your judgment? Who will accuse you for the destruction of nations that you made? Or who will come before you to plead as an advocate for the unrighteous?" (12:12). Likewise the book of Job asks, "He snatches away; who can stop him? Who will say to him, 'What are you doing?'" (9:12).

Paul, however, is not interested in resolving the tension between God's sovereign purpose and human freedom. For him, the very question betrays a profound misunderstanding of the relationship between the creature and the Creator, a rebellious response that Paul has already described in 1:18–32. Consequently, adopting the same form of address that he did in 2:1, 3 (*ō anthrōpe*), he asks, **On the contrary, mortal one, who are you to talk back to God?** (9:20a). To argue his point, Paul turns to a well-known metaphor for God: the potter who fashions his creation (see Jer. 18:1–12). Employing language found in two texts from Isaiah, but without any formal introduction to indicate that he is quoting Scripture, Paul asks: **What is molded does not say to the one who molded it, "Why did you make me thus?" does it?** (9:21b). The first part of the quotation is similar to the LXX text of Isa. 29:16: "Shall the thing formed say to the one who formed it?" (NETS). But whereas the LXX concludes with a declarative statement of defiance, "You did not form me," Paul concludes with a question in which the creature calls into question the wisdom of the Creator: "Why did you make me thus?" A somewhat similar question occurs in Isa. 45:9: "Does the clay say to the one who fashions it, 'What are you making?'" (NRSV). Paul's question, however, is more specific ("Why did you make me thus?") because he is responding to a particular interlocutor who dares to interrogate God.

J. Ross Wagner (2003, 65) points out that the text of Isa. 29:16 "is part of a larger narrative in Isaiah 28–29 in which Israel doubts God's wisdom and power to save them, trusting instead in their own schemes for deliverance." He further notes that "Isa. 45:9 likewise involves a disputation between God and his people; once again the issue revolves around Israel's persistent questioning of God's wisdom and power to save them." Although Paul has not identified his interlocutor, it appears that he is responding to those who question God's wisdom as announced in the gospel of God's righteousness.

Developing the metaphor of the potter further, Paul asks his interlocutor, **Does not the potter have authority over the clay to make from the lump a jar for special use and a jar for ordinary use?** (9:21). Here there are echoes of Jer. 18:6 ("Can I not do with you, O house of Israel, just as this potter has done? says the LORD. Just like the clay in the potter's hand, so are you in my hand, O house of Israel") and Wis. 15:7 ("A potter kneads the soft earth and laboriously molds each vessel for our service, fashioning out of the same clay both the vessels that serve clean uses and those for contrary uses, making all alike; but which shall be the use of each of them the worker in clay decides"). By emphasizing that the potter makes different kinds of jars from the same lump of clay, Paul recalls God's choice of Jacob over Esau (Rom. 9:10–13). Because God is the Creator, God is free to create as he does.

Having spoken of the potter's right to fashion different kinds of jars from the same lump of clay, Paul applies the metaphor of the potter to God (9:22–24). All translators struggle with these verses since Paul begins a conditional question in 9:22–23 that he never concludes, thereby requiring translators to supply something in order to make sense of these verses (see the discussion of Cranfield 1979, 492–97). Aware of this grammatical difficulty, the text of Vaticanus and the Vulgate omit the *kai* (and) that introduces 9:23. This results in a smooth translation, such as is found in 9:22–24 RSV: "What if God, desiring to show his wrath and to make known his power, has endured with much patience the vessels of wrath made for destruction, *in order to* make known the riches of his glory for the vessels of mercy, which he has prepared beforehand for glory, even us whom he has called, not from the Jews only but also from the Gentiles?" I have retained the *kai*, which is the more difficult and better-attested reading, and introduced the phrase "what if" at the beginning of 9:22 and 9:23 and made 9:24 the conclusion of 9:23: **What if God, although willing to show his wrath and make known his power, endured with great forbearance jars of wrath designed for destruction? And what if he has done this in order to make known the richness of his glory upon jars of mercy that he prepared for glory, namely us, whom he called not only from among the Jews but even from among the Gentiles?** (9:22–24). Paul's long and complicated argument can be paraphrased as follows: If God, like a patient potter, has not destroyed those "jars" that ought to have been destroyed so that he could manifest his glory to other "jars" that he has destined for glory, who are human beings to question God's wisdom? Like the potter, the Creator is free to do as he wishes with what he has created.

In this elaborate metaphor, the identity of the "jars of mercy" is clear. These jars, which are destined for God's glory, represent the community of Jewish and Gentile Christ-believers whom God has recently called in Christ. As for the "jars of wrath," although Paul never explicitly identifies them, they appear to represent that portion of Israel that has refused to believe in the gospel. The upshot of Paul's metaphor is this: God has borne and continues to bear with unrepentant Israel in order to manifest his glory toward those whom he has called and elected from among the Gentiles as well as from among the Jews. God's elective purpose, then, is still at work. To be sure, this puts Israel in a negative light and appears to transfer its elective status to this new eschatological community. But there is hope for Israel since God's elective purpose is still at work in a remnant.

In 9:25–29 Paul quotes from the prophets Hosea and Isaiah to persuade his audience that God's elective purpose is presently at work. In 9:25–26 he draws from Hosea to explain how God has created a community composed of Gentiles as well as Jewish Christ-believers. Then in 9:27–29 he twice quotes from Isaiah to show how God's elective purpose is at work to restore Israel.

Having identified the new community that God has called from among Gentiles and Jews as the "jars of mercy" who are destined for God's eschatological glory—yet another reference to the general resurrection of the dead—in 9:25–26 Paul enlists Hosea to confirm his argument: **As it says in Hosea** (9:25a). The quotation that follows is a mixed citation from Hosea 2:23 and Hosea 1:10, which Paul has edited for his purposes. Thus whereas Hosea 2:23 reads, "And I will have pity on Not pitied, and I will say to Not my people, 'You are my people'; and he shall say, 'You are my God'" (NRSV margin), Paul writes: **"I shall call one who is not my people, my people, and one who is not beloved, beloved"** (9:25b). In doing so, he (1) emphasizes God's elective call, (2) designates this people as God's people, and (3) speaks of God's love rather than of God's pity. In quoting Hosea 1:10, however, Paul remains close to the LXX text of Hosea (2:1 in the LXX): **"And it will happen in this place where it was said to them, 'You are not my people,' there they will be called children of the living God"** (9:26). The upshot of Paul's mixed quotation is that a people who formerly were not God's people have become God's people because God has elected them. But whereas in its historical context the text

of Hosea had in view the restoration of the northern tribes of Israel and the phrase "in this place" referred to Jerusalem (Fitzmyer 1993, 573), Paul envisages the restoration of Gentiles and Jews who were formerly alienated from God. Moreover, "this place" no longer refers to Jerusalem but to any place where God speaks to people and calls them to belong to this new people, be they Gentiles or Jews.

Having explained how God's elective purpose has resulted in the creation of a people that includes Gentiles as well as Jewish believers, in 9:27–29 Paul employs two quotations from Isaiah that deal more specifically with the destiny of Israel, thereby bringing the discussion begun in 9:6a (that God's word

Figure 10. The Prophet Isaiah, cathedral niche sculpture by Wiligelmo da Modena (fl. ca. 1099–ca. 1120), Modena, Italy. Quotations from Isaiah figure prominently in Paul's argument in the Letter to the Romans.

has not failed) to a conclusion. Paul uses the first quotation to show that a "remnant" remains, and the second to show that God has left Israel with "seed" or "descendants" (*sperma*). The gist of the argument, then, is that God's elective purpose is still at work *for Israel*, which will be saved through this remnant/seed.

The introduction to Paul's first quotation signals that he is now turning his attention to Israel: **Isaiah cries out on behalf of Israel** (9:27a). The quotation that follows is a shortened form of Isa. 10:22–23 and is close to the LXX, which reads as follows (with the portion omitted by Paul in brackets): "And if the people of Israel become like the sand of the sea, the remnant will be saved, for he is completing and cutting short a reckoning [with righteousness, because God will perform a shortened reckoning] in the whole world" (NETS). In addition to omitting the bracketed words, the first part of Paul's quotation is closer to the text of Hosea 2:1 LXX (1:10 Eng.; "And the number of *the sons of Israel* was like the sand of the sea," NETS) than it is to Isa. 10:22a ("And if *the people of Israel* become like the sand of the sea," NETS). The result is the following quotation: **"Even if the number of the children of Israel should be as the sand of the sea, only a remnant will be saved; for the Lord will accomplish his word completely and swiftly upon the earth"** (9:27b–28). The text of Isaiah originally referred to the remnant preserved at the time of the Assyrian captivity, but Paul identifies it as that portion of Israel—himself included (11:1)—that has believed in the gospel for whom God will "accomplish his word completely and swiftly [*syntelōn kai syntemnōn*]." Although this phrase—which occurs in Isa. 28:22 LXX; Dan. 5:26 LXX; and Dan. 9:24 Theodotion—has been interpreted in various ways (Cranfield 1979, 502; Fitzmyer 1993, 574; Jewett 2007, 603–4), I have taken it in a positive sense. God will accomplish his purpose on behalf of the remnant completely and swiftly.

Paul introduces his second quotation, this one from Isa. 1:9, in a way that highlights Isaiah's prophetic knowledge of God's divine plan: **Even as Isaiah foretold long ago** (9:29a). The text that follows essentially corresponds to the LXX: **"If the Lord of Hosts had not left us descendants, we would have become like Sodom, and we would be like Gomorrah"** (9:29b). But whereas Isaiah originally spoke of the preservation of a remnant at the time of the Assyrian captivity, Paul has in view the events of his own day. Thus he rereads and applies the text to the present situation of historical Israel. If God has not left a faithful remnant of believers from historical Israel, one would have to conclude that the word of God has failed. But that is not the case. The remnant of Israel that has believed in the gospel is the "seed"/"descendants" (*sperma*) that God has left for the restoration of all Israel. Thus Paul's argument has come full circle. Having maintained that Abraham's true *sperma* is found in the line of Isaac and Jacob, a descent of divine election, Paul here employs *sperma* once more to assure his audience that God's elective purpose has not failed. Israel was created by God's election, and Israel is being re-created by God's election through the remnant, the seed that God has preserved.

The train of thought in 9:1–29 can be summarized in this way: God's word has not failed in its purpose because God has always worked on the basis of election in creating, saving, and now restoring Israel through a remnant. That elective purpose was at work in the period of the patriarchs, the time of exodus, and it is presently at work in a chosen remnant. Those who view God's elective purpose as arbitrary and unjust do not understand that election is a manifestation of mercy, whereas those who object that it does away with human freedom challenge the one who has created them, the God whose elective purpose they do not understand.

Theological Issues

In an earlier period, when commentators focused on Rom. 1–8 as the theological heart of Paul's letter, Rom. 9–11 was often mined for its doctrine of predestination. In recent years, however, the pendulum has shifted. With a renewed appreciation for the central role that Paul's discussion of Israel plays in Rom. 9–11, commentators have highlighted the climactic role these chapters play in Paul's exposition of God's righteousness. In doing so, they have spoken less—if at all—about the predestination of the individual. For example, in his exposition of Rom. 9:6–29, James Dunn (1988, 2:562) writes, "Modern commentators should beware of generalizing too quickly from this passage.... A more extensive doctrine of election is not found here." In contrast to Dunn, Douglas Moo (1996, 598), who fully appreciates the centrality of Rom. 9–11 in Paul's argument, comments on 9:18: "It seems, then, that this text, in its context, provides important

John Calvin on Predestination

"As Scripture, then, clearly shows, we say that God once established by his eternal and unchangeable plan those whom he long before determined once for all to receive into salvation, and those whom, on the other hand, he would devote to destruction. We assert that, with respect to the elect, this plan was founded upon his freely given mercy, without regard to human worth; but by his just and irreprehensible but incomprehensible judgment he has barred the door of life to those whom he has given over to damnation. Now among the elect we regard the call as a testimony of election. Then we hold justification another sign of its manifestation, until they come into the glory in which the fulfillment of that election lies. But as the Lord seals his elect by call and justification, so, by shutting off the reprobate from knowledge of his name or from the sanctification of his Spirit, he, as it were, reveals by these marks what sort of judgment awaits them." (Institutes of the Christian Religion 3.21.7, Calvin 1960, 2:931)

exegetical support for the controversial doctrine of 'double predestination.'" Moo then refers his readers to Calvin's *Institutes of the Christian Religion* 3.21.5; 3.22.11; 3.23.1–14; 3.24.12–17.

Whether one agrees with Dunn or Moo, Rom. 9 has played a central role in the theological discussion of predestination; namely, that God has predestined the elect for salvation. In his description of what he calls the "Lutheran Paul," Stephen Westerholm (2004, 16–19, 54–55) recounts how Augustine and Calvin employed Romans in their teaching on predestination. In his survey of how commentators from Origen to the present have interpreted Romans, Mark Reasoner (2005, 85–86) highlights three loci that have played a central role in this discussion. The first "concerns providence (8:28) and the place of predestination within the order of salvation (8:29–30)." The second "concerns the status and function of the human will in salvation (9:16) and the significance of Paul's description of the hardening of Pharaoh's heart (9:17–18)." The third "concerns the significance of the potter and the clay analogy (9:20–21), the question of double predestination, the idea that God elects some people for salvation and others for damnation (9:22), the question of whether God elects people individually or corporately (9:22–23)." Finally, Steven Boguslawski (2008, 87–122) has recently summarized Thomas Aquinas's teaching of election and predestination as found in Aquinas's commentary on Rom. 9–11. These surveys are salutary reminders that whereas contemporary commentators rightly focus on Rom. 9–11 in terms of Paul's discussion of Israel, there is an important history of interpretation that has highlighted the divine sovereignty of God, an issue that is hardly unrelated to Paul's discussion of Israel.

Having traced Paul's train of thought in 9:1–29 in light of God's elective purpose for Israel and the nations, in this section I propose to turn to the question of predestination. In doing so, I do not pretend to resolve this issue. Rather, I seek to highlight what is at stake: God's sovereignty.

As noted above, Reasoner reminds us that there are three classic loci for this doctrine in Romans. In the first of these (8:28–30), Paul twice employs the verb "to predetermine," "to predestine" (*proorizō*), the only occurrences of this verb in Romans. In this text, he summarizes the whole sweep of God's redemptive plan: Those whom God foreknew, God predestined to be conformed to the image of his Son. Those whom God predestined, God called. Those whom God called, God justified. Thus the divine plan unfolds in this way: foreknowledge leads to predestination; predestination leads to election; and election leads to justification. The justified cannot boast in what they have done because God, who foreknew them, predestined and elected them to be justified.

In the second of these loci (9:16–19), Paul is no longer talking about the justified but about God's elective purpose on behalf of Israel. Although this text does not use the vocabulary of predestination, it has provided commentators with an opportunity to speak of predestination since Paul emphasizes God's utter sovereignty to have mercy on whom he will have mercy and to harden whom he will harden, without regard for human willing or striving. Thus the divine mercy is the manifestation of an utterly sovereign and gracious God, who does not grant mercy as something due. But what are we to say about God's equally sovereign decision to harden the hearts of others? Origen offers a solution that obviates the charge of injustice: "It is not, therefore, that God hardens whom he wants, but the one who is unwilling to comply with patience is hardened" (*Comm. Rom.* 7.16.8, trans. Scheck 2001–2, 2:118). Though Origen's solution is helpful, it is not the plain meaning of the Pauline text.

The third of these loci (9:20–23) is, in many ways, the most problematic, and it is this text more than any other that has spawned the doctrine of double predestination: God has destined some for eternal salvation and others for eternal damnation. The text begins with the metaphor of the potter, who has the right to create what he chooses from the same lump of clay. It concludes by asking what we are to say if God chose to create "jars of wrath" destined for destruction and "jars of mercy" destined for glorification. While the immediate application of the text refers to that portion of Israel that has not believed in the gospel ("the jars of wrath") and to the new eschatological people that God has created from among the Gentiles as well as from among the Jews ("the jars of mercy"), this text is also open to the doctrine of predestination in a most terrifying manner. God has predestined some people to salvation and others to damnation.

Many contemporary Christians stumble over the Pauline teaching of predestination, especially as formulated in the writings of the later Augustine and Calvin. Given modern sensibilities of fair play, there is nothing fair about this teaching, especially when it is expressed in terms of double predestination. So what is at stake? Why has predestination played such an important role in the interpretation of Romans? Westerholm (2004, 96) gets at the crux of the problem: "Augustine came to think that those who believe must have been enabled by God to do so; moreover, those who persevere in faith must have been furthered empowered to remain steadfast." Westerholm further notes, "For Calvin divine sovereignty is a still more central conviction. The notion that God's plans or activities are in any way contingent on human choices Calvin finds utterly preposterous." In other words, the central issue is the sovereignty and grace of God. If human beings can determine their eternal destiny, it would appear that God is no longer sovereign and God's grace is no longer necessary. But if God is sovereign, and if God's grace is necessary, then it would appear that there is some sense in which a doctrine of predestination is inescapable.

Much of the problem in the discussion of predestination has to do with the concept of "causality," since predestination suggests that God "causes" some to be saved and "causes" others to be damned. In reaction to this, Karl Barth (1933, 324–25) writes that Augustine and the Reformers represented the doctrine of predestination in mythological form as though it were a scheme of cause and effect, thereby robbing it of its significance. . . . Predestination means the recognition that love towards God is an occurrence, a being and having and doing of men, which takes place in no moment of time, which is beyond time, which has its origin at every moment in God Himself, and which must therefore be sought and found only in Him. . . . The truth of the love of men towards God is His Truth, not man's; in Him it is constituted and realized; He sees it and rewards it; He knows it; and it is existential only in Him. But the knowledge of God is eternal and unobservable: it occurs altogether beyond time.

If I have understood Barth correctly, predestination is not to be viewed in a mechanistic manner as if God were intervening and directing every action of every life. Rather, predestination is grounded in the ineffable mystery that is God, a mystery that cannot be confined or defined by time and space. Predestination, then, is a way of speaking of the mystery of the totally other God, who cannot be fully comprehended in time and space. Predestination is about God's love and grace. It is about the priority of God's love for us in the economy of salvation.

It is doubtful that Paul sought to develop a "doctrine" of predestination in Romans. His immediate purpose in Rom. 9 is to show that despite the failure of most of his contemporaries to believe in the Messiah, God's word has not failed. In his defense of God's word, the apostle focuses on God's elective purpose in creating, redeeming, and now restoring Israel. To make this argument, Paul draws from Israel's scriptures to show that the existence of Israel depends on God's grace. While the language of Rom. 9 has in view the historical people of Israel, it is (as the history of interpretation has shown) open to other interpretations as well. After all, Paul reread and reinterpreted Israel's scriptures in light of Christ's resurrection. Although later interpreters are not in the same privileged position as Paul, who saw the risen Christ, they can reread the text in ways that go beyond its strict historical meaning. They too can focus on God's elective purpose in their own day, an elective purpose rooted in the mystery of God, a mystery in which believers must trust. Understood in terms of the priority of God's grace, love, and mercy, then, predestination points to the mystery of God's eternal love for the creation that God has redeemed. To deny the priority of this love and grace is to assert the sovereignty and independence of the creature. It is to claim that there is no need for God.

Romans 9:30–10:21

The Reason for Israel's Failure

〔 〕

Introductory Matters

In 9:1–29 Paul addressed the question of Israel's failure to believe in the gospel by pointing to God's elective plan for Israel. Declaring that the word of God has not failed (9:6), the apostle employed an impressive array of scriptural quotations to show that God's elective purpose—which has always been at work in creating, sustaining, and renewing Israel—is still at work in the creation of a community of believers drawn from Gentiles as well as Jews. Having shown that God's word has not failed, Paul now focuses his attention on Israel's response to God's word (9:30–10:21). In doing so, he argues that the present situation is not a failure of God's word but Israel's failure to attain the goal of the law it so zealously pursues: the righteousness of God revealed in the death and resurrection of Christ. As in 9:1–29 Paul employs an extensive array of scriptural quotations to make his case. Before tracing his train of thought in 9:30–10:21, then, it will be helpful to preview these texts.

Paul introduces his first quotation in 9:33 in order to show that Scripture attests to Israel's failure or "stumbling." The quotation comes from two texts of Isaiah that Paul brings together on the basis of their common use of the word "stone." The primary text is Isa. 28:16, into which Paul incorporates the phrase "a rock one stumbles over" from Isa. 8:14. I have reproduced the larger context of both texts, italicizing the portion of the text that corresponds to Paul's citation. Although Paul tends to work with some form of the LXX, the text from which I am quoting for the sake of convenience (NRSV) is based on the Hebrew text:

> Therefore hear the word of the Lord, you scoffers who rule this people in Jerusalem. Because you have said, "We have made a covenant with death, and with Sheol we have an agreement; when the overwhelming scourge passes through it will not come to us; for we have made lies our refuge, and in falsehood we have taken shelter"; therefore thus says the Lord God, See, *I am laying in Zion a foundation stone*, a tested stone, a precious cornerstone, a sure foundation: "*One who trusts will not* panic." (Isa. 28:14–16)

> But the Lord of hosts, him you shall regard as holy; let him be your fear, and let him be your dread. He will become a sanctuary, a stone one strikes against; for both houses of Israel he will become *a rock one stumbles over*—a trap and a snare for the inhabitants of Jerusalem. And many among them shall stumble; they shall fall and be broken; they shall be snared and taken. (Isa. 8:13–15)

The historical context for these texts was Judah's refusal to trust that God would deliver it at the time of the Syro-Ephraimite war. In response to this failure of faith, Yhwh promises to lay a foundation stone in Zion (28:16), which Isa. 8:14 describes as "a rock one stumbles over." This rock is Yhwh, who will become a "sanctuary" for those who trust in him.

After employing this mixed quotation from Isaiah, Paul turns to the Torah itself to describe the righteousness of God that has caused Israel to stumble (Rom. 10:5–8). There are two speakers in this section: Moses and "the righteousness based on faith," whom Paul personifies. Quoting from Lev. 18:5, Paul allows Moses to speak first. Once more, I quote the fuller context:

> My ordinances you shall observe and my statutes you shall keep, following them: I am the Lord your God. You shall keep my statutes and my ordinances; *by doing so one shall live*: I am the Lord. (Lev. 18:4–5)

The context of Lev. 18 shows that obedience to the law results in life and blessing for Israel, but those who violate its precepts will "be cut off from the people" (Lev. 18:29).

After the testimony of Moses, Paul draws from Deut. 9:4 and 30:12–14 in order to allow "the righteousness based on faith" to describe itself:

> When the Lord your God thrusts them out before you, *do not say to yourself,* "It is because of my righteousness that the Lord has brought me in to occupy this land"; it is rather because of the wickedness of these nations that the Lord is dispossessing them before you. (9:4)

> Surely, this commandment that I am commanding you today is not too hard for you, nor is it too far away. It is not in heaven, that you should say, "*Who will*

go up to heaven for us, and get it for us so that we may hear it and observe it?"
Neither is it beyond the sea, that you should say, "Who will cross to the other
side of the sea for us, and get it for us so that we may hear it and observe it?"
No, *the word is very near to you; it is in your mouth and in your heart* for you
to observe. (30:11–14)

The quotation from Deut. 9:4 reminds Israel that its redemption is not the
result of its own righteousness, and the longer text of Deut. 30:11–14, which
Paul will interpret christologically, reminds Israel that the law that God has
given Israel is close at hand.

Having drawn a contrast between the words of Moses and the words of "the
righteousness based on faith" in Rom. 10:11, 13, Paul introduces two more
quotations to support what "the righteousness based on faith" says of itself.
The first is a reprise of Isa. 28:16, which Paul used in Rom. 9:33:

Therefore thus says the Lord GOD, See, I am laying in Zion a foundation stone,
a tested stone, a precious cornerstone, a sure foundation: "*One who trusts will
not panic.*"

However, whereas the Hebrew text reads "will not panic," Paul follows the LXX,
which reads, "and the one who believes in him will *not be put to shame*" (NETS).
In addition, he introduces the word "all"/"everyone" ("all who believe in him"),
which is found in the quotation from Joel that follows. The Joel quotation,
which Paul employs in Rom. 10:13, draws upon Joel 3:5 LXX (2:32 Eng.):

Then *everyone who calls on the name of the* LORD *shall be saved*; for in Mount
Zion and in Jerusalem there shall be those who escape, as the LORD has said,
and among the survivors shall be those whom the LORD calls. (NRSV)

These two quotations (from Isaiah and Joel), which have a similar structure,
support what Paul says about the relation between faith, confession, and
salvation in Rom. 10:9–11:

all	who believe in him	will not be ashamed
all	who call on the name of the Lord	will be saved

In 10:14–21 Paul employs quotations from Isaiah, Psalms, and Deuteronomy
to show that Israel has heard the gospel and has known from its own Scriptures
that the gospel would be preached to the Gentiles. The first quotation from
Isaiah occurs in Rom. 10:15, after Paul points to the need for people to preach
the gospel. But whereas the text of Isaiah has in view an individual who
announces the end of the exile, Paul's redaction of the text refers to a multitude
of preachers who proclaim the gospel:

How beautiful upon the mountains *are the feet of* the messenger who announces peace, *who brings good news*, who announces salvation, who says to Zion, "Your God reigns." (Isa. 52:7)

Explicitly referring to Isaiah for the first time since Rom. 9:29, in 10:16 Paul associates himself with the prophet's lament, a text that speaks about the redemption wrought by a suffering servant:

Who has believed what we have heard? And to whom has the arm of the LORD been revealed? (Isa. 53:1)

Raising the possibility that Israel has not believed because it has not heard the gospel, in Rom. 10:18 Paul quotes from Ps. 19:4 (18:5 LXX), which describes how creation announces the glory of God:

Day to day pours forth speech, and night to night declares knowledge. There is no speech, nor are there words; their voice is not heard; *yet their voice goes out through all the earth, and their words to the end of the world.* (Ps. 19:2–4)

Having determined that Israel has heard the gospel, Paul turns to the witness of Moses (Rom. 10:19) and Isaiah (Rom. 10:20–21) to assure his readers that Israel knew from its own Scriptures that the gospel would be preached to the Gentiles. The witness of Moses comes from Deut. 32:21:

He said: I will hide my face from them, I will see what their end will be; for they are a perverse generation, children in whom there is no faithfulness. They made me jealous with what is no god, provoked me with their idols. So *I will make them jealous with what is no people, provoke them with a foolish nation.* (32:20–21)

Next follows the witness of Isaiah. But whereas this text originally referred to Israel, Paul reads Isa. 65:1 as referring to the Gentiles and 65:2 as referring to Israel in order to show that Isaiah foresaw (and so Israel should have understood) the present situation:

I was ready to be *sought out by those who did not ask*, to be *found by those who did not seek me.* I said, "Here I am, here I am," to a nation that did not call on my name. (65:1)

I held out my hands all day long to a rebellious people, who walk in a way that is not good, following their own devices. (65:2)

It is apparent from Paul's use of Scripture in Rom. 9:30–10:21 that in his view Scripture contains the whole story of Israel. Accordingly, the present situation whereby Gentiles have attained righteousness and Israel has failed

Romans 9:30–10:21 in the Rhetorical Flow

The letter opening (1:1–17)

Gentiles and Jews in the light of God's wrath (1:18–3:20)

Gentiles and Jews in the light of God's righteousness (3:21–4:25)

The experience of salvation in the light of God's righteousness (5:1–8:39)

God's righteousness and the destiny of Israel (9:1–11:36)

    The mystery of divine election (9:1–29)

▶ **The reason for Israel's failure (9:30–10:21)**

    Israel's failure to attain righteousness (9:30–10:4)

        The present situation of Israel and the Gentiles (9:30–33)

            Gentiles have attained righteousness (9:30)

            Israel has not attained the goal of the law (9:31)

            The reason for this situation (9:32–33)

        The reason for Israel's failure (10:1–4)

            A personal interjection on Paul's part (10:1)

            A lack of discernment (10:2)

            A disregard for God's righteousness (10:3)

            Ignorance of the goal of the law (10:4)

    The righteousness that comes from faith (10:5–13)

        The testimony of Moses (10:5)

        The testimony of the righteousness based on faith (10:6–8)

        Confession and faith (10:9–10)

        The universal scope of this righteousness (10:11–13)

    Israel's disobedience (10:14–21)

        The relation between preaching and faith (10:14–15)

        Not all have obeyed (10:16–17)

        Question and response regarding the preaching of the gospel (10:18)

        Question and responses regarding Israel's knowledge (10:19–21)

to reach the goal of the law is not a puzzle for Paul. Reading Israel's Scripture in light of Christ, who is the goal of the law, Paul understands not only the past story of his people but also their present and future story.

Tracing the Train of Thought

Romans 9:30–10:21 consists of three units. In the first, Paul describes the ironic situation that has come upon Israel and the Gentiles (9:30–10:4). The Gentiles have attained righteousness without pursuing it, but Israel has failed to attain righteousness even though it pursued it (9:30–31). The reason for this is that Israel stumbled by pursuing righteousness as if it depended on "works" (9:32–33). In its misguided zeal for the law, it preferred its own righteousness to God's righteousness manifested in Christ, who is the goal of the law (10:1–4).

In the second unit, Paul describes the righteousness that comes from God (10:5–13). Drawing upon the testimony of Moses (10:5) and the testimony of the righteousness based on faith (10:6–8), Paul agues that this righteousness is close at hand. It requires one to confess that Jesus is Lord and to believe that God has raised him from the dead. Such confession and faith lead to salvation for all, for there is no distinction between Gentile and Jew (10:12–13).

In the third unit, Paul describes Israel's disobedience (10:14–21). He begins by discussing the intimate relation between faith and the preaching of the gospel (10:14–15). Next, with Isaiah, Paul laments that not all have been obedient to the message of Christ (10:16–17). Raising the possibility that Israel has not believed because it has not heard the gospel, he affirms that the gospel has been proclaimed throughout the earth (10:18). Paul then notes that Moses and Isaiah foretold that God would be revealed to the Gentiles and that Israel would be disobedient (10:19–21).

The argument of this section begins with a description of the ironic situation that has come upon Israel, which has failed to attain righteousness despite its zeal for the law (9:30–10:4), and it concludes with an explanation of Israel's refusal to embrace the gospel of God's righteousness (10:14–21). Between these two units, Paul's describes the righteousness based on faith that Israel has failed to attain (10:5–13).

9:30–10:4. This is the first of three units in which Paul argues that it is not God's word that has failed but Israel that has failed to submit itself to that word as revealed in Christ. The unit consists of two subunits, each of which deals with the reason for Israel's failure to attain the goal of the law. In the first, Paul describes the strange situation in which Israel finds itself vis-à-vis the Gentiles (9:30–33). Although Israel has been racing toward the goal of the law (righteousness), it has not crossed the finish line, whereas the Gentiles, who did not even enter the race for righteousness, have crossed the line and won the prize, which Paul describes as a righteousness based on faith. Paul's initial analysis of the situation is that Israel, like a racer who stumbles over an obstacle on the course, has stumbled over a stone/rock that Paul will identify as Christ (10:11). In the second subunit, Paul continues to address the problem of Israel's failure to attain the law's goal (10:1–4). Acknowledging Israel's zeal, he characterizes it as a zeal without discernment because, instead of hastening toward God's righteousness, Israel has pursued its own righteousness, unaware that the goal of the law—the finish line—is Christ.

Paul begins with a brief question that he has used several times in this letter (4:1; 6:1; 7:7; 8:31; 9:14): **Then what shall we say?** (9:30a). He raises the question in light of what he has said in 9:24–29: that God's elective purpose is now at work in a people called forth from the Gentiles as well as from a remnant of Israel. But instead of following the question with a false inference as he did in 6:1; 7:7; and 9:14, he provides his audience with the correct inference (Jewett 2007, 607). Accordingly, he replies: **That Gentiles who were not pursuing righteousness attained righteousness, a righteousness based on faith, but Israel, pursuing a law of righteousness, did not attain the law** (9:30a–31). Paul's response can be structured in this way:

Gentiles	*not* pursuing righteousness	attained righteousness
Israel	pursuing a law of righteousness	did *not* attain the law

Although the structure of Paul's answer reveals that there is a parallelism between 9:30b and 9:31, it is not what we expect. Instead of writing that Israel was pursuing righteousness, Paul writes that Israel was pursuing "a law of righteousness." And instead of writing that Israel did not attain righteousness, Paul writes that Israel "did not attain the law." It is not surprising, then, that some witnesses such as the Vulgate read, "a law of righteousness." But Paul has in view the climactic statement that **the goal of the law is Christ, leading to righteousness for all who believe** (10:4). It is best to deal with what he has written rather than what we think he should have said.

Paul's response to his question in 9:30–31 can be explained in this way: On the one hand, the Gentiles were not seeking righteousness. Nonetheless they attained a righteous relationship with God that Paul qualifies as "based on faith" (*ek pisteōs*), an expression that will appear again in 10:6. The righteousness that Paul has in mind should not be viewed as a moral or ethical quality of the individual. Drawing upon the Hebrew notion of "righteousness" (*ṣedeq*), which is a relational concept, Paul understands righteousness as a relation with God that is the outcome of God's saving activity (see Badenas 1985, 102). On the other hand, Israel was pursuing "a law of righteousness" (*nomon dikaiosynēs*). This expression, which occurs only here in the NT, is best construed "as the Torah viewed from the perspective of the *dikaiosynē* it promises, aims at, or bears witness to" (Badenas 1985, 104). Thus, in pursuing the law, Israel was pursuing righteousness—a right relationship with God. Paul writes that Israel "did not attain the law" rather than Israel "did not attain righteousness," which shows Paul's positive understanding of the law as meant to bring Israel to a right relationship with God. The goal of the law is righteousness, and Israel would have attained righteousness if it had attained the law. More precisely, Israel would have attained the righteousness based on faith that the Gentiles have already received if it had attained the goal of the law, which Paul will identify as Christ (10:4). Paul then is not disparaging the law, as many contemporary commentators correctly point out:

for the goal of the law is the righteousness based on faith, which the Gentiles have already received.

Having described the ironic situation in which Israel presently finds itself, Paul provides a first explanation for this puzzling set of circumstances (9:32). Continuing the metaphor of the race that he began with the verbs "to pursue" and "to attain" (9:30–31), Paul portrays Israel as having stumbled in its race to attain the goal of the law. In Greek the first part of the verse lacks a verb and reads: "because not from faith (*ek pisteōs*) but as from works (*hōs ex ergōn*)." Accordingly, I have supplied the verb "pursue": **Why? Because they did not pursue it on the basis of faith, but pursuing it as if it could be attained on the basis of works, they stumbled against the stone that causes one to stumble** (9:32). Using the same expression that he did to describe the righteousness that the Gentiles received, Paul draws a sharp contrast between pursuing the law on the basis of faith and pursuing it on the basis of works. In doing so, he is not criticizing Israel's pursuit of "the law of righteousness" but the manner in which Israel pursued that law: "as if it could be attained on the basis of works." But what do these expressions mean?

Paul establishes a contrast between *ek pisteōs* and *ex ergōn*: the first expression points to an approach that trusts and relies on God; the second points to an approach that can be described as a matter of human striving and exertion. But if God's elective purpose is a matter of "God's exercising mercy" rather than the result of human "willing or striving" (9:16), any attempt to pursue the law "as if it could be attained on the basis of works" misconstrues the goal and purpose of the law. For if righteousness is a relational concept that involves a right relationship with God rather than an ethical notion of personal achievement, and if all have sinned (3:9), then only God can bring about this right relationship. And if only God can effect this relationship, the proper response to what God has accomplished is trusting faith. Brendan Byrne (1996, 310) puts it well: "To seek righteousness on the basis of fulfilling the 'works of the law' is to refuse to admit that one is part of the sinful mass of humanity addressed by God's grace." Israel, then, has not stumbled because it tried to do the law but because of the manner in which it tried to do the law, as if human effort and striving could bring about a right relationship with God when the proper response is trusting in God, who effects this right relationship.

Having diagnosed the problem in 9:32, Paul provides a scriptural confirmation of his diagnosis. Beginning with a formal introduction indicating that he is quoting from Israel's scriptures, he writes: **as it is written: "Behold, I am laying in Zion a stone that causes one to stumble and a rock that causes offense, and the one who believes in it will not be put to shame"** (9:33). Paul's quotation draws from the texts of Isa. 8:14 and 28:16, with the latter supplying most of the material and the former providing the key phrase "the stone that causes one to stumble, a rock that causes offense." Since 1 Pet. 2:6 also uses these same texts, Paul may be drawing from a collection of scriptural texts that the early church assembled (Badenas 1985, 106). Others, however, argue that it was Paul who brought these texts together (Jewett 2007, 612–13). Whatever the answer, the more important question is the identity of the stone/rock over which Israel has stumbled. Although Paul does not identify the stone/rock here, his use of Isa. 28:16 in Rom. 10:11 ("For Scripture says, 'All who believe in him will not be put to shame'") leaves little doubt that he is referring to Christ. The "stone" that God laid in Zion (Jerusalem) and the "rock" that offended Israel, and in which Israel refused to believe, was Christ. Thus, just as Judah at the time of the Syro-Ephramite war refused to trust in Yhwh, its rock of refuge, so the Israel of Paul's day has refused to trust in Christ as the source of its salvation. Paul, however, is not merely drawing a lesson from the past. According to his rereading, Scripture was already speaking of contemporary Israel and Christ when Isaiah uttered these words. This is why it is not the word of God that has failed but Israel that has failed to heed God's word.

Having provided a first explanation for Israel's failure, Paul offers a second (in 10:1–4). This subunit begins with an expression of Paul's concern for his people (10:1), which is followed by three supporting statements, each beginning with *gar* (for), each statement supporting the one that precedes it. Accordingly, after expressing his concern for Israel (10:1), Paul supports this statement by acknowledging Israel's zeal, which he characterizes as undiscerning (10:2). Next, he explains that this zeal is undiscerning because it has not submitted to God's righteousness (10:3). Finally, he supports the latter claim by declaring that the law's goal is Christ, for the sake of righteousness for all who believe (10:4). Paul's train of thought can be structured in this way:

> Paul's concern for his people
> > *for* they are zealous, but their zeal is undiscerning
> > > *for* Israel did not submit to God's righteousness but sought its own
> > > > *for* the goal of the law is Christ, who brings righteousness

By means of this tightly knit argument, Paul explains the present situation in which Israel finds itself and what he meant when he wrote that Israel did not attain the law because it pursued it as if it were a matter of works.

Paul's argument begins with a statement that echoes his earlier expression of solidarity with Israel (9:1–3): **Brothers and sisters, my heart's desire and my prayer to God on their behalf is for their salvation** (10:1). The most striking aspect of this statement is Paul's desire and prayer for Israel's "salvation" (*sōtērian*), a noun that he has not employed since the thematic statement of 1:16 but which will play an important role in this chapter (10:10–11). The "salvation" Paul has in view is God's final work of redemption, which will occur when the dead are raised and death is defeated. Accordingly, although

Israel has not attained the righteousness it sought in its pursuit of "the law of righteousness," Israel has not been disqualified from the race; it is still possible for Israel to be saved. Indeed, Paul will affirm his confidence that all Israel will be saved (11:26). Byrne (1996, 309) puts it this way: "Israel may not have obtained righteousness but that is not tantamount to missing out, finally, on salvation."

Having assured his audience (most of whom were Gentile believers, some of whom were hostile to Israel) of his concern for Israel, Paul explains why he prays for the salvation of his people: **For I testify on their behalf that they have a zeal for God, but it is not guided by knowledge** (10:2). Although Israel has refused the gospel, it manifests an intense devotion to God through its ardor and zeal for the law. It is the same kind of zeal for the law that Paul exercised in the period before his call (Acts 22:3; Gal. 1:14; Phil. 3:6). But while zeal is a positive quality celebrated throughout Israel's history in figures such as Phinehas (Num. 25), Elijah (1 Kings 18), and Mattathias (1 Macc. 2), it is misdirected when it is not informed by knowledge. Aware of his own misdirected zeal for the law, Paul characterizes Israel's zeal in a similar way. It is a misguided zeal because it does not discern God's will presently at work in Christ.

Next, Paul explains why Israel's zeal was misguided: **For failing to recognize God's own righteousness and seeking to establish their own, they did not submit to God's righteousness** (10:3). With this statement, Paul establishes a strong contrast between two kinds of righteousness, much as he does in Phil. 3:8–9: "For his sake I have suffered the loss of all things, and I regard them as rubbish, in order that I may gain Christ and be found in him, not having a righteousness of my own that comes from the law, but one that comes through faith in Christ, the righteousness from God based on faith." In the text of Philippians, Paul is speaking about the gift of righteousness that comes from God (*tēn ek theou dikaiosynēn*), but here in Romans he refers to God's own righteousness (*dikaiosynē tou theou*) that he announced in 1:16–17 and celebrated in 3:21–26. Although some commentators (Cranfield 1979, 515) understand the Greek to mean "God's proffered gift of a status of righteousness in His eyes," it seems to me that the context argues for a reference to God's own righteousness, "the dynamic activity of God whereby he brings people into relationship with himself" (D. Moo 1996, 633). This understanding of righteousness will become apparent from what Paul writes in 10:4.

If this interpretation is correct, Paul faults Israel's zeal for failing to recognize God's salvific work in Christ. In refusing that manifestation of God's righteousness (a righteousness that came about apart from the law, though it was testified to by the law and the prophets; 3:21), Israel unwittingly preferred its own righteousness (which it pursued as if it were a matter of works; 9:32) to the saving righteousness that God manifested in Christ. Focusing on its distinctiveness as God's covenant people, Israel did not see that, in the crucified Christ, God was breaking down the barriers that separated Israel from the nations in order to bring all to salvation. So James Dunn (1988, 2:588) notes "that in seeking to 'establish' covenant righteousness as 'theirs' they failed to appreciate the full significance of the fact that only God's righteousness can 'establish' the covenant." In doing so, Israel did not "submit" to God's righteousness that was manifested in Christ.

With a statement that clarifies his earlier comment in 9:31 about Israel's failure to attain the law, Paul arrives at the climax of this unit: **For the goal of the law is Christ, leading to righteousness for all who believe** (10:4). This verse has been the subject of an intense debate chronicled by Robert Badenas (1985). The fundamental question is how to interpret the *telos*, which I have translated as "goal," but which can also be construed as "end" or "termination." Is Paul affirming that Christ is the end or termination of the law, in which case there would appear to be a sharp disjuncture between the dispensation of the law and the dispensation of Christ? Or is he declaring that the goal of the law has always been the Christ/Messiah, thereby highlighting the unity of God's salvific plan from the beginning? To answer this question, we must review what Paul has said about the relationship between Christ and the law.

At the outset of this letter, he spoke of the gospel as "previously promised through his prophets in the holy Scriptures" (1:2). Then he wrote that the "law and the prophets" witness to God's righteousness (3:21). After his discussion of God's righteousness in 3:21–26, Paul concluded that he was not "nullifying" but "confirming" the law (3:31), a statement he supported by showing how God had already declared Abraham righteous on the basis of faith (chap. 4). Finally, in his defense of the law in chapter 7, Paul insisted that the law is "holy" (7:12) and "spiritual" (7:14). Given this body of evidence, it seems unlikely that Paul argues for discontinuity between the revelation of God's will in Torah and the manifestation of God's righteousness in Christ. The "goal" of the law has always been Christ, "leading to righteousness for all who believe." This final phrase, which echoes Paul's thematic statement in 1:16 ("For I am not embarrassed by the gospel; for it is God's own power, resulting in salvation *for all who believe*, for the Jew first and then for the Greek"), provides us with a way to relate 10:4 to what Paul said earlier (9:31–32).

In 9:31–32 Paul described Israel as pursuing a "law of righteousness" but not attaining the law because it pursued it as if it were a matter of works. In light of what he writes in 10:4, it is evident (1) why Paul spoke of a "law of righteousness," (2) why he said that Israel did not attain the law, and (3) why Israel failed. First, Paul spoke of a "law of righteousness" because the true goal of the law is Christ, who brings righteousness to all who believe. Second, in saying that Israel did not attain the law, he meant that it did not attain the goal of the law, which is Christ. Third, Paul faults Israel not for trying to practice the law but for practicing it as if it were a matter of effort and striving when the righteousness that the law offers is accessible to all on the basis of faith. Accordingly, C. Thomas Rhyne (1985, 489) insightfully writes, "Thus, to attain the law and to receive righteousness by faith are practically identical!" Paul is neither denigrating the law nor faulting Israel for trying to observe it. Rather, his point is that Israel has failed to recognize the righteousness toward which the law has been directing it from the beginning. Israel has failed to understand that the goal of the law is Christ.

10:5–13. At the end of the last unit, Paul wrote, "The goal of the law is Christ, leading to righteousness for all who believe." Douglas Moo (1996, 645) notes that in this unit Paul explains the final words of 10:4, "leading to righteousness for all who believe." The question that Paul must answer is how Christ leads to salvation for all who believe. To respond to this question, he provides a description of "the righteousness that is based on faith," which has become available through Christ for all who believe. The unit consists of four subunits. In the first, Moses speaks of the righteousness that is based on the law (10:5). In the second, the righteousness that is based on faith speaks (10:6–8). In the third, Paul explains that the righteousness based on faith expresses itself in confession and faith, which lead to righteousness and salvation (10:9–10). Finally, Paul considers the universal scope of this righteousness (10:11–13). The problem this unit occasions is the relationship between the words of Moses (10:5) and the words of personified righteousness (10:6–8). Is Paul establishing a contrast between two antithetical ways of pursuing righteousness, or is he employing the words of the righteousness based on faith to interpret the words of Moses? Before answering this question, it is necessary to follow the train of Paul's thought.

Having declared that the goal of the law is Christ, Paul introduces a quotation from Moses, taken from Lev. 18:5, that promises life to those who do what the law commands: **For Moses writes about the righteousness that is based on the law: "The one who does these things will live by them"** (10:5). The quotation is similar to what Paul wrote in 2:13: "For it is not the hearers of the law who are righteous before God, but it is *those who do the law who will be justified*." In effect Paul states what most of his contemporaries would have accepted: obedience to the law leads to life and justification.

After Moses speaks on behalf of "the righteousness that is based on the law," the righteousness based on faith speaks. The words of personified righteousness echo the speech that Moses delivers to Israel in Deut. 30, when Israel was about to renew the covenant. Reminding Israel of the importance of obeying the law if it is to live in the land it is about to receive, Moses assures Israel that the commandment he is giving is "not too hard for you; nor is it too far away" (Deut. 30:11). Paul begins with Moses's warning in Deut. 9:4 that Israel must not say to itself that it is because of its own righteousness that God brought Israel into the land. Then, drawing from Moses's words in Deut. 30:11–14, he places the words of Deuteronomy in the mouth of the righteousness based on faith: **But now the righteousness based on faith speaks in this way: "Do not say in your heart, who will ascend into heaven?"** that is, who will bring Christ down? Nor does it say, "Who will descend into the abyss?" that is, who will bring Christ forth from the dead? But what does it say? "The message is near you, in your mouth and in your heart," that is, the message of faith that we proclaim (Rom. 10:6–8).

Paul's description of personified righteousness as "the righteousness based on faith" establishes a contrast with what he has just called "the righteousness that is based on the law" (10:5). But what is the contrast? Are there two kinds of righteousness, or is Paul speaking of the same righteousness pursued in two different ways? Whatever the answer, the structure of the text is clear. After a brief introduction, Paul proceeds by way of quotation and interpretation:

> Introduction of the righteousness based on faith (Rom. 10:6a)
> Quotation from Deut. 9:4 and 30:12 (10:6b)
> *Christological interpretation* (10:6c)
> Quotation based on Deut. 30:13 and Ps. 107:26 (10:7a)
> *Christological interpretation* (10:7b)
> Quotation from Deut. 30:14 (10:8a)
> *Christological interpretation* (10:8b)

After a brief introduction that alludes to Deut. 9:4, the initial words of the righteousness based on faith (Rom. 10:6b) draw upon Deut. 30:12, "It is not in heaven, that you should say, '*Who will go up to heaven* for us, and get it for us so that we may hear it and observe it?'" But whereas these words of Moses originally referred to "this commandment that I am commanding you today," Paul interprets them christologically, in terms of what later theology would call the incarnation: "that is, who will bring Christ down?" (Rom. 10:6c). The sense of Paul's interpretation is that there is no need for someone to ascend to heaven to bring the Messiah to Israel, for the Messiah has already appeared.

The next words of personified righteousness (9:7a) are not so closely related to the text of Deut. 30:13, which reads, "Neither is it beyond the sea, that you should say, '*Who will cross to the other side* of the sea for us, and get it for us so that we may hear it and observe it?'" But they are similar to the words of Ps. 107:26: "They went down to the depths." This imagery of descent better serves Paul's purpose since it establishes a contrast with ascending into heaven. But whereas the context of Deuteronomy concerns the commandment, Paul interprets the words of personified righteousness christologically (Rom. 10:7b). There is no need to descend into the abyss to raise the Messiah, because Christ has been raised from the dead.

Employing a strong adversative in 10:8a, "but what does it say?" (*alla ti legei*), Paul personifies righteousness as speaking the words of Deut. 30:14 ("No, the word is very near you: it is in your mouth and in your heart for you to observe"). Deuteronomy originally had in view the word of the commandment, but Paul interprets the words of personified righteousness christologically

(Rom. 10:8b). The "word" (*rhēma*) that is very near is "the word" or "the message of faith [*to rhēma tēs pisteōs*] that we proclaim."

Next, Paul illustrates just how close this *rhēma* is. It is not far or distant. It is not an esoteric message that one cannot understand or grasp. The message of faith that leads to salvation is as near as one's mouth and heart: **Because if you confess with your mouth that "Jesus is Lord," and if you believe in your heart that God raised him from the dead, you will be saved. For one believes in the heart, and this leads to righteousness; one confesses with the mouth, and this leads to salvation** (10:9–10). Paul structures these carefully crafted verses in a ring pattern whereby two references to confession with the mouth enclose two statements about faith in the heart:

> *confession with the mouth* that Jesus is Lord
> *faith in the heart* that he was raised leads to *salvation*
>   <u>for</u>
> *faith in the heart* leads to righteousness
> *confession with the mouth* leads to *salvation*

To understand the significance of this statement, it is helpful to recall Paul's description of unredeemed humanity, whose "senseless heart was darkened" (1:21) and whose mouths were filled with "curses and bitterness" (3:14). Under the power of sin, unredeemed humanity found itself estranged from its Creator. But now that humanity has been redeemed, those who confess with their mouth that Jesus is Lord and believe in their heart that God has raised him from the dead will be saved when God delivers them from the power of death at the general resurrection of the dead. Why? Because faith in the heart leads to righteousness, which is the new covenant relationship of peace and reconciliation that God establishes through Christ, and confession with the mouth leads to salvation. By speaking of the mouth and the heart, Paul highlights the dynamic nature of the Christian response that involves the whole person, beginning in the heart and sounding forth from the mouth as confession.

Finally, Paul turns his attention to the universal dimension of this righteousness that is available to all who believe and call upon the name of the Lord, Jew and Gentile alike. He begins by repeating the quotation from Isa. 28:16 LXX that he employed in Rom. 9:33. But this time he introduces the word "all," which is not present in the Isaiah quotation but is found in the text of Joel that Paul will soon quote: **For Scripture says, "All who believe in him will not be put to shame"** (10:11). In the LXX text of Isaiah, "him" refers to God, but Paul applies it to Christ. Next, he provides two supporting reasons why those who believe in Christ will not be ashamed. First, **For there is no distinction between Jew and Greek, for the same one is Lord of all and is generous toward all who call upon him** (Rom. 10:12). Echoing a theme he announced in 3:22–23 (that there is no distinction because all have sinned),

Paul reaffirms that there is no distinction between Jew and Greek because the same one—Christ—is Lord of all. In affirming this, Paul echoes what he wrote in 3:29. But whereas in 3:29 he declared that God is the God of the Gentiles as well as of the Jews, here he proclaims that Christ is the Lord of Jews and Gentiles alike, thereby highlighting Christ's godly status.

Picking up on the last phrase of 10:12 ("and is generous toward all who call upon him"), Paul quotes from Joel 3:5 LXX (2:32 Eng.), but without any indication that he is quoting from Scripture: **For all who call on the name of the Lord will be saved** (Rom. 10:13). The use of the verb "will be saved" and the designation "Lord" relate this verse to Paul's statement in 10:9 that those who confess that Jesus is Lord and believe that he has been raised will be saved. The emphasis on "all" here and in 10:11 points to the universal scope of this salvation that is available to "all" on the basis of faith, without distinction.

I summarize the train of thought in this unit as follows: The righteousness that is based on faith is not an esoteric teaching that cannot be appropriated. It is a matter of confessing that Jesus is *kyrios* (Lord) and believing that God raised him from the dead. Such faith and confession lead to the righteousness and salvation, which is available to all who call on the name of the Jesus, who is the Lord of all, of Jews and Greeks alike. But how are the words of Moses related to those of personified righteousness? Does Paul intend his audience to see an antithetical or a complementary relationship between the words of Moses and personified righteousness?

Most commentators maintain that Paul is establishing some sort of contrast between Moses and personified righteousness. Joseph Fitzmyer (1993, 589) writes that a "contrast is introduced between two aeons or two ways of attaining uprightness in God's sight." Brendan Byrne (1996, 317) notes, "Over against this 'doing' righteousness, based upon the law, Paul finds in Scripture the announcement of an alternative righteousness based upon faith." J. Ross Wagner (2003, 160), however, argues that Paul is using the quotation of personified righteousness to interpret the words of Moses, thereby redefining "doing" as believing and trusting. Likewise N. T. Wright (2002, 662) views the words of personified righteousness as a "modification, a redefinition" of Moses's words rather than as a "direct antithesis or contradiction." To be sure, there is a contrast between the words of Moses, who enjoins Israel to "do" the commandment, and the personified righteousness, which calls people to believe in and confess the gospel. The contrast, however, is not intended to criticize Moses or the law, nor is it meant to establish an opposition between "doing" and "believing." Rather, having identified Christ as the goal of the law, Paul shows how the law finds its goal in Christ. Through the words of personified righteousness, he explains that the commandment of which Moses spoke was Christ. This is why Paul identifies Christ as the goal of the law.

10:14–21. In the first two units of 9:30–10:21, Paul dealt with Israel's failure to attain the goal of the law that it so zealously pursued (9:30–10:4), and he described the righteousness based on faith that is available to all who believe and call on the name of the Lord (10:5–13). In the third and final unit of this section (10:14–21), he highlights Israel's disobedience in failing to accept the gospel that has been preached throughout the world. By focusing on the disobedience of Israel, Paul reinforces the argument he has been developing throughout chapters 9–10: it is not the word of God that has failed but Israel that has failed to embrace God's word as revealed in Christ, the Messiah.

This unit consists of four subunits. In the first, Paul employs a series of rhetorical questions to establish the relation between preaching and faith (10:14–15). In the second, he draws on a quotation from the prophet Isaiah to show that not all have been obedient to the gospel (10:16–17). In the third subunit, he maintains that the gospel has been preached to all, including Israel (10:18). Finally, he argues from Scripture that Israel should have known that the gospel would be preached to the Gentiles (10:19–21). Accordingly, Paul completes the indictment against Israel that he began in 9:30–10:4. Not only has Israel missed the goal of the law, but it has also been disobedient to the gospel that has been preached to it.

Having affirmed that all who call on the name of the Lord will be saved (10:13), Paul begins with four rhetorical questions that establish a relation between preaching and calling on the name of the Lord. But instead of beginning with preaching and concluding with calling on the name of the Lord, Paul starts at the end of the process—calling on the name—thereby relating what he will say to what he has just said in 10:13: **How then can they call on one in whom they have not believed? How can they believe in one they have not heard? How can they hear without a preacher? And how can they preach unless they are sent?** (10:14–15a). The sequence proceeds in the following way: First, someone must be sent to *preach* the gospel. Second, those who *hear* the preached gospel must *believe* in it. Having believed in the gospel, they can *call on* the one in whom they have believed and be saved. Thus Paul presents hearing the gospel as an offer of grace that makes the act of faith possible. If there is no one to preach the gospel, the gospel cannot be heard; if the gospel is not heard, people cannot believe in the one whom the gospel proclaims. And if they cannot believe in him, they cannot call on him as their Lord. But it is not only hearing the gospel that is an offer of grace; the sending of messengers to preach the gospel is also a manifestation of God's grace. This is why Paul concludes these questions with a quotation from Isa. 52:7: **As it is written, "How lovely are the feet of those who preach good things"** (10:15b). The text of Isaiah speaks of a single messenger who announces the end of Israel's exile, but Paul reads the text as a living word for his own day. The single "messenger" in Isaiah's text who proclaims the end of Zion's captivity becomes the numerous heralds of the gospel who proclaim the benefits of Christ's redemptive work ("the good things"). Thus Paul employs Scripture to explain what is happening at the present time as well as to draw examples from the past.

Although the gospel has been preached, Paul is aware that not all—especially his own people—have obeyed it. Consequently, having explained the importance of preaching and hearing the gospel, he begins with a strong adversative (*all' ou*) and announces, **But not all have obeyed the gospel** (10:16a). Since the Greek verb *hypakouō* (to obey) is a compound of *akouō* (to hear), Paul plays on what he has just said. Faith comes from "hearing" (*akouō*) the gospel, but if the gospel is to bear fruit, those who "hear" must "obey" (*hypakouō*) the word they have heard. Explicitly associating himself with Isaiah, and in order to confirm what he has just said, Paul writes, **For Isaiah says, "Lord, who has believed our message?"** (10:16b). This quotation from Isa. 53:1 occurs in the midst of the fourth and most elaborate of the Servant Songs, a passage that speaks of a mysterious suffering servant. It is difficult to say if Paul identified Christ as this servant, but it is apparent that he is reading the words of the prophet in reference to his own time. Thus Paul and Isaiah offer a common witness to Israel's failure to obey the gospel. As J. Ross Wagner (2003, 180) notes, "Isaiah remains a living voice for Paul, one who speaks alongside the apostle as an authoritative witness to the gospel."

Having proclaimed that not all have believed in the gospel, Paul begins with the particle *ara* to draw an inference from what he has just said: **Thus faith comes from what is heard, and what is heard comes through the message of Christ** (10:17). Faith depends on hearing the gospel, and hearing the gospel comes *dia rhēmatos Christou*, which can be taken as "the message about Christ" (Fitzmyer 1993, 598) or "the message of Christ," which is now spoken through the messengers noted above (Byrne 1996, 327; Cranfield 1979, 537). In either case, hearing the gospel plays an essential role in faith, for unless people hear the gospel, it is impossible for them to believe in it.

Picking up on the noun "hearing" (*akoē*) and beginning with another strong adversative (*alla*), Paul writes, **But I ask, did they not hear?** (10:18a) to which he immediately responds, **Indeed they did!** (10:18b). To substantiate his point, Paul quotes Ps. 18:5 LXX (19:4 Eng.) without any explicit indication that he is citing Scripture: **Their voice has gone forth throughout all the earth, and their message to the ends of the world** (10:18c). However, whereas the psalm personifies creation as proclaiming the glory of God, Paul reads the psalm in terms of the present situation. "Their voice" refers to the messengers of the gospel mentioned in 10:15. Both Israel and the Gentiles have heard the message that these messengers have brought to "the ends of the world." If people have not believed, it is because they have not obeyed (*hypakouō*), not because they have not heard (*akouō*).

To this point in his argument, Paul has not identified who has heard and disobeyed the gospel. But in 10:19–21 there is no question of whom he is speaking. Beginning with another strong adversative (*alla legō*), he makes an explicit reference to Israel: **But I ask, didn't Israel know?** (10:19a). In response, he brings forth two witnesses, Moses and Isaiah, to show that Israel knew—or should have known—that the gospel would be proclaimed to the Gentiles. Drawing from Deut. 32:21 LXX, he allows Moses to speak: **First Moses says, "I will make you jealous by means of a non-nation; by a nation without understanding I will incite you"** (Rom. 10:19b). Taking these words from the Song of Moses (Deut. 32), which recalls Israel's infidelity during the period of its wilderness wandering, Paul reads Scripture in light of Israel's present circumstances. For Paul, the text is a warning to contemporary Israel that God would make it jealous by the conversion of the Gentiles, a theme to which he will return in 11:11, 14.

Having presented the witness of Moses on behalf of the Gentiles, in 10:20–21 Paul brings forth the witness of Isa. 65:1–2, which he divides into two parts. He applies the first part to the Gentiles: **Then Isaiah dares to say, "I have been found by those who were not seeking me; I have revealed myself to those who were not asking for me"** (Rom. 10:20). These words are an unmistakable echo of the problem Paul raised in 9:30. There he said that the Gentiles, who were not pursuing righteousness, have attained it. Here he writes that God has been revealed to those who were not seeking him. Again, Paul reads the text in light of contemporary circumstances rather than in terms of their historical context. Accordingly, whereas the text of Isaiah originally referred to Israel, Paul applies it to the Gentiles. Given this daring exegesis, it is not surprising how he introduces this text: "Isaiah *dares* to say."

Paul completes his quotation of Isaiah, and this time he applies the text to Israel, as did Isaiah: **But to Israel he says, "The whole day long I have stretched out my hands to a disobedient and stubborn people"** (10:21). Yet in referring the words of Isaiah to Israel, Paul has in mind the present disobedience of his people to the gospel. Thus his argument has come full circle. Although Israel has been zealous for the law, Israel has not attained the righteousness that was the goal of the law, for its zeal was not guided by knowledge of God's plan (10:2), which Israel could have discerned in its own Scriptures: that the gospel would be proclaimed to the Gentiles. Israel—not the word of God—has failed because (1) Israel did not pursue the law on the basis of faith, and (2) Israel was disobedient to God's plan for the Gentiles that Scripture reveals.

Theological Issues

Scripture plays a central role in the argument that Paul makes in Rom. 9–11. Robert Badenas (1985, 90) notes, "Nowhere else in his writings does Paul quote from the OT so frequently as in Romans, and nowhere else in Romans does Paul quote the OT so frequently as in chs. 9–11." He also notes that Paul cites these passages "almost in a 'canonical' sequence, following the order of the history of Israel from Isaac to Elijah, in an arrangement which may hardly be taken as accidental or irrelevant." Given Paul's extensive use of Scripture in

Rom. 9–11, we must ask what this reveals about his understanding of Scripture. To respond to this question, I will summarize the narrative that Paul creates in Rom. 9–11 through these quotations.

The story that Paul creates has three movements: Israel's past (9:1–29), Israel's present (9:30–10:21), and Israel's future (11:1–36). The movement of 9:1–29 can be summarized in this way: First, after explaining his concern for his people (9:1–5), Paul quotes from Genesis and Malachi to explain how God's elective purpose "created" Israel (9:6–13). Second, he cites Exodus to show how that same elective purpose was at work to "sustain" Israel during the period of its exodus from Egypt (9:14–18). Third, he draws from the prophets, especially Isaiah and Hosea, to explain how God's elective purpose is still at work today in calling a people from among the Gentiles and Israel in order to "restore" Israel (9:19–29). Thus the first movement includes all that has happened from the creation of Israel to the present.

The second movement of the story begins with Israel's present situation (9:30–10:21). It develops in this way. First, Paul draws from the prophet Isaiah to explain why the greater part of Israel has failed to attain the righteousness based on faith that should characterize the restored Israel (9:30–10:4). Second, Paul draws from Leviticus and Deuteronomy to illustrate what he means by righteousness based on faith (10:5–10). Next, he employs texts from Isaiah and Joel to describe the universal scope of the salvation that this righteousness brings (10:11–13). Finally, Paul draws from Isaiah, Psalms, and Deuteronomy to demonstrate that Israel has heard the gospel of God's righteousness and was told that God would be revealed

Paul's Use of Scripture in Romans 9–11

Romans 9

Rom. 9:7	Gen. 21:12
Rom. 9:9	Gen. 18:10, 14
Rom. 9:12	Gen. 25:23
Rom. 9:13	Mal. 1:2–3
Rom. 9:15	Exod. 33:19
Rom. 9:17	Exod. 9:16
Rom. 9:20	Isa. 29:16; 45:9
Rom. 9:25	Hosea 2:23
Rom. 9:26	Hosea 1:10
Rom. 9:27–28	Isa. 10:22–23; Hosea 1:10
Rom. 9:29	Isa. 1:9
Rom. 9:33	Isa. 28:16; Isa. 8:14

Romans 10

Rom. 10:5	Lev. 18:5
Rom. 10:6–8	Deut. 9:4; 30:12–14
Rom. 10:11	Isa. 28:16
Rom. 10:13	Joel 2:32
Rom. 10:15	Isa. 52:7
Rom. 10:16	Isa. 53:1
Rom. 10:18	Ps. 19:3
Rom. 10:19	Deut. 32:21
Rom. 10:20	Isa. 65:1
Rom. 10:21	Isa. 65:2

Romans 11

Rom. 11:2	1 Sam. 12:22; Ps. 94:14
Rom. 11:3	1 Kings 19:10, 14
Rom. 11:4	1 Kings 19:18
Rom. 11:8	Isa. 29:10; Deut. 29:4
Rom. 11:9b–10	Ps. 69:22–23
Rom. 11:26–27	Isa. 59:20–21; 27:9
Rom. 11:34	Isa. 40:13
Rom. 11:35	Job 41:11

to the Gentiles (10:14–21). Israel, however, was disobedient. Thus the second movement deals entirely with Israel's present circumstances.

The third movement completes the story of Israel by looking to the future (11:1–36). It develops in this way: First, Paul quotes from the story of Elijah, as found in 1 Kings 19, to assure his readers that despite Israel's present unbelief, God has left a remnant, of whom Paul is a parade example, that points to salvation (11:1–6). Next, he draws from Deuteronomy, Isaiah, and Psalms to illustrate the blindness and hardening that has come upon the majority of Israel (11:7–24). Finally, Paul employs his favorite witness, Isaiah, in order to look to the future and assure his audience that all Israel will be saved (11:25–32). The chapter then concludes with a hymn of praise to God's inscrutable wisdom, with language drawn from Isaiah and Job (11:33–36). Thus, while the first movement has looked primarily to the past and the second to the present, the third movement completes the story by looking to the future.

From this overview it is apparent that Paul employs Scripture in Rom. 9–11 to create and tell the story of Israel's election, preservation, disobedience, hardening, and ultimate restoration in light of the righteousness that God has manifested in Christ. What has happened to Israel from the beginning, and what is presently occurring, is the result of an elective purpose that has been guiding Israel to the goal of the law—the righteousness of God revealed in the Messiah.

This reading of Rom. 9–11 shows that Paul is creating and developing a narrative of Israel in light of Christ. Scripture tells a story, and the story it tells is the narrative of God's dealings with Israel. But this narrative is not merely a recounting of Israel's past; it is also the story of God's present and future dealings with Israel. Rather than simply employ Scripture as a witness to the past, then, Paul reads it as God's living word that speaks to Israel's present and future as well as to its past. For example, the stone of which Isaiah spoke is Christ (Rom. 9:33); the words Moses spoke to Israel were about the righteousness that is based on faith (10:5–7); the preacher to whom Isaiah refers becomes those who are presently proclaiming the gospel (10:15); Ps. 19 testifies that this gospel has been proclaimed throughout the world (10:18); Moses is a witness to Israel's jealousy toward the Gentiles (10:19); and Isaiah testifies that God will reveal himself to the Gentiles, but Israel will remain disobedient (10:20–21).

Paul's quotations tend to follow the LXX, but he is not a slave to the LXX nor is he always precise in the way he quotes from it. At times he can meld two texts into one, as he does with Isa. 8:14 and 28:16 in Rom. 9:33. At other times, he can alter words to make his point, as happens with the text of Isa. 52:7 in Rom. 10:15, where he speaks of many preachers rather than of a single preacher. Paul can even apply a text to the Gentiles that, in its historical setting, originally spoke of Israel, as happens in Rom. 10:20, where he quotes from Isa. 65:1. If we ask how Paul can interpret Scripture in this way, the answer is twofold. First, since the goal of the law is Christ (10:4), all of Scripture speaks about Christ. Thus Paul can interpret the "stone" text of Isaiah in light of Christ. Second, Scripture is not a mere record of past events; it is also a living word. And because it is a living word, it speaks to every generation. For Paul, then, exegesis is not so much a matter of recovering the past as it is a task of interpreting the present. It is not so much a matter of reconstructing history as it is a process of constructing meaning for the present. Although contemporary interpreters may not be able to interpret Scripture as Paul did—given his privileged situation as a writer of Scripture—they can learn from him that if they read Scripture as only a historical account of the past, it is a dead word. But if they read it as God's word, it is a living word.

Romans 11:1–36

God's Irrevocable Call

⊡

Introductory Matters

Thus far, Paul's argument has proceeded in this way. In 9:1–29 he defended the constancy and integrity of God's word by showing that God has always worked on Israel's behalf through a process of divine election/selection. Then in 9:30–10:21 he turned his attention to Israel to show that it is not God's word that has failed but Israel that has failed to be obedient to that word. Now in 11:1–36 Paul comes to the crucial step in his argument that the word of God has not failed (9:6). Focusing his attention on God once more, he affirms that God has not rejected his people (11:1), that Israel has not stumbled so as to fall (11:11), and that all Israel will be saved (11:26), for the gifts and the call of God are irrevocable (11:29). In this exposition of God's faithfulness to Israel, Paul explains the role of Israel's disobedience in God's plan and how the selection of some results in salvation for all. The flow of these chapters, in which two expositions of God's fidelity enclose an exposition of Israel's disobedience, can be summarized in this way:

The past: *God's fidelity to Israel* manifested through election (9:1–29)

The present: *Israel's disobedience* manifested through seeking its own righteousness (9:30–10:21)

The future: *God's fidelity to Israel* manifested through mercy toward all (11:1–36)

As in the previous chapters, Paul makes extensive use of Scripture to develop his argument. Accordingly, I begin with an overview of the wider context of his scriptural citations. The portions of the citations that appear in Romans are italicized.

Paul's use of Scripture in Rom. 11 occurs in four blocks of material: his discussion of the remnant (11:1–6), his explanation of the hardening of Israel (11:7–10), his announcement of Israel's restoration (11:25–32), and his celebration of God's wisdom and knowledge (11:33–36). As in chapters 9 and 10, Paul draws from the Pentateuch, the Prophets (especially Isaiah), and the Psalms. But in Rom. 11 he cites the books of Samuel and Kings as well.

Paul's initial citation of Scripture occurs in 11:2 without any indication that he is quoting Scripture. Thus only the biblically literate members of his audience would have realized that he was quoting from Israel's scriptures. The quotation of 11:2 is usually attributed to 1 Sam. 12:22, which occurs in Samuel's farewell discourse to Israel. After hearing this discourse and being aware that they have sinned by demanding a king for themselves, the people ask Samuel to pray for them (1 Sam. 12:19). In response, the prophet assures them that God will not cast them away:

> And Samuel said to the people, "Do not be afraid; you have done all this evil, yet do not turn aside from following the LORD, but serve the LORD with all your heart; and do not turn aside after useless things that cannot profit or save, for they are useless. *For the LORD will not cast away his people*, for his great name's sake, because it has pleased the LORD to make you a people for himself." (1 Sam. 12:20–22)

A similar text occurs in Ps. 94:14. Making use of synonymous parallelism, the psalm assures the afflicted righteous that God will neither forsake his people nor abandon his heritage:

> *For the LORD will not forsake his people*;
>   *he will not abandon his heritage*;
> for justice will return to the righteous,
>   and all the upright in heart will follow it. (Ps. 94:14–15)

By means of these texts, Paul establishes the thesis of Rom. 11: God has not forsaken Israel.

Paul's use of Scripture in Rom. 11:3–4 builds upon his allusion to 1 Sam. 12:22 and Ps. 94:14. To illustrate that the Lord will not forsake his people, he recalls an episode in the life of the prophet Elijah, who mistakenly thought that he was the last faithful Israelite. Like many of Paul's contemporaries, Elijah wonders if God has forsaken his people. In the face of the prophet's discouragement, God assures him that there is a faithful remnant within Israel that has not worshiped Baal:

> At that place he came to a cave, and spent the night there. Then the word of the LORD came to him, saying, "What are you doing here, Elijah?" He answered, "I have

been very zealous for the L ORD, the God of hosts; for the Israelites *have* forsaken your covenant, *thrown down your altars, and killed your prophets with the sword. I alone am left, and they are seeking my life, to take it away.*" (1 Kings 19:9–10)

When Elijah heard it, he wrapped his face in his mantle and went out and stood at the entrance of the cave. Then there came a voice to him that said, "What are you doing here, Elijah?" He answered, "I have been very zealous for the L ORD, the God of hosts; for the Israelites *have forsaken your covenant, thrown down your altars, and killed your prophets with the sword. I alone am left, and they are seeking my life, to take it away.*" Then the L ORD said to him, "Go, return on your way to the wilderness of Damascus; when you arrive, you shall anoint Hazael as king over Aram. Also you shall anoint Jehu son of Nimshi as king over Israel; and you shall anoint Elisha son of Shaphat of Abel-meholah as prophet in your place. Whoever escapes from the sword of Hazael, Jehu shall kill; and whoever escapes from the sword of Jehu, Elisha shall kill. *Yet I will leave seven thousand in Israel, all the knees that have not bowed to Baal,* and every mouth that has not kissed him." (1 Kings 19:13–18)

Although this story, which marks the end of the prophet's career, is critical of Elijah, it serves Paul's needs. For if not even Elijah recognized that the Lord reserved a remnant for himself, it is not surprising that Paul's contemporaries (especially Gentile believers) are unaware of the faithful remnant of Israel in their midst.

Having spoken of the remnant, in 11:7–10 Paul employs two scriptural quotations to explain the hardening, which is best understood as a blindness to God's salvific work, that has come upon "the rest" of Israel. The first is a mixed quotation from Isa. 29:10 and Deut. 29:4. The quotation from Isaiah points to the blindness of Judah's prophets and seers to the salvation that God is about to bring to Jerusalem; in the citation from Deuteronomy, Moses tells Israel that, to this very day, the Lord has not given them an understanding mind. Both citations indicate that Israel's stupor is divinely imposed:

Stupefy yourselves and be in a stupor, blind yourselves and be blind! Be drunk, but not from wine; stagger, but not from strong drink! *For the L ORD has poured out upon you a spirit of deep sleep; he has closed your eyes,* you prophets, and covered your heads, you seers. (Isa. 29:9–10)

Moses summoned all Israel and said to them: You have seen all that the L ORD did before your eyes in the land of Egypt, to Pharaoh and to all his servants and to all his land, the great trials that your eyes saw, the signs, and those great wonders. *But to this day the L ORD has not given you* a mind to understand, or *eyes to see, or ears to hear.* (Deut. 29:2–4)

Paul complements this mixed quotation from Deuteronomy and Isaiah with a citation from Ps. 68:23–24 LXX (69:22–23 Eng.). In this psalm, which the early church applied to Jesus's passion, David utters an imprecation against his persecutors, asking God to darken their eyes so that they cannot see:

> *Let their table become a trap* before them, and a retribution and a stumbling block. *Let their eyes be darkened so that they cannot see, and bend their back permanently.* (NETS)

Like the mixed quotation from Isaiah and Deuteronomy, this quotation speaks of eyes that cannot see. But whereas the mixed quotation portrays Israel's blindness as divinely imposed, this one presents blindness as a punishment for evil behavior. The juxtaposition of these two texts allows Paul to show that the blindness of contemporary Israel is both divinely imposed *and* humanly deserved.

Paul does not make use of any explicit scriptural quotations in his warning to Gentile believers not to become haughty toward Israel (Rom. 11:13–24). But in 11:26–27 he supports his revelation that all Israel will be saved (11:26) with a mixed quotation that draws from Isa. 59:20–21 and 27:9. Isaiah 59 begins by describing the situation of Israel from which the people cannot free themselves. Accordingly, when God saw that "there was no one to intervene" (59:16), he put on "righteousness like a breastplate" (59:17) and intervened on Israel's behalf. The chapter concludes in this way:

> And he will come to Zion as Redeemer, to those in Jacob who turn from transgression, says the LORD. And as for me, *this is my covenant with them*, says the LORD: my spirit that is upon you, and my words that I have put in your mouth, shall not depart out of your mouth, or out of the mouths of your children, or out of the mouths of your children's children, says the LORD, from now on and forever. (59:20–21)

Isaiah 27 also speaks of how God will redeem Israel, which is portrayed as "a pleasant vineyard" (27:2). This wider context suggests that the manner in which God once restored the vineyard of Israel foreshadows the way in which God is about to regraft the disobedient portion of Israel into the olive tree:

> Therefore by this *the guilt of Jacob* will be expiated, and this will be the full fruit of *the removal of his sin*: when he makes all the stones of the altars like chalkstones crushed to pieces, no sacred poles or incense altars will remain standing. (27:9)

Having revealed the mystery of God's mercy toward Israel, Paul concludes with a benediction that celebrates God's knowledge and wisdom (Rom. 11:33–36). This benediction makes use of a text from Isa. 40:13 LXX (and perhaps Job 41:3—but not LXX) that points to the incomprehensibility of the Creator God, who is about to deliver Israel from exile. *"Who has known the mind of the Lord, and who has been his counselor to instruct him?"* (Isa. 40:13 NETS). But instead of introducing this text as coming from Isaiah or Scripture, Paul weaves

Romans 11:1–36 in the Rhetorical Flow

The letter opening (1:1–17)

Gentiles and Jews in the light of God's wrath (1:18–3:20)

Gentiles and Jews in the light of God's righteousness (3:21–4:25)

The experience of salvation in the light of God's righteousness (5:1–8:39)

God's righteousness and the destiny of Israel (9:1–11:36)

  The mystery of divine election (9:1–29)

  The reason for Israel's failure (9:30–10:21)

▶ God's irrevocable call (11:1–36)

  A remnant remains (11:1–6)

    Question and answer (11:1–2a)

    Elijah and the remnant (11:2b–4)

    Application to the present day (11:5–6)

  The hardening of "the rest" of Israel (11:7–10)

    "The rest" of Israel and "the elect" (11:7)

    Scriptural confirmation (11:8–10)

  The purpose of Israel's misstep (11:11–12)

    Question and response (11:11)

    What Israel's restoration will mean (11:12)

A warning to Gentile believers (11:13–24)

  Introduction (11:13–16)

    Paul's ministry to the Gentiles and concern for his people (11:13–14)

    What Israel's restoration will mean (11:15)

    The firstfruits and the root (11:16)

  The allegory of the olive tree (11:17–24)

    A warning not to boast against the branches (11:17–18)

    An objection to Paul's warning (11:19)

    Paul's response (11:20–24)

The revelation of the mystery of Israel (11:25–32)

  The mystery (11:25–27)

    Disclosure formula (11:25a)

    The temporary hardening of Israel (11:25b)

    The salvation of all Israel (11:26a)

    Scriptural confirmation (11:26b–27)

  Israel within God's plan (11:28–32)

    Enemies yet beloved (11:28)

    God's irrevocable call (11:29)

    As the Gentiles were disobedient and received mercy (11:30)

    So Israel has been disobedient in order to receive mercy (11:31)

    The role of disobedience in God's plan (11:32)

God's inscrutable wisdom (11:33–36)

  Three exclamations (11:33)

  Three questions (11:34–35)

  Three-part benediction (11:36)

it into his own argument, thereby leaving it to his biblically literate audience to draw the connection between the salvation that God brought to Israel at the time of the exile and the salvation that God is currently bringing in Christ.

As was the case in chapters 9–10, Scripture plays a central role in Paul's argument in chapter 11 by showing that what was written in the past speaks today. Scripture for Paul is a living word.

Tracing the Train of Thought

This section consists of six units. In the first, Paul raises the central question that drives the discussion forward: Has God rejected his people? (11:1–6). Responding with an emphatic no, he reminds his contemporaries of God's response to Elijah, who mistakenly thought that he was the last faithful Israelite. Just as God left a remnant of seven thousand faithful Israelites at that time, so God has left a faithful remnant at the present time.

In the second unit, Paul draws a contrast between this faithful remnant that has attained what Israel was seeking and "the rest" of Israel that, as Scripture attests, has been hardened (11:7–10). Asking if Israel's misstep means that it has irretrievably stumbled, Paul in the third unit holds out hope for "the rest" of Israel (11:11–12).

In the fourth unit, Paul interrupts his discussion about "the remnant" and "the rest" of Israel to warn Gentile believers not to boast in their new status at Israel's expense (11:13–24). Comparing them to wild olive shoots that have been grafted onto a cultivated olive tree, he assures them that God is powerful to graft onto the olive tree the natural branches—Israel—that were cut off.

Having warned his Gentile audience not to boast against Israel, Paul in the fifth unit reveals a mystery: all Israel ("the rest" as well as "the remnant") will be saved since God's call and gifts are irrevocable (11:25–32). For just as the disobedient Gentiles received mercy, so disobedient Israel will receive mercy. The revelation of the mystery of God's mercy leads to the final unit of this chapter, in which Paul stands in awe of God's wisdom and knowledge (11:33–36).

11:1–6. Paul begins this unit with a question that has been the subtext of his discussion since the beginning of chapter 9: **I ask, then, has God repudiated his people?** (11:1a). The question makes eminent sense in light of what Paul has said thus far: God is presently calling forth a people from the Gentiles as well as from the Jews (9:24), and whereas the Gentiles have attained a righteousness based on faith, Israel has not attained the goal of the law (9:31). Moreover, since Paul has just described Israel as a "disobedient and stubborn" people (10:21), it might seem that God has rejected Israel. But Paul, who has already hinted at Israel's restoration (9:27–29), cannot conceive of God repudiating his people. Indeed, the very manner in which he formulates this question (*mē apōsato*) anticipates a negative answer: "God has not repudiated his people, has he?" Accordingly, Paul replies with his favorite retort, **Of course not!** (11:1b). To substantiate his answer, he points to the evidence of his own life: **After all, I am an Israelite, the offspring of Abraham, a member of the tribe of Benjamin** (11:1c). Paul offers similar descriptions of himself in 2 Cor. 11:22 and Phil. 3:5. In those texts, he insists on his Israelite pedigree to defend his apostolic credentials, but here he highlights his pedigree in three ways in order to associate himself with his people. First, he is an Israelite like his compatriots (9:4). Second, he is the "offspring" (*sperma*) of Abraham, who was chosen by God's elective purpose (9:7–8); and so he belongs to the *sperma* that God has spared so that Israel will not disappear from the face of earth (9:29). Third, he belongs to the tribe of Benjamin, "the most Israelite of the tribes" (Fitzmyer 1993, 604), which Moses called "the beloved of the LORD" (Deut. 33:12), a tribe that was once on the verge of extinction (Judg. 20–21; Haacker 2003, 88). Paul himself, then, is living proof that God has not repudiated his people. Israel remains the people of God.

Paul states the answer to his question in a positive way as strongly as possible: **God has not repudiated his people whom he foreknew** (11:2a). In doing so, he draws from the language of 1 Sam. 12:22 and Ps. 94:14. In addition to using these texts, he adds the phrase "whom he foreknew" (*proegnō*), which echoes what he said earlier about the justified: "those whom God foreknew [*proegnō*], God predetermined to be conformed to the image of his Son so that the Son might be the firstborn among many siblings" (8:29). In light of this phrase, it becomes apparent why God has not repudiated his people: Israel is part of God's elective plan, predetermined to be conformed to the image of his Son. In this way, Paul suggests that Israel will share in God's final act of salvation: the resurrection of the dead.

Aware that his audience, especially its Gentile members, might find it difficult to understand why God would not reject a people whom Paul has just described as disobedient, Paul draws from an episode in Elijah's life as recounted in 1 Kings 19. In doing so, he returns to the theme of the "remnant" that he first broached in his Isaiah quotations in Rom. 9:27–29. At one of the lowest periods in Israel's history, it appeared that the prophet was the last Israelite faithful to Yhwh and that his death would signal the end of Israel as a nation that worshiped Yhwh. Paul reminds his audience of this story: **Do you not know what the Scripture says in the section dealing with Elijah, how he complains to God against Israel? "Lord, they have killed your prophets and razed your altars to the ground, and only I am left, and they seek my life"** (11:2b–3). In the original story, Elijah's words are a response to a question that God asks twice: "What are you doing here, Elijah?" (1 Kings 19:9, 13). But in his retelling of the story, Paul interprets the prophet's reply as a complaint against the people of Israel, using the same verb (*entynchanei*) that he employed to describe the intercession of the Spirit and Christ on behalf of the justified (8:27, 34). In addition to this, he omits Elijah's remark about the people forsaking God's covenant, and he reverses the order of the remarks in 1 Kings 19:10, 14 so that the killing of the prophets stands before the razing of the altars, thereby highlighting Elijah's claim that he is the only remaining prophet (Byrne 1996, 334).

The strong adversative (*alla*) that begins the next verse indicates that Paul's concern is to highlight the prophet's mistaken notion that he is the last faithful Israelite. Accordingly, he writes: **But what is the divine response to him?**

"I have left for myself seven thousand who have not bowed down to Baal" (11:4). Once more, Paul skips over material found in the original story, in which God commissions Elijah to anoint Hazael, Jehu, and Elisha (1 Kings 19:15–17), so that he can emphasize what is most important for his purposes: the seven thousand faithful Israelites whom Yhwh has reserved, unbeknownst to the prophet. To underline the importance of God's reply, Paul speaks of "the divine response" (*ho chrēmatismos*), a word used in 2 Macc. 2:4 to signal an authoritative oracular reply (Cranfield 1979, 546).

Having employed the biblical story of Elijah, Paul draws a lesson from this episode for his contemporaries: **In the same way, at the present time, there is a remnant selected by grace. But if it is by grace, then it is no longer on the basis of works, otherwise grace would not be grace** (11:5–6). There are two significant points here. First, Paul highlights the theme of the remnant, which he defines in terms of an election/selection based on grace. To do this he employs the expression *leimma kat' eklogēn*, which I have translated as "a remnant selected by grace" (see BDAG 590, s.v. *leimma*). This remnant refers to the portion of Israel that has believed in the Messiah and attained a righteousness based on faith. Paul uses the Elijah episode to suggest to his contemporaries that the remnant is greater than they imagine. Second, Paul highlights the "grace" or "favor" (*charis*) that God has extended to this faithful remnant of Israel. The remnant has been selected solely on the basis of God's favor, not because of anything it has accomplished; otherwise God's grace would not be a matter of favor. Here Paul echoes what he said earlier in 4:4, 6 about the graciousness of God's righteousness toward Abraham, and what he wrote in Gal. 3:18 about the inheritance being based on God's promise rather than on the law. Having introduced the theme of the remnant of Israel that has been selected on the basis of grace, Paul must now deal with the more difficult issue of "the rest" of Israel if he is to make his case that God has not repudiated Israel.

11:7–10. In the previous unit, Paul has argued that God, who has left a remnant selected by election, has not repudiated his people. But what does this mean for the rest of Israel? If only a remnant remains, it would appear that God has rejected his people, or at least the vast majority of them. Aware of this problem, Paul takes up the question of God's dealings with "the rest," the portion of Israel that has not accepted the gospel. Beginning with an expression that he has employed several times in this letter (*ti oun*: 6:1, 15; 7:7; 8:31; 9:14, 30), Paul states the paradoxical situation that presently characterizes Israel according to his gospel: **Then what? Israel did not obtain what it was seeking, but the elect obtained it. The rest were made calloused** (11:7). Here Paul echoes what he wrote in 9:30–31 about the ironic situation of Israel and the Gentiles: the Gentiles, who were not pursuing righteousness, have attained it; whereas Israel, who was pursuing a law of righteousness, did not reach the goal of that law. But here, as J. Ross Wagner notes (2003, 239), Paul is not talking about Israel and the Gentiles (even though the Gentiles are part of the elect; see Byrne 1996, 335) but about two groups *within* Israel, "the rest" and "the elect." While this elect group within Israel has attained what Israel was always seeking, the rest of Israel has been "made calloused" or "hardened," a point Paul also develops in 2 Cor. 3:12–18 (see especially 3:14).

To substantiate this claim, Paul introduces two scriptural quotations. The first reads: **As it is written, "God gave them a spirit of stupefaction, eyes that do not see and ears that do not hear, to this very day"** (Rom. 11:8). The text is introduced by a formula ("as it is written") that Paul frequently employs when he wants to alert his audience that he is quoting from Scripture (1:17; 2:24; 3:4, 10; 4:17; 8:36; 9:13, 33; 10:15). This particular quotation, however, is a conflation of Deut. 29:4, in which Moses testifies that "to this day the LORD has not given" Israel a "mind to understand, or eyes to see or ears to hear," and Isa. 29:10, in which Isaiah says that "the LORD has poured out upon" the prophets and seers of Judah "a spirit of deep sleep" because they have refused to acknowledge God's salvation on behalf of Jerusalem. Whether this conflation is the work of Paul or others, Paul's point is clear: God has imposed a hardening upon "the rest" of Israel "to this very day" so that it cannot understand what God is doing on its behalf.

However, lest it appear that this hardening is arbitrary, as if Israel were without guilt, Paul introduces a second quotation (Rom. 11:9). This quotation, which comes from Ps. 68:23–24 LXX (69:22–23 Eng.), presents this hardening as retribution: **And David says, "Let their banquet table become a snare and a trap, a cause for stumbling and retribution for them. Let their eyes become darkened so that they do not see, and let their backs be continually bent"** (Rom. 11:9–10). Paul makes use of this psalm text because, like the mixed quotation from Deuteronomy and Isaiah that speaks of eyes that do not see, this text refers to eyes that will be darkened so that they cannot see. Rereading the text in light of what is presently happening, Paul applies David's words about those who persecute the righteous to the portion of Israel that has not believed in the gospel. In doing so, he reprimands them for opposing the gospel (cf. 1 Thess. 2:14–16). In an interesting exegesis of this passage, Origen writes that the banquet table signifies "all the Scriptures that were in Israel's possession before the coming of the Lord." Origen then goes on to say that Scripture itself "becomes a snare for them when they read the things that have been prophesied about Christ" (*Comm. Rom.* 8.8.9–10, trans. Scheck 2001–2, 2:164). Although Paul may not have intended such an allegorical reading, Origen correctly understands that Paul is reading this text in terms of his contemporary circumstances.

11:11–12. What Paul has written in the previous section appears to militate against his thesis that God has not repudiated his people. For if a divinely imposed blindness has come upon a portion of Israel so that it cannot perceive the salvation that the gospel proclaims, how can Paul maintain that God has not abandoned his people? Aware of the problem he has created for himself,

Paul raises a second question. Employing the pattern that he used in 11:1 (question, response, explanation), he writes, **I ask, then, have they stumbled to the point of falling? Of course not! Rather, salvation has come to the Gentiles by their transgression in order to provoke them to jealousy** (11:11). As in 11:1, Paul phrases the question in a way that expects a negative answer: "They have not stumbled to the point of falling, have they?" He then responds in a manner that rules the question as being out of order before providing his audience with a more-detailed response. As he did in 9:30–32, Paul makes use of the metaphor of a race. Although Israel has stumbled, its fall has not disqualified it from the race. To the contrary, as Paul will now reveal, Israel's fall has played a role in God's salvific plan for the Gentiles and for Israel itself. Making use of a term ("transgression," *paraptōmati*) he has already employed on several occasions (4:25; 5:15, 16, 17, 18, 20), Paul explains the significance of Israel's "transgression" in preferring its own righteousness to God's righteousness disclosed in Christ. Because Israel has refused to believe in the gospel, salvation has come to the Gentiles, as illustrated in Acts 13:46, when Paul and Barnabas turn to the Gentiles after the Jewish populace of Pisidian Antioch rejects them. But this offer of salvation to the Gentiles is not the end of God's plan. Returning to the theme of jealousy that he introduced in Rom. 10:19, Paul discloses that salvation has come to the Gentiles for the purpose of making "them" (the rest of Israel) jealous of the salvation that the Gentiles have received. Israel's fall, then, is not the end of the race but a vital part of God's plan that includes salvation for the Gentiles as well as for the whole of Israel. Klaus Haacker (2003, 90) insightfully writes: "Thus, the problem of Israel's unbelief is removed from the moral level (where it had been placed at the end of chapter 10) back to the sphere of God's policy in ruling the history of the people he has chosen (see 9:6–29)."

Having explained that God has hardened the rest of Israel for the purpose of leading the Gentiles to salvation and making Israel jealous so that they would embrace the gospel, Paul turns his attention to Israel's restoration: **But if their transgression has resulted in riches for the world and their failure has resulted in riches for the Gentiles, how much more will their full number be?** (11:12). As he did in 5:9–10, 15, and 17, Paul employs an argument that moves from the lesser to the greater. If Israel's "transgression" and failure resulted in such "riches" for the Gentiles and the world, "how much more [*posō mallon*] will their full number be?" While "world" (*kosmos*) can refer to the physical world, as it does in 1:20, here Paul has in view the world of human beings, as in 3:6, 19. This interpretation is confirmed by what he writes about the reconciliation of the world in 11:15, a statement that echoes 2 Cor. 5:19: "In Christ God was reconciling the world [of human beings] to himself." The riches that Israel's transgression has brought to the world of human beings, then, is nothing less than the reconciliation of humanity to God. Thus, when Paul speaks of the riches that Israel's failure has brought to the Gentiles, he means their reconciliation to God, which they have already appropriated on the basis of their faith in God's righteousness. But if this is the result of transgression and failure, what will "their full number" (*to plērōma autōn*) bring? Although Paul will speak of "the full number of the Gentiles" in Rom. 11:25, here he has in view the full number of "the rest" of Israel that has been hardened at the present time. When that portion of Israel has played its role in God's plan, God's work of salvation will be complete.

11:13–24. Having explained that a divinely imposed blindness has come upon "the rest" of Israel in order to bring the Gentiles to salvation, and having suggested that this disobedient portion of Israel will be restored, in this unit Paul turns his attention to the Gentile believers in his audience in order to warn them not to boast against Israel. The unit begins with a brief introduction (11:13–16), in which Paul picks up the theme of Israel's restoration that he introduced in 11:12. He then develops an allegory about a cultivated olive tree from which branches have been cut off and replaced by branches that were grafted in from a wild olive tree (11:17–24). In this allegory the natural branches represent the portion of Israel that has not believed in the gospel, whereas the branches from the wild olive tree stand for Gentiles who have believed in the gospel. Whether or not Paul understood the horticulture of his day, the point he makes remains valid: as wondrous as the grafting of the Gentiles into the tree of Israel was, the regrafting of the portion of Israel that has not believed will be more wondrous. Thus Origen long ago noted that Paul, "by virtue of his apostolic authority," adapted the realities of the horticultural situation to his argument rather than his argument to the realities of the horticultural situation (*Comm. Rom.* 8.11.13, trans. Scheck 2001–2, 2:181).

Paul begins with a direct address to the members of his Gentile audience: **I am speaking directly to you Gentiles. Insofar as I am an apostle to the Gentiles, I honor my ministry in the hope that I might somehow incite my race to jealousy and save some of them** (11:13–14). This is the first time in the letter that Paul explicitly addresses the Gentile members of the Roman community. In doing so, he identifies himself as "an apostle to the Gentiles," thereby echoing what he said in 1:5 about his ministry to the Gentiles and anticipating what he will write in 15:16 (see also Gal. 2:7, 9). Although this address to the Gentile believers at Rome does not necessarily mean that the community was composed exclusively of Gentiles, it does suggest that Gentile believers were a significant component, perhaps the majority, of Paul's audience. In addressing the Gentiles, he assures them that while he honors his ministry to the Gentiles, his ministry to them does not exclude a continuing concern for Israel. Nor does his concern for Israel lessen his concern for them. For Paul, there is a relation between these two ministries that seems to have eluded his Gentile converts and Christians ever since. As Paul sees it, his Gentile ministry is necessary for Israel's salvation. Accordingly, he preaches the gospel to the Gentiles not only to bring them to salvation but also to make his kindred jealous of this salvation and so bring them to Christ.

Next Paul employs an argument from the lesser to the greater, as he did in 11:12, in order to explain the importance of bringing his own people to the salvation that the Gentiles already enjoy in Christ: **For if their repudiation has meant the reconciliation of the world, what will their acceptance mean if not life from the dead?** (11:15). On first reading, what Paul writes here appears to contradict what he said in 11:1: God has not "repudiated" (*apōsato*) his people. How, then, can Paul claim that their "their repudiation" (*apobolē autōn*) has led to the reconciliation of the world? While the majority of commentators interpret this repudiation as a temporary rejection, I am persuaded by those (such as Fitzmyer 1993, 612) who construe "their repudiation" as a subjective genitive; that is, *Israel's repudiation* of the Messiah has paradoxically resulted in the reconciliation of the world. If this interpretation is correct, the phrase "their acceptance" (*hē proslēmpsis*) should be taken in the same way: *their acceptance* of the Messiah. Thus Paul would be saying that if Israel's rejection of God's righteousness has paradoxically led to the world's reconciliation, consider what its acceptance of the gospel will mean: nothing less than "life from the dead." This final phrase, however, is open to diverse interpretations. While some argue that Paul is speaking of the new life in the Spirit, the type of argument that Paul is making here ("from the lesser to the greater") and the phrase "from the dead" (Dunn 1988, 2:658) suggest that the patristic interpretation of the phrase in terms of the general resurrection of the dead best expresses Paul's original meaning. So Origen (*Comm. Rom.* 8.10.8, trans. Scheck 2001–2, 2:175) notes, "It would seem absurd if their reception would not bestow something greater and more excellent to the world, seeing that their stumbling gave reconciliation to the world."

Paul provides one more argument to explain why he is so concerned for his own people: **If the first portion is holy, so is the whole batch; and if the root is holy, so are the branches** (11:16). There is general agreement that "the whole batch" and "the branches" refer to Israel, but there is little agreement about how to construe "the first portion" and "the root." There is further discussion as to whether Paul understands the "whole batch" and the "root" as referring to the same reality. There have been three suggestions for resolving this question: The first portion/root refers to (1) Christ, (2) the patriarchs, (3) the remnant of first Jewish converts (Bell 2005, 274–75). In my view, Paul's train of thought favors the following interpretation: Whereas the "first portion" refers to the remnant of Jewish converts that has already believed in the gospel, the root stands for the patriarchs from whom Israel has originated. If this interpretation is correct, Paul is affirming the following: Since the tiny remnant of Jewish converts that has believed in the gospel ("the first portion") is holy, this assures that the rest of Israel ("the whole batch") will be holy when it accepts the gospel. And since the patriarchs ("the root") are holy, this guarantees that the rest of Israel ("the branches") will be holy.

In this brief but dense subunit (11:13–24), Paul assures his Gentile audience that he honors and glorifies his ministry to them since it will ultimately bring Israel to salvation.

In the introductory portion of this unit (11:13–24), Paul used the plural form of "you" (*hymin*) in addressing his audience. Now, in the portion of this unit that develops the allegory of the olive tree (11:17–24), he makes use of the singular (*sy*). In doing so, he employs the "technique of speech-in-character" (Jewett 2007, 683–84) to address an imaginary interlocutor and discuss the issue of Jewish-Gentile relations in a nonthreatening manner. Making use of this rhetorical technique and the allegory of the olive tree, he will argue against Gentile boasting just as he has argued against Jewish boasting (2:17–29) in order to reaffirm the thesis he has been developing throughout this letter: Jewish and Gentile believers enjoy equal status because their new standing before God is a gift of sheer grace. The allegory begins with a warning to Paul's Gentile interlocutor not to boast against the branches that were cut off (11:17–18). Next, it allows the interlocutor to raise an objection (11:19). Paul then responds to this objection at length (11:20–24).

Paul begins his allegory with a conditional clause that describes the true situation of his Gentile interlocutor: **But if some of the branches were cut off and you, being from a wild olive tree, were grafted in among them and shared in the rich sap of the olive tree's root** (11:17). The manner in which the allegory begins thrusts Paul's interlocutor into the inferior position of being a branch from "a wild olive tree" that has been grafted among branches of a tree that Paul identifies as a cultivated olive tree (11:24). From the outset of the allegory, then, Paul reminds the interlocutor that he comes from the stock of a tree that "was notoriously *un*productive" (Dunn 1988, 2:661). The passive verbs in 11:17, *exeklasthēsan* (were cut off) and *enekentristhēs* (were grafted in)—verbs that will reoccur in 11:19–20, 23–24—are best construed as divine passives, with God as the unexpressed subject. God is the one who has "cut off" some of the branches in order to "graft in" branches from a wild olive tree. Robert Jewett (2007, 683–85) notes that while ancient writers disagreed about whether the grafting in of wild shoots produced richer fruit, Paul's allegory focuses on the manner in which the grafted-in branches draw from the rich sap of the olive tree's root, Israel's patriarchs. Thus, instead of commending his Gentile interlocutor for strengthening and enriching the tree, Paul reminds him that he draws upon, and is strengthened by, the rich heritage of Israel. Having made the interlocutor aware of his real situation "among the branches" of the tree that is Israel, Paul issues his warning: **Do not boast against the branches** (11:18a). The imperative recalls his earlier statement that boasting has been excluded through "the law of faith" (3:27). The "branches" to which Paul refers here include those that remain on the tree (the remnant

David Brühlmeier, commons.wikimedia.org

Figure 11. Olive trees. Paul compares the inclusion of the Gentiles in the salvation that springs from Israel to the grafting of a wild olive branch onto a cultivated olive tree.

that believes) as well as those that have been cut off (the rest of Israel that has been hardened).

Employing the verb "to boast" as a hook word, Paul introduces a second conditional clause, which exhorts his Gentile interlocutor to recall his relationship to the root of the tree should he be tempted to boast: **But if you should boast, recall that it is not you who support the root but the root that supports you** (11:18b). Envisioning a situation in which his Gentile interlocutor might boast of his new status, Paul returns to the metaphor of the root to remind the interlocutor of his relationship to the tree of Israel. As an engrafted branch, the interlocutor finds his support from the root of the tree of Israel: from Abraham, Isaac, and Jacob. Any notion that Paul has dismissed Israel's heritage and history is greatly mistaken.

Having reminded his interlocutor of his place on the tree of Israel, and having warned him not to boast against the branches of that tree, even if they have been cut off, Paul allows his interlocutor to raise an objection that may have been current among some members of Paul's Gentile audience: **Accordingly, you will say, "Branches were cut off in order that that I might be grafted in"** (11:19). Employing Paul's own description of the branches as "cut off," the interlocutor cleverly argues that God must have cut off branches to make room for Gentiles like himself. This objection is the seedbed for all theories of supersessionism. According to such claims, the engrafted branches (the church) have replaced Israel. What such theories forget, however, is that although "some" branches have been cut off, the root of the tree remains, and some branches were never cut off.

The objection of 11:19 gives Paul an opportunity to explain why the other branches were cut off (11:20), to warn the interlocutor that even he may not be spared (11:21), to recall the goodness and severity of God (11:22), and to conclude with the startling announcement that God has the power to graft in the seemingly dead branches that were cut off (11:23).

Paul's initial response to his interlocutor is a simple *kalōs*, **True enough** (11:20a), which on first reading suggests that he agrees with the analysis of his dialogue partner. But instead of saying that branches were cut off to make room for the branches from the wild olive tree, Paul provides another reason why they were cut off and others were grafted in: **They were cut off because of unbelief, but you stand firm by faith** (11:20b). The branches were not cut off to make room for new branches but because of their "unbelief" (*apistia*), and the interlocutor now resides in the tree that is Israel by means of faith (*pistei*; see 2 Cor. 1:24 for a similar phrase).

Paul has already spoken of Israel's unbelief as opposed to God's faithfulness (3:3), and he has pointed to the centrality of faith on numerous occasions (1:8, 12, 17; 3:22, 26, 28), especially in his discussion of Abraham. Now he reminds his interlocutor that the only difference between him and the branches that have been cut off is faith in God's righteousness as manifested in Christ. Consequently, Paul issues a further warning: **Do not be haughty, but fear** (11:20c). Paul will repeat the first part of this warning in 12:16. Here, however, he couples it with a second imperative. Instead of being haughty, the interlocutor should fear. While the object of this fear is not expressed, the context suggests that the interlocutor should fear God lest the same fate come upon him that came upon the branches that were cut off.

Paul supports what he has said with a warning that what God has done to the branches that have not believed, God can do to the interlocutor: **For if God did not spare the natural branches, perhaps he will not spare you** (11:21). The explicit mention of "God" in this verse confirms that the verbs "to cut off" and "to graft in" were indeed divine passives. The one who cut off the branches is the one who did not spare the branches. By describing the branches that were cut off as "natural branches," Paul alludes to the true situation of the interlocutor, who is not a natural branch on the tree of Israel. And by arguing from the greater (the natural branches) to the lesser (the unnatural branches), he intimates how much more readily God might cut off branches from a wild olive tree if they fall from faith.

In the next verse, Paul changes his tone. Having attacked the interlocutor's pride, he reminds him of the grace he has experienced: **See then the kindness and severity of God: on the one hand, severity toward those who have fallen; on the other hand, the kindness of God toward you** (11:22a). At the present time God has exhibited both "kindness" (*chrēstotēs*) and "severity" (*apotomia*): kindness toward those who have believed and severity toward those who have not. The kindness of God is God's goodness and generosity manifested as sheer grace and unmerited favor. Paul has already referred to this kindness in 2:4. The later Pauline literature continues to speak of it (Eph. 2:7; Titus 3:4), and Ps. 31:19 praises God for the greatness of the kindness that he shows toward those who *fear* him (precisely what Paul has exhorted his interlocutor to do). God has manifested severity by not sparing "the rest" of Israel that has been cut off on account of its unbelief. Paul assures his interlocutor that God will continue to manifest kindness toward him **if you persevere in his kindness** (11:22b). The Gentile interlocutor must persevere in faith by acknowledging that his present status is a result of divine favor. If the Gentile does not persevere in faith but boasts of his new status, his fate will be the same as the branches that God did not spare, **because even you can be cut off** (11:22c).

The final words of Paul's allegory are words of hope and resurrection rather than words of warning and fear. Employing the verb "to graft in" three times in 11:23–24, he reckons with the possibility that the branches that have been cut off can be grafted in again. As the distribution of the verbs "cut off" and "grafted in" shows, this allegory that began by affirming that some natural branches were "cut off" concludes with an assurance that they can be "grafted in":

11:17	natural branches <u>cut off</u>
	wild branches *grafted in*
11:19	natural branches <u>cut off</u>
	wild branches *grafted in*
11:20	natural branches <u>cut off</u> because of unbelief
11:23	natural branches can be *grafted in*
	for God is powerful to *graft them in*
11:24	wild branches were *grafted in,*
	how much easier to *graft in* natural branches

Aware that God's severity toward Israel is not God's final word, Paul writes: **And they, if they do not persist in unbelief, will be grafted in, for God has the power to graft them in again** (11:23). Paul, however, is no longer talking about the horticultural practices of his day, which could hardly envision a pile of dead, dried-up branches being grafted into a living tree. Echoing what he said of Abraham's faith in 4:21 ("He was convinced that [God] was able to do what he promised"), Paul expresses his own faith that God is able to graft in the branches that were cut off because of unbelief. Aware that what he has said contradicts the laws of horticulture, Paul makes use of another argument that moves from the lesser to the greater: **For if you were cut off from a natural wild olive tree and contrary to nature were grafted into a cultivated olive tree, how much more will the natural branches be grafted into their own olive tree** (11:24). By describing the tree as a "cultivated olive tree" (*kallielaion*), Paul not only draws a sharp contrast with the "wild olive tree" from which his Gentile interlocutor has come but also recalls the care with which God has tended the tree of Israel. The logic of Paul's argument does not rest on the horticultural practices of his day but on the power of God. If God could graft into the tree of Israel what did not belong to that tree by nature, how much easier it will be for God to regraft into the tree of Israel what belongs to it by nature.

11:25–32. Paul's dialogue with his Gentile interlocutor was something of an interlude in chapter 11, distinguished from the surrounding material of this chapter by its use of the second-person singular and its absence of scriptural quotations. By reminding his interlocutor that God is powerful to graft in those natural branches that were cut off from the tree that is Israel, Paul has prepared for this unit, which is the climax of the argument he has been making since the beginning of chapter 9. Having hinted at Israel's restoration in the previous unit, in this passage he reveals "the mystery" of Israel's restoration and salvation. The unit consists of two subunits. In the first, Paul discloses the mystery of Israel's restoration, which he supports with a mixed quotation from the book of Isaiah (11:25–27). In the second, he explains Israel's role in God's plan of salvation (11:28–32).

Paul begins with a disclosure formula: **I do not want you to be unaware of this mystery, brothers and sisters, lest you be wise in your own estimation** (11:25a). Next he reveals the mystery: **A hardening has come upon a portion of Israel until the full number of the Gentiles should enter in, and in this way all Israel will be saved** (11:25b–26a). Finally, he supports what he has just revealed by a quotation from Scripture: **As it is written: "The deliverer will come from Zion, and he will remove impiety from Jacob. And this will be my covenant with them, when I take away their sins from them"** (11:26b–27).

Paul's use of a disclosure formula in 11:25a (for other examples, see Rom. 1:13; 1 Cor. 10:1; 12:1; 2 Cor. 1:8; 1 Thess. 4:13) and his return to the second-person plural (*hymas*) signal a turning point in this chapter. The apostle to the Gentiles is about to reveal a "mystery" (*mystērion*) to the members of his predominantly Gentile audience lest they become like his arrogant interlocutor and consider themselves wiser than they truly are about Israel's fate. In saying that he is about to reveal a *mystērion*, Paul takes up the language of Jewish apocalyptic writings in which seers disclose heavenly secrets revealed to them about the fate and future of God's people. Although Paul does not inform his audience when or how this mystery was revealed to him, his language assures the Roman Christians that what he is about to say is not the outcome of personal reflection but something that God, or perhaps Christ, has communicated to him. Paul mentions other revelations in addition to his call in Gal. 2:2 and 2 Cor. 12:1–10.

The word "mystery" indicates that what Paul is about to communicate is inaccessible to human reason. The gospel is such a mystery. In 1 Cor. 2:1 Paul refers to his gospel about the crucified Messiah as "the mystery of God" (cf. 1 Cor. 1:23; 2:2), "God's wisdom, secret [*en mystēriō*] and hidden" (1 Cor. 2:7). Accordingly, Helmut Krämer (*EDNT* 2:448) writes, "This saving event is inaccessible to human reason because it appears to the reason to be foolishness." As a preacher of the gospel, Paul is a steward of "God's mysteries" (1 Cor.

4:1). At the end of Romans, he speaks of "the revelation of the mystery that was kept secret from all eternity, but is now revealed through the prophetic writings in accordance with the command of the eternal God in order that the obedience of faith might be made known to all the nations" (Rom. 16:25–26). Colossians and Ephesians develop this concept in a similar vein in terms of "the fully developed plan of revelation, which was once hidden but now has been revealed" (Krämer, *EDNT* 2:448).

The mystery that Paul reveals here unfolds in two phases. First, a hardening has come upon a part of Israel until the full number of the Gentiles enters into the tree that is Israel. Second, once this full number has entered, all Israel will be saved. Although the text of 11:25 could be construed as a "*partial* hardening has come upon Israel" (so Dunn 1988, 2:679; Fitzmyer 1993, 621), Paul's description of the blindness that has been imposed on "the rest of Israel" (11:7–10) suggests that he is speaking of a *part* of Israel, since a remnant has believed in the gospel (11:5). The "full number of the Gentiles," which echoes the full number of Israel that Paul has mentioned in 11:12, is a number known only to God. When that number enters in, "all Israel will be saved." Although the meaning of "all Israel" has been contested (see Cranfield 1979, 576–77; and Reasoner 2005, 121–28, for a fuller discussion), the argument of this chapter indicates that Paul is speaking of ethnic Israel, which includes not only the remnant that has believed but also the vast majority that has not. Historical Israel (past, present, and future) will be the beneficiary of God's salvation.

Paul grounds this amazing revelation in a mixed quotation drawn from Isa. 59:20–21 and 27:9. Although the Hebrew text of Isa. 59:20 reads, "and he shall come *to* Zion as redeemer," and the LXX reads, "and the one who delivers will come *for* Zion's sake" (NETS)—God being the subject in both texts—Paul writes, "The deliverer will come *from* Zion," referring to Christ. Although it is not clear whether "Zion" refers to the earthly or the heavenly Jerusalem (see Gal. 4:25–26, where Paul distinguishes between the "present Jerusalem" and "the Jerusalem above"), it appears that he has Christ's parousia in view. According to the mystery that Paul reveals, then, the full entrance of the Gentiles into the eschatological people of God will inaugurate the parousia, when all Israel will be saved. If this reading is correct, it helps to explain why Paul has exulted in his ministry to the Gentiles: the entrance of their full number will inaugurate the salvation of his own people.

Having disclosed the mystery of how Israel will be saved, in 11:28–32 Paul reviews and previews Israel's role in God's plan. He employs two neatly balanced phrases (*kata men to euangelion . . . kata de tēn eklogēn*) to structure his first statement: **With reference to the gospel, they are enemies for your sake, but with reference to their election, they are beloved because of the patriarchs** (11:28). Looking at Israel's history from two vantage points, the gospel and God's election of Israel, Paul affirms that from the vantage point of the gospel, the majority of Israel stands in opposition to God's righteousness revealed in

Christ. But since their opposition has led to salvation for the Gentiles, Paul describes this enmity as being for the sake of the Gentiles. From the vantage point of Israel's election (see 9:11; 11:5, 7), however, the people of Israel remain "beloved" (*agapētoi*) of God—the same adjective Paul used in 1:7 when addressing the Romans—because of the root of the tree, the patriarchs, who gave them life. The sentence is structured as follows:

enemies	for the sake of Gentile salvation
beloved of God	for the sake of the patriarchs

Paul provides his audience with supporting evidence for what he has just said: **For the gifts and call of God are irrevocable** (11:29). While the "gifts of God" refer to the privileges of Israel that Paul enumerated in 9:4–5, the "call of God" refers to Israel's election, which was not listed among those gifts since God's election of Israel is the source of the gifts and privileges God has bestowed on Israel. Paul's insistence that the gifts and call are "irrevocable" (see 2 Cor. 7:10 for Paul's only other use of the word) highlights the fidelity and uprightness of the God of Israel: God will not forsake the people he has chosen. Consequently, even though Israel has not been faithful to God, God remains faithful, as Paul noted in 3:3–4.

Having assured his audience that Israel will be saved because God's call is irrevocable, Paul addresses the question of Israel's disobedience and the role this disobedience has played in God's plan (11:30–32). Paul again carefully structures the material, drawing a comparison between the former situation of his Gentile readers (*hōsper . . . pote*; 11:30) and the present situation of Israel (*houtōs . . . nyn*; 11:31) before explaining the role of disobedience in God's plan (*gar . . . hina*; 11:32).

In 11:30–32 Paul summarizes the whole scope of salvation history to explain why God's gifts and call are irrevocable. First, he recalls the past situation of his Gentile audience: **For just as you were once disobedient to God but now have received mercy because of their disobedience** (11:30). Juxtaposing the themes of disobedience and mercy that have played a central role in this letter, he reminds his audience how they have received mercy as a result of Israel's disobedience to the gospel.

Next, Paul points to the present situation of the majority of Israel that ironically finds itself in the former situation of the Gentiles: **so now they have been disobedient in respect to the mercy shown to you in order that they might be shown mercy** (11:31). This verse presents a translation problem that I have resolved by taking the phrase *tō hymeterō eleei* (in respect to the mercy shown to you) with what comes before ("they have been disobedient"). If the phrase is taken with the purpose clause that follows ("in order that they might be shown mercy"), the meaning is that they have been disobedient in order that they might receive mercy by the mercy shown to you. C. E. B. Cranfield (1979, 582–86) and Joseph Fitzmyer (1993, 627–28) support this second meaning. But if I am correct, the meaning of the verse is that the majority of Israel has been disobedient by opposing the mercy shown to the Gentiles. Without Israel knowing it, God's purpose has been to extend mercy to Israel just as he has extended mercy to the Gentiles.

How can this be? Why would God make people disobedient in order to be merciful to them? Paul provides an answer. Employing the verb that he used in Gal. 3:22–23, where he writes that God confined all under the power of sin so that the promise might be based on faith, Paul affirms: **For God has confined all to disobedience so that he might have mercy on all** (11:32). God's plan then works in a paradoxical way that was already implied in Paul's Adam-Christ comparison, where human disobedience became the occasion for God to manifest mercy. All were imprisoned in disobedience and rebelled against God, first the Gentiles and now Israel. But just as Gentile disobedience became the occasion for God to manifest mercy to the Gentiles, so Israel's disobedience has become the occasion for God to show mercy to Israel as well.

11:33–36. Having revealed the mystery of God's plan for Israel and the nations in the preceding unit, in this unit Paul concludes with a hymn-like passage that serves as a fitting conclusion not only to chapters 9–11 but to everything he has said thus far about the manifestation of God's righteousness in Christ (Fitzmyer 1993, 633). Although exegetes disagree as to whether Paul is the author of this passage—with Jewett (2007, 714) arguing against Pauline composition—all acknowledge the poetic nature of this text, which begins with three exclamations of praise (11:33), turns to three rhetorical questions (11:34–35), and concludes with a three-part benediction (11:36). Within the context of Rom. 9–11, the hymn serves as a forceful reminder to the Romans that even though the mystery has been revealed to them, God's righteous activity in Christ ultimately remains beyond human comprehension.

The passage begins with the first of three exclamations that highlight three aspects of God's attributes: **Oh the depths of the wealth and of the wisdom and of the knowledge of God!** (11:33a). Paul has already spoken of the "wealth" (*ploutos*) of God's kindness (2:4) and glory (9:23) and most recently of the enrichment/wealth that has come to the world and the Gentiles through Israel's transgression (11:12). Here he refers to the wealth of God's mercy that has been extended to Gentile and Jew despite their disobedience (11:30–32). Although Paul has not yet explicitly mentioned God's wisdom or knowledge in this letter, they are the foundation of God's astonishing plan for Israel that Paul has just revealed. Given the incomprehensibility of God, no one, not even Paul, can fully comprehend God's plan.

Paul introduces two more exclamations that focus on what has been the outcome of God's activity: **How unfathomable are his decrees and inscrutable his ways!** (11:33b). Here Paul employs two adjectives in alliterative fashion:

anexeraunēta (unfathomable) and *anexichniastoi* (inscrutable). God's "decrees" are synonymous with God's "ways" since both refer to the manner in which God has manifested his saving righteousness in Jesus Christ. God's decrees/judgments are unfathomable because he declares the ungodly righteous (4:5; 5:6), and his ways are inscrutable because God has imprisoned all in disobedience in order to extend mercy to all (11:32).

After these three exclamations, Paul asks three rhetorical questions, each question corresponding to one of the aspects of God listed in 11:33a (Jewett 2007, 714). The first question corresponds to the third aspect (God's knowledge): **Who has known the mind of the Lord?** (11:34a). The second question corresponds to the second aspect (God's wisdom): **Or who has been his counselor?** (11:34b). And the third question corresponds to the first aspect (God's wealth): **Or who has given him anything, and it will be returned to him?** (11:35). Although Paul does not introduce the material of these verses as Scripture, in 11:34 he follows Isa. 40:13 LXX rather closely: "Who has known the mind of the Lord, and who has been his counselor to instruct him?" (NETS). The background of the text in 11:35 is not clear, although many suggest Job 41:11: "Who has confronted me that I should repay? Everything under heaven belongs to me!" (NET). But even if Paul's audience was not aware that he was quoting from Scripture, its members would surely have understood that these questions had special poignancy for them and anyone who questions God's redemptive plan. God's knowledge and wisdom are beyond comprehension, and the wealth of God's generosity is so far beyond what humans can give God that no one can expect anything in return. All is grace.

After these three exclamations and questions, Paul concludes with a tripartite benediction: **Because all things come from him and exist through him and are for him. To him be the glory forever. Amen** (11:36). Paul employs similar language in 1 Cor. 8:6: "Yet for us there is one God, the Father, *from whom are all things* and *for whom we exist*, and one Lord, Jesus Christ, *through whom are all things and through whom we exist*." But whereas in the text of 1 Corinthians, Paul presents Christ as the agent of God's creative work, here he speaks of God: God is the origin, God is the agent, and God is the goal of all that happens. The only appropriate response, then, is to give God the glory, even when one does not comprehend the full scope of God's plan.

Theological Issues

Romans 9–11 is Paul's most extended discussion of Israel, as is evident from his use of "Israel." Eleven of the seventeen uses of "Israel" in the Pauline writings occur in these three chapters, the other six being 1 Cor. 10:18; 2 Cor. 3:7, 13; Gal. 6:16; Eph. 2:12; and Phil. 3:5. In our discussion of these chapters, we have seen that although Paul's discussion of Israel begins with a lament about the failure of the majority of his people to accept the gospel (9:1–5), it concludes with the revelation of the mystery that "all Israel will be saved" (11:25–27). To arrive at this conclusion, however, it was necessary for Paul to show that it is not the word of God that has failed but Israel that has failed to obey God's word. To explain how this failure came about, Paul argued that Israel sought its own righteousness rather than God's righteousness. Consequently, at the present time a "hardening" has come upon Israel so that it cannot understand. Nevertheless, there is a faithful remnant from Israel, preserved by God's grace, that has heeded God's word. This remnant belongs to a people whom God has called forth not only from Jews but from the Gentiles as well (9:24–25). Although Paul does not identify this people as the "church" (*ekklēsia*)—a word that does not occur in Romans apart from 16:1, 4, 5, 16, 23—it is not unreasonable to assume that he would so identify them if he were asked. In light of this, I pose the following question: How does Paul understand the relationship between Israel and this people whom God has called forth, the church? (For a full treatment of this issue, see W. Campbell 2006.)

Paul's understanding of the church, let alone his understanding of the relationship of the church to Israel, is complicated. Given the constraints of space, I will make only two points here. First, although Paul usually speaks about the church as a local congregation that resides in a particular place (1 Cor. 16:1, 19; 2 Cor. 8:1), his use of "the church of God" (1 Cor. 1:2; 10:32; 15:9) and "the body of Christ" (1 Cor. 12:27) intimates that the church is, in some way, more than the local congregation. The church is also universal in scope, an aspect of the church that Ephesians and Colossians highlight when they identify it as the body of the cosmic Christ, and Christ as the head of this body (Eph. 1:22; Col. 1:18). Second, although Paul speaks of "the Israel of God" (Gal. 6:16), by which he means the community of Jewish and Gentile believers whom God has called forth, he never calls the church "the new Israel." For Paul, the church is that community of believers who are sanctified in Christ and call upon the name of the Lord Jesus Christ (1 Cor. 1:2). The church is the body of Christ (Rom. 12:4–5; 1 Cor. 12:27), the temple of God (1 Cor. 3:16). How, then, is this community related to Israel? Has the church replaced Israel in God's plan of salvation? Is it a community that exists alongside Israel, independent of Israel? Or is there some other way to explain the relation between Israel and the church?

Although it is not Paul's purpose to answer these question in Rom. 9–11, what he says about Israel and the eschatological people that God has called forth from among the Gentiles as well as from among the Jews provides us with some guidance for formulating an answer. In what follows, I focus on three points: (1) Paul's understanding of "the remnant" of Israel that has believed in the gospel, (2) Paul's understanding of the Gentiles who have believed in the gospel, (3) Paul's understanding of "the rest" of Israel that has been disobedient by pursuing its own righteousness rather than accepting God's righteousness revealed in Christ.

In regard to the first point, Paul is quite insistent that a remnant remains, of which he is an example (11:1–5). Consequently, it is not as though the whole of Israel has refused to believe. For Paul, this remnant is the "seed" that assures the survival of historical Israel. The first portion guarantees that the whole batch, the rest of Israel, is holy. This remnant has not been cut off from the tree that is Israel, a tree rooted in the patriarchs; this remnant belongs to Israel. But this remnant also belongs to the people that God has called forth from among Gentiles as well as Jews (9:24). Consequently, it belongs to the church of God, and Paul would certainly identify it as such. This remnant that belongs to Israel, however, is not a new or alternate Israel. Rooted in Abraham, Isaac, and Jacob, it is Israel.

In regard to the second point, Rom. 9–11 affirms that in addition to this remnant, there are Gentiles who have attained to God's righteousness, even though they were not seeking that righteousness. Like the remnant, they have been called forth to be part of God's eschatological people, composed of Gentiles as well as Jews. But in addition to Paul's important statement about this people, which he describes in 9:24–26, Paul's allegory of the olive tree clearly affirms that these Gentile believers have been grafted into the cultivated olive tree that is Israel. Like the remnant, then, they are part of Israel (but not a new Israel), rooted in the patriarchs. Unlike the remnant, however, Gentile believers have been grafted into a tree to which they do not belong by nature. They belong to Israel, but they are not and cannot be Jewish.

In regard to the third point—the rest of Israel that has been disobedient and upon whom a hardening has come—Paul affirms three things. First, the rest of Israel does not belong to the people that God has called forth from among the Gentiles as well as from the Jews. Second, because of their unbelief, they have been cut off like branches from the tree that gave them life. Third, the hardening that has come upon them is temporary, because when the full number of the Gentiles is grafted into the tree, then the branches that were cut off will be grafted in again. Although Paul says that "the rest" have been "cut off," he continues to call them "Israelites" (9:4), enumerating the gifts that God has bestowed upon them because of their election. More important, as Paul has shown in chapter 11, their disobedience paradoxically plays a positive role in the salvation of the Gentiles, just as the salvation of the Gentiles plays a positive role in Israel's redemption. Thus, even though Paul says that they have been "cut off" from the tree, he strongly affirms that God has not rejected his people (11:1) and that they have not stumbled to the point of falling once and for all (11:11). The rest of Israel remains Israel, the people of God. And the election of the rest is secure because God's call is irrevocable. The status of these three groups can be summarized in this way:

The Remnant of Israel

belongs by birth to the tree of Israel; it has not been cut off

belongs to a people whom God has called from Gentiles and Jews, the church

The Gentiles

have been grafted into the tree of Israel

belong to a people whom God has called from Gentiles and Jews, the church

The Rest of Israel

belongs by birth to the tree of Israel; it has been cut off

will be regrafted into the tree to which it belongs by birth

In light of these observations, I propose four theses about *Paul's understanding* of Israel and the church. I emphasize the words "Paul's understanding" because I am focusing on the historical meaning of Rom. 9–11. Later, I will suggest some applications of these theses for the present day.

1. *The church is not the new Israel.* There is no place in Rom. 9–11 or anywhere in Paul's writings where the apostle equates Israel and the church. Israel refers to a historical people with a past, a present, and a future. The church refers to the eschatological people of God that has already made its appearance and will find its completion when all Israel will be saved. At that moment, Israel and the church will converge.

2. *Historical Israel remains God's people.* Although Israel has not believed in the gospel, Israel remains God's people since the call and the gifts of God are irrevocable. To deny Israel's status as God's people (here I am referring to the Jewish people rather than to the modern state of Israel) is to call into question the faithfulness and uprightness of God.

3. *Although Gentile believers have been grafted into Israel, they are not Israelites.* For Paul, the Gentile members of the congregations that he calls "the churches of God" belong to the historical people of Israel. This, however, does not mean that they have become Jews or have replaced the Jewish people. Paul is insistent that Gentiles should maintain their own identity rather than adopt a Jewish identity. But by God's grace, Gentiles have been given a place in the tree that is Israel.

4. *Israel and the church overlap.* The church is not Israel, and Israel is not the church. But there is an overlap between Israel and the church that does not entail one enveloping the other. Because of the believing remnant and those Gentiles who have been grafted into Israel, something

of the church resides in Israel, and something of Israel resides in the church.

While my observations have attempted to summarize how Paul understood the relation between Israel and the church in his time, they have implications for contemporary Christianity and Judaism, both of whose circumstances have greatly changed since the time of Paul. I mention three points made from the perspective of a believing Christian in the hope that they will strengthen the relations between Jews and Christians. First, the Jewish people remain God's covenant people, chosen by divine election; God has not and will not repudiate them. Second, while Christians sometimes refer to the church as the new Israel, they need to be careful when they employ this expression. If one understands it to mean that the church is rooted in Israel, then this designation may be of some value for Christians. But if they understand it to mean that the church has "replaced" the historical people of Israel, they are claiming more than Paul affirms. Third, the continued existence of Israel in the Jewish people is God's mystery with which Christians must grapple, a mystery of divine election that should remind Christians of their origins and preclude every temptation toward any kind of anti-Semitism. In God's way (not our way), in God's time (not our time), in God's wisdom (not our wisdom), all Israel will be saved.

PART 5

Romans 12:1–15:13

God's Righteousness and the
Moral Life of the Justified

⌘

In the fifth and final part of Romans, Paul presents his readers with an extended moral exhortation in which he urges them to live a morally good life made possible by the saving righteousness that God has manifested in Christ's death and resurrection. Accordingly, I have titled this part of the letter "God's Righteousness and the Moral Life of the Justified." In doing so, I am highlighting two things: (1) the thematic role that the righteousness of God plays throughout this letter, and (2) the integral role that the moral life plays in Paul's exposition of the gospel. Rather than serving as an appendix that is unrelated to Paul's gospel of God's righteousness, this exhortation provides a fitting conclusion to his exposition of the gospel by explaining how God's saving justice unfolds in the life of the Christian community.

There is general agreement among commentators that this exhortation consists of two sections. In the first, which I have titled, "Love and Obedience in the New Age" (12:1–13:14), Paul focuses on the topics of love and nonretaliation in order to exhort his audience to live as a community of believers who form one body in Christ. Believers live in this way when they offer themselves as living sacrifices to God and allow themselves to be transformed by the renewal of their minds, which God's saving justice makes possible (12:1–2).

Believers ought to live in this way because the time for their eschatological salvation is at hand (13:11–14).

In the second section, which I have titled "Welcoming One Another according to the Example of Christ" (14:1–15:13), Paul's exhortation becomes more specific as he deals with a problem within the Roman community. Adjudicating between two factions that he identifies as the strong and the weak, he exhorts the Roman Christians not to judge or scandalize one another because of differing opinions regarding diet and the observance of particular days but to sustain and receive one another as Christ has received them (15:7–13). Paul's exhortation to receive one another as Christ has received them grounds this section in the gospel of God's saving justice.

Although the second section of Paul's moral exhortation is more specific than the first, this does not mean that the first section presents timeless truths and the second section is merely concerned with a particular community problem. Although general in nature, the moral exhortation of 12:1–13:14 also deals with a specific issue, the payment of taxes (13:1–7), whereas the second exhortation (14:1–15:13), which is more specific in content, concludes with a statement that summarizes Paul's gospel of God's righteousness (15:7–13). Thus N. T. Wright (2002, 701–2) notes "that chapters 12 and 13 are more general, laying foundations, though not without an eye to the particular situation, and that chapters 14 and 15 are more specific, though not without an eye to other situations . . . and other related issues."

Romans 12:1–13:14

Love and Obedience in the New Age

Introductory Matters

Paul's teaching in Rom. 12:1–15:13 is usually identified as paraenesis, a species of moral exhortation that encourages people to continue in a particular way of life. The purpose of paraenesis, then, is not so much to provide new instruction as it is to encourage people to do what they already know they ought to do. David Aune (2003, 334) lists five characteristics of paraenesis: (1) It "is traditional, reflecting conventional wisdom, generally approved by society." (2) It "is applicable to many situations." (3) It "is so familiar that it is often presented as a 'reminder.' " (4) It "can be exemplified in exceptional people who are models of virtue." (5) It "is usually transmitted by people who are regarded as socially and morally superior to those they address."

Because Paul must encourage his congregations to maintain the new faith they have so recently embraced, paraenesis plays an important role in his letters. The paraenesis of some letters is a clearly defined unit that occurs toward the end of the letter (Rom. 12:1–15:13; Gal. 5:1–6:10; Col. 3:1–4:6; Eph. 4:1–6:20), but in other letters, paraenesis occurs throughout the letter (1 and 2 Corinthians, Philippians). And in the case of 1 Thessalonians the whole letter is paraenetic (Stowers 1986, 96). Accordingly, while there is a temptation to think that Paul reserves his ethical teaching for the final part of his letters, after he has completed his doctrinal exposition, he actually employs paraenesis in a variety of ways, depending upon the needs of his audience.

In the case of Romans, Paul reserves his paraenesis for the end of the letter in order to show the Romans how the gospel he proclaims can work itself out in their community life if they allow themselves to be transformed by the renewal of their minds, which God has made possible in Christ. To accomplish this, Paul must do several things. First, he must employ traditional topics with which the community is familiar. Accordingly, he reminds the Romans of the gifts they have received for building up the community, the centrality of love and nonretaliation, the imminence of their salvation, and the example of Christ. Second, on the basis of what he knows about the community from others, he must tailor this material to the specific situation of the Roman community. Accordingly, he discusses the question of paying taxes to the Roman authorities and the tensions within the community between those whom he calls the weak and the strong. The result is a paraenesis that, although tailored to the needs of the community, is meaningful to others as well.

Those who read through this paraenesis should avoid two extremes: (1) treating this paraenesis as if it were a summary or compendium of Paul's ethics, (2) viewing this paraenesis as so situational that it has little or no meaning for those who read Romans today. The goal of Rom. 12:1–15:13 is not to lay down the foundation for ethics but to show the intimate relationship between the gospel and life. By providing this paraenesis, Paul shows the Romans that the gospel he preaches is the deepest source of the moral life. For those who want to construct a Pauline ethic, the best starting points are chapter 6, where Paul speaks about the moral life in relation to baptism, and chapter 8, where he discusses the moral life in relation to the Spirit. It is in these chapters rather than chapters 12–13 that one finds the proper starting point for Pauline ethics.

The manner in which Paul relates gospel and paraenesis in Romans goes beyond the use of paraenesis in the Greco-Roman world. For while Paul's paraenesis makes use of traditional topics that would have been familiar to his readers, and while he can legitimately present himself as the embodiment of the teaching he presents, he configures his paraenesis in terms of God's righteousness. Accordingly, although much of Paul's moral exhortation would have been familiar to the Romans from what other Christian teachers had taught them, the manner in which he relates his moral exhortation to his gospel of God's righteousness would not have been familiar to them. The uniqueness of Paul's paraenesis, then, is the way he relates it to his gospel: the justified can live in Christ, the eschatological human being, because God has overcome the power of sin that held sway over Adamic humanity.

Tracing the Train of Thought

This section consists of six units. The first is the foundation for all that follows (12:1–2). It exhorts the justified to offer their redeemed bodies as a living

Romans 12:1–13:14 in the Rhetorical Flow

The letter opening (1:1–17)

Gentiles and Jews in the light of God's wrath (1:18–3:20)

Gentiles and Jews in the light of God's righteousness (3:21–4:25)

The experience of salvation in the light of God's righteousness (5:1–8:39)

God's righteousness and the destiny of Israel (9:1–11:36)

God's righteousness and the moral life of the justified (12:1–15:13)

▶**Love and obedience in the new age (12:1–13:14)**

Paul's fundamental moral exhortation (12:1–2)

Offer your body as a sacrifice to God (12:1)

Be transformed by the renewal of your mind (12:2)

Living as one body in Christ (12:3–8)

Think humbly of yourself (12:3)

Supporting reason (12:4–5)

Application (12:6–8)

Genuine love (12:9–21)

First set of maxims (12:9–13)

Second set of maxims (12:14–21)

Subordination to those in authority (13:1–7)

Initial exhortation to be subject to governing authorities (13:1a)

A supporting argument (13:1b–2)

A further argument in diatribal form (13:3–5)

The application of the argument to the question of taxes (13:6–7)

Love as the fulfillment of the law (13:8–10)

An initial exhortation to love one another (13:8a)

Supporting argument (13:8b–10)

The moral life in light of the end (13:11–14)

The nearness of the hour (13:11)

Two sets of contrasts (13:12)

Exhortation to live accordingly (13:13–14)

sacrifice to God and to be transformed by the renewal of their minds so that they can discern God's will. In the second unit, Paul provides an example of how a renewed mind results in a new kind of community life (12:3–8). Since believers are one body in Christ, they should serve one another by exercising the gifts they have received for the sake of one another. In the third unit, Paul provides a series of maxims to illustrate how the renewed mind can transform the life of the community so that each member is concerned for the needs of others and no one seeks to retaliate when injured (12:9–21). This first maxim—that love should be genuine (12:9)—functions as the leitmotif for the maxims that follow, each of which illustrates that nature of genuine love. The fourth unit is related to Paul's injunction in the previous unit not to retaliate. It exhorts believers to be subject to the governing authorities and to pay taxes (13:1–7). The fifth unit is related to the fourth by the catchword "owe" (13:8–10). Believers are to pay taxes to those to whom they are *owed* (13:7); and they are to *owe* no other debt than to love one another (13:8), for love is the fulfillment of the law. In the final unit, Paul reminds the Romans that they are to live a morally good life since the hour of their salvation is closer than when they first embraced the faith (13:11–14). Like the opening unit (12:1–2), this one points to the eschatological dimension of the moral life that the new age has made possible.

12:1–2. All commentators recognize the importance of these verses for Paul's moral exhortation. More than an introduction to what he is about to say, they relate what he will say (12:3–15:14) to what he has already said in Rom. 1–11, thereby reinforcing the intimate relation that he draws between the gospel and the morally good life. In the first verse, Paul exhorts his audience to offer their bodies as a living sacrifice to God, a striking metaphor suggesting that the morally good life of the justified is an act worship: **Therefore, brothers and sisters, I exhort you through God's compassion to offer your bodies as a living sacrifice, holy and pleasing to God—your spiritual worship** (12:1). In the second verse, he employs two imperatives, one negative, the other positive, to exhort the community: **Do not conform yourselves to this age but be transformed by the renewal of your mind so that you may discern God's will: what is good, what is pleasing, what is perfect** (12:2). By focusing on the "body" in the first verse and the "mind" in the second, Paul accomplishes two things: First, he indicates that the moral life encompasses the entire person as an embodied and thinking self. Second, he draws an implicit contrast between redeemed and unredeemed humanity.

The opening words of Paul's exhortation in 12:1 relate what he is about to say to what he has already said in two ways. First, the conjunction *oun* (therefore) signals that he is drawing an inference from what he has written thus far. Second, the phrase *dia tōn oiktirmōn* ("through God's compassion," usually translated "through the mercies of God") suggests that Paul is drawing this inference on the basis of the compassion that God has manifested toward humanity in Jesus Christ. Because of this compassion, Paul can confidently exhort the Romans "to offer" (*parastēsai*) their bodies as "a living sacrifice . . . to God."

Paul's exhortation that the Romans offer their bodies as a living sacrifice to God (12:1) echoes his exhortation that they should no longer present (*paristanete*) the members of their bodies as instruments of wickedness in the service of sin but present (*parastēsate*) themselves to God (6:13). The use of "body" (*sōma*), by which Paul means the embodied self, recalls earlier uses of this term in 1:24 (where he describes humanity as dishonoring the body by impurity), in 6:6 (where he speaks of the body as dominated by sin), in 6:12 (where he exhorts the Romans not to let sin rule in their mortal body), and in 7:24 (where unredeemed humanity asks who will redeem it from the body doomed to death).

By echoing these texts, Paul draws a striking contrast between the justified and the unredeemed. Before being incorporated into Christ, the unredeemed dishonored their bodies and presented the parts of their bodies as instruments of wickedness in the service of sin, but thanks to God's compassion in Christ, they can now offer their redeemed bodies to God as a "living sacrifice" that is "holy and pleasing to God." Paul calls this sacrifice their "spiritual worship" (*logikēn latreian*). By a "living sacrifice" (*thysian zōsan*), he means a sacrifice "that does not die as it is offered but goes on living and therefore continues in its efficacy" (D. Moo 1996, 751) because the believer now lives in newness of life (Cranfield 1979, 600). Such a sacrifice stands in stark contrast to the sacrifices of the temple cult that were put to death before they were offered. Only a living sacrifice, characterized by newness of life, is holy and pleasing to God, because it is an act of "spiritual worship." Although commentators disagree about the meaning of this phrase, which many translate as "rational worship," the sense is worship that accords with thinking beings who freely offer themselves in God's service.

The use of "worship" to describe the morally good life establishes a contrast with Paul's earlier description of unredeemed humanity. Those under the wrath of God "dishonored their bodies" (1:24) and "worshiped and served the creature rather than the Creator" (1:25), but the justified worship God in a way that is pleasing to God by offering themselves as a living sacrifice through a morally good life.

Having spoken of the new situation of the justified in terms of the embodied self, Paul turns his attention to the justified as thinking beings, encouraging the Romans not to conform themselves to this age but to be transformed by the renewal of their mind so that they can discern God's will (12:2). The injunction not to be conformed to "this age" (*tō aiōni toutō*) recalls the contrast that Paul established between those in Adam and those in Christ (5:12–21). When they were in Adam, those who are now justified belonged to the old age. But inasmuch as the old age has not yet disappeared, it is still possible for those in Christ to fall back and be reconfigured to Adamic humanity. If they are to avoid this, they must discern God's will. This is why Paul urges his converts to "be transformed" (*metamorphousthe*; cf. 2 Cor. 3:18) by the renewal of their mind. For only when the mind has been renewed can thinking beings know what is good, pleasing, and perfect in God's sight.

In summoning the Romans to be transformed by the renewal of their mind, Paul recalls his earlier description of humanity under the wrath of God (Furnish

1968, 102–4). When humanity did not glorify or thank God as God, it gave itself to futile speculations and its senseless heart was darkened. Thinking itself wise, it was actually foolish (1:21–22). And because humans *did not discern* what is true about God, God "delivered them over to their *undiscerning mind* to do what is not proper" (1:28). The justified, however, have died with Christ so that, just as he was raised from the dead, they might walk in "newness of life" (*en kainotēti zōēs*, 6:4). By urging the Romans to be transformed by the renewal of their mind, then, Paul exhorts them to live the newness of life that their baptism into Christ's death has made possible. By doing so, they will "discern" (*dokimazein*) God's will in a way that those who possessed the law could not (2:18).

To summarize, in these two verses Paul describes the morally good life as an act of worship made possible by God, whose compassion in Christ enables believers to present their embodied selves as a living sacrifice to God and discern God's will through their renewed mind.

12:3–8. Having introduced his exhortation by placing all that he will say in the context of the new situation in which the justified find themselves (12:1–2), Paul summons the Romans to live as one body (12:3–8). By doing so, they will show that they are being transformed by the renewal of their minds that has been made possible through their participation in Christ's death. The train of thought in this unit proceeds in three steps. First, Paul exhorts the Romans to think humbly of themselves (12:3). Second, he supports this exhortation by drawing an analogy between the human body and the believing community, which is one body in Christ (12:4–5). Finally, he applies the analogy to the Romans by encouraging them to use their diverse gifts for the sake of one another (12:6–8).

Paul begins his exhortation with an introduction that reminds the Romans of the grace that has been given to him: **Through the grace that has been given to me, I say to each one of you** (12:3a). Although he does not specify the grace that has been granted him, he is undoubtedly referring to his apostleship. In 15:15, after he has completed this paraenesis, he will make a similar statement in order to explain why he has written so boldly. Next, Paul employs a negative imperative followed by a strong adversative to exhort the Romans not to think more highly of themselves than they ought: **do not think more of yourself than what you should think, but think in a way that you think sensibly in accord with the measure of faith that God has apportioned to each one** (12:3b). My rather wooden translation seeks to reproduce the play on words found in the Greek text: "do not think more" (*mē hyperphronein*), "should think" (*dei phronein*), "but think" (*alla phronein*), "think sensibly" (*eis to sōphronein*). Paul's injunction to think sensibly is related to his exhortation that the Romans should be transformed by the renewal of their mind (12:2); the transformation that Paul has in view involves a new way of thinking about oneself in relation to others. Paul will employ the verb *phronein* (to think) two more times (12:16), thereby indicating how important this new way of thinking is for him.

The curious phrase that qualifies how the Romans are to think sensibly ("in accord with the measure of faith [*metron pisteōs*] that God has apportioned to each one") can be construed in several ways (Cranfield 1979, 613–16), only two of which I will present. First, if "faith" is understood as the act of believing and "measure" is construed as how much of this gift of believing one has received, the meaning would be that each one is to think in proportion to the gift of believing that God has granted, the presupposition being that people have received different capacities for believing. Second, if "faith" is understood as the content of what is believed and "measure" as a norm, then the meaning would be that each one is to think in accord with the norm of what is to be believed. Reliable commentators have adopted some form of the first interpretation, but I am inclined to adopt the second because it provides the Romans with a more objective norm for thinking about themselves in relation to one another.

Having enjoined the Romans to adopt a new way of thinking about themselves in accord with the norm of faith, Paul draws an analogy between the body understood as a physical organism and the community understood as a body: **For just as we have many members in one body, and not all of the members have the same function, so we who are many are one body in Christ and individually members of one another** (12:4–5). The first part of the analogy (which Paul draws out in greater detail in 1 Cor. 12:14–26) needs little explanation: each member of the human body has a different function for the good of the whole body. On the basis of this example, Paul draws out his analogy: the Christian community is a body in which each individual is joined to every other member of the community. Although such an analogy would have been familiar to the Romans since "the comparison of the 'body politic' to the human body was well known in the Greco-Roman world" (Tobin 2004, 391), the addition of the phrase "in Christ" adds a new dimension to this metaphor. Without explicitly saying that the members of his audience are "the body of Christ" in the way that he does in 1 Cor. 12:27, Paul points out that their unity as a body derives from their existence in Christ.

Having explained why they should think in a new way about themselves within the context of their community, Paul applies his analogy to their situation: **We have different gifts according to the grace given to us. If we possess the gift of prophecy, let us use it in agreement with faith. If we possess the gift of service, let us use it in service. If we possess the gift of teaching, let us use it in teaching. If we possess the gift of consoling, let us use it in consoling. Let the giver give generously. Let the leader lead with all diligence. Let the one who is merciful be merciful cheerfully** (12:6–8). The gifts that Paul mentions are hardly exhaustive, and others can be found in the lists of 1 Cor. 12:4–11 and Eph. 4:11. Paul names seven gifts: (1) *prophecy*, the gift to discern

God's will and plan through the power of the Spirit; (2) *service*, the gift to be of assistance to others within the community; (3) *teaching*, the gift to instruct others by explaining the faith; (4) *consoling*, the gift of comforting others; (5) *giving*, the gift of almsgiving; (6) *leading*, the gift of leadership, in this instance perhaps oversight of the community's alms; and (7) *mercy*, the gift of performing acts of mercy for others. Without identifying the giver of these gifts, Paul notes that they are possessed "according to the grace [*kata tēn charin*] given to us," thereby indicating that each gift is a particular manifestation of God's favor.

Since Paul's purpose is to encourage the unity of the community, he does not merely list the gifts; he also exhorts the Romans to exercise them for the good of all. In three instances (service, teaching, and consoling), his statement is rather banal and repetitive. In three others (giving, leading, merciful), he explains how these gift should be exercised. In the case of prophecy, he adds, "Let us use it in agreement with faith" (*kata tēn analogian tēs pisteōs*; lit., "according to the analogy of faith"). As with the expression "the measure of faith," the precise meaning of these words is disputed. On the one hand, they could mean "in accordance with the faith (understood as the act of believing) that one has received," thereby suggesting that one prophesies according to the gift one has to believe. On the other hand, the phrase could mean "in right relationship to the faith (understood as the content of what is believed)," thereby suggesting that prophecy should be in accordance with what is believed. As my translation indicates, I favor the latter position since the content of faith provides the recipients of the letter with a more objective norm.

To summarize, by exhorting the Romans to think in a new way that will allow them to live as one body in Christ, Paul provides a concrete example of what it means to be transformed by the renewal of their minds.

12:9–21. Having provided his audience with an example of community life guided by the renewed mind that transforms believers, Paul introduces a series of maxims to assist the Romans in living as one body in Christ (12:9–21). There is little agreement among commentators as to the internal structure and cohesion of this passage. For example, James Dunn (1988, 2:737) characterizes the passage as a loosely constructed paragraph, whereas Robert Jewett (2007, 756) argues that "it is artfully constructed for rhetorical impact and closely related to the tensions between the Christian groups in Rome." There is some agreement, however, that there is a minor break between 12:13 and 12:14. In 12:9–13 Paul employs a series of participial phrases that function as imperatives; in 12:14–21 he disrupts this pattern with a series of imperatival infinitives.

In terms of content, the unit is guided by Paul's initial injunction that love should be without pretense (12:9a). All of the maxims in the first subunit (12:9–13) focus on life within the community, and some of those in the second (12:14–21) focus on the community in relation to its enemies, enjoining the

Romans not to retaliate or seek vengeance. By introducing the theme of nonretaliation in the second subunit, Paul prepares for the next, in which he will counsel the Romans to be subject to and pay taxes to the governing authorities (13:1–7). My discussion focuses on twelve maxims that Paul proposes to the Romans.

Paul's initial maxim serves as the leitmotif for what follows. It begins with a simple statement, *hē agapē anypokritos* (lit., "love [is] without pretense"), that nearly all translations render as an imperative: **Let love be without pretense** (12:9a). In 2 Cor. 6:6 Paul describes his own love in this way. The adjective is also employed by 1 Pet. 1:22 in relation to love and by 1 Tim. 1:5; 2 Tim. 1:5; and James 3:17 in relation to faith, thus suggesting that faith and love can be practiced in ways that are hypocritical if one is not careful. To explain what he means by genuine love, Paul exhorts the Romans: **Hate what is evil. Hold fast to what is good** (12:9b). In doing so, he reminds them of

> **Twelve Maxims**
>
> 1. Let love be sincere (12:9).
> 2. Be devoted to one another in love (12:10).
> 3. Be zealous in serving the Lord (12:11).
> 4. Persevere (12:12).
> 5. Contribute to the needs of others (12:13).
> 6. Do not retaliate (12:14).
> 7. Empathize with others (12:15).
> 8. Do not be high-minded (12:16).
> 9. Do not retaliate (12:17).
> 10. Be at peace with all (12:18).
> 11. Do not avenge yourselves (12:19–20).
> 12. Do not be conquered by evil (12:21).

the ongoing struggle that the attainment of genuine love involves, and he implicitly warns them that love can be lost if one does not exhibit a vehement dislike (*apostygountes*) for what is evil and an active clinging (*kollōmenoi*) to what is good.

In his second maxim, Paul exhorts the Romans: **Be devoted to one another in mutual love** (12:10a). The use of *philadelphia* ("mutual love"; lit., "brotherly love") invokes the kind of love ordinarily reserved for family members, but which Paul and other Christian writers apply to the love that ought to characterize the "new family" of those in Christ (see 1 Thess. 4:9; Heb. 13:1; 1 Pet. 1:22). Paul specifies that such love entails **outdoing one another in honoring one another** (12:10b). Thus, whereas those who are conformed to this age seek their own honor, those who are transformed by the renewal of their mind seek the honor of others.

Although Paul's third and fourth maxims do not speak of love, they provide the community with six injunctions to preserve the fervor that is necessary for maintaining the kind of community that Paul envisions. The first three emphasize the importance of preserving the community's initial fervor by avoiding the indolence that prevents one from serving the Lord: **Do not be slack in zeal, be aglow in the Spirit, serve the Lord** (12:11). The second three provide advice for maintaining zeal in the face of the difficulties that believers will inevitably encounter: **Rejoice in hope, persevere in affliction, continue in prayer** (12:12). Hope (5:2, 4, 5; 8:20, 24) and affliction (5:3; 8:35) have been major themes in this letter. In light of what Paul has already said about them, it is apparent that he encourages the community to continue in prayer and persevere in affliction in their hope for the general resurrection of the dead.

The fifth maxim is more clearly related to the theme of genuine love, enjoining the community, **Contribute to the needs of the holy ones, pursue hospitality** (12:13). Although "the holy ones" (*tōn hagiōn*) could mean all Christians since all who belong to Christ are "holy" because they have been set aside and consecrated for service to him, here "the holy ones" may refer to the members of the different Roman house churches, some of whom were better off than others. The injunction to "pursue hospitality" was especially important in the ancient world, where Christian missionaries depended on the hospitality of others (Heb. 13:2; 3 John 5–8). But here the injunction may also have in view the need for the members of the different Roman house churches to be hospitable toward one another (see Rom. 15:7, where Paul will exhort the Romans to receive one another as Christ has received them).

Paul's sixth maxim marks a change of style and content that signals the beginning of the second subunit (12:14–21). Employing an imperatival infinitive rather than a participial infinitive, he explains how genuine love deals with those who persecute and abuse the community: **Bless those who persecute you; bless and do not curse them** (12:14). This carefully balanced couplet echoes Jesus's teaching as found in the Sermon on the Mount and the Sermon on the Plain, but it does not reproduce his explicit teaching "Love your enemies" (Matt. 5:44; Luke 6:28). It does, however, explain that genuine love requires believers to ask God to bestow favor rather than evil upon those who persecute them.

The seventh maxim is another carefully balanced couplet that begins with an imperatival infinitive: **Rejoice with those who are rejoicing, weep with those who are weeping** (12:15). The object of the maxim, however, is not clear since it could refer to those within the community as well as those outside the community. In the case of the eighth maxim (12:16), however, it appears that Paul does have the community in view. Like the maxims in the first subunit, this one makes use of a participial imperative. As he did in 12:3, Paul highlights the importance of thinking in a new way that reflects the renewed mind. This maxim has four lines, with a negative imperative standing at the end of the second and fourth lines:

> *Think* [*phronountes*] in the same way toward each other.
> *Do not think* [*mē phronountes*] in a way that is haughty,
> but associate with those who are lowly.
> *Do not consider yourself wise* [*mē ginesthe phronimoi*] in your own
> estimation. (12:16)

With his ninth maxim, Paul returns to the theme of nonretaliation, echoing what he wrote in 1 Thess. 5:15: **Do not render evil for evil to anyone; have in mind to do what is good in the sight of all** (12:17). As in other maxims, the second part, which echoes the LXX form of Prov. 3:4, helps to clarify the first. Not only are believers not to retaliate. Rather, they are to give careful thought to what is good in the sight of others, an injunction that reflects Paul's own behavior (2 Cor. 8:21). The tenth maxim, which also appears to have those outside the community in view, is closely related to this maxim: **If possible, to the extent that it is in your power, be at peace with everyone** (12:18). The initial qualification, however, suggests that this may not always be possible if, for example, it requires believers to compromise what they believe.

Paul's eleventh maxim is his longest, differing from the others in two ways. First, he addresses the Romans as "beloved. " Second, he supports his injunction not to seek vengeance with a scriptural quotation that is a conflation of Deut. 32:35 and Prov. 25:21–22a LXX. The maxim begins with a negative participial imperative: **Beloved, do not seek to avenge yourselves** (12:19a). This is followed by a strong adversative that is supported by a scriptural quotation: **but allow "the wrath" to take its course. For it is written, "Punishment belongs to me, I will exact repayment," says the Lord. But if your enemy is hungry, feed him. If he is thirsty, give him something to drink. For by doing this, you will pile blazing coals upon his head** (12:19b–20). "The wrath," which has played such a prominent role in this letter (1:18; 2:5, 8; 3:5; 5:9; 9:22), refers to God's wrath. As in the rest of Romans, it is a metaphor for God's judgment rather than an emotion of God. The final remark about piling "blazing coals" upon the enemy's head has been construed in different ways: (1) as a metaphor for the punishment that God will bring upon one's enemy; (2) as a metaphor for the shame that will come upon one's enemy, perhaps leading the enemy to repentance.

The twelfth and final maxim is so closely related to the eleventh that one could easily read the two as one: **Do not be conquered by evil, but conquer evil by what is good** (12:21). This neatly balanced couplet provides the ultimate rationale for avoiding vengeance. To participate in evil is to be conquered by it, whereas to refuse to retaliate is to conquer evil by good, as Christ did.

To summarize, through these maxims Paul shows the community how those with a renewed mind are transformed rather than conformed to this age.

13:1–7. Having exhorted the Christians at Rome to practice genuine love and not to retaliate or avenge themselves, Paul takes up a specific issue: the obligation of the justified to submit themselves to the authorities that rule over them by paying taxes and revenues (13:1–7). Although the moral exhortation that he gives here appears to have been occasioned by, and tailored to, the needs of the Roman Christians, it has commanded "the sustained attention of interpreters in the last two millennia" (Reasoner 2005, 129) because of what it says about the source of political authority and the obligation that believers have toward that authority, a topic that I will consider under "Theological Issues."

The unit consists of four subunits: an initial exhortation that functions as a thesis statement (13:1a), a supporting argument for the thesis (13:1b–2), a further argument that exhibits characteristics of a diatribe (13:3–5), and the application of the thesis to the question of paying taxes and revenues (13:6–7).

Paul begins by announcing his thesis: **Let everyone be subject to the governing authorities** (13:1a). Two points are important here. First, the subject that Paul has in view is the thinking and willing self (*pasa psychē*; lit., "every soul"), which I have translated as "everyone." By highlighting the reflecting self as the subject of this unit, Paul relates this exhortation to his opening injunction that believers should be transformed by the renewal of their minds (12:2). Second, in exhorting the reflecting self to "subject" (*hypotassesthō*) itself to the governing authorities, Paul reminds believers that they are part of an ordered society in which they should find and acknowledge their place. Accordingly, he is not so much summoning the Romans to obey the governing authorities (although this is not excluded) as he is exhorting them to find their place in an ordered society and live accordingly. The "governing authorities" (*exousiais hyperechousais*) to which they are to submit are not angelic powers but human rulers who exercise "a variety of imperial and local offices" (Jewett 2007, 788) within the Roman Empire.

Paul supports his injunction in two ways. First, he points to God as the source of all authority: **for there is no authority except that appointed by God, and those that exist have been put in place by God** (13:1b). In making this statement, Paul is not breaking new ground but affirming what Israel's scriptures already teach. For example, God's personified wisdom proclaims, "By me kings reign, and rulers decree what is just; by me rulers rule, and nobles, all who govern rightly" (Prov. 8:15–16). Similarly, Daniel reveals to Nebuchadnezzar, "He [God] changes times and seasons, deposes kings and sets up kings; he gives wisdom to those who have understanding" (Dan. 2:21). And again, "You [Nebuchadnezzar] shall be made to eat grass like oxen, and seven times shall pass over you, until you have learned that the Most High has sovereignty over the kingdom of mortals and gives it to whom he will" (4:32). The notion that all authority comes from God, which is difficult for contemporary readers to understand, derives from Paul's understanding of God as the source and origin of all things (1 Cor. 8:6).

Second, having affirmed that God is the source of all authority, Paul draws out the consequences of opposing those who are in authority: **Consequently, the one who resists the governing authority resists God's ordinance, and those who resist will bring judgment upon themselves** (13:2). The resistance that Paul has in view is more than disobedience; it is a refusal to acknowledge one's role within the ordered structure of society, which derives from God's ordinance. Playing on the root of the verb "to resist" and of the noun "ordinance," Paul writes that "the one who resists" (*antitassomenos*) resists God's "ordinance" (*diatagē*), by which he means the divine decree that accounts for the structure of society. Those who oppose this ordinance bring "judgment" (*krima*) upon themselves. This judgment is God's own judgment rather than the punishment that those in authority mete out (Cranfield 1979, 664).

Addressing an imaginary interlocutor who is fearful of the authorities, Paul reverts to the style of the diatribe in his second argument (13:3–5). The material unfolds in four movements: a thesis statement (13:3a), a question and response (13:3b), a supporting reason for submitting to those in authority (13:4), and a conclusion (13:5). The thesis statement provides the Romans with a positive reason for subjecting themselves to the governing authorities: **For rulers are not an occasion of fear when it is a matter of good conduct but when it is a matter of bad conduct** (13:3a). What Paul writes here is similar to the text of 1 Pet. 3:13, "Now who is going to harm you if you are enthusiastic for what is good?" (NAB). Although the argument of this unit may appear naive, given the manner in which governments often exercise authority, it is premised on Paul's contention that all authority derives from God. This enables the apostle to affirm that believers who do what is right need not fear those who rule.

Having presented his thesis, Paul employs the diatribe style to question his imaginary interlocutor: **You do not want to fear the ruling authority? Then do what is good, and you will receive its approval** (Rom. 13:3b). Both the question and answer are premised on Paul's thesis that all authority comes from God. Consequently, since rulers have received their authority from God, only those who do evil need fear them. Those who do good need not be fearful, for they will meet with the authority's approval. The language of "approval" (*epainon*) also occurs in 1 Pet. 2:13–14, which stands as a close parallel to this text: "For the Lord's sake accept the authority of every human institution, whether of the emperor as supreme, or of governors as sent by him for the punishment of evildoers and the *approval* of those who do good."

Having explained why those who do good need not fear those who rule over them, Paul in 13:4 provides his audience with a supporting reason for what he has said. This carefully constructed verse uses three clauses, each introduced by the conjunction "for" (*gar*). The first *gar* clause supports what Paul has just said in the previous verse: **for it is God's servant for your sake, for what is good** (13:4a). There is no need to fear the one who rules, *for* the ruling authority is God's "servant" (*diakonos*) for what is good. Once more it is imperative to recall Paul's working premise that God is the source of all authority. On the basis of the premise, Paul affirms that God employs those who rule as his servants to assure the social order necessary for people to attain the good that God wills for them. Next, Paul issues a warning: **But if you do what is evil, then be afraid** (13:4b), which he explains by a second *gar* clause: **for it is not without reason that it holds the power of the sword** (13:4c). Employing the sword as a metaphor for the authority that rulers have to inflict punishment, Paul reminds his audience of the legitimate power that rulers have "to coerce recalcitrant citizens to maintain order and strive for the common good" (Fitzmyer 1993, 668). In the third *gar* clause, Paul explains why rulers inflict punishment. Again describing the ruler as God's servant, Paul writes: **for it is God's servant as an agent that punishes with a view to retribution for those who do evil** (13:4d). Accordingly, the ruler works as God's servant in two ways. First, the ruler is God's servant so that people can attain what is good (13:4a). Second, the ruler is God's servant as "an agent that punishes" (*ekdikos*) those who do evil for the purpose of "retribution" (*orgēn*). Given the rulers' role to punish, there should be no need for individuals to take vengeance (as Paul exhorted in 12:14, 17, 19–21) since God is already working through his servants to punish those who do evil.

Making use of the coordinating conjunction *dio* (therefore), Paul draws his conclusion: **Therefore, it is necessary to be subject, not only on account of retribution but also for the sake of conscience** (13:5). This verse suggests that there is an inherent necessity (*anankē*) in the social order, and it provides two reasons why Paul's audience must be subject to the ruling authorities: the first is external, the second internal. On the one hand, believers should fear "retribution" (*orgēn*), by which Paul means God's wrath and judgment, as well as the punishment that rulers can inflict. On the other hand, they should be subject "for the sake of conscience." Here "conscience" refers to the knowledge and moral awareness that the reflecting self has about the structure of society and its role within this order.

The use of the infinitive "to be subject" (*hyptassesthai*) in 13:5 echoes the imperative "be subject" in 13:1a, thereby enclosing verses 1–5 in a literary bracket. Verses 6–7, then, function as a conclusion that applies the teaching of verses 1–5 to the specific circumstances of the Roman Christians, some of whom may have questioned the propriety of paying taxes to the Roman Empire. There are two parts to this subunit. In the first, Paul draws a specific conclusion: **This is why you pay taxes** (13:6a). What Paul means is that the Roman Christians ought to pay taxes because of their place in the social hierarchy he has just described. To support this conclusion, he introduces another *gar* clause: **for those in authority are God's ministers, devoting themselves to this very thing** (13:6b). Having called the ruler God's "servant" (*diakonos*) in 13:4, Paul now identifies rulers as God's "ministers" (*leitourgoi*), which can refer to those who carry out a public service for the city or state as well as to those who minister within the religious cult. In saying that they devote themselves "to this very thing," Paul has in view the collection of taxes, although he is surely not limiting their role to this.

In the second part of this subunit, Paul begins with an imperative that introduces a neatly balanced fourfold command: **Pay to everyone what is owed to them: tax to the one who is due tax, revenue to the one who is due revenue, respect to the one who is due respect, honor to the one who is due honor** (13:7). "Tax" (*phoron*) refers to the tribute or tax that is owed to the state; "revenue"

Erich Lessing/Art Resource, NY

Figure 12. Tax collection in the Roman Empire, from a funeral stele (second to third century), Rheinisches Landesmuseum, Trier, Germany. Paul tells Roman Christians to pay their taxes as a way of saying that even though Christians belong to the new creation, they continue to live in the world.

(*telos*) refers to indirect taxes, such as toll taxes and custom duties. In addition to this external duty of paying taxes and revenues, Paul exhorts his audience to give "respect" and "honor" to those to whom it is due, to each in accordance with the role that each one plays in the hierarchical order of society, in which some authorities are due greater respect than others.

13:8–10. With this unit, Paul returns to the theme of love that he has introduced in 12:9, where he exhorted the Romans to let their love be without pretense. But whereas he made use of a number of maxims in 12:9–21 to illustrate what he meant by sincere love, here he discusses the relation between love and the Mosaic law, a topic that he also broaches in the paraenesis of Galatians (Gal. 5:13–14). Ernst Käsemann (1980, 361) views this text as problematic because there is no polemic against the law, and he concludes that Paul must be following "a catechetical tradition of Jewish Christianity (cf. Matt. 5:17ff.). . . . From all this it follows that here, in distinction from 12:1f., Paul does not present his own argument but simply points the community to a familiar tradition." But since Paul makes a similar point about the relation of love and the law in Gal. 5:13–14, which is a polemical letter, it appears that this teaching is more Pauline than Käsemann allows.

The unit begins with an initial exhortation (13:8a) that Paul supports by arguing that love is the fulfillment of the law (13:8b–10). This unit is carefully tied to the preceding one by the verb "owe" in 13:8, which echoes "owed" in 13:7. Having urged the Romans to pay everyone what is owed to them, Paul exhorts them, **Owe nothing to anyone except to love one another** (13:8a). The implication of the injunction is that while believers must discharge all of their debts, they are allowed to maintain the debt of love because it is an obligation that never ends for those who live in the sphere of Christ. The ongoing nature of this debt is apparent from what Paul writes to the Galatians when he tells them not to let their freedom become an opportunity for the flesh "but through love become slaves to one another" (Gal. 5:13).

In support of his exhortation Paul explains: **for the one who loves the other has fulfilled the law** (13:8b). The use of *peplērōken* (has fulfilled) here echoes what Paul said earlier about the just requirement of the law being fulfilled in the believer (8:4). But whereas in 8:4 he wrote that God fulfilled that requirement by sending his Son in the flesh in order to conquer sin, here he implies that believers *fulfill* the law—not by *doing* its individual commandments but by loving the other. To explain how loving the other fulfills the law, Paul introduces a subsidiary argument that begins with the conjunction *gar*: **For the commandments, "Do not commit adultery, do not murder, do not steal, do not covet"—and any other commandment—are summed up in this phrase, "You shall love your neighbor as yourself"** (13:9). The commandments that Paul lists here follow the wording and order of the Decalogue according to Deut. 5:6–21 LXX. Paul, however, quotes only four of them (Deut. 5:17, 18, 19, 21). Employing a new verb, he affirms that all of the commandments are "summed up" (*anakephalaioutai*) in the injunction of Lev. 19:18, "You shall love your neighbor as yourself." The use of the verb "summed up" (used in Eph. 1:10 in reference to all things being summed up or recapitulated in Christ) presents love of neighbor as the essential content of the law. A similar statement occurs in Gal. 5:14. In Galatians, however, Paul writes, "The whole law is *fulfilled* [rather than summed up] in one statement, namely, 'You shall love your neighbor as yourself'" (NAB).

Paul concludes his argument with a negative definition of love: **Love does not harm the neighbor** (13:10a). On the basis of this, he writes, **Therefore love is the fulfillment of the law.** This negative definition of love recalls Paul's description of love in 1 Cor. 13:4b–6: "Love is not envious or boastful or arrogant or rude. It does not insist on its own way; it is not irritable or resentful; it does not rejoice in wrongdoing." The final phrase of this unit echoes the opening of the unit, thereby placing Paul's central argument within an artful literary bracket:

Love and Law

"In fact, put love in for each of the commandments of the law and see how easily they can all be fulfilled. Can one who loves his neighbor murder him? Certainly no one would kill the one he loves. Love, therefore, is the means by which what is commanded, 'You shall not murder,' is fulfilled. And again, does a man who loves his neighbor commit adultery with his wife? Certainly not. If you love your neighbor, then you will not commit adultery. In a similar way as well the one who loves his neighbor does not steal his possessions; and he who loves his neighbor does not bear false testimony against him. The same thing applies to the other commands of the law. If there is love toward one's neighbor, they are kept without any effort." (Origen, *Comm. Rom.* 9.31.1, trans. Scheck 2001–2, 2:229)

> For the *one who loves* the other has *fulfilled the law* (13:8).
> The commandments are *summed up* in *love your neighbor* (13:9).
> *Love* is the *fulfillment of the law* (13:10).

To summarize, although those who are in Christ have been justified on the basis of faith rather than on the basis of *doing* the works of the law, the justified are not antinomians. In Christ and empowered by the Spirit, they *fulfill* the essential demands of love by the love commandment. As Joseph Fitzmyer (1993, 677) notes, "Love is the way Pauline faith works itself out (Gal 5:6); it thus becomes 'the deeds' of which Jas 2:18 speaks."

13:11–14. With this unit, Paul draws the first section of his paraenesis (12:1–13:14) to a close. In the opening verses of this section, he has exhorted the Romans not to be conformed to this age but to be transformed by the renewal of their minds (12:1–2), thereby pointing to the new age that has dawned for those who are in Christ. In these verses, he views all that he has said against the horizon of the final or eschatological salvation that awaits those who are in Christ. The unit begins with a reminder of the eschatological hour (13:11). Following this reminder, there are two contrasts: night and day, putting aside and putting on (13:12). On the basis of these contrasts, Paul exhorts the Romans to behave as during the day rather than as during the night (13:13) by clothing themselves with the Lord Jesus Christ (13:14). Because this unit makes use of several baptismal motifs, it is not surprising that some have seen the echoes of an ancient baptismal hymn here (Jewett 2007, 817–18).

The opening words of this passage in Greek, which I translate as **Aware of the time, act in this way** (13:11a), lack a verb. The sense, however, is that the Romans should act in the way that Paul has described, especially the way of love, because the critical moment (*ton kairon*) is at hand. To explain what he means, Paul writes, **because it is already the hour for you to arise from sleep; for our salvation is nearer than when we first began to believe** (13:11b). The mention of "salvation" (*sōtēria*) recalls other statements that Paul has made about salvation: that the gospel is the power of God that leads to salvation (1:16), the assurance of salvation that belongs to the justified and reconciled (5:10–11), and the hope of final salvation (8:14–39). This salvation is nothing less than the life that comes with resurrection from the dead. Given the nearness of the hour, Paul exhorts the community "to arise" (*egerthēnai*), a word that would surely have recalled their promised resurrection from the dead. Ephesians 5:14, which also contains strong baptismal motifs, is more explicit: "Sleeper, awake! *Rise from the dead*, and Christ will shine on you" (emphasis added).

Playing on the theme of slumber, Paul introduces the first of two contrasting statements: **The night is almost over, and the day is at hand** (13:12a). Whereas the night corresponds to the old age to which believers are not to conform themselves, the day corresponds to the new age that will be ushered in by the

Lord's parousia. For Paul, the coming day has moral and ethical implications for those who await the parousia. Employing the metaphor of putting on and taking off clothing, Paul writes: **Therefore, let us put aside deeds that belong to the darkness, and let us put on the armor that belongs to the light** (13:12b). The injunction to put aside the deeds that belong to darkness highlights Paul's moral realism. Even though believers have been justified, it is possible for them to fall back. The injunction to put on the armor that belongs to the light points to the eschatological battle that believers must face. For other injunctions to put aside an old way of life that belongs to the old age, see Eph. 4:22; Col. 3:8–9; James 1:21; and 1 Pet. 2:1. For injunctions to put on a way of life appropriate for the new age, see Eph. 6:11–18; Col. 3:10–17; and 1 Thess. 5:8.

Having exhorted the Romans to set aside the deeds that belong to darkness, Paul further exhorts them, **Let us behave properly as we would in the day, not in carousing and drunkenness, not in sexual immorality and indecency, not in strife and jealousy** (13:13). The conduct that Paul describes here is the kind of behavior that people do in the night, under the cover of darkness, lest their deeds be exposed. To live properly, as in the day, is to live in a way that is "honorable" (*euschēmonōs*), and so without shame. It was the reading of this verse in a garden in Milan that led Augustine to his conversion. Employing a strong adversative (*alla*), Paul presents the alternative to such shameful behavior: **Rather, clothe yourselves with the Lord Jesus Christ and give no forethought to the flesh for the purpose of arousing its desires** (13:14). The language of clothing oneself (*endysasthe*) occurs frequently in the Pauline Letters. In Gal. 3:27 it is explicitly related to baptism: the baptized have clothed themselves with Christ. In 1 Cor. 15:53–54 it is used in reference to the mortal body that must put on imperishability and immortality if death is to be overcome. And in Col. 3:10 it points to the "new self" with which believers were clothed at their baptism into Christ. Although Paul knows that the Romans have already been clothed with Christ through their baptism, he enjoins them to repeat this action by living morally good lives that are no longer directed by

---

Romans 13:13 and the Conversion of Augustine

"Eagerly then I returned to the place where Alypius was sitting; for there had I laid the volume of the Apostle when I arose thence. I seized, opened, and in silence read that section on which my eyes first fell: Not in rioting and drunkenness, not in chambering and wantonness, not in strife and envying; but put ye on the Lord Jesus Christ, and make not provision for the flesh, in concupiscence. No further would I read; nor needed I: for instantly at the end of this sentence, by a light as it were of serenity infused into my heart, all the darkness of doubt vanished away." (Conf. 8.12, trans. Pusey 1949, 167)

the desires that the flesh arouses—"flesh" being understood as what is mortal and corruptible and so opposed to God's Spirit.

To summarize, in this final unit Paul provides the Romans with an eschatological view of the moral life. Since they are living in the last hour of the old age, when the darkness is already passing away and the light of the day is already appearing, they are to live "in the day," as people who have been clothed with Christ through their baptismal death, which foreshadows their resurrection.

Theological Issues

In tracing the train of thought in Rom. 13:1–7, I have purposely refrained from discussing the theological significance of this text. But now, having listened to what the text says, we can consider the theological issues it raises. For even though this passage consists of a mere seven verses, it has had an enormous impact on the life of the church. At times, it has been seen as the biblical starting point for constructing a doctrine of church and state; and at times, it has been invoked to legitimate obedience and subservience to oppressive regimes. For if all authority has been appointed by God, and if the governing authorities are God's servants, then it seems that there is no recourse but to obey such authorities, no matter how dishonest and corrupt they may be.

Aware of the difficulties that this text presents, scholars have striven mightily to interpret its meaning and authority as Scripture for the contemporary church (see Furnish 1985, 115–39; Schelkle 1973, 333–50). Most acknowledge that Paul was addressing a situation that was specific to the circumstances of the Roman community: the need to pay taxes. Accordingly, in tracing the train of thought in this passage, I noted that the final two verses (13:6–7) apply the teaching of the first five verses. Paul's primary purpose in calling the Romans to be subject to the governing authorities, then, was to lay the foundation for his more-specific injunction to pay taxes and revenues to those to whom they are due.

Given the multiple ways in which rulers have abused their authority throughout the centuries (one thinks especially of the totalitarian regimes of the twentieth century), and given the specific circumstances that Paul was addressing (the payment of taxes and revenues to the Roman Empire), it is tempting to dismiss this text as devoid of theological content and assert that Paul's teaching is naive and purely time-conditioned. For if Paul knew what we know today, he would surely not have written as he did. Such an approach, however, may itself be naive. More important, it runs the risk of overlooking the theological dimension of Paul's exhortation. To explain what I mean, I propose to review the context and occasion of the text before drawing out its theological meaning as the church's Scripture.

Although distinctive in content, Rom. 13:1–7 is not an isolated unit within the paraenesis of 12:1–13:14. It stands between Paul's foundational exhortation that believers are to offer themselves as a living sacrifice to God as they are transformed by the renewal of their minds (12:1–2) and Paul's teaching about the nearness of their salvation. Thus, in his classic essay on this text, Ernst Käsemann (1969a, 199) writes, "Even obedience to earthly authority is regarded by Paul as a fragment of the Christian's worship of God in the secularity of the world." The underlying theological issue, then, is the relation between this world and the new age. Firmly convinced that believers have been transferred from the realm of Adam to the realm of Christ, and having encouraged them not to conform themselves to this age but to be transformed by the renewal of their mind, it is not Paul's purpose to call believers out of the world as if they no longer had any responsibility to the present creation. This is why Käsemann (1969a, 211) writes, "It is for the sake of this determining of Christian existence in the world that Paul sets himself so passionately against the separation of creation and the new age."

Paul was keenly aware that believers are already, in some sense, citizens of heaven (Phil. 3:20). Likewise, he firmly believed that "the present form of this world is passing away" (1 Cor. 7:31). But he was not ready to dispense believers from their obligations to the created order. For example, although his personal preference was for a celibate life so that he could serve the Lord single-mindedly, he recognized the enduring importance of marriage (1 Cor. 7). Likewise, although he knew that believers were already participating in the new age through the gift of the Spirit, he recognized the necessary role that governing authorities play in maintaining an ordered society.

Although Paul benefited from Roman protection because he was a Roman citizen (Acts 16:37; 22:25–29; 23:27), he was not naive about the brutality and tyranny of the Roman Empire, having "endured injustice at the hands of governing authorities in his own missionary work" (Schreiner 2001, 449). Moreover, it was the Roman governor, Pontius Pilate, who sentenced Jesus to be crucified. But just as Jesus told Pilate that he would have no power over him unless it were given to him from above (John 19:11), so Paul was firmly convinced that all power comes from God, even when that power is misused and abused, as it often was by the Roman Empire. Paul, then, did not write these words naively; for he understood that those in authority did not always act properly.

To grasp what Paul says in this text, we must distinguish between "being subject" to the authorities and "obeying them" in all that they command. While being subject inevitably involves some kind of obedience, it should not be confused with blindly obeying them in every instance. Victor Furnish (1985, 126) puts it well: "To 'be subject' means to acknowledge the reality of the political structure under which one stands, and to respect it. One might, for example, 'disobey' a law of the state and still 'be subject' to the political structure." Like the apostles, Paul would have understood that there are times when believers must "obey God rather than any human authority" (Acts 5:29).

By enjoining believers to be subject to the governing authorities, and in viewing those authorities as God's servants, Paul was affirming that God is the source of all authority and that all authority is meant to serve God's purpose. While the governing authorities may not acknowledge this, and while they may refuse to act as God's servants, Paul was firmly convinced that the authority to govern derived from God. Moreover, like other biblical writers, he understood that God could use even rebellious authorities to carry out the divine plan, as happened with Pharaoh at the time of the exodus (Exod. 9:16, quoted in Rom. 9:17) and Cyrus at the time of the exile (Isa. 45:1, 13).

The theme of being subject to the governing authorities is also found in the Letter to Titus and 1 Peter. In Titus, Paul instructs his young associate, "Remind them to *be subject* to rulers and authorities, to be obedient, to be ready for every good work" (3:1, emphasis added). Similarly, Peter exhorts the recipients of his letter, "For the Lord's sake accept the authority of every human institution, whether of the emperor as supreme, or of governors, as sent by him to punish those who do wrong and to praise those who do right. For it is God's will that by doing right you should silence the ignorance of the foolish" (1 Pet. 2:13–15). In the text of 1 Peter, however, the motivation for accepting authority has become more pragmatic: to silence the criticism of nonbelievers.

When all is said and done, Rom. 13:1–7 is not a theological tract about the relationship between church and state. There is, as Joseph Fitzmyer (1993, 662) reminds us, no mention of the state in this text. Nor, for that matter, is there any reference to the church. The theological contribution of the text, in my view, is threefold. First, it testifies that even though Christians belong to the new creation, they continue to live in a world that is passing away. Accordingly, those who drop out of the present social order or refuse to find their place within it, because they maintain that they belong to the new creation and the old is passing away, have misunderstood the nature of Paul's gospel, which can be summarized in the expression "already but not yet." Although believers are a new creation in Christ, they still live in the created order.

Second, this text testifies to God's concern for the created order in which human beings live. In affirming that God is the source of all authority, it proclaims that a structured social order in which human beings can live peacefully is part of God's creative plan. This affirmation, however, does not mean that God determines the specific form that the social order will take; this God leaves to human beings. But it is an affirmation that a structured social order is willed and made possible by God's authority.

Third, what Paul says in this text is a warning to governing authorities that their authority is not their own (Furnish 1985, 135–36). Whatever authority they possess comes from God and is intended to be exercised for God's purpose.

That this does not work out in practice does not mean that God is not the source of all authority any more than the denial of God's existence means that God does not exist. Paul's gospel proclaims what reality looks like when viewed from the perspective of the gospel. The goal of the new obedience that Paul proclaims is to live in accord with that reality.

Romans 14:1–15:13

Welcoming One Another
according to the Example of Christ

Introductory Matters

This material constitutes the second section of Paul's paraenesis. But whereas the first section (12:1–13:14) dealt with a number of different topics, this section concerns itself with a single issue that I have titled "Welcoming One Another according to the Example of Christ." Like the first section of Paul's paraenesis, it also stands under the overall theme that controls the entire paraenesis: the need for believers to offer themselves as a spiritual sacrifice to God and to be transformed by the renewal of their minds rather than conform themselves to the present age (12:1–2). To fulfill this injunction, the Roman Christians must welcome one another as Christ has welcomed them.

This section of Paul's paraenesis stands at the center of a lively debate about Paul's purpose in writing to the Romans that has been chronicled in the volume edited by Karl Donfried (1991). The two major questions surrounding this section can be stated in this way: (1) Is Rom. 14:1–15:13 a general paraenesis, or is it intended to address a specific problem in the Roman church? (2) Who are "the weak" and "the strong" to whom Paul refers in these verses?

Although the majority of commentators maintain that Paul was addressing a specific problem, some argue that Rom. 14:1–15:13 is a general moral exhortation. For example, Robert Karris (1991, 66) maintains that "Rom. 14:1–15:13 should be analyzed for what it is: general, Pauline paraenesis and not so many pieces of polemic from which a scholar may reconstruct the positions of the parties in Rome who occasioned this letter." In his view, Paul is essentially repeating, rephrasing, and echoing arguments he originally made in 1 Cor. 8:9 and 10:23–11:1 (Karris 1991, 75). He further notes that even though this paraenesis may have been addressed "to possible situations within the Roman community," it is also applicable to "any Christian community" (83), and it "has no specific referent within the Roman community" (84). Brevard Childs (2008, 171) has recently echoed similar sentiments: "I judge therefore that it is a basic exegetical error to assume that Paul is addressing specific contingent events in Romans 14–15 in accordance with his approach in Corinthians. The majority of modern commentators are misled when they extrapolate from a few vague hints in chapters 15–16 to posit that Paul's use of weak and strong reflects a specific controversy in Rome between Jewish and Gentile Christians."

The majority of contemporary commentators, however, urge that Paul is responding to a specific situation in Rom. 14:1–15:13. For example, A. J. M. Wedderburn (1991a, 34) concludes that "the information given in Rom. 14 can be fitted coherently into a situation in which Christians are involved who were disposed to adopt a rigorous, ascetic form of Jewish practice. These formed at least part of the ranks of the 'weak,' who might well also have included Christians adopting a less rigorous form of Jewish observance." Francis Watson (1991, 206) writes about the purpose of this paraenesis: "Thus, Rom. 14:1–15:13 addresses itself not to tensions between Jewish and Gentile Christians within a single congregation (the usual view), but to the problem of two separate congregations who regard each other with suspicion and who hold no common worship."

Although most commentators argue that Rom. 14:1–15:13 is determined by a specific situation at Rome, there is disagreement about the precise nature of that situation and the identity of "the weak" and "the strong." For example, while most see this paraenesis as responding to tensions within the community, Watson (1991, 212) views it as addressing a conflict between two different congregations: "Jewish Christians, who comprised the remnants of the original Roman congregation, and Gentile Christians who were Paulinists—converts and associates of Paul." Similarly, while most argue that "the weak" were Jewish Christians who observed the dietary and ritual prescriptions of the law, and "the strong" were Gentile Christians who found no need to do so, others assess the ethnic makeup of these groups differently. For example, A. Andrew Das (2007, 264) argues that both the weak and the strong were Gentile believers. The former had a deep appreciation of Judaism and its practices because they had been closely associated with the synagogue, whereas the latter did not. Mark Nanos (1996) introduces an entirely new dynamic when he urges that whereas "the strong" refers to Christians, "the weak" refers to those Jews at Rome who are not believers in Christ. In this scenario, Paul is "a champion

Three Ways of Viewing the Weak and the Strong

The Weak	The Strong
law-observant Jewish Christians	nonobservant Gentile Christians
law-observant Gentile Christians	nonobservant Gentile Christians
Jews who do not believe in Christ	Jews and Gentiles who believe in Christ

of Israel's historical faith" (Nanos 1996, 165) who reminds the Christians at Rome "to embrace the principles of love that were inherent in the intentions of the apostolic decree" (157).

Because the historical background of Rom. 14:1–15:13 and the identity of "the weak" and "the strong" are disputed, I will summarize the evidence before offering any remarks about this section's historical setting. First, Paul's primary audience appears to be the strong since they must make the greater sacrifice if tensions are to be relieved (14:1). This does not mean that Paul never addresses the weak; he does in 14:4, 10. But his primary audience remains the strong. Second, Paul identifies "the weak" in several ways: they eat only vegetables (14:2); they observe certain days as more important than other days (14:5); they do not appear to drink wine (14:21). Third, Paul identifies himself with the strong, who believe that they are free to eat all foods and need not observe certain days (15:1). Fourth, the reason the weak and the strong act differently has to do with their faith convictions of what is and is not permitted (14:5). Fifth, Paul imputes good motives to both the weak and the strong: both seek to praise God (14:6). Sixth, the strong act wrongly when, by insisting on their faith, their freedom becomes a stumbling block for the weak (14:15). The weak act wrongly when they act on the basis of what others are doing rather than on the conviction that comes from faith (14:23). Seventh, Paul is convinced that nothing in itself is unclean, but he does not insist on his personal freedom and scandalize the believer for whom Christ died (14:14). Eighth, Paul grounds his exhortation not to judge others in the lordship of Christ (14:7–9), God's judgment (14:10–12), and the kingdom of God (14:17). Ninth, Paul makes extensive use of Scripture to persuade the strong and the weak (14:11; 15:9–12). Tenth, his goal is to bring the weak and the strong to accept each other as Christ has accepted them (15:7).

Although Paul's paraenesis in 14:1–15:13 is general enough to apply to different situations, thereby allowing it to function as moral exhortation for other congregations as well, the references to abstaining from certain foods and observing certain days give it a specificity suggesting that Paul is addressing certain tensions among the Romans. Although these tensions were known

Romans 14:1–15:13 in the Rhetorical Flow

The letter opening (1:1–17)

Gentiles and Jews in the light of God's wrath (1:18–3:20)

Gentiles and Jews in the light of God's righteousness (3:21–4:25)

The experience of salvation in the light of God's righteousness (5:1–8:39)

God's righteousness and the destiny of Israel (9:1–11:36)

God's righteousness and the moral life of the justified (12:1–15:13)

  Love and obedience in the new age (12:1–13:14)

▶**Welcoming one another according to the example of Christ (14:1–15:13)**

  An exhortation not to judge one another (14:1–12)

    An exhortation to welcome the weak (14:1)

    Initial application of the exhortation (14:2–3)

    Question and supporting reason (14:4)

    Further application of the exhortation (14:5–6)

    Supporting evidence for the application (14:7–9)

    Question and supporting reason (14:10–12)

  An exhortation not to scandalize one another (14:13–23)

    An initial exhortation not to scandalize one another (14:13)

    First explanation (14:14–18)

      Paul's personal conviction (14:14)

      Supporting reason for the initial exhortation (14:15)

      A further exhortation (14:16)

      Supporting reasons related to the kingdom of God (14:17–18)

    Second explanation (14:19–23)

      An exhortation to build up one another (14:19)

      A warning not to destroy God's work (14:20)

      Curbing one's convictions for the sake of others (14:21–22a)

      Two kinds of behavior (14:22b–23)

  An exhortation to support the weak (15:1–6)

    An exhortation for the strong to bear with the weak (15:1–2)

    The example of Christ (15:3)

    The purpose of what is written in Scripture (15:4)

    A prayer-wish (15:5–6)

  An exhortation to receive one another (15:7–13)

    An exhortation based on the example of Christ (15:7)

    Why Christ became a servant of the circumcised (15:8–9a)

    Scriptural confirmation (15:9b–12)

    A prayer-wish (15:13)

to the Romans and so needed no explanation, their precise nature remains a matter of conjecture for contemporary readers. Consequently, I am inclined to negotiate a middle way between those who view this text as merely general paraenesis and those who employ it to identify the specific historical episode that occasioned Paul's Letter to the Romans. First, I view those whom Paul describes as weak with respect to faith as Jewish and/or Gentile believers who observed Jewish dietary laws and festivals because of a deep personal conviction born of attachment to a Jewish way of life, which they related to their faith in Christ, whereas those whom Paul describes as strong with respect to faith represent Jewish and/or Gentiles believers who have never observed, or no longer found it necessary to observe, these practices because of similar deep convictions about their faith in Christ. Since it is apparent from Rom. 16 that the Roman Christians belonged to different house churches, it is probable that the divisions were between house churches, some composed of the strong and others of the weak. But it is also possible that the strong and weak belonged to the same house church. While this situation would have been of concern to Paul because it divided the Christian believers in Rome, I do not see this situation as *the* occasion for this letter in which Paul is primarily concerned to present his gospel to the Romans.

Tracing the Train of Thought

This section consists of four units, each one beginning with an exhortation. In the first, Paul exhorts his audience to refrain from judging one another (14:1–12). Those who are strong in respect to their faith should welcome those who are weak in respect to faith since each person acts in accordance with one's own faith in Christ. Moreover, since judgment belongs to God, believers must refrain from judging one another. In the second unit, Paul exhorts the stronger members of the community not to scandalize the weaker members (14:13–23). Accordingly, they must not place obstacles before the weak. Although Paul is personally convinced that all things are clean, he does not want the strong to destroy the faith of those for whom Christ died. Food becomes unclean for a person when that person eats because of another's example rather than from conviction born of faith. Whatever does not proceed from the conviction of faith, therefore, is sin. In the third unit, Paul exhorts the strong to sustain the weak because this is what Christ did (15:1–6). To support his argument, Paul points to Scripture, which was written to provide believers with hope. In the last unit, he exhorts the weak and the strong to welcome each other according to the example of Christ, who became a servant of the Jewish people so that the Gentiles might praise God (15:7–13).

14:1–12. Paul's rhetorical goal in this unit is to convince the strong not to despise the weak, and the weak not to judge the strong. To accomplish this, he begins by exhorting the strong to receive the weak (14:1). He then applies this exhortation to the situation of the weak and the strong (14:2–3). Next, he reprimands the weak for judging the strong (14:4). Following this reproach, he applies his exhortation to the weak and the strong a second time (14:5–6). He then supports this application with a christological argument based on the lordship of Christ (14:7–9). Finally, Paul addresses a rebuking question to both the weak and the strong, which he supports by an argument from Scripture (14:10–12). The argument of this unit, then, makes use of an initial exhortation, two applications, two rebuking questions, and two theological arguments.

Paul's initial exhortation sounds the theme that he will develop throughout this paraenesis: **Welcome the person who is weak in respect to faith, but not for the purpose of quarreling about opinions** (14:1). Later Paul will encourage the strong to bear with the scruples of the weak (15:1), and he will exhort both the weak and the strong to welcome each other as Christ has welcomed them (15:7). In this way, he brackets his paraenesis with exhortations to welcome the weak (14:1) and to welcome one another (15:7). Here to welcome others is to be understood in terms of hospitality: receiving another into "one's home or circle of acquaintances" (BDAG 883, s.v. *proslambanō*, def. 4). Although Paul does not identify his target audience, it is apparent from 15:1 that he is addressing believers with whom he has a certain affinity because he too is strong in respect to his faith.

The designation "weak in respect to faith" may have been a pejorative phrase that the strong applied to those who did not share their views since it is unlikely that one group would identify itself in this way (Jewett 2007, 834; Keck 2005, 336). A similar phrase occurs in 4:19, where Paul says that Abraham did not grow weak in faith when he considered his aged body and Sarah's barren womb. But whereas in Rom. 4:19 Paul had in view Abraham's faith in God's promises, here the apostle employs "faith" in the sense of *tharreō* ("to be confident," Lagrange 1922, 323). Thus the epithet does not indicate a lack of faith in Christ but a more cautious assessment of the implications of faith in Christ (D. Moo 1996, 836). Joseph Fitzmyer (1993, 688) describes the weak as not having "really grasped what is meant by uprightness through faith." M.-J. Lagrange (1922, 322) suggests that they were not strong enough in their Christian convictions to judge solely from the point of view of faith.

Paul encountered a similar, but more serious, problem at Corinth that dealt with participation in cultic meals and the consumption of food sacrificed to idols. In response to that crisis, he sought to protect "the weak" (1 Cor. 8:9). But instead of referring to the weak in respect to faith, he spoke of the weak in respect to their conscience that did not allow them to eat food that had been sacrificed to idols (8:10). Although different, the situation in Romans is analogous. The expression, "the weak in respect to faith," refers to a weakness related to a conscience that will not take a certain course of action because it is not convinced that such an action is in accord with authentic faith in Christ. Thus we could say that the weak are strong in their personal convictions of what faith in Christ does *not* allow them to do. Paul's admonition not to welcome the weak for the "purpose of quarreling about opinions" suggests that the gatherings of certain believers were becoming the occasion for the strong to dispute with the weak about what faith in Christ allowed.

Paul now applies his exhortation to a specific instance. **One person believes that he is allowed to eat anything, while the one who is weak eats only vegetables. The one who eats is not to disdain the one who refrains from eating, and the one who does not eat is not to judge the one who eats, for God has welcomed him** (14:2–3). The person who believes that he can eat anything represents the strong, while the one who eats only vegetables represents the weak. The former, like Paul, is convinced that all food is clean (14:14), whereas the latter is not. Rather than adjudicate this dispute and impose his own view, Paul advises the strong, whose robust conscience might incline them to look down upon others, not to "disdain" the weak. And he admonishes the weak, whose more delicate conscience might incline them to be judgmental, not to "judge" the strong. Employing the same verb he did in 14:1 ("welcome"), Paul supports this advice with a short but powerful *gar* clause, "*for* God has welcomed him." Believers, then, do not welcome one another because they share the same views but because God has already welcomed them despite their diverse views. Paul's argument can be summarized in this way: God has welcomed you; therefore you are to welcome one another.

Although it is impossible to know with assurance the precise circumstances that occasioned Paul's remarks, many commentators suggest that some of the Roman Christians who still practiced the dietary prescription of the law (be they Jews or Gentiles) refrained from eating meat sold in the market because they were not confident that it was ritually clean. Therefore, to avoid unclean meat, they ate vegetables, as did Daniel and his compatriots, lest they defile themselves with food from the royal table (Dan. 1). Despite his firm conviction that the justified are no longer under the law, Paul does not dispute this practice since he understands that it rests on a conviction of what the weak believe their faith in Christ entails rather than on a lack of faith in Christ.

Having made the first of what will be two applications, Paul employs the diatribe form to ask: **Who are you to judge another person's house servant? He will stand or fall before his own lord, and he will stand because the Lord is able to make him stand** (14:4). Although it is possible that Paul is addressing both the strong and the weak in this question (Byrne 1996, 412), the use of the verb "to judge," which recalls the advice that he has just given to the weak, suggests that Paul is addressing the weak (Cranfield 1979, 802; Keck 2005, 339; Lagrange 1922, 324). The use of this verb also recalls Paul's earlier diatribal warning in 2:1, 3, about judging others. In this instance, however, Paul employs the metaphor of a master and a slave in order to draw an analogy between believers and their

Lord. Just as the household servant of one master has no right to judge the household servant of another master, so the weak have no right to judge the strong since they are only fellow household servants. To support his position, Paul reminds the weak that just as a household slave stands (is approved) or falls (is disapproved) before his own master, so it will be with everyone who stands before God's judgment seat (14:10). Expressing his confidence in the final outcome, Paul insists that the household servant (the strong) will stand because of the Lord's help. In this last use of "lord," Paul is clearly referring to the Lord, though it is not clear if he has God or Christ in view.

After his accusing question, Paul introduces a second example to show how the exhortation of 14:1 is to be applied to the strong and the weak: **One person judges that one day is more important than another, another person judges that every day is the same. But let each one be completely convinced in one's own mind. The one who thinks a particular day is more important considers it as such for the sake of the Lord, and the one who eats, eats for the sake of the Lord, for one gives thanks to God. The one who does not eat, does not eat for the sake of the Lord and gives thanks to God** (14:5–6). As with the application in 14:2–3, Paul contrasts the behavior of the weak and the strong without criticizing either the one or the other. The person who observes one day as more important than others represents the position of the weak, whereas the one who considers all days the same represents the position of the strong. Like the first application, this application is vague, and how one interprets it depends, in some measure, on one's reconstruction of the events underlying this passage. However, while some think that he is referring to pagan festivals and others urge that he is speaking of days of abstinence, most commentators believe that Paul has in view Jewish festivals required by the law (Cranfield 1979, 705; D. Moo 1996, 842).

No matter what days Paul has in view, the advice he gives is quite explicit, and it can be applied by analogy to other situations. First, he insists that no matter how one evaluates such days, it is imperative that a person "be completely convinced in one's own mind" (14:5b). Such conviction derives from faith in Christ. Consequently, if the weak observe such days, they must do so on the basis of their faith in Christ, and if the strong do not, they too must act on the basis of their faith in Christ. Second, Paul is careful to impute the best of motives to both the weak and the strong. Returning to the theme of eating, even as he deals with the theme of observing certain days, he insists that both the weak and the strong act on behalf of the Lord whether or not they eat certain foods and observe certain days. In support of this, he notes that when both eat, they give thanks to the Lord: the weak for their meatless meal, the strong for the food they eat (14:6). Thus it is apparent to Paul that each group acts out of devotion to the Lord.

Having applied his exhortation to the situation of the weak and the strong, Paul supports what he has just said with a profound theological reflection on the lordship of Christ to show the weak and the strong that they should not think merely of themselves to the detriment of others (14:7–9). The language of living and dying, which I have italicized for emphasis, plays an important role in these carefully structured verses. Paul develops his argument in four movements. The first opens with a contrast between living and dying: **None of us *live for ourselves*, and none of us *die for ourselves*** (14:7). While someone unfamiliar with Paul's thought might have expected him to continue, "We live and we die for the sake of others," the apostle supports this opening statement with a christological insight. Accordingly, in the second movement he writes: **For insofar as *we live*, *we live* for the Lord, and insofar as *we die*, *we die for the Lord*** (14:8a). To understand what Paul intends here, it is helpful to recall what he writes in 2 Cor. 5:14–15: "For the love of Christ urges us on, because we are convinced that one has died for all; therefore all have died. And he died for all, *so that those who live might live no longer for themselves, but for him who died and was raised for them*." Making use of his Adam Christology, Paul points to the representative nature of Christ's death: because he died for all, all have died in and with him.

From this insight, Paul concludes, as he does here, that the purpose of human life is now determined by the pattern of Christ's death and resurrection. The purpose of life is not to live for ourselves but for Christ, the progenitor of the new humanity. Accordingly, in the third movement of his argument, Paul draws this conclusion: **Therefore, whether *we live* or whether *we die*, we belong to the Lord** (14:8b). Such a statement, however, can be true only if Christ has conquered death. Accordingly, the fourth movement of Paul's argument points to the purpose of Christ's death. It was a death that conquered death, thereby enabling Christ to rule over the dead, who will be raised with him, as well as the living, who already share in his resurrection life: **For this is why *Christ died* and *lives again*, so that he might exercise lordship over the *dead* and the *living*** (14:9). Origen provides an insightful commentary on this text:

> For no one provides a pattern of death for himself, but he takes it up from Christ, who alone has died to sin, so that he too, by imitation of him, can become estranged from sin and dead to it. Moreover, we do not have the pattern of life from ourselves, but we have received it from the resurrection of Christ. . . . So then, the newness of life by which we live in Christ through faith in his resurrection is attributed to the Lord, since it receives a commencement from him, not from us. (*Comm. Rom.* 9.39.2, trans. Scheck 2001–2, 2:39)

If the weak and the strong remember that the pattern of their own lives has been determined by the one who is the Lord of the living and the dead, they will set aside their disputes in order to live for him.

Having provided the strong and the weak with a christological argument based on the lordship of Christ, Paul employs the style of the diatribe to ask the strong and the weak an accusing question: **Who are you to judge your brother or sister? Or who are you to hold your sister or brother in disdain? For we will all stand before the judgment seat of God** (14:10). In light of Paul's use of "judge" and "disdain" in 14:3 (where he exhorts the weak not to *judge* the strong, and the strong not to *disdain* the weak), I conclude that the first part of his question is addressed to the weak and the second part to the strong. But now, for the first time since the beginning of this paraenesis (12:1), Paul employs the designation *adelphos* (lit., "brother") to remind the weak and the strong that despite their differences over food and days, they are brothers and sisters to each other in a new family whose kinship is determined by the blood of Christ, which was shed on the cross. In support of his question, he reminds both that they will stand before "the judgment seat of God." Paul makes a similar reference to the judgment that awaits the justified in 2 Cor. 5:10. But there he writes that "all of us must appear before the judgment seat *of Christ*." And in 1 Cor. 4:5 he warns the Corinthians not to judge him before the Lord comes at the parousia when he "will bring to light the things now hidden in darkness and will disclose the purposes of the heart." The point Paul makes here is similar. It is foolish to judge one another since everything will be revealed before the only judicial bench that matters, the judgment seat of God.

In support of his argument, Paul introduces a scriptural quotation to remind his audience that no one will escape God's judgment: **For it is written: "As I live, says the Lord, every knee will bow to me, and every tongue will acknowledge God"** (Rom. 14:11). The first part of this quotation comes from Isa. 49:18, a text in which God assures the inhabitants of Jerusalem that they will experience salvation: "Lift up your eyes all around, and see them all; look, they have gathered and have come to you. *I live, says the Lord*; you shall clothe yourself with all of them and put them on like a bride's ornament" (NETS). The second part of the quotation (which Paul also employs in Phil. 2:10–11) comes from Isa. 45:23, a text in which God assures Israel of his saving righteousness: "By myself I swear, 'Verily righteousness shall go forth from my mouth; my words shall not be turned back, *because to me every knee shall bow and every tongue shall acknowledge God*'" (NETS). The emphasis on salvation and righteousness in these texts suggests that Paul's composite quotation should be interpreted in light of God's saving righteousness as well. The weak and the strong will stand before the judgment seat of God and, at that moment, when the righteousness of God is revealed, all will worship God. If the weak and strong keep this eschatological vision before them, they will refrain from judging one another. To seal his argument, Paul concludes, **Thus each one of us will give an account of ourselves before God** (Rom. 14:12). Here Paul's subtle shift from the second-person singular in 14:10 to the first-person plural serves to unite the weak and the strong into one group in which each must account for what he or she has done (see 2 Cor. 5:10b for a similar statement).

14:13–23. Having concluded the last unit with a warning that everyone will stand before the judgment seat of God, Paul begins this unit by exhorting the weak and the strong not to judge each other (14:13a). He then introduces the theme that controls the rest of the unit: the strong should not scandalize the weak (14:13b). Paul develops this theme in two closely related ways (Wright 2002, 740). First, he warns the strong not to destroy the weak by insisting on their convictions about dietary prescriptions, since the kingdom of God is not about what believers eat and drink (14:14–18). Second, he encourages the strong to build up the community rather than destroy God's work (14:19–23).

The use of the conjunction *oun* (therefore) at the beginning of this unit indicates that Paul is drawing a conclusion based upon what he has just said in the first unit: **Therefore, let us no longer judge one another** (14:13a). But whereas Paul's earlier exhortations not to judge (14:4, 10) appear to have been directed at the weak, here he addresses the strong as well as the weak. Since everyone must stand before the judgment seat of God, no one is in a position to judge another. Playing on the Greek verb *krinein* (to judge), which he uses in the sense of "determine," Paul employs a strong adversative (*alla*) to introduce the theme of this unit: **rather, determine to do this: not to place any obstacle or enticement to sin in the way of your brother or sister** (14:13b). The manner in which Paul formulates this theme indicates that he is addressing the strong, who are in danger of scandalizing the weak by insisting that they (the strong) can eat any food and that they need not observe some days as more important than others.

Before developing his theme, Paul introduces a parenthetical remark that reveals his personal conviction: **I know and am fully persuaded in the Lord Jesus that there is nothing unclean in itself, unless someone considers it unclean; then it is unclean for that person** (14:14). The manner in which Paul introduces this remark is significant. His knowledge and conviction derive from his intimate relationship with the risen Lord Jesus, which persuades him "that there is nothing unclean in itself." Thus Paul has arrived at this conviction not by a process of rational deduction but on the basis of his relationship to Christ, which leads him to a personal conviction about what faith in Christ entails. Paul, however, is aware that there are others whose faith in Christ has not brought them to a similar conclusion. Consequently, despite his personal convictions, he understands that if another person thinks that something is unclean, it is unclean for that person. The issue, then, is not faith in Christ but the different convictions that derive from faith.

Paul's use of the adjective *koinon* (unclean) here is a strong argument that the apostle has the dietary prescriptions of the law in view. The same word plays a prominent role in the story of the conversion of Cornelius in the Acts of the Apostles. Peter insists that he has never eaten anything "unclean" (*koinon*; Acts 10:14 and 11:8), and he explains that God has shown him that he should not call anyone profane or unclean (10:28). Furthermore, in the Gospel of

Mark, Jesus affirms that what enters a person from the outside cannot defile (*koinōsai*) that person (7:18), a statement that the evangelist interprets as a pronouncement that all foods are clean (7:19).

Having stated his own position regarding food without insisting that the weak adopt his position, Paul presents a supporting argument for his statement in Rom. 14:13b that the strong should not scandalize the weak: **For if your fellow believer is irritated because of food you eat, you are no longer conducting yourself according to love. Do not destroy, for the sake of food, that one for whom Christ died** (14:15). For the first time, Paul introduces the noun "food" (*brōma*) into the discussion, a further indication that the central issue has something to do with the dietary prescriptions of the Mosaic law. He then argues that if the weak person is "irritated" (*lypeitai*; lit., "grieved" or "saddened," but the context suggests a stronger verb; so Dunn 1988, 2:820) by what the strong eat, then the strong are no longer acting in accordance with the genuine love that Paul has described in chapters 12–13. Those who practice genuine love do not consider themselves wise in their own estimation (12:3, 16) nor do they harm their neighbor in any way (13:10). To secure his argument, Paul relates the issue of scandalizing the weak to his gospel that Christ died *for us*. Accordingly, he warns the strong that if they irritate the weak by insisting on their right to eat whatever they wish, they risk destroying someone for whom Christ died (*hyper hou Christos apethanen*). The use of this traditional formula, which is found in 1 Cor. 15:3, recalls Paul's earlier statements about Christ's death (Rom. 5:6, 8; 14:9) and echoes the warning that he gave those in Corinth who thought they were more knowledgeable than others: "So by your knowledge those weak believers *for whom Christ died* are destroyed" (1 Cor. 8:11).

Drawing a conclusion from what he has just said, Paul introduces a further exhortation: **Therefore, do not let your good be reviled** (Rom. 14:16). The precise meaning of this enigmatic statement is debated. While some maintain that "your good" refers to the freedom of the strong, born of faith, that all foods are clean (Fitzmyer 1993, 697; D. Moo 1996, 855), others argue that the "good" refers to the gospel, the covenant blessings, the state of salvation that the strong enjoy (Cranfield 1979, 717; Dunn 1988, 2:821; Käsemann 1980, 376). Although it is probably impossible to break this impasse, I am inclined to adopt the first position. The strong should not let their freedom, which is a good thing born of the gospel, be reviled by insisting and arguing about their rights in public settings where the weak will be scandalized. Accordingly, in some instances it is better to curb one's legitimate rights than to insist on them without regard for others.

Next, Paul presents two closely related arguments in support of what he has just said. The first has to do with the kingdom of God, the second with service to Christ. First, the strong are not to let their freedom in regard to dietary prescriptions become an occasion for revilement, **For the kingdom of**

God is not about food and drink but about righteousness and peace and joy in the Holy Spirit (14:17). Drawing from a central theme of Jesus's teaching, Paul reminds the strong that life in the sphere of God's rule is not about eating and drinking but about the new creation that Christ, the eschatological Adam, has introduced through his saving death and resurrection. Paul's description of the kingdom is a summary of the gospel: (1) *righteousness* is God's saving righteousness, which has been manifested in Christ and communicated to the justified; (2) *peace* is the reconciliation that God effects through the death and resurrection of his Son; and (3) *joy* is the hallmark of the Spirit, who grants the newness of life that the justified and reconciled enjoy. Accordingly, although there are only a few references to the kingdom of God in the Pauline Letters (1 Cor. 4:20; 6:9, 10; 15:50; Gal. 5:21; Eph. 5:5; Col. 4:11; 1 Thess. 2:12; 2 Thess. 1:5; 2 Tim. 4:1), the underlying reality of the kingdom plays a central role in Paul's thought. For just as John employs the concept of "life" to describe the reality of the kingdom, so Paul describes the reality of the kingdom in terms of righteousness, peace, and joy. Insofar as believers are in Christ, the kingdom is a present reality for them. Its final consummation, however, will not occur until the parousia and the general resurrection of the dead.

Paul's second argument in support of his exhortation in Rom. 14:13b is related to what he has just said about the kingdom of God: **The one who serves Christ in this way is pleasing to God and approved by human beings** (14:18). "This way" refers to what Paul has just written about righteousness, peace, and joy. But now he applies these concepts to the moral life of the believer. Those who belong to a kingdom defined by God's righteousness, peace, and joy serve Christ and are approved by others when they live lives characterized by the righteousness, peace, and joy that define the kingdom of God. Such people do not insist on "their good" when the exercise of that good might destroy the one for whom Christ died.

To sum up, just as Paul grounded his exhortations in the first unit in the lordship of Christ and God's judgment, so he roots his exhortation in this unit in the death of Christ and the kingdom of God.

In 14:19–23 Paul provides the strong with a second reason not to scandalize the weak. Although closely related to what he has just said, his argument in this subunit introduces a slightly different perspective by focusing on the need to build up the community.

Paul begins with an initial exhortation that is positive in nature and grows out of what he has written. Having pointed to peace as an essential mark of the kingdom of God, he begins, **Therefore, let us pursue peace and mutual edification** (14:19). Paul's train of thought is clear. Since God's own peace is one of the defining marks of the kingdom of God, those who belong to the kingdom should pursue peace and reconciliation with one another. When applied to the strong, this means that the strong should be reconciled with the weak (although what Paul writes here can also be applied to the weak as well). In addition to pursuing peace, the strong must seek "mutual edification." The Greek word that I have translated as "edification" (*oikodomēs*) occurs frequently in the Corinthian correspondence in connection with "building up" and "edifying" the church (1 Cor. 14:3, 5, 12, 26; 2 Cor. 10:8; 12:19; 13:10), which Paul understands as God's "building" (*oikodomē*, 1 Cor. 3:9). Read in light of this vocabulary, Paul is calling on the strong to build up the Christian community at Rome by being reconciled with the weak.

Next, in a verse that echoes Rom. 14:15, Paul writes, **Do not destroy God's work for the sake of food. All things are clean, but evil for the one who eats thereby causing an offense to others** (14:20). This difficult verse presents two problems. The first has to do with the meaning of "God's work." Some argue, in light of the exhortation for mutual edification, that "God's work" refers to the church (Byrne 1996, 421; Dunn 1988, 2:825; Käsemann 1980, 378; D. Moo 1996, 860); others maintain that Paul has the weak in view since he has just warned the strong in 14:15 not to destroy the one on behalf of whom Christ died (Cranfield 1979, 723; Fitzmyer 1993, 698). Both interpretations make good exegetical sense, but the manner in which this verse echoes 14:15 persuades me to adopt the latter. The second problem concerns the meaning of *dia proskommatos* (lit., "because of offense," or "for the sake of offense"). I have interpreted it as referring to the strong who, in the process of eating, cause offense to the weak, but others construe it as referring to the weak who eat because they have been misled by the example of the strong. Brendan Byrne (1996, 415) translates the text in this sense: "in the case of the one who eats as a result of being made to stumble." Although both readings are grammatically sound and make good sense, Paul's focus on the strong in this unit suggests that he has in view the actions of the strong, rather than the weak. If this interpretation is correct, he is saying that even though all foods are clean, the strong should not destroy the weak by insisting that they (the strong) can eat whatever they wish. For even though the strong know that all food is clean (as does Paul), eating such food is wrong when it offends the weak.

Having warned the strong not to scandalize the weak, Paul encourages them to curb what, under other circumstances, would be their legitimate right: **It is good not to eat meat or drink wine or anything in which your brother or sister takes offense. The faith you have, keep to yourself before God** (14:21–22a). Earlier Paul affirmed his conviction that nothing is unclean in and of itself (14:14) and spoke of "food" (14:15a), but now he speaks of meat and wine and affirms that it is good to refrain from these if they offend one's brother or sister. While the law did not prohibit the drinking of wine, the weak may have refrained from wine because they feared that it had been defiled by idolatrous worship (Dunn 1988, 2:827). The use of the singular (*ho adelphos sou*) here, as in 14:15, personalizes Paul's instruction by reminding the strong that the weak person is *your* brother or sister. In 1 Cor. 8:13 Paul makes a similar statement about the need to restrain one's freedom: "Therefore, if food is a cause of their falling, I will never eat meat, so that I may not cause one of them to fall."

In advising the strong to keep their "faith" to themselves before God, Paul is not referring to their faith in Christ but to their convictions regarding food and drink that result from their faith in Christ. For example, if the strong find themselves in a social situation at which the weak are present, the strong should refrain from entering into disputes about food (14:1), and they should abstain from foods that scandalize their fellow believers in Christ.

Paul concludes this unit with a statement that contrasts two kinds of behavior: **Blessed are those who do not condemn themselves by what they approve. But those who waver as they eat condemn themselves because they do not act from faith. Everything that is not from faith is sin** (14:22b–23). Paul's use of *krinōn* (condemn/judge) and *katakekritai* (condemn/judge) in these verses echoes the verbs *krinōmen* (judge) and *krinate* (determine) at the beginning of this unit (14:13), thereby bracketing the passage with words whose root meaning is "to judge." The beatitude that Paul formulates in 14:22b states a general principle that could be applied to the weak as well as to the strong, although it may have the strong in view here. Applied to the strong, it pronounces a blessing on those who are able to eat all foods without condemning themselves because they have made their decision in accordance with the conviction that comes from faith. The contrasting statement of 14:23a, however, has in view those who are not sure whether they should eat certain foods but eat them nonetheless. Although it appears that Paul has the weak in view here, the statement could also apply to the strong.

Paul's final statement in 14:23b has played an important role in the history of theology since, on face value, it implies that anything that does not come

Two Views of Romans 14:23

"We gather from all this that even the good works of unbelievers are not good works of theirs, but are the good works of Him who makes good use of evil men. But their sins are sins of theirs, by which they do good things in an evil way, because they do them, not with a believing but with an unbelieving will, that is, with a foolish and harmful will. No Christian doubts that a tree that can bring forth only bad fruit, that is, only sins, is a bad tree. For, whether you will or not, 'All that is not from faith is sin.' Therefore, God cannot love those trees, and, if they remain such as they are, He plans to cut them down, because 'Without faith it is impossible to please God.'" (Augustine, C. Jul. 4.32, trans. Schumacher 1957, 196)

"'For whatsoever is not of faith is sin.' For when a person does not feel sure, nor believe that a thing is clean, how can he do else than sin? Now all these things have been spoken by Paul of the subject in hand, not of everything." (John Chrysostom, *Hom. Rom.* 26.23, *NPNF²* 11:531)

from faith is sinful. Understood in this sense, the implication would be that all actions apart from Christian faith are sinful, making it impossible for non-Christians to please God. Although Augustine understood the text in this way, Chrysostom did not. But since Paul has used "faith" in a rather restricted way throughout this discussion (the conviction born of faith), this statement should be interpreted more restrictively: Whatever believers do that does not come from a conviction that derives from their faith in Christ is sinful.

At the end of chapter 14, a few manuscripts introduce the doxology that is found at the end of the letter (16:25–27). I will discuss the significance of this textual variant for the history of the transmission of the text of Romans when I consider the introductory matters pertinent to the closing of the letter (15:14–16:27).

15:1–6. This unit is the first of two conclusions to Paul's discussion of the weak and the strong. A second conclusion follows in 15:7–13. Both units exhibit a similar structure: an exhortation in which Paul points to the example of Christ (15:1–2, 7), a supporting argument grounded in Scripture (15:3–4, 8–12), and a short prayer-wish in which he prays for the recipients of this letter (15:5–6, 13).

Paul begins with a direct appeal to the strong: **We who are strong ought to bear with the weaknesses of those who are not strong rather than please ourselves** (15:1). Although Paul has identified one group as "the weak" at the outset of this discussion (14:1–2), this is the first time that he explicitly identifies the other group as "the strong" (*hoi dynatoi*). Moreover, whereas in 14:14 he has implicitly associated himself with the strong, here he explicitly identifies himself with them. Like the strong, Paul's faith has convinced him that he is free to eat every kind of food. But instead of trying to persuade the weak to adopt his position, he exhorts the strong to bear with the "weaknesses" of those with whom they do not agree. By "weaknesses," Paul means the inability of those who are not strong (*tōn adynatōn*) to eat certain foods without a sense of having violated the Mosaic law. Given this situation, the strong should "bear" (*bastazein*) with the weak rather than please themselves by insisting on their rights. Paul employs the same verb in Gal. 6:2, "*Bear* one another's burdens, and in this way you will fulfill the law of Christ." Using "please" as a hook word, he explains what he means in a positive statement: **Let each one of us please our neighbor for the sake of what is good for the purpose of edification** (Rom. 15:2). Paul's use of "neighbor" here recalls his earlier injunction that "love does not harm the neighbor" (13:10), who, in this instance, is the weak person. The positive "good" that Paul has in view is that the weak will become conformed to the gift of justification that God has already bestowed upon them in Christ (Légasse 2002, 890). In this way the weak person, and so the whole community, will be edified and built up.

Continuing to employ the hook word "please," Paul supports his exhortation by pointing to the example of the Messiah, which he grounds with a scriptural quotation: **For the Christ did not please himself, but as it is written, "The insults of those who insulted you have fallen upon me"** (15:3). Here the use of the definite article with "Christ" suggests that Paul is employing *Christos* in a titular sense. It is not just someone called Christ who did not please himself; it is the Christ, the Messiah. To illustrate what he means, Paul quotes from Ps. 68:10 LXX (69:9 Eng.), which, at this point, does not deviate from the Hebrew text. The lament of a righteous sufferer who is being unjustly persecuted, this psalm is alluded to in the passion narratives. But whereas in the passion narratives there is only an allusion to this psalm in connection with the sour wine that Jesus's persecutors offered him (Matt. 27:34, 48; Mark 15:23, 36; Luke 23:36; John 19:29), here Paul interprets the psalm christologically by making Jesus the speaker. According to this reading, Jesus was aware that the insults and ridicule he bore were directed against God. Therefore, on the basis of Jesus's example, Paul calls on the strong to take upon themselves the ridicule and insults that are presently directed against the weak because of their dietary habits. By doing so, the strong will imitate the example of the Messiah.

To support his christological reading of Ps. 68 LXX (Ps. 69 Eng.), Paul reminds his audience that Scripture is a living word that was written with them in view: **For whatever was previously written was written for our instruction** (15:4a). Paul made a similar statement in 4:23–25, in his discussion of Abraham's faith, where he concluded that the text of Gen. 15:6 (that God credited Abraham's faith as righteousness) was not written only for Abraham's sake but also for all who believe in the one who raised Jesus from the dead. Paul makes a similar statement about the purpose of Scripture in 1 Cor. 9:9–11 when he applies the text of Deut. 25:4 (that one should not muzzle the ox) to the right of apostles to receive support for preaching the gospel. For Paul, Scripture is a living word **so that through patient endurance and the consolation that comes from the Scriptures, we might have hope** (Rom. 15:4b). "Patient endurance," "consolation," and "hope" are important concepts that Paul develops throughout his letters, especially in Rom. 5:1–5, where he relates affliction, endurance, and hope to one another, and in 2 Cor. 1:3–11, where he thanks God for the consolation he has received in the midst of his apostolic sufferings. Here, however, Paul relates these concepts to the Scriptures by affirming that the teaching of Scripture is a source of patient endurance and consolation that provides believers with hope. Paul's train of thought can be summarized in this way: Inasmuch as Scripture teaches us how God has fulfilled his promises in the past, it provides us with the consolation that enables us to endure our present suffering patiently in the sure hope that God will continue to fulfill his promises. Accordingly, if God has vindicated the rejected Messiah, who bore the insults of others, God will surely vindicate the strong who bear the insults hurled against the weak.

Paul concludes this unit with the first of four prayer-wishes, the other three being 15:13, 33; and 16:20: **May God, the source of patient endurance and** consolation, grant you to think about one another in the same way according to the pattern of Christ Jesus (15:5). In the other three prayer-wishes, Paul speaks of "the God of hope" and "the God of peace," but here he describes God as the one who is the source of steadfast endurance and consolation, thereby echoing what he has just said about the Scriptures. Since God is the author of Scripture, these descriptions of Scripture and God are intimately related to each other. Paul prays that the strong and the weak will "think about each other in the same way," a phrase that echoes his exhortation in 12:16. Similar injunctions are found in 1 Cor. 1:10; Phil. 2:2; 4:2. More important, the pattern for this behavior is "Christ Jesus," which can also be rendered as "Messiah, Jesus."

The ultimate purpose of Paul's prayer, however, is not the unity of the community but the glory of God. Accordingly, he concludes his prayer with a purpose clause: **in order that with one mind and in one voice you may praise the God and Father of our Lord Jesus Christ** (15:6). If the community is divided, there will always be something lacking in its worship. But when both the weak and the strong praise God as a community united in faith, then God and Jesus Christ will be praised. The manner in which Paul associates Jesus with God as the object of praise is an important christological statement, for it implies that the community worships the risen Lord as it does God the Father.

15:7–13. In recent years many scholars (Dunn 1988, 2:844–45; Fitzmyer 1993, 705–6; Kirk 2008, 49; J. R. Wagner 2003, 307; Wright 2002, 744) have argued that this unit has a triple function: to conclude Paul's discussion of the weak and the strong (14:1–15:13), to conclude his paraenesis (12:1–15:13), and to conclude the argument of the letter (1:18–15:13). The unit does recapitulate one of the central issues of the letter: the unity of Jewish and Gentile believers in Christ. Moreover, it echoes several themes that have occurred throughout the letter, such as the truth of God, God's promises, and the Davidic origins of the Messiah. Others, however, note that "many of the letter's key themes are also omitted" (D. Moo 1996, 874) and argue that this unit, along with 15:1–6, is better seen as the conclusion to Paul's paraenesis rather than as "a *recapitulatio* of the entire letter" (Lambrecht 2003, 172). Like the previous unit, this one begins with an exhortation (15:7) that is supported by a scriptural argument (15:8–12) before closing with a prayer-wish (15:13).

Employing the same verb (*proslambanesthe*) that he used at the beginning of this section (14:1), Paul draws his final conclusion: **Therefore, welcome one another for the glory of God as the Christ welcomed you** (15:7). But whereas in 14:1 Paul spoke directly to the strong, encouraging them to welcome those who are weak in respect to faith, here he addresses the weak as well as the strong. As in 15:1, the motivation for this exhortation is christological. Since "the Messiah" (*ho Christos*) has welcomed them for the glory of God, the weak and strong should welcome each other for the glory of God rather than "for the purpose of quarreling about opinions" (14:1).

In 15:8–12 Paul presents a supporting argument for this exhortation, which he grounds in four scriptural quotations, each related to the other by the use of "Gentiles" (*ethnē, ethnesin*). These verses form a single sentence, which begins with a description of how the Messiah has welcomed both Jews and Gentiles (15:8–9) and concludes with scriptural quotations from the Law, the Prophets, and the Psalms (15:10–12).

Paul begins his supporting argument with a solemn declaration of the Messiah's ministry toward Israel: **For I affirm that the Christ became a minister to the circumcised for the sake of God's truth in order to confirm the promises made to the patriarchs** (15:8). In this initial statement, Paul portrays the Messiah as having become a *diakonon* for the circumcised, by which he means the Jewish people. While *diakonon* could also be translated as "servant," I have rendered it as "minister" since Paul has in view the Messiah's work among his people. The use of the perfect tense *gegenēsthai* (became) points to the enduing nature of this ministry (Légasse 2002, 899). Not only was the Messiah a minister to his people; he also continues to be so. By identifying the Jewish people as the circumcised, Paul highlights the mark of circumcision that separated them from the Gentiles, and he echoes his earlier references to circumcision in chapters 2–4. By affirming that the purpose of the Messiah's ministry was "for the sake of God's truth" (*hyper alētheias theou*), he recalls his earlier statements about the truth or faithfulness of God (1:25; 3:7). And by saying that the purpose of this ministry was to confirm the promises made to the patriarchs, he recalls the many promises that God made to Israel. Thus Paul highlights an important aspect of Jesus's earthly ministry: his ministry to Israel, by which he showed God's faithfulness to his promises (Matt. 10:5–6; 15:24).

The connection between 15:8, in which Paul speaks of the Messiah's ministry to the uncircumcised, and 15:9, in which he refers to the Gentiles, has proven to be one of the most intractable problems in exegesis. The difficulty arises because there appears to be an ellipsis between the two verses that makes it necessary for translators to supply what they think has been omitted. Most commentators, however, would agree with Byrne (1996, 429) that "Paul is saying something about the purpose of Christ's ministry, . . . first in relation to the Jewish people, . . . then in relation to the Gentiles." The difficulty, however, is that 15:8 employs a purpose clause in reference to the Messiah's ministry to the Jewish people ("in order to confirm the promises made to the patriarchs"), whereas the next verse begins with an adversative statement: **the Gentiles, however, praise God for his mercy** (15:9a). If we respect this adversative clause, Paul's train of thought is as follows: The Messiah welcomed the circumcised by ministering to them in order to confirm the promises that God made to them. As for the Gentiles, although the Messiah did not minister to them in the same way, the Gentiles praise God for the mercy that has been bestowed upon them (see Lambrecht 2003, 170). For even though they were only a wild olive shoot, they have been grafted into the tree of Israel by the

Messiah's death and resurrection (11:17), in which they have encountered God's saving righteousness (9:30) and mercy (11:30).

To confirm that the Gentiles are presently praising God, Paul turns to Scripture, which he again interprets christologically: **as it is written: "Therefore, I will praise you among the Gentiles, and I will sing to your name"** (15:9b). Here Paul quotes from Ps. 17:50 LXX (18:49 Eng.), a royal psalm in which the king thanks God for delivering him from his enemies. Having been saved, the king extols God among the nations and praises his name. If Paul is reading this text christologically, the speaker is the risen Christ, the Messiah, who praises God's name among the Gentiles (so Byrne 1996, 432).

Having quoted from the Psalms, Paul turns to the Law to substantiate his argument: **And again it says, "Rejoice, O Gentiles, with his people"** (Rom. 15:10). With this text of Deut. 32:43 LXX, which is part of the Song of Moses, Paul introduces a new element. The speaker now invites the Gentiles to rejoice with "his people," that is, the people of Israel. But who is the speaker? If Paul is reading the text christologically, it is the risen Christ who is inviting the Gentiles to join in a chorus of praise with the people of Israel since they too have experienced God's salvation. The third quotation, which comes from the shortest psalm of the Psalter, Ps. 116:1 LXX (117:1 Eng.), makes a similar point: **And again, "Praise the Lord all the Gentiles; let all the peoples praise him"** (Rom. 15:11). Here the psalmist invites all the nations to praise Yhwh for his steadfast love toward Israel because the faithfulness of the Lord endures forever. Paul, however, again reads the text christologically. Thus it is the risen Christ who invites "the Gentiles" (*ta ethnē*) and "all the peoples" (*pantes ho laoi*) to praise God in a joint chorus. In the psalm, "all the peoples" refers to the Gentiles, but here Paul has in view the people of Israel.

The speaker of the last quotation, taken from Isa. 11:10 LXX, is no longer the Messiah but Paul's favorite prophet, Isaiah: **And again, Isaiah says, "The root of Jesse will appear, the one raised up to rule the Gentiles; in him the Gentiles will hope"** (Rom. 15:12). Paul's use of the LXX here is important since it allows what J. Ross Wagner (2003, 319) calls "a delicious double-entendre" inasmuch as the phrase "the one raised up" (*ho anistamenos*) would have undoubtedly called to mind the Lord's resurrection, a reading that the Hebrew text of Isaiah does not allow: "On that day the root of Jesse *shall stand as a signal to the peoples*; the nations shall inquire of him, and his dwelling shall be glorious" (Isa. 11:10 NRSV). Understood christologically, then, this text points to the witness of Isaiah, who proclaims the appearance of the risen Messiah, who now rules over the Gentiles as the exalted Lord. J. R. Daniel Kirk (2008, 54) summarizes the essential message of these scriptural citations: "The creation of a mixed people of God ruled by the resurrected Messiah vindicates God's faithfulness to the promises contained in Scripture."

Having explained how Christ has received both the Jewish people and the Gentiles into a community of believers, ruled by the Messiah, who praise God's name, Paul concludes this unit with a prayer-wish: **May the God of hope fill you with all joy and peace in believing, so that you may abound in hope by the power of the Holy Spirit** (Rom. 15:13). Echoing the theme of hope mentioned in 15:4, Paul identifies God as "the God of hope," by which he means the source of all hope. Paul's prayer for the recipients here echoes his earlier description of the kingdom of God, which, he said, consists of righteousness, peace, and joy in the Holy Spirit (14:17). Thus Paul prays that by welcoming each other as the Messiah has welcomed them, the weak and the strong will enter into the fullness of God's kingdom.

Theological Issues

Although Paul's discussion of the weak and the strong deals with a practical issue, it raises an important theological question: What is the nature of the freedom that believers enjoy in Christ? This question arises because of Paul's teaching on justification by faith. If believers are no longer under the law because they belong to Christ, then are they not free in regard to the matters that deal with the law? Moreover, since believers belong to the new humanity that their risen Lord has initiated, are they not free from all things that pertain to the old humanity? Put another way, can the freedom and new life that believers enjoy in the Spirit be circumscribed in any way? While one can imagine Paul's answering these questions in favor of the freedom that believers enjoy in Christ, his discussion in Rom. 14:1–15:13 shows that there are moments when it is necessary to restrain one's personal freedom for the good of the body of believers.

But isn't such a stance a betrayal of the Pauline gospel, an admission that a gospel of Christian freedom is, when all is said and done, an impossibility? Although this may have been the reaction of some of Paul's supporters, the apostle knew better. Having recently defended the rights of his Gentile converts at Galatia to be incorporated into Christ without becoming circumcised and adopting a Jewish way of life, Paul was not about to surrender "the truth of the gospel" (Gal. 2:5, 14). But his experience at Corinth had also taught him how those who insisted on their superior knowledge could harm the body of Christ. Accordingly, in his Letter to the Romans, the apostle frames the question of freedom within the context of the messianic community of Jews and Gentiles, which is meant to worship God with a single voice. The freedom that believers enjoy in Christ, Paul insists, is not an absolute freedom to do whatever one wants. It is a freedom to live in a community of Gentiles and Jews where each graciously acknowledges the differences of the other so that the entire community can worship God in the voice of its messianic Lord.

The freedom that Paul envisions is a freedom to relinquish, at least temporarily, one's legitimate rights so that the community can worship as one body.

It is a freedom that recognizes that, at times, it may be necessary to restrain oneself for the good of the other since all are not at the same level of maturity in the Christian life.

If the question at Rome had been whether Gentile believers could worship Christ without submitting to circumcision and the Mosaic law, there is no doubt where Paul would have stood. But that was not the question. The issue at Rome was whether the weak and the strong could form a united community that glorifies God with a single voice. Aware that the strong were in a position that allowed them greater freedom, Paul adopted the only solution that conformed to the pattern of the Messiah's life. Rather than impose his views, Paul exhorted those who agreed with him to follow the example of the Messiah, who did not seek to please himself.

The exercise of freedom within the church remains an enduring challenge for those who believe in Christ—especially when believers are convinced of the righteousness of their cause. But when the exercise of freedom comes at the cost of injuring others or of dividing the church, it is not the freedom that Paul envisions.

Romans 15:14–16:27

The Letter Closing

⊡

Introductory Matters

Having presented his gospel about God's saving righteousness to the Christ-believers at Rome, Paul ends his letter with an extended conclusion (15:14–16:27), which recalls many of the themes in the letter opening (1:1–17), thereby framing and enclosing the body of the letter (1:18–15:13). Before tracing Paul's train of thought in this conclusion, however, it will be helpful to consider three introductory issues: the doxology of 16:25–27, the formal elements of this conclusion, and the relationship between the conclusion and the letter opening.

The Doxology of Romans 16:25–27

Although the textual tradition that underlies most contemporary editions of Romans concludes the letter with the doxology of 16:25–27, this doxology occurs in several other places in the manuscript tradition. And in a few instances it does not occur at all. Bruce Metzger (1994, 471) summarizes the different places that the doxology is found as follows:

1:1–16:23 plus the doxology
1:1–14:23 plus the doxology plus 15:1–16:23 plus the doxology
1:1–14:23 plus the doxology plus 15:1–16:24

> 1:1–15:33 plus the doxology plus 16:1–23
> 1:1–14:23 plus 16:24 plus the doxology

As this summary shows, the doxology appears in several places. In addition to coming at the end of chapter 16, it can be found at the end of chapter 14, at the end of chapter 15, as well as at the end of chapters 14 *and* 16.

The different places in which the doxology occurs in the textual tradition suggest to some that Romans may have circulated in three different forms: chapters 1–14, chapters 1–15, and chapters 1–16. Origen, for example, reports that the second-century heretic Marcion employed an edition of Romans that contained only fourteen chapters:

> Marcion, by whom the evangelical and apostolic Scriptures have been interpolated, completely removed this section from the epistle; and not only this but he also cut up everything from the place where it is written, "But all that is not from faith is sin," to the end. But in other copies, i.e., in those that have not been desecrated by Marcion, we find this section itself placed in different locations. For in several manuscripts, after the passage cited above, that is, "All that is not from faith is sin," immediately joining this is rendered, "now to him who is able to strengthen you." But other manuscripts contain it at the end, as it now stands. (Origen, *Comm. Rom.* 10.43.2, trans. Scheck 2001–2, 2:307–8)

In the oldest extant manuscript of the Pauline Letters, the Chester Beatty Papyrus 𝔓⁴⁶ (dated to about AD 200), the doxology occurs at the end of chapter 15, which suggested to T. W. Manson (1991) the following: (1) that Paul's Letter to the Romans originally consisted of fifteen chapters, (2) that Marcion subsequently excised chapter 15 because of its OT quotations, and (3) that chapter 16 was originally a cover letter to Ephesus intended to introduce Paul's Letter to the Romans (which he maintains originally consisted of chaps. 1–15) to the Ephesians since it was a summing up of his gospel.

Although this is an attractive interpretation of the manuscript tradition, Manson's proposal has been criticized (Cranfield 1975, 5–11; Gamble 1977, 15–35; Lampe 1991). In my view, Peter Stuhlmacher presents a more persuasive account of the textual history. He argues that Marcion excised chapters 14–15 from the original version of Romans, which consisted of chapters 1–16. Later, however, Marcion's version was supplemented by the addition of chapter 15, as can be seen in 𝔓⁴⁶. "Finally, the entire length of the letter is reconstituted, except that now the statement of praise which concludes chapter 16 (= 16:25–27) either appears twice, that is, after chapters 14 and 16 . . . or only after chapter 14, with a different benediction following 16:23, 'May the grace of our Lord Jesus Christ (be) with you all. Amen' (16:24)" (Stuhlmacher 1994, 245).

To summarize, although the original text of Romans consisted of sixteen chapters, it appears that other editions of the letter circulated, one with only fourteen chapters, another with only fifteen, all of which had the doxology in different places.

The Formal Elements of 15:14–16:27

The closings of Paul's letters vary in length, those of Romans, 1 Corinthians, and Galatians being the longest (Rom. 15:14–16:27; 1 Cor. 16:1–24; Gal. 6:11–18), and those of 2 Corinthians, Philippians, and 1 Thessalonians being shorter (2 Cor. 13:11–13; Phil. 4:21–23; 1 Thess. 5:26–25). Moreover, Paul and other early Christian writers did not follow the conventions of closings for Hellenistic letters as closely as they imitated other formal elements in Hellenistic letters (Doty 1973, 39). Nevertheless certain formal elements occur with some regularity in the Pauline letter closing: a grace benediction, the wish of peace, greetings, the holy kiss, an autographic conclusion, notices of a hortatory nature, travel plans, and requests for prayers. Having cataloged these elements of the Pauline letter closing, Harry Gamble (1977, 65–83) contends that the major components exhibit the following sequence: hortatory remarks, a peace wish, greetings, the holy kiss, grace benediction.

Romans possesses the following formal elements: the announcement of Paul's travel plans (15:22–29), a request for prayers (15:30–33), a commendation (16:1–2), greetings to the recipients (16:3–15), an injunction to exchange a holy kiss (16:16), a concluding exhortation (16:17–20), greetings from those with Paul (16:21–23), a grace wish (which is not present in the best manuscripts; 16:24), and a doxology (16:25–27). The most distinctive element of this letter closing is the extended list of greetings in 16:3–15. The inclusion of this formal element, however, makes eminent sense in the case of Romans because it allows Paul to establish rapport with the Romans, whom he has not yet visited, by showing that he knows many of them. Likewise, given Paul's plans to visit Spain and the controversy that may have attended his impending visit to Rome, it is understandable that he discusses his travel plans in such detail in this letter. The most anomalous element of the letter closing, however, is the benediction, which replaces the more traditional grace wish. It is, however, a majestic conclusion to a magnificent letter.

The Letter Opening and the Letter Closing

In addition to its length, one of the most distinctive characteristics of the letter closing of Romans is the way in which it echoes the letter opening, thereby forming an artful literary frame around the body of the letter. While these echoes occur throughout the conclusion, they are especially evident when Paul discusses his apostolic commission and travel plans (15:14–29). In the letter opening, Paul speaks of the favor or grace of apostleship he has received (1:5); then, in the letter closing, he refers to that favor once more

(15:15) to explain why he has written so boldly (15:14–21). In a similar vein, in the letter opening he tells the Romans of his long-standing desire to visit them but says that he has been prevented from doing so until now (1:13); then in the letter closing he explains what has prevented him from coming to them (15:17–22). He then goes on to reveal, for the first time, that he will go to Spain from Rome (15:22–29). Thus one of the main purposes of the letter closing is to complete and explain themes found in the letter opening. Below I have listed several examples of how the letter conclusion echoes the letter opening:

15:15	because of *the favor given to me* by God
1:5a	through whom we have *received the favor of apostleship*
15:16	*serving the gospel of God in a priestly capacity* so that the *sacrificial offering* of the Gentiles might be pleasing
1:9	God, whom *I worship spiritually by proclaiming the gospel*
15:18	for the *obedience of the Gentiles*
1:5b	*the obedience that comes from faith, among all the Gentiles*
15:19	I have fully proclaimed *the gospel of Christ*
1:3	*a gospel about his Son*
15:22	*I have been detained* for a long time from coming to you
1:13b	*until now I have been prevented* from doing so
15:24a	*I hope*, in passing through, *to see you*
1:11a	*I long to see you*
15:24b	after first *enjoying your company* for a while
1:12	*to be encouraged by you* through our mutual faith
16:19	your obedience has become *known to all*
1:8b	your faith has been *proclaimed throughout the world*
16:25a	to the one who is able *to strengthen you* in accordance with my gospel
1:11b	that I might impart to you some spiritual favor in order *to strengthen you*
16:25b	in accordance with *the revelation of the mystery* that was kept secret
1:17	for in it God's righteousness *is revealed*
16:26a	but now revealed through the *prophetic writings*
1:2	previously promised *through his prophets in the holy Scriptures*
16:26b	that *the obedience that comes from faith* might be made known to *all the Gentiles*
1:5b	*the obedience that comes from faith,* among *all the Gentiles*

To summarize, Paul has adapted the letter closing of Romans to his circumstances. On the one hand, he employs the letter closing to recall and expand upon motifs found in the letter opening. On the other, he uses the letter closing to establish rapport with the Romans so that they will understand why he has written so boldly and why he is about to visit them.

330

Romans 15:14–16:27 in the Rhetorical Flow

The letter opening (1:1–17)

Gentiles and Jews in the light of God's wrath (1:18–3:20)

Gentiles and Jews in the light of God's righteousness (3:21–4:25)

The experience of salvation in the light of God's righteousness (5:1–8:39)

God's righteousness and the destiny of Israel (9:1–11:36)

God's righteousness and the moral life of the justified (12:1–15:13)

▶ **The letter closing (15:14–16:27)**

  Paul's travel plans (15:14–33)

    Paul's missionary commission (15:14–21)

      His confidence in the Romans (15:14)

      Why he has written so boldly to them (15:15–16)

      His boast in Christ (15:17–19)

      His missionary strategy (15:20–21)

    Paul's plans to visit Rome and Spain (15:22–24)

      His long-standing desire to visit Rome (15:22)

      Now free to visit Rome on his way to Spain (15:23–24a)

      Why he is coming to Rome (15:24b)

Paul's immediate plans (15:25–29)

  His ministry to Jerusalem (15:25)

  Gentile participation in the collection (15:26–27)

  His plans to visit Rome and then Spain (15:28–29)

A request for prayers (15:30–33)

  A request to join him in prayer (15:30)

  The reason for the request (15:31–32)

  A prayer-wish (15:33)

Commendation of Phoebe and greetings to those in Rome (16:1–16)

  Commendation of Phoebe (16:1–2)

  Greetings to those in Rome (16:3–16)

A warning (16:17–20)

  Against those who cause divisions (16:17)

  Supporting reason for the warning (16:18)

  Why Paul rejoices and what he wishes (16:19)

  What God will do (16:20a)

  Grace wish (16:20b)

Greetings from those with Paul (16:21–23)

[Grace (16:24)]

Doxology (16:25–27)

Tracing the Train of Thought

The closing of Paul's Letter to the Romans consists of five units (six if we count the grace wish of 16:24, which is not found in all manuscripts). In the first unit, which consists of four subunits (15:14–33), Paul reminds the Romans of his missionary commission (15:14–21), announces his plans to visit Rome before going to Spain (15:22–24), discusses his imminent journey to Jerusalem (15:25–29), and asks the Romans to join him in praying that his ministry to Jerusalem will succeed (15:30–33). In the second unit, which consists of two subunits (16:1–16), he commends Phoebe to the Romans (16:1–2) before extending greetings to numerous believers (16:3–16). In the third unit, the apostle warns the Romans to avoid those who would cause divisions among them (16:17–20). In the fifth, he sends greetings from those who are with him in Corinth (16:21–23). Finally, he concludes with a doxology (16:25–27).

15:14–33. Having completed his paraenesis with a rather forceful exhortation that has been directed primarily at the strong, Paul begins his closing statement by affirming his confidence in the Romans: **I myself am confident about you, my brothers and sisters, that you are full of goodness, filled with all knowledge, capable of admonishing one another** (15:14). Although Paul has implicitly reprimanded the Roman Christians for not welcoming one another as they should, he expresses his supreme confidence in the transformation that has already occurred in their lives. This is why he speaks of their goodness, their knowledge, and their ability to admonish one another. "Goodness" is a gift of God, the fruit that the Spirit produces in the justified (Gal. 5:22). By attributing such goodness to the believers at Rome, Paul affirms that they are no longer in the dire situation of unredeemed humanity, which cries out, "For I know that nothing that is good dwells in me, that is, in my flesh" (Rom. 7:18). By writing that they are "filled with all knowledge," he implicitly contrasts them with unredeemed humanity, which claims to be wise but is foolish (1:22), and whose mind is incapable of discerning good from evil (1:28). Finally, by saying that the Romans are capable of admonishing one another, Paul acknowledges their spiritual maturity (see 1 Cor. 4:14 and Col. 3:16, where Paul admonishes others; 1 Thess. 5:12, where leaders admonish others; and 1 Thess. 5:14 and 2 Thess. 3:15, where believers admonish one another).

Aware that there is a tension between his expansive statement of confidence in the Romans and what he has just written about the strong and the weak, Paul explains why he has written as he has: **But I have written rather boldly to you on some points by way of reminding you because of the favor given me by God to be a minister of Christ Jesus to the Gentiles, serving the gospel of God in a priestly capacity so that the sacrificial offering of the Gentiles might be pleasing, sanctified by the Holy Spirit** (Rom. 15:15–16). Paul begins by acknowledging that he has written rather daringly "on some points" (here I have taken *apo merous* with the verb rather than with the next phrase) for someone who did not establish, and has not even visited, the church at Rome. But he immediately explains this boldness in terms of the "grace" (*charin*) that God has given to him. This *charin* is the grace of his apostleship that Paul mentioned at the outset of the letter (1:5; for other references to the grace given to Paul, see 12:3; 1 Cor. 3:10; Gal. 2:9; Eph. 3:2, 7).

Employing a series of cultic metaphors, Paul makes three statements about the grace of his apostleship. First, this "grace" has made him a "minister" (*leitourgon*) of Christ Jesus to the Gentiles." Second, he exercises his ministry to the Gentiles by serving the gospel in a priestly capacity (*hierourgounta*). Third, the purpose of this ministry is to present the Gentiles as a "sacrificial offering" (*prosphora*) that is pleasing to God and sanctified by the Holy Spirit.

This is not the first time that Paul has used cultic language. In Rom. 3:25 he employed the ritual background of the Day of Atonement to explain the significance of Christ's death. In 12:1 he described the morally good life as an act of worship when he urged the Roman Christians to offer themselves to God as "a living sacrifice, holy and pleasing to God—your spiritual worship." The use of cultic imagery here, then, is not surprising. Similar imagery can be found in Phil. 2:17 and 25. Although Paul was not a priest, and could not be a priest since he belonged to the tribe of Benjamin rather than to the tribe of Levi, he employs cultic language here and elsewhere to highlight the new creation that God has brought about through the death and resurrection of Christ. In this new age, the eschatological people of God, believers drawn from Gentiles as well as Jews, is the temple of God and the dwelling place of God's Spirit (1 Cor. 3:16). In this temple, believers offer themselves to God as a living sacrifice, and by proclaiming the gospel, Paul acts in a priestly capacity. The reason why Paul has spoken so boldly, then, is this: he is Christ's minister whose service to the gospel is a priestly ministry inasmuch as he offers the Gentiles to God as a pleasing sacrifice. Because the Roman Christians have been drawn, at least in part, from the Gentiles, Paul is under obligation to them as well (Rom. 1:5–6).

After reminding the Romans of the grace of apostleship that God has given him, Paul draws a conclusion from what he has said: **Therefore, in Christ Jesus I have this boast in regard to what pertains to God** (15:17). Paul boasts in his ministry to the Gentiles, but his boasting is not grounded in what he has done. Rather, he boasts about what God has done in Christ. This is Paul's boast, however, only and insofar as he is and remains in the sphere of Christ. To explain what he means by this boast, Paul writes, **For I will not be so bold as to speak of anything but what Christ has accomplished in me for the obedience of the Gentiles, in word and deed, by the power of signs and wonders, by the power of God's Spirit** (15:18–19a). Paul's boast is about what Christ has accomplished in him to bring about "the obedience of the Gentiles." This obedience is "the obedience that comes from faith" of which Paul spoke in the letter opening (1:5). It is an obedience that came about as the result of God's powerful work, which has been manifested in "word and deed" (the proclamation of the gospel and the effect of that gospel on the lives of those who have embraced it) and "by the power of signs and wonders" (the signs pointing to God's work and the wonders leading people to praise God). The power behind all of this, however, is not Paul's own power but the power of God's Spirit. Making use of a result clause, Paul explains the outcome of his ministry: **so that from Jerusalem, around about as far as Illyricum, the gospel of Christ has been preached** (15:19b). Although the precise meaning of this statement is not clear, the gist of Paul's words is that he has preached the gospel from Jerusalem in the south to (but probably not into) the Roman province of Illyricum, which lies to the north and west of Greece and in Paul's

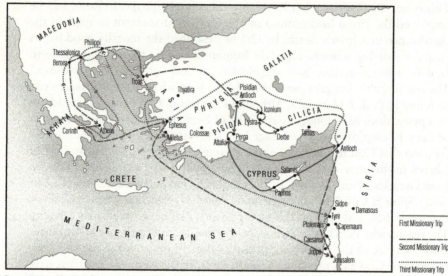

Figure 13. Map of Paul's missionary work in Asia Minor and Greece.

day consisted of the Roman provinces of Macedonia and Achaia. In doing so, he established congregations in the eastern basin of the Mediterranean, a territory that includes modern-day Turkey and Greece.

In the final part of this subunit (15:14–21), Paul explains what his missionary strategy has been: **Thus I have aspired not to preach where Christ is already known, lest I should build on another's foundation** (15:20). Rather than proclaim the gospel where Christ is already known, Paul has opened mission fields where the gospel has not yet been heard. In 2 Cor. 10:15–16 the apostle enunciates a similar strategy as he distinguishes himself from the missionary interlopers who have come to Corinth and disturbed the community that he established there: "We do not boast beyond limits, that is, in the labors of others; but our hope is that, as your faith increases, our sphere of action among you may be greatly enlarged, so that we may proclaim the good news in lands beyond you, *without boasting of work already done in someone else's sphere of action*" (emphasis added). In Romans, however, Paul provides a scriptural warrant for this strategy. Quoting from Isa. 52:15 LXX, which will be his final scriptural citation, Paul writes: **Rather, as it is written, "Those who were not told about him will see, and those who have not heard will understand"** (Rom. 15:21). Paul has already drawn from Isa. 52 in 2:24 in connection with Jewish disobedience to the law, and in 2 Cor. 6:17 in his exhortation to the Corinthians to separate themselves from those who would defile them. Here, however, he focuses on a text of Isa. 52 that stands at the beginning of the fourth Servant Song (Isa. 52:13–53:12). Once more the LXX serves Paul's purpose since it explicitly refers to the servant in a way that the Hebrew text does not. The Hebrew of Isa. 52:15, as translated by NRSV, reads, "for *that which* had not been told them they shall see, and *that which* they had not heard they shall contemplate." The LXX, as translated in NETS, reads, "because those who were not informed *about him* shall see and those who did not hear shall understand." Paul's christological reading of Isaiah identifies the servant as Christ and provides the apostle with a prophecy of his own ministry. For by preaching Christ to those who have not yet heard of him, Paul fulfills Isaiah's words.

To summarize, in Rom. 15:14–21 Paul explains why he has written so boldly: he has received the grace of apostleship to preach the gospel to the Gentiles, among whom are the Romans (1:5–6).

In the next subunit (15:22–24), Paul returns to a theme that he introduced in the opening of this letter: his intention to visit Rome (1:11–15). In the introduction to the letter, Paul said that he had often intended to come to Rome but has been prevented from doing so (1:13), and here he explains why he has been prevented from visiting them: **For this reason, I have been detained many times from coming to you** (15:22). Paul has been detained because of his missionary work in the East. **But now, no longer having any room in these regions, and having longed to come to you for many years . . .** (15:23). He, of course, does not mean that he has preached to everyone in the eastern basin of the Mediterranean. But the work he has done is sufficient to ensure that the gospel will grow and increase. Accordingly, having finished his pioneering missionary work in the East, he is now free to come to Rome.

The grammatical connection between 15:23 and 15:24 is problematic since Paul never completes the sentence that he begins in 15:23, leading some manuscripts to introduce the phrase, "I shall come to you," toward the beginning of 15:24. To establish a smooth connection between these two verses, I have done something similar, as the brackets in my translation indicate: **[I shall come to you] as I go to Spain. For I hope to see you as I pass through and be sent on my way by you, after I have enjoyed your company for a while** (15:24). This is the first time that Paul reveals his plans to go to Spain, although the Romans may have already known his plans from Paul's associates, Phoebe, Prisca, and Aquila (16:3). Moreover, since his primary focus in this letter closing is his visit to Rome, Paul discloses these plans in a rather oblique way. In doing so, it becomes apparent that he is not coming to Rome to build on the foundation that others have laid, since the goal of his journey is Spain, where he hopes to preach to those who have not yet heard of Christ. Earlier, Paul wrote that the purpose of his visit would be to strengthen the Roman Christians and to be encouraged by them, as well as to encourage them (1:11–12). Now he adds that he hopes to enjoy their company for a while before being sent by them on his way. Douglas Moo (1996, 901) notes that the verb Paul uses here, "be sent on my way" (*propemphthēnai*), often implies missionary support. If this is so, Paul is coming to Rome to seek assistance for his Spanish mission as well as to visit the church at Rome.

In the first two subunits, Paul spoke of his missionary commission (15:14–21) and of his plans to visit Rome on his way to Spain (15:22–24). In this third subunit he discloses his immediate plans (15:25–29). Before visiting Rome and Spain, he must go to Jerusalem. Paul begins with a strong adversative statement: **But now, at the present time, I am going to Jerusalem to minister to the holy ones** (15:25). The use of *diakonōn*, which I have rendered as "to minister," signals that his visit to Jerusalem is for the purpose of ministering and serving the needs of the poor, as he will explain in the following verses. The "holy ones" (*hagiois*) to whom he will minister are the circumcised Christ-believers at Jerusalem. Like all believers, they are not called "the holy ones" or "the saints" because of their personal holiness but because they have been set aside and consecrated for service to God through the death of Christ and the gift of the Spirit.

In the first of three clauses that begin with *gar* (for), Paul explains why he is going to Jerusalem at this time: **for Macedonia and Achaia have determined to contribute to the poor among the holy ones in Jerusalem** (15:26). Macedonia refers to the Roman province in northern Greece, where Paul established congregations in Philippi and Thessalonica, and Achaia refers to the Roman province in the south of Greece, where he founded a vibrant though sometimes contentious congregation at Corinth. Although the Corinthians appear to have responded with enthusiasm to Paul's original request that they contribute to the needs of "the holy ones" in Jerusalem, the difficulties that Paul experienced with the community, as chronicled in 2 Corinthians, delayed the completion of the collection. In 2 Cor. 8–9, therefore, after these issues were resolved, Paul tells the Corinthians that the Macedonians have already made their contribution to this collection (2 Cor. 8:1–5), and he urges the Corinthians to complete the work of the collection that they had begun a year earlier (2 Cor. 8:6–11). Romans 16:23 indicates that Paul is writing from Corinth, and his report that Achaia and Macedonia have contributed to this collection suggests that the Corinthian crisis has been resolved in his favor. This is why Paul is now bringing a collection of money from his Gentile congregations for "the poor among the holy ones in Jerusalem." While this last phrase could be construed as "the poor who are the holy ones," I have interpreted it as "the poor *among* the holy ones," the sense being that not all of the Jerusalem believers were poor.

Making use of two more *gar* clauses, Paul explains the significance of this collection: **For they have resolved to do this and are indebted to them. For if the Gentiles have shared in their spiritual gifts, they ought to minister to them in material things** (15:27). First, Paul emphasizes the resolve (*eudokēsan*, lit., "they were pleased") of the Macedonians and Achaians to contribute to the collection, thereby dispelling any notion that they were forced to do so. Second, he argues that if his Gentile converts have shared in the spiritual gifts of the Jerusalem Christ-believers, they ought to assist them in their time of

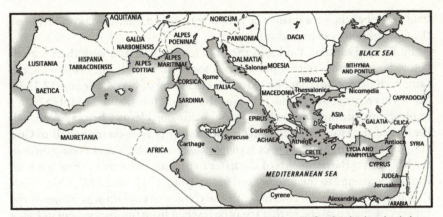

Figure 14. Map of Paul's proposed journey. Paul's journey to Spain would have entailed traveling from Corinth to Jerusalem, in the eastern region of the empire, then west to Rome. From Rome, he would have traveled to Spain, in the western region of the empire (see Hispania Tarraconensis on this map).

need. After all, it is a small thing for Gentile believers to share their material resources (*sarkikois*, lit., "fleshly things") with the Jerusalem church since the circumcised have shared their "spiritual gifts" (*pneumatikois*) with them. As Paul sees it, there ought to be a reciprocity between Jewish and Gentile believers, a point he makes in 2 Cor. 8:12–14. The collection is of supreme importance for Paul because, if it is accepted, it will signify the unity in Christ that binds his Gentile congregations with the Jewish Christ-believers of Jerusalem.

Having explained why he is about to go to Jerusalem, Paul draws a conclusion from what he has said: **Therefore, when I have completed this and safely delivered this gift for them, I shall go to Spain by way of you. And I know that when I come to you, I shall come with the fullness of Christ's blessing** (Rom. 15:28–29). The manner in which Paul describes his travel plans here indicates that Rome is only a stopping-off point on his journey to Spain. It is, however, an important stopping point since Paul hopes to come to the Romans with "the fullness of Christ's blessing." This difficult expression can be construed in at least two ways: (1) Paul will come with the fullness of the blessing that comes from Christ because his ministry in Jerusalem has been successful (Stuhlmacher 1994, 243); (2) Paul will bring the Romans the fullness of Christ's blessing by imparting some spiritual favor in order to strengthen them as he promised in 1:11 (Fitzmyer 1993, 723). Before this happens, however, he must complete his mission to Jerusalem and "seal this fruit for them" (*sphragisamenos autois ton karpon touton*), a phrase that I have rendered as "and safely delivered this gift for them." According to my construal, Paul employs the sealing metaphor to describe the final act in his service to the believers at Jerusalem. By personally bringing the collection to them, he will certify that it has reached its intended recipients. (See 2 Cor. 8:19–23, where

Paul describes the precautions he is taking to ensure that the contribution of the Corinthians is delivered safely.)

In the final subunit, Paul asks the Romans to assist him with their prayers before he concludes with a prayer-wish for them (15:30–33). Employing the same verb (*parakalō*) that he used at the beginning of his paraenesis (12:1), he frames his request in a manner that involves God, Jesus, and the Holy Spirit: **I implore you, brothers and sisters, through our Lord Jesus Christ and through the love of the Holy Spirit to assist me with your prayers on my behalf to God** (15:30). The verb that Paul uses (*synagōnisasthai*), which occurs only once in the NT, invites the recipients of the letter to play an active role in praying with Paul by pointing "to the urgent need for assistance" (Jewett 2007, 934). Next, Paul introduces two interrelated purpose clauses to explain why he needs the support of their prayers: **so that I may be rescued from the disobedient in Judea and my service to Jerusalem may be acceptable to the holy ones, in order that through God's will I might come in joy and be refreshed by your company** (15:31–32). First, despite his own enthusiasm for the collection, Paul is not sure how the circumcised Christ-believers of Jerusalem will receive the gift of his Gentile converts. Although some will surely accept this gracious gift, since it was the pillar apostles who required it (Gal. 2:9–10), Paul is fearful that some—the disobedient—will refuse his gift, because they oppose his Gentile ministry. Second, Paul asks the Romans for their prayers so that he can come to them "in joy" and be refreshed by them. Here Paul relates the joy of his visit to Rome to the success of his ministry in Jerusalem. If the latter fails, then the former will not be as joyful and refreshing as he hopes it will be.

Having requested the prayers of the Romans, Paul ends this unit (15:14–33) with a prayer-wish just as he concluded the previous section (14:1–15:13) with a prayer-wish (15:13): **The God of peace be with all of you. Amen** (15:33).

16:1–16. Having explained his missionary commission (15:14–21), disclosed his travel plans (15:22–29), and requested their prayers (15:30–33), Paul commends Phoebe to the Romans (16:1–2) before greeting several of them by name (16:3–16). In doing so, he indicates that even though he has never visited them, he is personally acquainted with many of them.

Paul's commendation of Phoebe has three parts. The first is the commendation proper: **I commend to your our sister Phoebe, who is also a minister of the church at Cenchreae** (16:1). In commending her, Paul identifies Phoebe in two ways. First, he calls her "our sister," thereby indicating that she belongs to the fellowship of those who are brothers and sisters to one another because they have become members of a new family in Christ. Thus, even though Phoebe is not one of them, she is their sister in Christ. Second, he informs them that she is a "minister" (*diakonos*) of the church at Cenchreae, a Corinthian harbor on the southeastern side of the isthmus that connects southern Achaia to northern Achaia and to Macedonia further north. According to Acts 18:18, before sailing for Syria, Paul had his hair cut at Cenchreae because of a vow he had taken. Although Paul may have been the founder of the church at Cenchreae, Phoebe was its *diakonos*, a term that Robert Jewett (2007, 944) takes as "an official title of leadership." In 1 Cor. 3:5 and 2 Cor. 3:6, Paul employs *diakonos* in speaking of his own ministry, and in the opening of the Letter to the Philippians (1:1), he greets the Philippians along with their "bishops and deacons" (*episkopois kai diakonois*), terms that indicate positions of leadership within that community.

In the second part of the commendation, Paul explains why he is commending Phoebe to them: **in order that you might receive her in the Lord in a manner worthy of the holy ones and assist her in whatever matter she may need your assistance** (16:2a). Here Paul makes two points. First, he wants the Romans to welcome Phoebe in a way that is worthy of her Christian dignity as one of "the holy ones." Second, he wants them to assist her in the task for which she has come to Rome. Although Paul does not explain what this task is, what he has just said about his plans to go to Spain by way of Rome suggests that Phoebe has come to Rome to make remote preparations for Paul's mission to Spain. If this is the case, then Phoebe may have been in Rome to seek the moral and material support of the Roman Christians for Paul's mission to Spain by encouraging some of them to accompany him as interpreters and evangelists.

In the final part of the commendation, Paul provides a supporting reason for commending Phoebe: **For she has been a patroness to many, including myself** (16:2b). The designation of Phoebe as a "patroness" indicates that she is a woman of considerable financial resources. For, in addition to hosting a community of believers in her home, she has also supported Paul in his work. That she is now in Rome suggests that she will also support him in his mission to Spain. If Phoebe is also the bearer of the Letter to the Romans, as many commentators suggest (Stuhlmacher 1994, 246), she has come to Rome with a double mission: (1) to deliver and interpret the Letter to the Romans, (2) and to make remote preparations for Paul's mission to Spain. It is not without reason, then, that in commenting on this text, Origen (*Comm. Rom.* 10.17.2, trans. Scheck 2001–2, 2:290) wrote, "This passage teaches with apostolic authority that women are likewise appointed to the ministry of the Church."

Following his commendation of Phoebe, Paul greets several people at Rome in order to deepen his relationship with those who have heard his gospel proclaimed to them through this letter (16:3–16). The structure of this subunit is determined by the aorist imperative *aspasasthe* (greet), which occurs sixteen times. By using this imperative, Paul invites the Romans, who belong to different house and tenement churches, to greet one another in his name (Jewett 2007, 951–52). Thus these greetings, which conclude with an exhortation to exchange a "holy kiss" (16:16), encourage the Romans to overcome whatever tensions have arisen among them, especially between the strong and the weak.

Before tracing the train of thought in this text, it will be helpful to tease out some observations about the Roman Christians from this list of names. First,

Paul says something about those whom he greets in the first part of this list, but in the last part he merely lists names, which may suggest that he knows of these people but is not personally acquainted with them (16:14–15). Second, the manner in which Paul greets (a) the church in the house of Prisca and Aquila, (b) those who belong to the household of Aristobulus, (c) those who belong to the household of Narcissus, (d) those listed in 16:14, and (e) those listed in 16:15 indicates that there are at least five different groups of believers at Rome. Furthermore, as Peter Lampe (1991, 230) notes, if we suppose that those who do not belong to any of these five groups belong to one or more other groups, "the result is at least seven separate groups" at Rome. Third, since many of the people in this list bear names that were used for slaves and for freedmen and freedwomen, it appears that several of the Roman Christians were slaves, had been slaves, or were descended from slaves. Fourth, while the majority of names are Greek and Latin, which points to a Gentile background, the designation of Andronicus, Junia, and Herodion as Paul's "compatriots" indicates that there were Jewish Christians as well as Gentile Christians among the Romans whom Paul was addressing. Fifth, several of the people that Paul names are actively involved in the work of evangelization. He calls Prisca, Aquila, and Urbanus his "coworkers." Andronicus and Junia are apostles. Mary, Tryphaena, Tryphosa, and Persis have worked hard for the Lord. Apelles has been tested in some way for Christ. Rufus is chosen or elect, and his mother has been a mother to Paul as well. Thus, in addition to five men (Aquila, Urbanus, Andronicus, Apelles, and Rufus), Paul highlights the service of seven women in addition to Phoebe (Prisca, Junia, Mary, Tryphaena, Tryphosa, Persis, and the mother of Rufus). The number of women that Paul identifies as engaged in the work of the gospel highlights the prominent role that women played in the Pauline mission.

Paul's first and most extensive greeting is to Prisca and Aquila: **Greet Prisca and Aquila, my coworkers in Christ Jesus, who, for the sake of my life, endangered their own lives, for whom not only I but all the churches among the Gentiles render thanks, and greet the church in their house** (16:3–5a). According to Acts 18:2–3, Aquila was a native of Pontus who had recently come to Corinth from Italy with his wife, "Priscilla" (the diminutive form of Prisca), because the Roman emperor Claudius had expelled the Jews from Rome. Since they practiced the same trade as Paul, he stayed with them when he was at Corinth in the early fifties. By the midfifties, they appear to be the leaders of a house church at Ephesus, according to 1 Cor. 16:19. But now, as Paul writes Romans, they are in Rome once more where they are hosting yet another church in their house. Whereas Acts tends to speak of "Priscilla and Aquila," Paul refers to them as "Prisca and Aquila"; perhaps Prisca is listed first because of her higher social rank. In calling them his "coworkers" (*synergous*), a term he frequently employs (1 Cor. 3:9; 2 Cor. 1:24; 8:23; Phil. 2:25; 4:3; Col. 4:11; 1 Thess. 3:2; Philem. 1, 24), Paul identifies them as evangelists who have worked alongside him in preaching the gospel. They are especially dear to Paul, and to all of the Gentile churches among whom they have labored, because they have risked their lives for Paul. Where and when, Paul does not say. But given the many hardships that Paul has endured (2 Cor. 11:23–28), they would have had many opportunities to assist him. Paul's greeting to "the church in their house" is the first use of *ekklēsia* in reference to the Christians at Rome.

Paul extends his second greeting to Epaenetus: **Greet Epaenetus, beloved to me, who is the first convert for Christ in Asia** (16:5b). Paul calls Epaenetus "beloved" because he was Paul's first convert in Asia. He makes a similar statement about Stephanas, whose household comprised Paul's first converts in Achaia (1 Cor. 16:15). Since Epaenetus came from Asia, he may have been a member of the church that met in the home of Prisca and Aquila in Ephesus. If so, he may also belong to the church that meets in their home at Rome.

Paul's third greeting is to Mary: **Greet Mary, who has worked earnestly for you** (16:6). His description of her suggests that she has played an important role among the Christians in Rome. Since her name has both a Hebrew (Miriam) and Latin (Maria) background, it is not possible to say with assurance if she is a Jewish or Gentile believer.

In his fourth greeting, Paul mentions a second married couple: **Greet Andronicus and Junia, my compatriots and fellow prisoners, who are prominent among the apostles, and who were in Christ before me** (16:7). Although some have tried to interpret the name "Junia" as masculine ("Junias"), this is unlikely since, while there are over 250 examples of "Junia," no example of "Junias" has been found among Roman inscriptions (Jewett 2007, 961). Paul identifies this couple in four ways. First, they are his "compatriots" (*syngeneis*), which, in light of 9:3, indicates that they are Jewish Christians. Second, on one or more occasions they were imprisoned with him. Third, like Paul they are numbered among the apostles, by which Paul means someone who has seen the Lord (1 Cor. 9:1) or has been commissioned for special work but is not one of the Twelve (compare 1 Cor. 15:5 with 15:7). Fourth, they believed in Christ before Paul did. Their prominence among the "apostles" suggests a special standing due, perhaps, to their work and suffering for the gospel.

Paul's fifth greeting is brief: **Greet Ampliatus, my beloved in the Lord** (16:8). Like Epaenetus, he is addressed as "beloved," which has the sense of dear or close friend. But this time Paul adds "in the Lord," thereby indicating the nature of their friendship. Ampliatus, which means "ample," was a common slave name.

Paul extends his sixth greeting to two people: **Greet Urbanus our coworker in Christ and my beloved Stachys** (16:9). Urbanus, whose name means "refined" or "elegant in manner," appears to have been more actively engaged in the work of the gospel, whereas Stachys, whose name refers to a head or ear of grain, is designated as a close friend of Paul.

Paul's seventh greeting is to Apelles, whose name was common among Jews (see BDAG 101, s.v. *Apellēs*): **Greet Apelles, tested in Christ** (16:10a). By saying that Apelles was "tested" (*dokimon*) in Christ, Paul implies that Apelles is a tried and true Christian because of what he has endured for the Lord.

In his eighth greeting, Paul appears to address a group of believers who belong to a particular household: **Greet those who belong to the household of Aristobulus** (16:10b). Since he addresses those who belong to the household of Aristobulus, it is unlikely that Aristobulus is a believer. But some of the members of his household are. Although Paul is aware of this group of believers, he does not appear to know anyone who belongs to it personally.

Paul's ninth greeting is addressed to Herodion: **Greet Herodion my compatriot** (16:11a). Like Andronicus and Junia, he is identified as a compatriot, which indicates that he too is a Jewish believer in Christ.

Paul's tenth greeting is similar to his eighth: **Greet those from the household of Narcissus who are in the Lord** (16:11b). Like Aristobulus, Narcissus (who bears a name frequently found among slaves and freedmen) is not a Christian. But some of the members of his household are, and these are the people whom Paul greets.

In his eleventh and twelfth greetings, Paul greets three women, all of whom have worked on behalf of the gospel: **Greet Tryphaena and Tryphosa, who have worked hard in the Lord. Greet beloved Persis, who has worked earnestly in the Lord** (16:12). Whereas Tryphaena means "dainty," Tryphosa means "luscious." All three are either slaves or freedwomen (Lampe 1991, 228). Like Epaenetus, Ampliatus, and Stachys, Persis is called "beloved," indicating friendship with Paul.

Paul's thirteenth greeting is to a mother and her son: **Greet Rufus, who is outstanding in the Lord, and his mother and mine** (16:13). In the Markan passion narrative, the man who carries the cross for Jesus is identified as Simon, the father of Alexander and Rufus (Mark 15:21). Although some commentators are reluctant to connect the two persons named Rufus (Fitzmyer 1993, 741), others are not (Jewett 2007, 269). Rufus is called "outstanding" (*eklekton*, lit., "elect" or "chosen") in the Lord. While all believers are elect and chosen in the Lord, the use of the adjective here suggests a certain prominence. His mother, who is not named, has been of service to Paul. Thus he refers to her as his mother too.

In his fourteenth greeting Paul lists a number of Christians who appear to belong to a particular group: **Greet Asyncritus, Phlegon, Hermes, Patrobas, Hermas, and the brothers and sisters with them** (16:14). That he greets these five men and then those with them may signify that these five play a leadership role within this group.

Paul's fifteenth greeting is also addressed to five people: **Greet Philologus and Julia, Nereus and his sister, and Olympas and all the holy ones with them** (16:15). If Philologus and Julia are a married couple, as the conjunction *kai* may indicate, this would be the third couple that Paul greets. That he does not address the sister of Nereus by name suggests that Paul is not personally familiar with her or with this group. As in 16:14, the reference to other people, in this case "the holy ones with them," may indicate that the people named here play a leadership role in this group of believers.

In his sixteenth and final greeting that uses the imperative, Paul instructs all of the Romans: **Greet one another with a holy kiss** (16:a). This command is significant if there are tensions among the different groups of believers at Rome since it would require the members of the different groups to extend a "holy kiss" to one another. Although the precise significance of this kiss is unknown, the designation of it as "holy" indicates that it was not an erotic kiss but a kiss by which believers express their unity with one another. Other references to such a kiss are found in 1 Cor. 16:20; 2 Cor. 13:12; 1 Thess. 5:26; 1 Pet. 5:14.

Making use of the present indicative rather than the aorist imperative, Paul concludes his greetings in a more general way: **All the churches of Christ greet you** (Rom. 16:16b). While this greeting is universal in scope, one suspects that Paul has in view the many Gentile congregations he has established or with which he is associated.

16:17–20. This brief exhortation, which warns the Romans to watch out for those who would cause dissensions and lead them into sin, has puzzled commentators. On the one hand, this warning seems out of place and unrelated to what Paul has just written. On the other, it stands between the greetings of 16:3–16 and those of 16:21–23. It is not surprising, then, that several commentators view this unit as a non-Pauline interpolation that comes from a later period. Robert Jewett (2007, 985, 988), for example, entitles this unit "The Church's Campaign against Heretics," and he assigns it "to the group that produced the Pastoral Epistles toward the end of the first century." Arguing that the benediction of 16:25–27 as well as this passage are non-Pauline interpolations, he maintains that the original ending of the letter consisted of the greetings (16:3–16, 21–23) followed by an epistolary benediction, which is found in 16:20b in some manuscripts and in 16:24 (in a slightly longer form) in others. Although this rearrangement of the text provides a more satisfying ending to Romans inasmuch as it connects the greeting of 16:3–16 with those of 16:21–23 and concludes the letter with a grace wish rather than the benediction of 16:25–27, the manuscript tradition attests to the constant presence of 16:17–20a in Romans. Moreover, there are other instances of brief exhortations in the conclusion of Paul's Letters (1 Cor. 16:13–18; 2 Cor. 13:11). Accordingly, while I recognize the problems that this unit presents, I treat it as part of the original letter.

The unit begins in a way that recalls the beginning of the exhortation in 12:1: **I exhort you, brothers and sisters, watch out for those who cause dissensions and enticements contrary to the teaching that you have learned. Avoid them!** (16:17). But whereas 12:1 exhorted the Romans to live in accordance with the divine mercy they have experienced in Christ, this exhortation is monitory in nature, similar to the kinds of warnings found in 1 Cor. 5:11; 2 Cor. 11:13–15; Gal. 1:9. Unlike these warnings, however, the warning of Romans is more general in nature and seemingly unrelated to the previous discussion of the weak and the strong. The Romans are to avoid those who would cause divisions and entice them to sin since such behavior is opposed to the pattern of the teaching to which they were handed over at their baptism (Rom. 6:17).

To support his exhortation, Paul provides the Romans with a brief description of the underlying motives of these would-be troublemakers: **For such people do not serve our Lord Christ but their own bodily appetites, and through refined speech and flattery they lead astray the hearts of the unsuspecting** (16:18). Paul's portrayal of those who would divide the Romans is reminiscent of his description of the "superapostles" whom he confronted at Corinth (2 Cor. 11:13–14). Like the superapostles, these people would, if given the opportunity, ingratiate themselves to the community by their skillful rhetoric. His warning about the false teachers who would require the Philippians to become circumcised is similar. Such people conduct themselves as "enemies of the cross of Christ," he writes, and "their god is their belly" (Phil. 3:18–19). The Greek *koilia* (belly) occurs here in Rom. 16:18 as well, where I have rendered it "bodily appetites."

Having warned the Romans of those who would divide them, Paul expresses his confidence in them just as he did in 1:8 and 15:14: **Your obedience has become known to all; therefore I rejoice because of you** (16:19a). Paul's reference to their obedience recalls the theme of "the obedience that consists in faith" that he first announced in 1:5. His expression of joy tempers his warning and suggests that he is giving the Romans pastoral advice rather than scolding them. Employing language that is similar to, though not necessarily dependent upon, Jesus's words in Matt. 10:16, Paul writes: **I would like you to be wise in regard to what is good, and innocent in regard to what is evil** (Rom. 16:19b). In saying that he wants them to be "wise in regard to what is good," Paul is not implying that they are not good, for he has already affirmed that they are "full of goodness" (15:14). Rather, he expresses his hope that they will be able to discern between those who truly serve Christ and those who only serve themselves.

Confident of God's victory, Paul writes: **God, who is the source of peace, will quickly trample Satan under your feet** (16:20a). As in 15:33, Paul identifies God as the "God of peace" (see also Phil. 4:9; 1 Thess. 5:23). I have rendered this expression as "God, who is the source of peace," because God is the one who has reconciled humanity to himself with the result that the justified are at peace with God (Rom. 5:1). Employing an image that is reminiscent of Gen. 3:15 ("he [a descendant of Eve] will strike your head, and you [the serpent] will strike his heel"), Paul provides the Romans with a vision of God's apocalyptic victory over Satan. Although this is the first reference to Satan in Romans, Satan appears with some frequency in the Pauline Letters (1 Cor. 5:5; 7:5; 2 Cor. 2:11; 11:14; 12:7; 1 Thess. 2:18; 2 Thess. 2:9; 1 Tim. 1:20; 5:15).

This unit concludes with a grace wish: **The grace of our Lord Jesus be with you** (Rom. 16:20b). Such grace wishes occur at the end of every Pauline letter except Romans (1 Cor. 16:24; 2 Cor. 13:13; Gal. 6:18; Eph. 6:24; Phil. 4:23;

Col. 4:18; 1 Thess. 5:28; 2 Thess. 3:18; 1 Tim. 6:21; 2 Tim. 4:22; Titus 3:15; Philem. 25), unless Jewett (2007, 986–88, 998–1002) is correct in identifying Rom. 16:17–20a and 16:25–27 as non-Pauline interpolations.

16:21–23. After the brief exhortation of 16:17–20, Paul resumes the greetings that he interrupted after 16:16b. The unit exhibits a tripartite structure: greetings from four individuals who are with Paul (16:21), greetings from the scribe who has written this letter (16:22), greetings from three more individuals who are with Paul (16:23). Thus this section consists of greetings from eight individuals who are with Paul.

My coworker Timothy greets you, as do my compatriots Lucius and Jason and Sosipater (16:21). In this initial greeting, pride of place is given to Timothy, whom Paul identifies as his "coworker." Timothy is named as the cosender of six of the Pauline Letters (2 Corinthians, Philippians, Colossians, 1 and 2 Thessalonians, Philemon) and as the recipient of two others (1 and 2 Timothy). He was Paul's envoy to the Thessalonians (1 Thess. 3:2, 6), the Corinthians (1 Cor. 4:17), and the Philippians (Phil. 2:19). According to the Acts of the Apostles, he was with Paul during his second and third missionary journeys (16:3; 19:22; 20:4), but after that there is no mention of him in Acts. Next, Paul sends the greetings of three other persons whom he identifies as "my compatriots" (*hoi syngeneis mou*), thereby signifying their Jewish background. Acts 13:1 speaks of Lucius of Cyrene, a prophet and teacher in the church at Antioch, but it is unlikely that he is the same person listed here since Paul identifies him only as a compatriot. The Jason who is mentioned here, however, is probably the Jason who hosted Paul and Silas at Thessalonica, according to Acts 17:5–7, 9. Sosipater is often identified with Sopater, a man from Beroea who accompanied Paul on his journey from Greece to Syria (Acts 20:4–6). These three men may have been in Corinth because they were about to accompany Paul on his journey to Jerusalem with the collection.

I, Tertius, the writer of this letter, greet you in the Lord (Rom. 16:22). This greeting provides us with an insight into the composition of this letter. While it is possible that Paul outlined the contents of this letter for Tertius and then entrusted the actual writing of it to him, it is more likely that Tertius was the scribe to whom Paul dictated the letter over several weeks or months, testing and trying out phrases for their rhetorical effect before Tertius wrote them down. Given the work involved in such a task, it is appropriate that Tertius, who appears to be a Christian, greets the Romans as well.

Gaius, my host, greets you, as does the whole church. Erastus, the city treasurer, greets you, as does our brother Quartus (16:23). Although persons by the name of Gaius appear in Acts 19:29; 20:4; and 3 John 1, the Gaius named here is undoubtedly the Corinthian whom Paul baptized (1 Cor. 1:14). He is now Paul's host at Corinth, from where Paul writes this letter. The phrase, "the whole church," suggests that Gaius is the host of a church, or of the whole church, at Corinth, although some interpret the phrase to mean that Gaius

Figure 15. The Erastus Inscription. This inscription, unearthed at Corinth in 1929, mentions the aedile "Erastus" as one who laid the pavement at his own expense. (The Latin reads: "Erastus pro aedilit[ate] s[ua] p[ecunia] stravit.") Archaeologists estimate that the pavement was laid around AD 50, so this could be the same Erastus mentioned in Rom. 16:23.

"had the reputation of extending hospitality to Christian travelers from all over the world" (Jewett 2007, 980–81). Acts 19:22 refers to Erastus and Timothy as Paul's assistants, and 2 Tim. 4:20 speaks of Erastus as remaining in Corinth. Here he is identified as the "city treasurer" (*oikonomos*). He is often identified with the Erastus mentioned in a famous inscription that reads: "Erastus in return for his aedileship laid (the pavement) at his own expense" (Murphy-O'Connor 1983, 37). Quartus, who is identified as a "brother," by which Paul means a fellow Christian, is not otherwise mentioned in the NT.

[16:24.] At this point some manuscripts introduce a grace wish: **The grace of our Lord Jesus Christ be with all of you. Amen** (16:24). While this grace wish provides a fitting ending to Paul's greetings, most commentators view it as a later addition because of the inferior quality of the textual witnesses that support it.

16:25–27. As I noted in the section on introductory issues, this doxology occurs in different places in the manuscript tradition. In addition to its position here, which is attested to by a number of strong textual witnesses, it occurs after 14:23 and 15:33. Given the distinctive style and length of this benediction, as well as the different places that it appears in Romans, most commentators question its Pauline origin. It does, however, recapitulate many of the letter's themes: the gospel, the revelation of the mystery, the prophetic scriptures, the obedience of faith. Although somewhat rambling, the benediction exhibits the following structure: an initial ascription to God (16:25a), an excursus about the mystery revealed through the gospel (16:25b–26), and an ascription of praise to God offered through Jesus Christ (16:27).

The benediction begins by pointing **To the one who is able to strengthen you** (16:25a). By identifying God as "the one who is able [*tō dynamenō*] to strengthen [*stērixai*]" the recipients of the letter, the benediction echoes the letter opening, in which Paul expresses his desire to impart some spiritual favor to the Romans so that he might "strengthen" them (1:11). It also recalls his description of the gospel as the manifestation of "the power of God" (*dynamis theou*) that leads to salvation (1:16).

Having identified God as the one who is able to strengthen the recipients of the letter, the benediction explains how God will strengthen them: **in accordance with my gospel, that is, the proclamation of Jesus Christ, in accordance with the revelation of the mystery that was kept secret from all eternity but is now revealed through the prophetic writings in accordance with the command of the eternal God, in order that the obedience of faith might be made known to all the nations** (16:25b–26). Here the benediction makes four points, each one echoing important themes found in the letter. First, God will strengthen the recipients through Paul's gospel, which is Paul's preaching about Jesus the Messiah. Here the benediction echoes the use of "my gospel" in 2:16, as well as the multiple uses of "gospel" in the letter opening (1:2, 3, 9, 15, 16). Second, the gospel is the revelation of a mystery that has been hidden. Here the benediction echoes the theme of the mystery that Paul has announced in 11:25. Third, the mystery has now been revealed through the prophetic writings according to the command of the eternal God. Here the benediction echoes Paul's insistence that Israel's scriptures bear witness to the gospel (1:2; 3:21). Fourth, God's purpose in revealing this mystery through the gospel was to make the obedience of faith known among the Gentiles. Here the benediction echoes the theme of the obedience of faith announced in 1:5.

Having explained how God will strengthen the recipients through the gospel, the benediction concludes by ascribing praise to God through Jesus Christ: **to God who alone is wise, to him, through Jesus Christ, be glory forever. Amen** (16:27). In describing God as "wise," the benediction recalls Paul's own wonder in the face of the depth of the wisdom and knowledge of God (11:33–36). In ascribing glory to God, the benediction does what rebellious humanity refused to do: glorify God (1:22–23). Thus the benediction reminds both the recipients of the letter and the readers of this commentary of the true purpose of human existence: to glorify God through Jesus Christ.

Theological Issues

Although the Pauline collection for the poor among the "holy ones" of Jerusalem may appear to be a minor matter, it had a profoundly religious meaning for Paul, and it is intimately related to the central theme of this letter: God's saving righteousness on behalf of Gentiles and Jews. Deeply aware that he had been entrusted with the gospel to the uncircumcised just as Peter had been entrusted with the gospel to the circumcised (Gal. 2:7), Paul did not abandon his own people, as Rom. 9–11 testifies. Nor did he view his gospel as doing away with, or voiding, the promises that God made to Israel. Consequently, even though many of his contemporaries—Jewish Christians as well as the Jews who did not believe in Christ—saw him as an apostate from Judaism, Paul understood his gospel as establishing the deepest meaning of the law (3:31), which, in his view, reached its salvation-historical terminus in the appearance of the Messiah (10:4). The Jerusalem collection, then, was more than a charitable donation. Given his understanding of the gospel of God's saving righteousness in Jesus Christ for Gentile and Jew alike, Paul saw it as a concrete expression of the visible unity between Gentile and Jew in Christ. This, of course, was the essence of the gospel he preached, a gospel that Paul describes as the power of God that leads to salvation for the Jewish people first because of their privileged role in salvation history and only then for the Gentiles (1:16).

By bringing the collection to Jerusalem, then, Paul was doing something far more important than bringing relief to the poor of that city. He was fulfilling the prophecy of Isaiah in a symbolic way: "In the days to come the mountain of the LORD's house shall be established as the highest of the mountains, and shall be raised above the hills; all the nations shall stream to it" (Isa. 2:1). The reason, then, that Paul devotes so much of his time and effort to encouraging his Gentile converts to contribute to the collection (1 Cor. 16:1–4; 2 Cor. 8–9) is that he seeks to establish an enduring "communion" (*koinōnia*) in Christ between his Gentile congregations and the Jewish-Christian community of Jerusalem, from which the gospel went forth. Thus God will be praised by a united chorus of Gentile and Jewish believers.

Christianity did not develop in the way Paul hoped it would. Jewish Christianity is a phenomenon of the past, and Gentile Christianity has long since become the dominant form of faith in Christ. Paul's theological understanding of the Jerusalem collection, however, stands as a stark reminder that the continuing separation between Gentile and Jew is not what the Pauline gospel envisioned. Although Paul was deeply pained that the majority of his compatriots did not accept the saving righteousness that God manifested in Christ, he continued to preach a gospel that embraces the whole of humanity—Gentile as well as Jew—in the new human being, the eschatological Adam. Although this gospel has sometimes been used to exclude and separate people, its true meaning is found in a salvation that embraces all people. For Paul, this meant overcoming the division between Gentile and Jew that, from his Jewish perspective, divided the world. In our day, the dividing lines have become more complex. But the gospel that Paul proclaimed remains the same: the salvation that God offers in and through Christ is not intended for the few but for the many. It is not a salvation based on what people do or fail to do, but on what God has already done for them. It is a salvation that summons people to unity by confessing that all, without exception, stand in need of God's saving grace.

The Jerusalem collection was not, and it could never be, a minor issue for Paul since it pointed to the purpose of God's saving righteousness in Christ: the unity of all people—Gentiles as well as Jews—in the human being who has already entered into the fullness of God's glory.

Soli Deo gloria

Bibliography

Aageson, James W. 1986. "Scripture and Structure in the Development of the Argument in Romans 9–11." *Catholic Biblical Quarterly* 48:265–89.

Achtemeier, Paul J. 1985. *Romans*. Interpretation: A Bible Commentary for Teaching and Preaching. Atlanta: John Knox.

Agersnap, Søren. 1999. *Baptism and the New Life: A Study of Romans 6.1–14*. Aarhus: Aarhus University Press.

Aland, Kurt, and Barbara Aland. 1989. *The Text of the New Testament: An Introduction to the Critical Editions and the Theology and Practice of Modern Textual Criticism*. 2nd rev. and enlarged ed. Grand Rapids: Eerdmans.

Aletti, Jean-Noël. 1991. *Comment Dieu est-il juste? Clefs pour interpréter l'épître aux Romains*. Parole de Dieu. Paris: Seuil.

———. 1998. *Israël et la loi dans la lettre aux Romains*. Lectio divina 173. Paris: Cerf.

———. 2002. "Rm 7.7–25 encore une fois: Enjeux et propositions." *New Testament Studies* 48:358–76.

Arichea, D. C. 1988. "Who Was Phoebe? Translating *Diakonos* in Romans 16.1." *Bible Translator* 39:401–9.

Aune, David E. 2003. *Westminster Dictionary of New Testament and Early Christian Literature and Rhetoric*. Louisville: Westminster John Knox.

Badenas, Robert. 1985. *Christ the End of the Law: Romans 10.4 in Pauline Perspective*. Journal for the Study of the New Testament: Supplement Series 10. Sheffield: JSOT Press.

Bailey, J. N. 2004. "Paul's Political Paraenesis in Romans 13:1–7." *Restoration Quarterly* 46:11–28.

Baker, Murray. 2005. "Paul and the Salvation of Israel: Paul's Ministry, the Motif of Jealousy, and Israel's Yes." *Catholic Biblical Quarterly* 67:469–84.

Balch, David L. 1998. "Romans 1:24–27, Science, and Homosexuality." *Currents in Theology and Mission* 25:433–40.

Barrett, C. K. 1957. *A Commentary on the Epistle to the Romans*. 2nd ed. Black's New Testament Commentaries. London: Black.

Barth, Karl. 1933. *The Epistle to the Romans*. Translated by Edwyn C. Hoskyns. 6th ed. London: Oxford University Press.

———. 1959. *A Shorter Commentary on Romans*. Translated by D. H. van Daalen. Richmond, VA: John Knox.

Bassler, Jouette M. 1982. *Divine Impartiality: Paul and a Theological Axiom*. Society of Biblical Literature Dissertation Series 59. Chico, CA: Scholars Press.

Baudry, G.-H. 1997. "Le baptême: Mise au tombeau avec le Christ." *Esprit et vie* 107:120–27.

Baur, Ferdinand Christian. 1836, repr. 1963. "Über Zweck und Veranlassung des Römerbriefes und die damit zusammenhängenden Verhältnisse der römischen Gemeinde." Pages 147–266 in vol. 1 of *Ausgewählte Werke in Einzelausgaben*. Edited by Klaus Scholder. 5 vols. Stuttgart: Frommann, 1963–75.

Bechtler, Steven Richard. 1994. "Christ, the *Telos* of the Law: The Goal of Romans 10:4." *Catholic Biblical Quarterly* 56:288–308.

Beker, J. Christiaan. 1980. *Paul the Apostle: The Triumph of God in Life and Thought*. Philadelphia: Fortress.

Bell, Richard H. 2005. *The Irrevocable Call of God: An Inquiry into Paul's Theology of Israel*. Wissenschaftliche Untersuchungen zum Neuen Testament 184. Tübingen: Mohr Siebeck.

Betz, Hans Dieter. 2000. "The Concept of the 'Inner Human Being' (*ho esō anthrōpos*) in the Anthropology of Paul." *New Testament Studies* 46:315–41.

Bird, Michael F. 2006. *The Saving Righteousness of God: Studies on Paul, Justification and the New Perspective*. Paternoster Biblical Monographs. Waynesboro, GA: Paternoster.

Black, C. Clifton. 1984. "Pauline Perspectives on Death in Romans 5–8." *Journal of Biblical Literature* 103:413–33.

Black, Matthew. 1989. *Romans*. 2nd ed. New Century Bible Commentary. Grand Rapids: Eerdmans.

Boers, Hendrikus. 1994. *The Justification of the Gentiles: Paul's Letters to the Galatians and Romans*. Peabody, MA: Hendrickson.

———. 2001. "The Structure and Meaning of Romans 6:1–14." *Catholic Biblical Quarterly* 63:664–82.

Boguslawski, Steven C., OP. 2008. *Thomas Aquinas on the Jews*. A Stimulus Book. New York: Paulist Press.

Bornkamm, Günther. 1991. "The Letter to the Romans as Paul's Last Will and Testament." Pages 16–28 in *The Romans Debate*. Edited by Karl P. Donfried. Revised and expanded ed. Peabody, MA: Hendrickson.

Branick, Vincent P. 1985. "The Sinful Flesh of the Son of God (Rom. 8:3): A Key Image of Pauline Theology." *Catholic Biblical Quarterly* 47:246–62.

Bray, Gerald, ed. 1998. *Romans*. Ancient Christian Commentary on Scripture: New Testament 6. Downers Grove, IL: InterVarsity.

———. 2009. *Commentaries on Romans and 1–2 Corinthians*. By Ambrosiaster. Ancient Christian Texts. Downers Grove, IL: InterVarsity.

Bryan, Christopher. 2000. *A Preface to Romans: Notes on the Epistle in Its Literary and Cultural Setting*. Oxford: Oxford University Press.

Bultmann, Rudolf. 1951. *Theology of the New Testament*. Translated by Kendrick Grobel. Vol. 1. London: SCM.

Byrne, Brendan. 1996. *Romans*. Sacra pagina 6. Collegeville, MN: Liturgical Press.

Calvert-Koyzis, Nancy. 2004. *Paul, Monotheism and the People of God: The Significance of Abraham Traditions for Early Judaism and Christianity*. Journal for the Study of the New Testament: Supplement Series 273. London: T&T Clark International.

Calvin, John. 1960. *Institutes of the Christian Religion*. Translated by Ford Lewis Battles. Edited by John T. McNeill. 2 vols. Library of Christian Classics 20–21. Philadelphia: Westminster.

Campbell, Douglas A. 1994. "Romans 1:17—A Crux Interpretum for the *Pistis Christou* Debate." *Journal of Biblical Literature* 113:265–85.

———. 1997. "False Presuppositions in the *PISTIS CHRISTOU* Debate: A Response to Brian Dodd." *Journal of Biblical Literature* 116:713–19.

Campbell, William S. 1991. *Paul's Gospel in an Intercultural Context: Jew and Gentile in the Letter to the Romans*. Studies in the Intercultural History of Christianity 69. Frankfurt: Lang.

———. 2006. *Paul and the Creation of Christian Identity*. Library of New Testament Studies 322. London: T&T Clark.

Cervin, Richard S. 1994. "A Note Regarding the Name 'Junia(s)' in Romans 16.7." *New Testament Studies* 40:464–70.

Childs, Brevard S. 1962. "Adam." Pages 42–44 in vol. 1 of *The Interpreter's Dictionary of the Bible*. Edited by G. A. Buttrick. 4 vols. Nashville: Abingdon.

———. 2008. *The Church's Guide for Reading Paul: The Canonical Shaping of the Pauline Corpus*. Grand Rapids: Eerdmans.

Cosgrove, Charles H. 1996. "Rhetorical Suspense in Romans 9–11: A Study in Polyvalence and Hermeneutical Election." *Journal of Biblical Literature* 115:271–87.

———. 1997. *Elusive Israel: The Puzzle of Election in Romans*. Louisville: Westminster John Knox.

Cranfield, C. E. B. 1975. *Introduction and Commentary on Romans I–VIII*. Vol. 1 of *A Critical and Exegetical Commentary on the Epistle to the Romans*. International Critical Commentary. London: T&T Clark International.

———. 1979. *Commentary on Romans IX–XVI and Essays*. Vol. 2 of *A Critical and Exegetical Commentary on the Epistle to the Romans*. International Critical Commentary. London: T&T Clark International.

———. 1985. *Romans: A Shorter Commentary*. Grand Rapids: Eerdmans.

Dahl, Nils Alstrup. 1977. "The Missionary Theology in the Epistle to the Romans." Pages 70–94 in *Studies in Paul*. Minneapolis: Augsburg.

Das, A. Andrew. 2007. *Solving the Romans Debate*. Minneapolis: Fortress.

Davies, M. 1995. "New Testament Ethics and Ours: Homosexuality and Sexuality in Romans 1:26–27." *Biblical Interpretation* 3:315–31.

De Bruyn, T. 1993. *Pelagius's Commentary on St. Paul's Epistle to the Romans*. Oxford Early Christian Studies. Oxford: Clarendon.

Deidun, T. J. 1981. *New Covenant Morality in Paul*. Analecta biblica 89. Rome: Biblical Institute Press.

Derrett, J. Duncan. 1994. "'You Abominate False Gods; but Do You Rob Shrines?'" *New Testament Studies* 40:558–71.

Dillon, Richard J. 1998. "The Spirit as Taskmaster and Troublemaker in Romans 8." *Catholic Biblical Quarterly* 60:682–702.

———. 2000. "The 'Priesthood' of St Paul, Romans 15:15–16." *Worship* 74:156–68.

Dodd, Brian. 1995. "Romans 1:17—A Crux Interpretum for the *Pistis Christou* Debate?" *Journal of Biblical Literature* 114:470–73.

Dodd, C. H. 1932. *The Epistle of Paul to the Romans*. Moffatt New Testament Commentary. London: Hodder & Stoughton.

Donfried, Karl P., ed. 1991. *The Romans Debate*. Revised and expanded ed. Peabody, MA: Hendrickson.

Doty, William G. 1973. *Letters in Primitive Christianity*. Philadelphia: Fortress.

Dunn, James D. G. 1988. *Romans*. 2 vols. Word Biblical Commentary 38A–B. Dallas: Word.

———. 1998. *The Theology of Paul the Apostle*. Grand Rapids: Eerdmans.

Ehrensperger, Kathy, and R. Ward Holder, eds. 2008. *Reformation Readings of Romans*. New York: T&T Clark International.

Elliott, Neil. 2008. *The Arrogance of Nations: Reading Romans in the Shadow of Empire*. Minneapolis: Fortress.

Epp, Elton J. 2005. *Junia: The First Woman Apostle*. Minneapolis: Fortress.

Esler, Philip F. 2003. *Conflict and Identity in Romans: The Social Setting of Paul's Letter*. Minneapolis: Fortress.

Fee, Gordon D. 1994. *God's Empowering Presence: The Holy Spirit in the Letters of Paul*. Peabody, MA: Hendrickson.

Fiorenza, Elisabeth Schüssler. 1986. "Missionaries, Apostles, Coworkers: Romans 16 and the Reconstruction of Women's Early Christian History." *Word and World* 6:420–33.

Fitzmyer, Joseph A. 1989. *Paul and His Theology: A Brief Sketch*. 2nd ed. Englewood Cliffs, NJ: Prentice-Hall.

———. 1993. *Romans: A New Translation with Introduction and Commentary*. Anchor Bible 33. New York: Doubleday.

———. 1995. *Spiritual Exercises Based on Paul's Epistle to the Romans*. New York: Paulist Press.

Furnish, Victor P. 1968. *Theology and Ethics in Paul*. Nashville: Abingdon.

———. 1985. *The Moral Teaching of Paul: Selected Issues*. 2nd ed. Nashville: Abingdon.

Gagnon, Robert A. J. 2000. "Why the 'Weak' at Rome Cannot Be Non-Christian Jews." *Catholic Biblical Quarterly* 62:64–82.

Gamble, Harry, Jr. 1977. *The Textual History of the Letter to the Romans: A Study in Textual and Literary Criticism*. Studies and Documents 42. Grand Rapids: Eerdmans.

Garlington, D. B. 1990. "*HIEROSYLEIN* and the Idolatry of Israel (Romans 2.22)." *New Testament Studies* 36:142–51.

Gathercole, Simon J. 2002. *Where Is Boasting? Early Jewish Soteriology and Paul's Response in Romans 1–5*. Grand Rapids: Eerdmans.

Getty, Mary Ann. 1988. "Paul and the Salvation of Israel: A Perspective on Romans 9–11." *Catholic Biblical Quarterly* 50:456–69.

Gignac, A. 1994. "Le Christ, *telos* de la Loi (Rm 10,4), une lecture en termes de continuité et de discontinuité, dans le cadre du paradigme paulinien de l'élection." *Science et esprit* 46:55–81.

Gillman, Florence Morgan. 1987. "Another Look at Romans 8:3: 'In the Likeness of Sinful Flesh.'" *Catholic Biblical Quarterly* 49:597–604.

Graves, Robert. 1979. *Suetonius: The Twelve Caesars.* Translated by Robert Graves. Revised, with an introduction by Robert Grant. London: Penguin Books.

Grayston, Kenneth. 1997. *The Epistle to the Romans.* Epworth Commentaries. London: Epworth.

Greenman, Jeffrey P., and Timothy Larsen, eds. 2005. *Reading Romans through the Centuries: From the Early Church to Karl Barth.* Grand Rapids: Brazos.

Gregory, Bradley C. 2008. "Abraham as the Jewish Ideal: Exegetical Traditions in Sirach 44:19–21." *Catholic Biblical Quarterly* 70:66–81.

Grelot, Pierre. 1989. "Une homélie de saint Paul sur le baptême: Épître aux Romains, ch. 6,1–23." *Esprit et vie* 99:154–58.

———. 2001. *L'épître de saint Paul aux Romains: Une lecture pour aujourd'hui.* Versailles: Saint-Paul.

Grieb, A. Katherine. 2002. *The Story of Romans: A Narrative Defense of God's Righteousness.* Louisville: Westminster John Knox.

Grindheim, Sigurd. 2005. *The Crux of Election: Paul's Critique of the Jewish Confidence in the Election of Israel.* Wissenschaftliche Untersuchungen zum Neuen Testament 2. Tübingen: Mohr Siebeck.

Guerra, A. J. 1988. "Romans 4 as Apologetic Theology." *Harvard Theological Review* 81:251–70.

———. 1990. "Romans: Paul's Purpose and Audience with Special Attention to Romans 9–11." *Revue biblique* 97:219–37.

Haacker, Klaus. 2003. *The Theology of Paul's Letter to the Romans.* New Testament Theology. Cambridge: Cambridge University Press.

———. 2006. *Der Brief des Paulus an die Römer.* Theologischer Handkommentar zum Neuen Testament 6. Leipzig: Evangelische Verlagsanstalt.

Hahn, Ferdinand. 2002. *Theologie des Neuen Testaments.* 2 vols. Tübingen: Mohr Siebeck.

Harrington, Daniel. J. 1998. *Romans: The Good News according to Paul.* Hyde Park, NY: New City.

Hay, David M., and E. Elizabeth Johnson, eds. 1995. *Romans.* Vol. 3 of *Pauline Theology.* Minneapolis: Fortress.

Heil, John P. 1987. *Paul's Letter to the Romans: A Reader-Response Commentary.* New York: Paulist Press.

———. 2001. "Christ, the Termination of the Law (Romans 9:30–10:8)." *Catholic Biblical Quarterly* 63:484–98.

———. 2002. "From Remnant to Seed of Hope for Israel: Romans 9:27–29." *Catholic Biblical Quarterly* 64:703–20.

Hengel, Martin. 1977. *Crucifixion in the Ancient World and the Folly of the Message of the Cross*. Translated by John Bowden. Philadelphia: Fortress.

Hodge, H. Grose, trans. 1927. *Cicero: The Speeches*. Loeb Classical Library. Cambridge, MA: Harvard University Press.

Hofius, Otfried. 1990. "'All Israel Will Be Saved': Divine Salvation and Israel's Deliverance in Romans 9–11." *Princeton Seminary Bulletin Supplement* 1:19–39.

Holmes, Michael W., ed. 2007. *The Apostolic Fathers: Greek Texts and English Translations*. 3rd ed. Grand Rapids: Baker Academic.

Horst, Pieter W. van der. 2000. "'Only Then Will All Israel Be Saved': A Short Note on the Meaning of *kai houtōs* in Romans 11:26." *Journal of Biblical Literature* 119:521–25.

Hultgren, Arland. J. 1985. *Paul's Gospel and Mission: The Outlook from His Letter to the Romans*. Philadelphia: Fortress.

Hvalvik, Reidar. 1990. "A 'Sonderweg' for Israel: A Critical Examination of a Current Interpretation of Romans 11.25–27." *Journal for the Study of the New Testament* 38:87–107.

Jervell, Jacob. 1991. "Romans 14:1–15:13 and the Occasion of Romans." Pages 53–64 in *The Romans Debate*. Edited by Karl P. Donfried. Revised and expanded ed. Peabody, MA: Hendrickson.

Jervis, L. Ann. 1991. *The Purpose of Romans: A Comparative Letter Structure Investigation*. Journal for the Study of the New Testament: Supplement Series 55. Sheffield: JSOT Press.

Jewett, Robert. 2007. *Romans*. Hermeneia. Minneapolis: Fortress.

Karris, Robert J. 1991. "Romans 14:1–15:13 and the Occasion of Romans." Pages 65–84 in *The Romans Debate*. Edited by Karl P. Donfried. Revised and expanded ed. Peabody, MA: Hendrickson.

Käsemann, Ernst. 1969a. "Principles of the Interpretation of Romans 13." Pages 196–216 in *New Testament Questions of Today*. Translated by W. J. Montague. Philadelphia: Fortress.

———. 1969b. "'The Righteousness of God' in Paul." Pages 168–82 in *New Testament Questions of Today*. Philadelphia: Fortress.

———. 1980. *Commentary on Romans*. Translated and edited by Geoffrey W. Bromiley. Grand Rapids: Eerdmans.

Keck, Leander E. 1989. "'Jesus' in Romans." *Journal of Biblical Literature* 108:443–60.

———. 2005. *Romans*. Abingdon New Testament Commentaries. Nashville: Abingdon.

Kertelge, Karl. 1991. "The Sin of Adam in the Light of Christ's Redemptive Act according to Romans 5:12–21." *Communio* 18:502–13.

Kim, Johann D. 2000. *God, Israel, and the Gentiles: Rhetoric and Situation in Romans 9–11*. Society of Biblical Literature Dissertation Series 176. Atlanta: Society of Biblical Literature.

Kim, Seyoon. 1997. "The 'Mystery' of Rom. 11.25–6 Once More." *New Testament Studies* 43:412–29.

Kirby, John. T. 1987. "The Syntax of Romans 5.12: A Rhetorical Approach." *New Testament Studies* 33:283–86.

Kirk, J. R. Daniel. 2008. *Unlocking Romans: Resurrection and the Justification of God.* Grand Rapids: Eerdmans.

Kümmel, Werner Georg. 1974. *Römer 7 und das Bild des Menschen im Neuen Testament: Zwei Studien.* Theologische Bücherei 53. Munich: Chr. Kaiser.

Lagrange, M.-J. 1922. *Saint Paul, Épître aux Romains.* 3rd ed. Études bibliques. Paris: Lecoffre.

Lambrecht, Jan. 1990. "The Groaning Creation: A Study of Rom. 8:18–30." *Louvain Studies* 15:3–18.

———. 1992. *The Wretched "I" and Its Liberation: Paul in Romans 7 and 8.* Louvain Theological and Pastoral Monographs 14. Louvain: Peeters.

———. 2003. "The Confirmation of the Promises (Romans 15, 8)." Pages 167–73 in *Understanding What One Reads: New Testament Essays.* Louvain: Peeters.

Lambrecht, Jan, and Richard W. Thompson. 1989. *Justification by Faith: The Implications of Romans 3:27–31.* Zacchaeus Studies: New Testament. Wilmington, DE: Glazier.

Lampe, Peter. 1991. "The Roman Christians of Romans 16." Pages 216–30 in *The Romans Debate.* Edited by Karl P. Donfried. Revised and expanded ed. Peabody, MA: Hendrickson.

Landes, Paula Fredriksen. 1982. *Augustine on Romans: Propositions from the Epistle to the Romans, Unfinished Commentary on the Epistle to the Romans.* Society of Biblical Literature Texts and Translations: Early Christian Literature Series. Chico, CA: Scholars Press.

Leenhardt, Franz J. 1995. *L'épître de Saint Paul aux Romains.* 3rd ed. Commentaire du Nouveau Testament 2. Geneva: Labor et Fides.

Légasse, Simon. 1991. "Être baptisé dans la mort du Christ: Étude de Romains 6,1–14." *Revue biblique* 98:544–59.

———. 2002. *L'épître de Paul aux Romains.* Lectio divina: Commentaires 10. Paris: Cerf.

Lodge, John G. 1996. *Romans 9–11: A Reader-Response Analysis.* University of South Florida International Studies in Formative Christianity and Judaism 6. Atlanta: Scholars Press.

Longenecker, Bruce W. 1989. "Different Answers to Different Issues: Israel, the Gentiles and Salvation History in Romans 9–11." *Journal for the Study of the New Testament* 36:95–123.

———. 1993. "*Pistis* in Romans 3.25: Neglected Evidence for the 'Faithfulness of Christ'?" *New Testament Studies* 39:478–80.

———. 1997. "Prolegomena to Paul's Use of Scripture in Romans." *Bulletin for Biblical Research* 7:145–68.

Luther, Martin. 1961. *Luther: Lectures on Romans.* Translated and edited by Wilhelm Pauck. Library of Christian Classics 15. Philadelphia: Westminster.

Malina, Bruce J. 2002. "The New Testament and Homosexuality? Part 1: The Social System behind Romans 1. Part 2: The Traditions Influencing Paul's Thinking in Romans 1." *Verbum et ecclesia* 23:141–50, 393–407.

Manson, T. W. 1991. "St. Paul's Letter to the Romans—and Others." Pages 3–15 in *The Romans Debate.* Edited by Karl P. Donfried. Revised and expanded ed. Peabody, MA: Hendrickson.

Marcus, Joel. 1989. "The Circumcision and the Uncircumcision in Rome." *New Testament Studies* 35:67–81.

Martens, John. W. 1994. "Romans 2.14–16: A Stoic Reading." *New Testament Studies* 40:55–67.

Marxsen, Willi. 1968. *Introduction to the New Testament: An Approach to Its Problems.* Tanslated by G. Buswell. Philadelphia: Fortress.

McDonald, Patricia M., SHCJ. 1990. "Romans 5:1–11 as a Rhetorical Bridge." *Journal for the Study of the New Testament* 40:81–96.

Metzger, Bruce M. 1994. *A Textual Commentary on the Greek New Testament.* 2nd ed. Stuttgart: Deutsche Bibelgesellschaft/United Bible Societies.

Metzger, Bruce M., and Bart D. Ehrman. 2005. *The Text of the New Testament: Its Transmission, Corruption, and Restoration.* 4th ed. New York: Oxford University Press.

Miller, James C. 2000. *The Obedience of Faith, The Eschatological People of God, and the Purpose of Romans.* Society of Biblical Literature Dissertation Series 177. Atlanta: Society of Biblical Literature.

———. 2001. "The Romans Debate: 1991–2001." *Currents in Research: Biblical Studies* 9:306–49.

Moiser, Jeremy. 1990. "Rethinking Romans 12–15." *New Testament Studies* 36:571–82.

Moo, Douglas. 1986. "Israel and Paul in Romans 7.7–12." *New Testament Studies* 32:122–35.

———. 1996. *The Epistle to the Romans.* New International Commentary on the New Testament. Grand Rapids: Eerdmans.

Moo, Jonathan. 2008. "Romans 8.19–22 and Isaiah's Cosmic Covenant." *New Testament Studies* 54:74–89.

Morgan, Robert. 1995. *Romans.* New Testament Guides. Sheffield: Sheffield Academic Press.

Morris, Leon. 1988. *The Epistle to the Romans.* Pillar New Testament Commentary. Grand Rapids: Eerdmans.

Mounce, Robert H. 1995. *Romans.* New American Commentary 27. Nashville: Broadman & Holman.

Murphy-O'Connor, Jerome. 1983. *St. Paul's Corinth: Texts and Archaeology.* Good News Studies 6. Wilmington, DE: Glazier.

Nanos, Mark. D. 1996. *The Mystery of Romans: The Jewish Context of Paul's Letter.* Minneapolis: Fortress.

———. 1999. "The Jewish Context of the Gentile Audience Addressed in Paul's Letter to the Romans." *Catholic Biblical Quarterly* 61:283–304.

Neuner, J., and J. Dupuis. 1996. *The Christian Faith in the Doctrinal Documents of the Catholic Church.* Edited by Jacques Dupuis. 6th rev. and enlarged ed. New York: Alba House.

Nolland, J. 2000. "Romans 1:26–27 and the Homosexuality Debate." *Horizons in Biblical Theology* 22:32–57.

Nygren, Anders. 1949. *Commentary on Romans.* Translated by Carl C. Rasmussen. Philadelphia: Fortress.

Petersen, A. K. 1998. "Shedding New Light on Paul's Understanding of Baptism: A Ritual-Theoretical Approach to Romans 6." *Studia theologica* 52:3–28.

Porter, Calvin. L. 1994. "Romans 1.18–32: Its Role in the Developing Argument." *New Testament Studies* 40:210–28.

Pusey, Edward B., trans. 1949. *The Confessions of Saint Augustine*. Modern Library. New York: Random House.

Quesnel, Michael. 2003. "La figure de Moïse en Romains 9–11." *New Testament Studies* 49:321–35.

Reasoner, Mark. 1999. *The Strong and the Weak: Romans 14.1–15.13 in Context*. Society for New Testament Studies Monograph Series 103. Cambridge: Cambridge University Press.

———. 2005. *Romans in Full Circle: A History of Interpretation*. Louisville: Westminster John Knox.

Rhyne, C. Thomas. 1985. "*Nomos Dikaiosynēs* and the Meaning of Romans 10:4." *Catholic Biblical Quarterly* 47:486–99.

Ridderbos, Herman. 1975. *Paul: An Outline of His Theology*. Translated by John Richard de Witt. Grand Rapids: Eerdmans.

Rosner, Brian S., ed. 1995. *Understanding Paul's Ethics: Twentieth Century Approaches*. Grand Rapids: Eerdmans.

Sanday, William, and Arthur Headlam. 1902. *A Critical and Exegetical Commentary on the Epistle to the Romans*. 5th ed. International Critical Commentary. Edinburgh: T&T Clark.

Scheck, Thomas P., trans. 2001–2. *Origen: Commentary on the Epistle to the Romans*. 2 vols. Fathers of the Church 103–4. Washington, DC: Catholic University of America Press.

Schelkle, Karl Hermann. 1973. *Morality*. Vol. 3 of *Theology of the New Testament*. Translated by William A. Jurgens. Collegeville, MN: Liturgical Press.

Schlatter, Adolf. 1995. *Romans: The Righteousness of God*. Translated by S. S. Schatzmann. Peabody, MA: Hendrickson.

Schmithals, Walter. 1975. *Der Römerbrief als historisches Problem*. Studien zum Neuen Testament 9. Gütersloh: Gerd Mohn.

Schnackenburg, Rudolf. 1964. *Baptism in the Thought of St. Paul: A Study in Pauline Theology*. Translated by G. R. Beasley-Murray. New York: Herder & Herder.

Schnelle, Udo. 2005. *Apostle Paul: His Life and Theology*. Translated by M. Eugene Boring. Grand Rapids: Baker Academic.

Schreiner, Thomas R. 1998. *Romans*. Baker Exegetical Commentary on the New Testament 6. Grand Rapids: Baker Academic.

———. 2001. *Paul, Apostle of God's Glory in Christ*. Downers Grove, IL: InterVarsity.

Schumacher, Matthew A, trans. 1957. *Saint Augustine against Julian*. Fathers of the Church 15. Washington, DC: Catholic University of America Press.

Scroggs, Robin. 1983. *The New Testament and Homosexuality: Contextual Background for Contemporary Debate*. Philadelphia: Fortress.

Segal, Alan F. 1990. "Paul's Experience and Romans 9–11." *Princeton Seminary Bulletin Supplement* 1:56–70.

Seifrid, Mark A. 1992. "The Subject of Rom. 7:14–25." *Novum Testamentum* 34:313–33.

———. 2007. "Romans." Pages 607–94 in *Commentary on the New Testament Use of the Old Testament.* Edited by C. K. Beale and D. A. Carson. Grand Rapids: Baker Academic.

Smiga, George. 1991. "Romans 12:1–2 and 15:30–32 and the Occasion of the Letter to the Romans." *Catholic Biblical Quarterly* 53:257–73.

Sonderland, Sven K., and N. T. Wright, eds. 1999. *Romans and the People of God: Essays in Honor of Gordon D. Fee on the Occasion of His 65th Birthday.* Grand Rapids: Eerdmans.

Song, Changwon. 2004. *Reading Romans as a Diatribe.* Studies in Biblical Literature 59. New York: Peter Lang.

Starnitzke, Dierk. 2004. *Die Struktur paulinischen Denkens im Römerbrief: Eine linguistische-logische Untersuchung.* Beiträge zur Wissenschaft vom Alten und Neuen Testament 163. Stuttgart: Kohlhammer.

Stirewalt, Martin Luther, Jr. 1991. "The Form and Function of the Greek Letter-Essay." Pages 147–71 in *The Romans Debate.* Edited by Karl P. Donfried. Revised and expanded ed. Peabody, MA: Hendrickson.

Stowers, Stanley Kent. 1981. *The Diatribe and Paul's Letter to the Romans.* Society of Biblical Literature Dissertation Series 57. Chico, CA: Scholars Press.

———. 1984. "Paul's Dialogue with a Fellow Jew in Romans 3:1–9." *Catholic Biblical Quarterly* 46:707–22.

———. 1986. *Letter Writing in Greco-Roman Antiquity.* Library of Early Christianity 5. Philadelphia: Westminster.

———. 1994. *A Rereading of Romans: Justice, Jews, and Gentiles.* New Haven, CT: Yale University Press.

Stuhlmacher, Peter. 1994. *Paul's Letter to the Romans: A Commentary.* Translated by Scott J. Hafemann. Louisville: Westminster John Knox.

———. 2001. *Revisiting Paul's Doctrine of Justification: A Challenge to the New Perspective; With an Essay by Donald Hagner.* Downers Grove, IL: InterVarsity.

Swanson, Reuben J., ed. 2001. *New Testament Greek Manuscripts: Variant Readings Arranged in Horizontal Lines against Codex Vaticanus: Romans.* Wheaton: Tyndale House.

Talbert, Charles H. 2002. *Romans.* Smyth & Helwys Bible Commentary. Macon, GA: Smyth & Helwys.

———. 2003. "Tracing Paul's Train of Thought in Romans 6–8." *Review and Expositor* 100:53–63.

Thackeray, H. St. J., trans. 1926. *Josephus.* Vol. 1, *The Life; Against Apion.* Loeb Classical Library. London: Heinemann.

Thielman, Frank. 1989. *From Plight to Solution: A Jewish Framework for Understanding Paul's View of the Law in Galatians and Romans.* Supplements to Novum Testamentum 61. Leiden: Brill.

Thompson, Richard. W. 1986. "How Is the Law Fulfilled in Us? An Interpretation of Rom. 8:4." *Louvain Studies* 11:31–40.

Tobin, Thomas H. 1993. "Controversy and Continuity in Romans 1:18–3:20." *Catholic Biblical Quarterly* 55:298–318.

———. 2004. *Paul's Rhetoric in Its Context: The Argument of Romans*. Peabody, MA: Hendrickson.

Toney, Carl N. 2008. *Paul's Inclusive Ethic: Resolving Community Conflicts and Promoting Mission in Romans 14–15*. Wissenschaftliche Untersuchungen zum Neuen Testament 2/252. Tübingen: Mohr Siebeck.

Trakatellis, Demetrius. 1992. *Being Transformed: Chrysostom's Exegesis of the Epistle to the Romans*. Brookline, MA: Holy Cross Orthodox Press.

Viagulamuthu, X. P. B. 1992. *Offering Our Bodies as a Living Sacrifice to God: A Study in Pauline Spirituality Based on Romans 12,1*. Tesi Gregoriana, Serie Spiritualità 7. Rome: Editrice Pontificia Università Gregoriana.

Wagner, Günter. 1967. *Pauline Baptism and the Pagan Mysteries: The Problem of the Pauline Doctrine of Baptism in Romans VI.1–1, in the Light of Its Religio-Historical "Parallels."* Translated by J. P. Smith. Edinburgh: Oliver & Boyd.

Wagner, J. Ross. 1997. "The Christ, Servant of Jew and Gentile: A Fresh Approach to Romans 15:8–9." *Journal of Biblical Literature* 116:473–85.

———. 2003. *Heralds of the Good News: Isaiah and Paul in Concert in the Letter to the Romans*. Novum Testamentum Supplements 101. Boston: Brill.

Walker, William O. 1999. "Romans 1.18–2.29: A Non-Pauline Interpolation?" *New Testament Studies* 45:533–52.

Watson, Francis. 1991. "The Two Roman Congregations: Romans 14:1–15:13." Pages 203–15 in *The Romans Debate*. Edited by Karl P. Donfried. Revised and expanded ed. Peabody, MA: Hendrickson.

Wedderburn, A. J. M. 1983. "Hellenistic Christian Traditions in Romans 6?" *New Testament Studies* 29:337–55.

———. 1991a. *The Reasons for Romans*. Studies of the New Testament and Its World. Edinburgh: T&T Clark.

———. 1991b. "Purpose and Occasion of Romans Again." Pages 195–202 in *The Romans Debate*. Edited by Karl P. Donfried. Revised and expanded ed. Peabody, MA: Hendrickson.

Westerholm, Stephen. 2004. *Perspectives Old and New on Paul: The "Lutheran" Paul and His Critics*. Grand Rapids: Eerdmans.

Witherington, Ben, III, with Darlene Hyatt. 2004. *Paul's Letter to the Romans: A Socio-Rhetorical Commentary*. Grand Rapids: Eerdmans.

Wright, N. T. 2002. "The Letter to the Romans." Pages 393–770 in vol. 10 of *The New Interpreter's Bible*. Edited by Leander E. Keck. Nashville: Abingdon.

Index of Subjects

Index of Modern Authors

Index of Scripture and Ancient Sources

Old Testament

Deuterocanonical Books

New Testament

Old Testament Pseudepigrapha

Dead Sea Scrolls

Apostolic Fathers

Ancient Authors